34.95

683638

JOB STRESS
IN A
CHANGING WORKFORCE

INVESTIGATING GENDER, DIVERSITY, AND FAMILY ISSUES

EDITED BY

GWENDOLYN PURYEAR KEITA AND

JOSEPH J. HURRELL, JR.

AMERICAN PSYCHOLOGICAL ASSOCIATION
WASHINGTON, DC

Murrell Library
Missouri Valley College
Marshall, Missouri

Published by
American Psychological Association
750 First Street, NE
Washington, DC 20002

Copies may be ordered from
APA Order Department
P.O. Box 2710
Hyattsville, MD 20784

In the United Kingdom and Europe, copies may be ordered from
American Psychological Association
3 Henrietta Street
Covent Garden, London
WC2E 8LU England

Typeset in Century Schoolbook by Easton Publishing Services, Inc., Easton, MD

Printer: Data Reproductions Corporation, Rochester Hills, MI
Cover designer: Minker Design, Bethesda, MD
Technical/production editor: Molly R. Flickinger

Library of Congress Cataloging-in-Publication Data
Job stress in a changing workforce : investigating gender, diversity, and family
  issues / edited by Gwendolyn Puryear Keita and Joseph J. Hurrell, Jr.
      p.   cm.
   Includes bibliographical references and index.
   ISBN 1-55798-271-6 (acid-free paper)
   1. Job stress—United States.   2. Work—Psychological aspects.   3. Corporate
culture—United States.   4. Work and family—United States.   I. Keita,
Gwendolyn Puryear.   II. Hurrell, Joseph J., Jr.
HF5548.85.J654   1994
158.7—dc20   94-31026
                                                                          CIP

British Cataloguing-in-Publication Data
A CIP record is available from the British Library.

Printed in the United States of America
First edition

Contents

Contributors

Carolyn M. Aldwin, *Department of Applied Behavioral Sciences, University of California, Davis*

Marjorie Armstrong-Stassen, *Faculty of Business Administration, University of Windsor, Ontario, Canada*

Emin Babakus, *Department of Management, Memphis State University, TN*

Julian Barling, *School of Business, Queen's University, Kingston, Ontario, Canada*

Rosalind C. Barnett, *Center for Research on Women, Wellesley College, Wellesley, MA*

Rabi S. Bhagat, *Department of Management, University of Memphis, TN*

Ronald J. Burke, *Department of Organizational Behavior and Industrial Relations, York University, North York, Ontario, Canada*

Sylvie Carrier, *Department of Psychology, University of Montreal, Quebec, Canada*

Nancy J. Chapman, *Department of Urban Studies and Planning, Portland State University, OR*

Jagdeep Chokkar, *Department of Organizational Behavior, Indian Institute of Management, Ahmedabad, India*

John M. Cornwell, *Department of Psychology, Tulane University, New Orleans, LA*

Johanne Dompierre, *Department of Industrial Relations, Université Laval, Ste-Foy, Quebec, Canada*

Fritz Drasgow, *Department of Psychology, University of Illinois, Urbana-Champaign*

Louise F. Fitzgerald, *Department of Psychology, University of Illinois, Urbana-Champaign*

David L. Ford, Jr., *School of Management, University of Texas, Dallas*

Len Frey, *Department of Management, Memphis State University, TN*

Reinhard Fuchs, *Institute for Psychology, Free University, Berlin, Germany*

M. Jesus Gonzalez Fernandez, *Department of Psychology, University of Madrid, Spain*

Sally Grant, *Child Development Centre, Cornwall General Hospital*

Beth L. Green, *Community Program Evaluation Project, University of Pittsburgh, PA*

Sara E. Gutierres, *Social and Behavioral Sciences, Arizona State University—West, Phoenix*

André Hahn, *Institute for Psychology, Free University, Berlin, Germany*

Charles L. Hulin, *Department of Psychology, University of Illinois, Urbana-Champaign*

Joseph J. Hurrell, Jr., *National Institute for Occupational Safety and Health, Cincinnati, OH*

Pekka Huuhtanen, *Department of Psychology, Institute of Occupational Health, Helsinki, Finland*

Berit Ingersoll-Dayton, *School of Social Work, University of Michigan, Ann Arbor*

Keith James, *Department of Psychology, Colorado State University, Fort Collins*

Susan E. Jennings, *Senior Vice President, Value Health Sciences, Inc., Santa Monica, CA*

Gwendolyn Puryear Keita, *Public Interest Directorate, American Psychological Association, Washington, DC*

E. Kevin Kelloway, *Department of Psychology, University of Guelph, Ontario, Canada*

Francine Lavoie, *School of Psychology, Université Laval, Ste-Foy, Quebec, Canada*

Mohale Mahanyele, *Manpower Assignments Consultants, Johannesburg, South Africa*

Thomas W. Mangione, *Senior Research Scientist, JSI Research and Training Institute, Inc., Boston*

Lyne Marcil, *Department of Psychology, Wayne State University, Detroit, MI*

Anthony J. Marsella, *Department of Psychology, University of Hawaii, Manoa*

Nancy L. Marshall, *Center for Research on Women, Wellesley College, Wellesley, MA*

Carol A. McKeen, *School of Business, Queen's University, Kingston, Ontario, Canada*

Rebecca L. Miles, *Department of Psychology, Wayne State University, Detroit, MI*

J. Donald Millar, *National Institute for Occupational Safety and Health, Centers for Disease Control and Prevention, Atlanta, GA*

Margaret B. Neal, *Institute on Aging, Portland State University, Portland, OR*

B. Habil Ninokumar, *Universität der Bundeswehr, Hamburg, Germany*

Michael P. O'Driscoll, *Department of Psychology, University of Waikato, Hamilton, New Zealand*

Esther M. Orioli, *Essi Systems, Inc., San Francisco, CA*

Rebecca A. Parker, *Department of Applied Behavioral Sciences, University of California, Davis*

Christie Partlo, *Department of Psychology, Ohio State University, Newark*

Larry E. Pate, *Department of Management, University of Utah, Salt Lake City*

Cynthia A. Piltch, *Senior Research Associate, Health Policy Institute, Brandeis University, Waltham, MA*

Lovinia Plimpton, *Department of Psychology, University of Montana, Missoula*

Ethel Roskies, *Department of Psychology, University of Montreal, Quebec, Canada*

Paul A. Ryder, *Faculty of Business and Hotel Management, Griffith University, Gold Coast, Australia*

Delia S. Saenz, *Department of Psychology, Arizona State University, Tempe*

Ralf Schwarzer, *Institut for Psychology, Free University, Berlin, Germany*

Sara Staats, *Department of Psychology, Ohio State University, Newark*

Jefferson L. Sulzer, *Department of Psychology, Tulane University, New Orleans, LA*

Lois E. Tetrick, *Department of Psychology, Wayne State University, Detroit, MI*

Karen F. Trocki, *Essi Systems, Inc., San Francisco, CA*

Christine M. Van Dosen, *Department of Psychology, Wayne State University, Detroit, MI*

Diana Chapman Walsh, *President of Wellesley College, Wellesley, MA*

Kevin C. Wooten, *School of Business and Public Administration, University of Houston—Clear Lake, Houston, TX*

Foreword

In recent years, millions of people in the industrialized world have experienced enormous personal change because of major shifts in the global economy. These changes have left many with a well-founded sense of vulnerability that is particularly evident in the work arena. Although those who lose their jobs are especially vulnerable and experience a number of related stressors, such as the break up of the family unit and an abrupt departure from the mainstream, for many millions of employed workers who are still employed, the fear of such losses is a daily companion. The rising costs of health care, child care, elder care, food, and housing affect even more workers and leave them vulnerable to health problems known to be caused by stress. The modern occupational plague of job stress affects workers in vast numbers. A recent survey by the Northwestern National Life Insurance Company[1] revealed that 27% of American workers considered their jobs to be their greatest single source of stress. In light of tenuous and declining incomes, fading fringe benefits, and rising costs, this epidemic of stress-related conditions is no surprise. The current era of global economic uncertainty, which seems to have affected every nation on earth, underscores the relevance of protecting the most vulnerable.

Psychologists cannot change the state of the economy or reduce the costs of health care, child care, education, housing, and food—these problems involve complex social issues that require action far beyond our scope. But we can help the vulnerable in society by recommending changes in the workplace. Most people spend the majority of their waking hours at work, and in America more people work today than ever before. In fact, nearly 200 million Americans work regularly. For these people, health psychologists can make a difference. The challenge is to see working people for what they really are: a nation's most valuable resource. This view lies behind the Preamble of the Occupational Safety and Health Act of 1970,[2] whose mission is "to assure safe and healthful working conditions and to preserve our human resources" (p. 1590). This notion is not mere altruism. In recent years, the idea of preserving human resources has become more and more widely accepted as a practical necessity for economic success. Respect for people, empowerment of each individual, continuous improvement, the quest for knowledge and balance, and teamwork—all of these principles are essential in the philosophy of "quality" management that has become so popular. Ensuring safe and healthful working conditions is not simply a question of removing hazards. It also means enabling people to experience positive benefits of work—the blessings of a sense of achievement and of making a meaningful contribution to worthwhile human endeavors.

The National Institute for Occupational Safety and Health (NIOSH) and

---

[1] Northwestern National Life Insurance Company. (1993). *Fear and violence in the workplace.* Minneapolis, MN: Author.

[2] Occupational Safety and Health Act of 1970, Pub. L. No. 91-596, Preamble, 84 Stat. 1590 (1971).

the American Psychological Association (APA) have a history of collaborating on efforts to promote the mental and physical well-being of workers. This partnership in prevention led to APA–NIOSH sponsorship of the conference *Stress in the 90s: A Changing Workforce in a Changing Workplace*, which provided the original forum for the ideas in this book. I welcome the publication of these much-needed research data on how work stress affects the individual worker. The chapters that follow explore issues of workforce diversity—such as gender, culture, and age—as well as the complex interface between work and family. Those concerned about occupational safety and health will find these data to be invaluable as they attempt to make more informed recommendations for the prevention of job stress.

J. Donald Millar
Director, National Institute for
Occupational Safety and Health,
Centers for Disease Control,
Atlanta, Georgia

Preface

A physically and mentally healthy workforce is one of a country's most valuable assets. However, there are signs that work-related psychological disorders are a serious threat to the well-being of any workforce: Workers' compensation claims for psychological disorders are at unprecedented levels, and the number of books on the popular market about managing stress attest to national concern about the problem. Stresses and strains in the workforce manifest themselves in reduced productivity, increased absenteeism due to illness, and, most important, a decreased sense of personal well-being and effectiveness. Because of demographic changes, the profile of today's workforce looks very different from that of the previous generation. Women, members of ethnic minority groups, and older adults form a greater percentage of the total workforce today, with wide-reaching ramifications for the family and the community at large. These workers are subject to a number of particular job-related stresses by virtue of their group membership.

The relationship between these changes in the workforce and reported stress are dynamic and complex. Researchers are only just beginning to understand the nature of the interactions, and much work remains to be done. However, as the chapters in this book show, considerable progress in understanding some of these relationships is being made at the microlevel.

This book owes its existence to a partnership that began 6 years ago. At that time, the American Psychological Association (APA) joined with the National Institute for Occupational Safety and Health (NIOSH) to address the problem of job stress by implementing ideas contained in a compendium of national strategies for the prevention of work-related disorders.[1]

The first product of the APA–NIOSH partnership was a jointly sponsored national conference in 1990 titled *Work and Well-Being: An Agenda for the 1990s.* This conference attracted over 400 participants from around the globe, and its proceedings were subsequently published in two APA books. The first suggested ways of improving the organization of work and described surveillance and mental health delivery systems to help prevent job stress and associated health disorders.[2] The second presented a series of international reports on occupational mental health risks and interventions.[3] The conference also provided the impetus for the initiation of a graduate fellowship program

---

[1] National Institute for Occupational Safety and Health. (1988). Prevention of occupationally-generated illnesses: A proposed synoptic national strategy to reduce neurotoxic disorder in the U.S. workplace. In *Proposed national strategies for the prevention of leading work-related diseases and injuries, part 2* (NTIS No. PB89–130348, pp. 31–50). Cincinnati, OH: Author.

[2] Keita, G. P., & Sauter, S. L. (Eds.). (1992). *Work and well-being: An agenda for the 1990s.* Washington, DC: American Psychological Association.

[3] Quick, J. C., Murphy, L. R., & Hurrell, J. J., Jr. (Eds.). (1992). *Stress and well-being at work: Assessments and interventions for occupational mental health.* Washington, DC: American Psychological Association.

in occupational health psychology; the start-up of a new journal, the *Journal of Occupational Health Psychology;* and a 1992 conference on job stress.

The 1992 conference, *Stress in the 90s: A Changing Workforce in a Changing Workplace,* drew a large number of top-level international submissions. The chapters in this volume are derived from that conference and were selected because their focus transcended the nature of the job itself and evaluated the interaction between the individual worker, the work environment, and the nonwork environment. The contributors are all distinguished experts from the field of industrial and organizational psychology, and they present original research studies that will be of great benefit to the field.

We thank several anonymous reviewers for their valuable suggestions for chapter revisions included in this volume, Judy Nemes of the American Psychological Association for her extensive editorial support in preparation of this volume, and Lynn Letourneau for her assistance with administrative details.

Gwendolyn Puryear Keita
Joseph J. Hurrell, Jr.

Introduction

In recent years, occupational stress and workplace wellness have become issues of central concern for management, labor, and the individual worker. In fact, Ilgen (1990) called the health of a nation's workers one of the most significant issues of the times. The National Institute for Occupational Safety and Health (1988) has identified psychological disorders as one of the 10 leading work-related diseases in the United States. Mental disorders are the most prevalent disabling condition among recipients of disability allowances from the Social Security Administration, accounting for 21% of all allowances. Estimated annual costs exceed $15 billion in disability payouts and lost wages, excluding health care costs and productivity losses (Social Security Bulletin, 1989). Northwestern National Life Insurance Company (1991), a major United States underwriter for workers' compensation insurance, reported that 13% of the claims it indemnified in 1990 involved stress-related disorders, an increase of 6% from 1982. In a national survey of American workers, Northwestern found that 72% of the workers surveyed experienced frequent stress-related physical or mental conditions that could increase health costs. Almost one half reported feeling that their jobs were very or extremely stressful, and over one fourth saw their jobs as the single greatest cause of stress in their lives.

What are the reasons for this epidemic of stress-related disorders? Although researchers still have much to discover about the complex interrelationship between workplace stress and psychological symptoms, a number of economic and demographic trends have clearly contributed to the problem. Work as it has traditionally been known has changed markedly over the past decade, continues to change at a rapid pace, and is characterized by an atmosphere of uncertainty. The U.S. economy is no longer dominated by manufacturing, and an ever-increasing number of workers are employed in service-producing industries. This sector of the economy is projected to account for nearly 94% of all newly created jobs between 1990 and 2005, with its share of all jobs expected to rise from 69% in 1990 to 73% in 2005 (U.S. Department of Labor, 1992). This change has had a dramatic impact on the kinds of jobs that are available, the type of worker employed, and the characteristics of the workplace. Of particular concern is the fact that workers in service industry jobs are at increased risk for psychological disorders (Colligan, Smith, & Hurrell, 1977; Landy, 1992). Although further research is needed to clarify the reasons for increased stress among service workers, "burnout" appears to be a particular problem for this sector of the working population. Part of the reason for this may be that service workers' job training often places great emphasis on the technical aspects of the job, while offering little training in the interpersonal skills that are such a crucial part of their work, thereby creating a gap between workers' skills and job requirements (Landy, 1992).

In addition, intensified international competition has led to the restructuring of many American corporations. This restructuring process often involves voluntary mergers, corporate takeovers, downsizing, and bankruptcies, contributing to the creation of an uncertain work climate for many (Landy, Quick, & Kasl, 1994). Other major challenges to workers include the increased use of computer technology in the workplace and the gap between the new skills demanded by employers and the actual skills possessed by workers (Herold, 1990; Landy et al., 1994).

Against this background, the face of the U.S. national workforce has changed, with the fastest growing segments of the working population being women, ethnic minorities, and older workers. Roberts (1993) noted that managing diversity may be the greatest challenge facing America as it begins the 21st century. Women are expected to account for 62% of the 26 million net increase in the civilian labor force between 1990 and 2005. Their share of the labor force has grown from only 38% in 1970, to 42% in 1980, and 45% in 1990. It has been projected that women will compose 47% of the labor force by the year 2005 (U.S. Department of Labor, 1992).

Labor force participation rates are expected to grow faster for ethnic minority women than for their White counterparts. Women of Hispanic origin as well as Asian and other women (Native Americans, Alaskan Natives, and Pacific Islanders) are projected to show the fastest growth in labor force participation rates between 1990 and 2005—both at 80%. Black women's labor force growth during this period has been estimated at 34%, which will also exceed the average for all women (i.e., 26%; U.S. Department of Labor, 1992).

This trend toward faster labor force growth among ethnic minority groups is not limited to women, however. As a result of revised immigration regulations and changing birth and death rates, Blacks (not just African Americans), Latinos, and Asians are represented in larger proportions of the population and the workforce. The Urban Institute (Edmonston & Passel, 1992) has projected that between 1990 and 2040, the number of Asian Americans will grow fivefold, from 7 million to 35 million, and Hispanics will nearly triple in number to 54 million, surpassing African Americans as the largest ethnic minority group. The number of African Americans is expected to increase from 30 million to 44 million, whereas numbers of Native Americans are expected to stay about the same, at approximately 2 million. Non-Hispanic Whites will continue to make up the majority of the population, growing from 187 million to 211 million.

This trend toward a vastly more diverse workforce is not just occurring in the United States, but is evident in most parts of the industrialized world. Large numbers of men and women are migrating to leading industrialized countries to find work and a chance for better opportunities. The resulting population shifts are having drastic effects on the workplace and the nations themselves. Although the specific immigrant or ethnic groups may differ from country to country, many of the problems and benefits created by the large influx of workers from different cultures will be similar. Moreover, many of these workers will experience stress related to their own immigrant, ethnic minority, or lower socioeconomic status; to possible racial or ethnic group discrimination; or to the diverse expectations and cultures of different workers. Ethnic minority women and men are especially vulnerable to being in jobs with hazardous work conditions and are more likely to be unemployed. Essentially, much of the ethnic minority workforce remains overrepresented in low-paying, low-skill, high risk, and hazardous occupations for which there is a more than adequate supply of replacement labor (Bullard & Wright, 1986–1987).

The average age of U.S. workers is also changing, resulting in the so-called graying of the workforce. The proportion of the American population over age 65 is larger than ever before, and this age group is growing faster than any other (Roberts, 1993). Demographers have predicted that between 2010 and 2030, the number of Americans 54 and older will mushroom by 30 million as baby boomers "turn the age pyramid upside down" (Roberts, 1993, p. 233). According to labor force statistics (U.S. Department of Labor, 1992), the median age of people in the labor force will rise from 36.6 years in 1990 to 40.6 years in 2005. By the year 2005, nearly 70% of U.S. workers will be in the 25- to 54-year-old age group—the prime working age. The percentage of workers 55 years of age and over will also rise, from 12.3% in 1990 to 14.7% in 2005. Again, this reflects a global phenomenon. The world's population is growing older, driven by declining fertility and expanding life spans in industrialized nations (Roberts, 1993). Although fertility and longevity are the two variables that universally drive median age, it is important to note that these variables differ by race, ethnicity, gender, and geography, with women living longer than men, and Whites living longer than Blacks and Hispanics (Roberts, 1993).

As a result of these changes in employee demographics, and particularly because of the increasing numbers of women in the workforce, balancing the demands of work and family has become a major challenge for many working adults (Williams & Alliger, 1994). Although occupying multiple roles may have psychological benefits, there is growing evidence that there are both individual and organizational costs associated with, for example, simultaneously occupying the roles of worker, spouse, and caregiver (Greenhaus & Parasuraman, 1986). Moreover, work and nonwork experiences clearly have reciprocal effects (Barling & McEwan, 1992). Although it is quite clear that the effects of stressful employment spill over to affect family members and family functioning (Piotrkowski, 1979), the magnitude and nature of these effects remain unclear. The reverse effects—of nonwork experiences on the work organization—are less clear. However, it seems reasonable to expect that such factors as child- and elder-care difficulties may have very important organizational consequences, affecting such factors as job satisfaction and productivity.

Despite radical changes in the makeup of the workforce and the availability of new research findings on occupational stress and workplace wellness—many of which have already prompted changes in some industries—the traditional research focus has changed slowly. Sufficient data still do not exist on the particular stresses experienced by the female, ethnic minority, and aging workers who will make up a large percentage of the workforce in years to come. Researchers also need to know more about the stresses that arise from balancing work and family life and that may spill over from either of these domains into the other. The purpose of this book is to help fill that gap by presenting new research that sheds light on some of these issues. The chapters that follow are organized around two broad stress-related themes: workforce diversity and the interface between work and nonwork life. The first section has three parts, containing chapters on gender, culture and ethnicity, and aging. The second section includes two parts, exploring work and family functioning and work and family conflict, respectively.

Part I looks at gender issues. Women's occupational health is a relatively new area of study. Much of the research in the past focused on job-related variables for men and on home- and family-related variables for women (Amaro, Russo, & Johnson, 1987). More recently, researchers have begun to understand how the characteristics of women's work and their employment settings might relate to risk for stress and ill-health. A number of researchers have proposed that women not only experience the same stressors as men but also face additional stress and strain as a result of their entry into male-dominated and patriarchal organizations (Jick & Mitz, 1985; Nelson & Hitt, 1992). Gender discrimination, including sexual harassment, is a stressor that mainly affects women.

Although the relationship between women's employment and their physical and psychological well-being is not clear-cut, studies presented in the Gender part of this book help to clarify some of the ambiguity. New methodology that increases the number and types of stressors examined shows that women do generally experience greater mental distress than men and helps clarify other differences in women and men, such as in the relationship between work and well-being. The use of methodologies allowing for simultaneous measurement of multiple coping constructs and different categories of stress symptomatology outcome furthers the understanding of similarities and differences between women and men in coping behaviors related to job stress and their effectiveness. Moreover, information is provided here that should lead to improvements in stress management programs developed for women. A common thread running through the chapters is the similarity between men and women with regard to work-related issues and mental distress—including the importance of family and work to both and the experience of stress from both arenas. Part I also includes a chapter on a topic that is too often overlooked: sexual harassment and its impact on the worker and the organization.

Part II continues the examination of coping strategies, social support, and the overall relationship between workplace stress and psychological and physical well-being. However, the chapters focus on cross-cultural and ethnic minority issues and populations. As noted previously, the workforce is becoming increasingly more diverse with regard to individuals with different cultural and ethnic backgrounds. However, occupational stress researchers have almost ignored these changes. Chapters in this part of the book help inform the research on similarities and differences across cultures and ethnic groups on several key issues within the occupational stress arena. Research on African Americans and Hispanics is included, as is a cross-cultural study of job stress and coping in seven different countries. The researchers in this part are helping to find more satisfactory answers to a variety of questions: Are there differences in coping behavior and effectiveness in moderating occupational stress for different cultures and ethnic groups? Are there differences in the social support-stress relationship for different ethnic groups? What are some of the factors most important for understanding occupational stress and health for different ethnic groups? Are these factors the same as or different from those for White Americans? Another important question addressed in this part is the importance of perceived discrimination in the workplace. Discrimination against minority group individuals appears to be stressful not only for the ethnic minority group individuals but for White workers as well.

Part III addresses issues of aging. Relatively little is known about the particular stresses experienced by older workers and about the impact that a "graying" workforce will have on industries. The research presented in the three chapters of this part extends understanding of these issues. It goes beyond information provided in extant research on the relationship between age and job loss to provide specific information about the needs of older job losers and ways to negate the effects of anxiety and depressive affect that have already proved to be major concerns. Likewise, although data clearly indicate that female workers and older workers are growing in number, a side effect that seems to be important but has been totally ignored is the large number of working widows. (Because women tend to live longer than men, and widows are less likely than widowers to remarry, there are likely to be many more widows than widowers and relatively large numbers in the labor force given women's increased representation in the labor force.) Research presented in Part III provides some of the earliest information available on this growing population. Given the paucity of information available in the United States, data are also provided on research ongoing in Finland concerning attitudes of older workers toward early retirement as part of a national program to develop an agenda for addressing the needs of that country's aging population.

In Part IV, the impact of work on family functioning is examined. The data show us that the workforce of today is a patchwork of many kinds of families facing diverse circumstances. Perhaps the most familiar and common model of the family includes two working parents who are struggling to find time for the competing demands of career building, home maintenance, and child raising. One can easily add to this model, however, to include the single man or woman who has chosen to forgo marriage and children for the sake of career success, the unemployed parent who must struggle to maintain high self-esteem in a work-dominated culture, and the children who must fend for themselves because the conditions of parents' work do not allow for sickness and the need to nurture. What is the effect of these competing demands? What is the relationship between job stress and violent behavior directed at spouses and children? How do family-friendly policies affect productivity? And, perhaps most important (though beyond the scope of this book), in a culture that professes to deify family values, why are family needs so often dismissed? These are some of the questions that will guide current and future research efforts.

In Part V, researchers take these issues a step further by focusing on work and nonwork conflict. Research could be productively applied to many questions regarding this conflict. How do the conditions of work thwart or further the developmental tasks of adulthood? How do individuals resolve conflicts between the demands of work and the needs of self, spouse, and children? If individuals choose to forgo either work or family obligations, are they at greater or lesser risk for stress-related psychological disorders?

The answers to these questions will provide clues to the complex psychosocial and behavioral refinements necessary for maximizing the skills of a diverse workforce while minimizing stress-related disorders. Lowman (1993) wrote:

> a fulfilling life role achieved through productive work should be the legacy and expected birthright of each adult, given that life without purpose is generally life lived unhappily and not lived well. . . . By better understanding the conditions and demands of work that are most apt to contribute to fulfillment for workers across the spectrum, we will make significant gains in understanding the psychological well-being of both individuals and society. (p. 3)

Gwendolyn Puryear Keita
Joseph J. Hurrell, Jr.

References

Amaro, H., Russo, N. F., & Johnson, J. (1987). Family and work predictors of psychological well-being among Hispanic women professionals. *Psychology of Women Quarterly, 11,* 505–521.

Barling, J., & MacEwan, K. E. (1992). Linking work experiences to facets of marital functioning. *Journal of Organizational Behaviour, 13,* 673–683.

Bullard, R. B., & Wright, B. H. (1986–1987). Blacks and the environment. *Humboldt Journal of Social Relations, 14,* 165–184.

Colligan, M. J., Smith, M. J., & Hurrell, J. J., Jr. (1977). Occupational incidence rates of mental health disorders. *Journal of Human Stress, 3,* 34–39.

Edmonston, B., & Passel, J. S. (1992). *The future of the immigrant population of the United States* (PRIP-UI-19). Washington, DC: Urban Institute.

Greenhaus, J. H., & Parasuraman, S. (1986). A work-nonwork interactive perspective of stress and its consequences. *Journal of Organizational Behaviour Management, 8,* 37–55.

Herold, D. M. (1990). Using technology to improve our management of labour market trends. *Journal of Organizational Change Management, 3,* 2.

Ilgen, D. R. (1990). Health issues at work: Opportunities for industrial/organizational psychology. *American Psychologist, 45,* 273–283.

Jick, T. D., & Mitz, L. F. (1985). Sex differences in work stress. *Academy of Management Review, 10,* 408–420.

Landy, F. J. (1992). Work design and stress. In G. P. Keita & S. L. Sauter (Eds.), *Work and well-being: An agenda for the 1990s* (pp. 119–158). Washington, DC: American Psychological Association.

Landy, F., Quick, J. C., & Kasl, S. (1994). Work, stress and well-being. *International Journal of Stress Management, 1,* 33–73.

Lowman, R. L. (1993). *Counseling and psychotherapy of work dysfunctions.* Washington, DC: American Psychological Association.

National Institute for Occupational Safety and Health. (1988). Prevention of occupationally-generated illnesses: A proposed synoptic national strategy to reduce neurotoxic disorder in the U.S. workplace. In *Proposed national strategies for the prevention of leading work-related diseases and injuries, part 2* (NTIS No. PB89-130348, pp. 31–50). Cincinnati, OH: Author.

Nelson, D. L., & Hitt, M. A. (1992). Employed women and stress: Implications for enhancing women's mental health in the workplace. In J. C. Quick, L. R. Murphy, & J. J. Hurrell, Jr. (Eds.), *Stress and well-being at work: Assessments and interventions for occupational mental health* (pp. 164–177). Washington, DC: American Psychological Association.

Northwestern National Life Insurance Company. (1991). *Employee burnout: America's newest epidemic.* Minneapolis, MN: Author.

Piotrkowski, C. S. (1979). *Work and the family system.* New York: MacMillan.

Roberts, S. (1993). *Who we are: A portrait of America.* New York: Times Books.

Social Security Bulletin. (1989). *Annual statistical supplement, 1989* (DHHS Publication No. 13-11700). Washington, DC: U.S. Government Printing Office.

U.S. Department of Labor, Women's Bureau. (1992). *Women workers outlook to 2005.* Washington, DC: Author.

Williams, K. J., & Alliger, G. M. (1994). Role stressors, mood spillover, and perceptions of work-family conflict in employed parents. *Academy of Management Journal, 37,* 837–868.

WORKFORCE DIVERSITY

Part I ———————————————

Gender

Introduction

One of the major changes taking place in the work world over the past 3 decades has been the tremendous growth in the participation of women in the paid labor force. Although women's numbers have increased markedly, the research expanding gender issues has been limited. In the five chapters of this part, the authors attempt to expand the knowledge of gender issues in research on occupational stress and workplace wellness.

Despite the fact that a number of studies have recently appeared focusing on the relationship between gender, family roles, and occupational stressors, several basic questions remain unanswered. For example, it is still not known whether women suffer from greater occupational stress than men. Similarly, although there has been a good deal of research on how coping strategies mitigate work stress, little attention has been paid to gender differences in coping with this kind of stress. In a complex, large-scale study, Trocki and Orioli attempt to clarify a number of aspects of these relationships.

Next, Parker and Aldwin track changes in role meaning among adult men and women over the past 3 decades, using two measures of role meaning—perceived primary source of life satisfaction and aspiring to professional careers. They also examine the relationship between role meaning and the appraisal of stress.

The next chapter provides an examination of gender differences in the relationship between work and personal factors associated with mental distress. More specifically, Piltch, Walsh, Mangione, and Jennings examine whether there are gender differences in levels of mental distress and, if so, whether these differences are related to levels of social support, the presence of dependent children at home, or conflict between work and family obligations. In addition, Piltch et al. expand the Karasek job strain model to incorporate additional structural and personal factors, in an attempt to better explain variations in mental distress among women.

Fitzgerald, Hulin, and Drasgow then address an issue of increasing importance in the workplace, sexual harassment. After reviewing the research on sexual harassment and the effects of harassment on work and the organization, Fitzgerald et al. describe an integrated model of the antecedents and outcomes of sexual harassment in organizations. They develop a theoretical model integrating the sexual harassment variables, outline a set of measures to assess the model, and discuss practical problems of conducting sexual harassment research in organizations.

In the final chapter in this part, Schwarzer, Hahn, and Fuchs examine gender differences in a sample of East German citizens who migrated to West Berlin shortly before or after the opening of the Berlin Wall. Their research is part of a longitudinal study launched to gain detailed information about the adaptation and coping processes of refugees and migrants from East Germany. Schwarzer et al. specifically address gender differences in the effects of unemployment, social resources, and health at three points in time over roughly a 2-year period.

1

Gender Differences in Stress Symptoms, Stress-Producing Contexts, and Coping Strategies

Karen F. Trocki and Esther M. Orioli

The second half of the twentieth century has been a time of profound change for women. In 1950, less than one quarter of married women were in the labor force. Today, over 58% of married women work, and 75% of them work full-time (U.S. Bureau of Labor Statistics, 1992). The proportion of women with young children who work has also risen dramatically. In 1950 only 12% of women with preschool children worked; now, 60% of these women work. An even larger proportion of women with school-age children now work—75%, up from 28% in 1950. As women have moved into paid employment, there has been some increase in the home roles of husbands and fathers. Still, women continue to carry the larger workload at home (Crosby, 1988; Martin & Roberts, 1984; Oakley, 1974; Pleck, 1985), making them candidates for poorer physical and mental health arising from work–family role conflict, role strain, and fatigue from sheer overwork.

Research on gender and the stressors associated with work and family roles has been the theme of numerous articles and books (Barnett, Biener, & Baruch, 1987; Eckenrode & Gore, 1990). In spite of this attention, several very basic questions remain unanswered or inadequately addressed. Baruch, Biener, and Barnett (1987) noted that research on occupational stress has focused primarily on men and that many gaps and biases exist. Surprisingly, one of the unanswered questions is whether women suffer from greater "occupational stress" than men. In a recent meta-analysis, Martocchio and O'Leary (1989) could find only 15 studies of gender differences in occupational stress that offered sufficiently adequate methodologies for their findings to be trusted. About half of these studies used all or part of the Maslach Burnout Inventory (Maslach & Jackson, 1981), and the rest used a variety of measures, including blood pressure, psychosomatic complaints, the Center for Epidemiologic Studies—Depression Scale, physiological symptoms, and psychiatric symptoms. Martocchio and O'Leary (1989) stated that "the widely held belief that there are sex differences in occupational stress was not supported" (p. 498). However, they noted that the lack of a consistent pattern is not irrefutable evidence that gender differences do not exist, only evidence that there needs to be more systematic research on the topic conducted with comparable measures and comparable populations.

This lack of support for gender differences in occupational stress is in contrast to a relatively long tradition of findings in which women have fared more poorly than men (or, are more willing to admit to problems) on mental health measures (Gove & Geerken, 1979; Gove & Tudor, 1973, 1984; Kessler & McRae, 1981). In addition, women have been shown to have higher rates of morbidity and to use doctors more than men, but to have greater longevity (Anderson & Anderson, 1979; Clarke, 1983; Gove, 1978; Nathanson, 1975). Paradoxically, women in the labor force—precisely the women one would expect to be most overloaded—have generally been found to be healthier than women who do not work (Verbrugge & Madans, 1985; Waldron & Herold, 1986; Warr & Parry, 1982). In general, occupational roles have been associated with good psychological health in women, although studies controlling for age, marital status, and presence or absence of children (Arber, Gilbert, & Dale, 1985) have found that women with multiple obligations (especially single mothers) do, in fact, show poorer health than nonworking, age-matched counterparts.

Over and above the issue of whether women exhibit greater occupational stress is whether women who successfully cope with these multiple stressors use different strategies from men or from women who are "unsuccessful" copers. Again, most research on coping strategies and work has been done on men (Goldberger & Breznitz, 1982; Holt, 1982). A fair amount of attention has been focused on the importance of social support as a moderator of stress (Pearlin & Johnson, 1977), and women are thought to be better at seeking out support from others when it is needed (Belle, 1987). But Belle also noted that the demands of social network obligations can be sources of stress too. Although social support appears to buffer negative life events, the role of social support and support seeking as a moderator of occupational stress has not been established (Barrera, 1988). Coping skills, life outlook, powerlessness, self-esteem, alienation, personality, and Type A (hurried, competitive, and angry) behavior patterns are just a few of the factors that are known to moderate or buffer stress symptoms (Holahan & Moos, 1987; Holt, 1982). To date, however, relatively little attention has been paid to gender differences in modes of coping with occupational stress other than social support (Frone, Russell, & Cooper, 1991).

Our purpose in this study was to investigate gender differences in a sample comprised largely of professional and administrative workers by using an omnibus stress instrument that incorporates a diverse selection of measures thought to be symptoms of stress, indicators of environmental stressors, or measures of coping mechanisms. We examined four questions: (a) Are there gender differences in the existence of levels of environmental stressors, stress symptoms, and types of coping strategies used? (b) If gender differences are found, are there structural variables (e.g., marital status, childbearing status, age, managerial status, occupational level, workload, and income) or contextual variables (e.g., work pressures or family pressures) that are related to these symptoms and are there different patterns for men and women? (c) What specific work pressures are predictive of higher symptomology, and do the patterns of association differ for men and women? and (d) Are there gender differences in the relation of various coping factors to stress symptoms?

Method

Materials

The instrument used in this study was StressMap®[1] (Essi Systems, 1984). StressMap was originally created to gain a broad overview of stress and its various components. In developing the instrument, researchers comprehensively reviewed the literature on stress in humans, identifying over 75 different scales, factors, and influences from a wide variety of disciplines and specialties. An initial pool of items was created that was thought to comprehensively assess these various constructs and that took into account the work and family environment, experience of changes, individual differences in coping resources, and world outlook as well as measures of symptoms thought to be indicative of chronic exposure to stressors. After reviews by experts, pretesting with diverse populations, and initial factor analyses, the number of items was reduced to 274. The instrument was first normed on an American population (in the mid-1980s) and then, recently, was renormed on an employed Canadian population (the current study sample). Scale-score distributions, reliability coefficients, intercorrelations among scales, and patterns of association to demographic and work variables were similar in both countries (Essi Systems, 1994).

The instrument has 21 subscales that are divided into four different categories: (a) environmental stressors, (b) coping resources, (c) inner world—thoughts and feelings (outlook and dispositional characteristics), and (d) symptoms of distress. Alpha coefficients were calculated for each scale, and all scales showed coefficients greater than .70. Table 1 shows the scales within each of the four broad topic areas, the number of items in each scale, and their reliability coefficients.[2] Test–retest reliability for StressMap is good—greater than .70 on most scales. In a 6-week retest with no specific interventions in between, 80% of the scales showed reliabilities greater than .70, with Work Pressures (.89) and Behavioral Symptoms (.88) the highest. Various forms of validity testing have also been done. The symptomology scales are strongly associated with self-perceived health, doctor visits, and absenteeism.

Additional reliability checks have been done on other populations. More than 150 respondents kept daily records of emotional fluctuations in 3 separate weeks over the course of a year, followed by administration of StressMap. Daily records of emotional symptoms correlated with the StressMap Emotional Symptoms scale as follows: .38 for the two measurement points farthest apart, .54 for the interim measurement, and .62 for the closest points. In addition, a

---

[1] StressMap is a registered trademark of Essi Systems, 70 Otis Street, San Francisco, CA 94103.

[2] Further information on the theoretical background of StressMap can be obtained by contacting Essi Systems.

Table 1. Descriptive Characteristics for Subscales of StressMap®

Category & subscales	No. of items	α
Environmental stressors		
Work Changes	9	.73
Work Pressures	28	.89
Work Satisfaction	15	.82
Personal Changes	18	.70
Personal Pressures	12	.78
Personal Satisfaction	14	.90
Coping resources		
Self-Care	16	.73
Direct Action	13	.78
Support Seeking	9	.78
Situation Mastery	14	.75
Adaptability	8	.78
Time Management	11	.80
Inner world—thoughts and feelings		
Self-Esteem	8	.76
Positive Outlook	8	.74
Personal Power	8	.81
Connection–Alienation	9	.76
Expression	8	.79
Compassion–Anger	9	.80
Symptoms of distress		
Physical Symptoms	15	.74
Behavioral Symptoms	18	.70
Emotional Symptoms	23	.91

group of telephone operators identified as "highly stressed" was tested, and the average StressMap scores for these group members were at the extremes of the distribution (upper or lower 20%) on the symptomology scales (Essi Systems, 1994). Finally, StressMap has been used effectively to measure change over time in stress reduction programs (McCue & Sachs, 1991).

Overall scores are calculated for each subscale by summing all items. Responses to each item are made on 4-point scales ranging from 0 to 3; the maximum score for each subscale is the number of items multiplied by 3. The environmental pressures and changes scales, the inner world scales, and the symptomology scales are all scored so that a higher score reflects a poorer situation or more symptoms. The environmental satisfactions scales and the coping resources scales are scored so that a higher score reflects greater resources.

Sample

A sample of 28 different organizations representing a range of industries and sizes of companies was drawn randomly (but proportionate to size, so that larger firms had a greater chance of selection) from the large client list of the Center for High Performance (CHIP), a Canadian stress management and human resources firm. Within each selected organization, the contact person (usually the personnel director or human resources coordinator) was asked to randomly choose a sample of employees (larger companies were asked to draw larger samples). The contact person sent employees the StressMap questionnaire and asked them to return it directly to CHIP by mail. CHIP then forwarded the instruments to Essi Systems. In all, 1,500 instruments were distributed, and 61% (914) were returned. On the basis of knowledge about the companies themselves and through comparisons with national statistics, nonresponse was found to be higher among those in blue-collar occupations and with less education. However, this appears not to have resulted in any noticeable gender-specific biases. The employed men and women did not differ on most demographic characteristics, except that the women earned less, and a smaller proportion of women were in managerial occupations—patterns typical in Canada as well as in the United States.

The sample was evenly divided between men and women (51% and 49%, respectively), and 89% of the respondents were of European background. All respondents were between the ages of 18 and 65 years, with nearly 70% between 30 and 49 years of age. The sample was well educated, with over 50% having graduated from college or completed some postgraduate education. Most respondents were married or "partnered" (75%), and the remainder were evenly divided between never married and formerly married. Forty-four percent lived with children. Nearly two thirds of the sample held some sort of management responsibility: 11% were entry-level managers, 33% were middle managers, and 19% were upper-level managers. More than 90% of the sample worked full-time, and, of the total, nearly 20% put in 50 work hours or more per week. In contrast to the sample characteristics, a general population survey of Canada (Statistics Canada, 1989) showed that in the working population, 88% were of European background, 55% were between 30 and 49 years of age, 18% had university degrees, 60% were married, and 40% had children. The labor force characteristics of the study sample showed them to be heavily clustered in the administrative and management levels (41%, in comparison with 14% of the general working population) and in the professional or technical specialties (33% in the sample vs. 21% in the general population). This sample also had high income levels: 84% made over $30,000 per year in personal earnings, whereas only 68% of households of the Canadian working population had combined incomes over $30,000. In summary, in comparison with the general population, members of the stress survey sample tended to be clustered in middle age; were more likely to be married; were better educated, primarily in administrative and professional occupations; and had higher income levels. Thus, care should be taken in generalizing the stress survey results to the working population as a whole. Given its higher proportion of white-collar workers, this is the part of the population to which our findings can be addressed with the most confidence.

Results

The first question to be addressed was whether there were any differences between men and women in the number and type of stressors they perceived in their environment. For our purposes, the *environment* included work and personal domains (i.e., primarily family issues as well as general interpersonal relationships and personal problems). Table 2 shows that women self-reported more work and personal changes and perceived more work and personal pressures. The largest differences were on the Personal Changes and Personal Pressures scales. There were no gender differences on the two satisfaction scales. Table 2 also shows the mean scores for the three symptomology scales. Women had significantly higher symptoms scores than men on all three scales. The scale on which there was the smallest difference was the behavioral scale. On the emotional scale, the differences were quite substantial (men = 16.6 and women = 21.4).

The next table (Table 3) shows results for the 12 different constructs related to coping with, moderating, or buffering stressors. On 10 of the 12 scales, there were significant gender differences; however, in all instances, the real scale difference averaged about 1 point. Women had more favorable scores than men on self-care and support seeking. Men had more favorable scores on all of the other scales where differences were observed. There were no gender differences on positive outlook and compassion–alienation.

These first two data tables show that the women perceived more pressures and changes, had somewhat lower coping resources (except for self-care and social support), and also had more symptoms. However, before examining the interrelationship of the different sets of variables in StressMap it was important to determine the extent to which personal as opposed to occupational structural factors might be associated with higher levels of symptoms. We performed a series of multivariate regression analyses, using background information on personal status (age, marital status, and childbearing status) and

Table 2. Mean Scores for Environmental Stressors and Symptoms of Distress Scales

Subscale	Men (n = 428)		Women (n = 423)		t	df
	M	SD	M	SD		
Environmental stressors						
Work Changes	6.90	4.89	8.06	5.23	−3.31**	833
Work Pressures	22.10	12.22	24.62	13.44	−2.82*	819
Work Satisfaction	33.49	6.29	34.06	6.19	−1.34	874
Personal Changes	9.52	6.23	12.00	7.14	−5.35**	830
Personal Pressures	9.72	5.85	11.90	6.36	−5.27**	873
Personal Satisfaction	33.33	6.09	32.91	6.45	0.96	839
Symptoms of distress						
Physical Symptoms	7.30	4.83	9.00	5.05	−5.01**	853
Behavioral Symptoms	12.35	5.33	13.77	5.77	−3.67**	823
Emotional Symptoms	16.55	9.24	21.44	11.42	−6.75**	813

Note. Higher scores indicate greater stress, more symptoms, or more negative attitudes except on the Work and Personal Satisfaction scales. Actual sample sizes varied from scale to scale.
*p < .01.   **p < .001.

Table 3. Mean Scores for Coping Resources and Inner World Scales

Subscale	Men (n = 428)		Women (n = 423)		t	df
	M	SD	M	SD		
Coping resources						
Self-Care	33.55	6.16	34.70	6.13	−2.78**	881
Direct Action	27.29	4.81	26.36	4.98	2.81**	866
Support Seeking	16.80	3.69	17.72	3.52	−3.78***	883
Situation Mastery	19.73	5.18	18.83	5.42	2.51**	874
Adaptability	16.78	3.27	16.12	3.56	2.85**	887
Time Management	21.16	4.65	20.48	4.81	2.11*	873
Inner world—thoughts and feelings						
Self-Esteem	9.40	3.75	10.23	4.47	2.98**	864
Positive Outlook	6.36	3.67	6.45	4.05	−0.35	876
Personal Power	7.36	3.98	8.01	4.58	−2.25*	874
Connection–Alienation	8.76	4.59	8.76	4.91	−0.01	867
Expression	11.31	4.58	10.43	4.44	2.91**	880
Compassion–Anger	6.84	4.19	7.68	4.57	−2.84**	884

Higher scores on coping scales indicate a better ability to cope with stress. Higher scores on the inner world scales indicate greater stress, more symptoms, or more negative attitudes. Actual sample sizes varied from scale to scale.

*$p < .05$.   **$p < .01$.   ***$p < .001$.

work factors (occupational status, management status, hours worked, and income) as predictors of symptoms of distress. None of these variables were very good predictors for men. In only one analysis (with emotional symptoms as dependent) did any individual variable show a significant relationship. Men who lived with a spouse had fewer emotional symptoms, and, even in that instance, the overall equation was not significant. For women, the number of hours worked predicted physical and behavioral symptoms (the more hours, the more symptoms). Emotional symptoms, however, were associated with being younger and having children. But even here, only a small proportion of the variance in the Emotional Symptoms scale was accounted for by these structural factors.

It was thus necessary to turn to other specific work and personal stressors as measured by our instrument to understand the relationship of work and personal life to stress symptoms. Because we were faced with the problem of women having heavier demands than men with respect to family roles, we needed to control for family factors to determine if greater levels of symptoms were due to occupational stress. First, we conducted a series of analyses of covariance (ANCOVAs) to see whether a significant gender effect would exist once personal changes, pressures, and satisfactions were controlled for (entered as covariates). There was such an effect: Women still had significantly higher scores on all three symptom scales after we controlled for personal factors. However, when we conducted a second set of ANCOVAs—adding work changes, pressures, and satisfactions—there was still a significant gender difference on physical and emotional symptoms, indicating that there was additional variance attributable to gender not explained by either set of variables. When we conducted multivariate regression analyses separately for men and women, women did have more variance explained by personal factors. However, when work factors were entered, the change in the squared multiple correlation was very similar for men and women on physical symptoms (an increment of .039 for men, and .038 for women) and on emotional symptoms (.1038 for men, and .0915 for women), but was different on behavioral symptoms (.0938 for men, and .1309 for women). Entering the interaction of work and personal life variables added little to the explained variance. Thus, women had higher symptoms in response to stress, some of which was due to added personal factors and some of which was due to unexplained factors. However, the attribution of greater stress symptoms directly related to work pressures for women appears to be limited to the behavioral symptoms.

Table 4 shows the results of using the first six scales of StressMap— environmental stressors—as predictors in a series of stepwise multivariate regression analyses. We completed these analyses to identify the most parsimonious models. It has already been established in earlier research (Goldberger & Breznitz, 1982) that all of these factors have something to do with stress, but the primacy of each factor and the degree of overlap of these constructs

Table 4. Regression of Environmental Stressors Scales on Distress Symptoms: Stepwise Multiple Regression Analyses for Each Gender

	β	
Environmental stressor	Men	Women
Physical Symptoms		
Personal Pressures	.24***	.18**
Work Pressures	.18**	.23***
Work Changes	.15**	
Personal Changes		.18**
R^2	.18	.20
Behavioral Symptoms		
Work Pressures	.40***	.38***
Personal Pressures	.23***	.19***
Personal Satisfaction		−.14**
Work Changes		.11*
R^2	.29	.37
Emotional Symptoms		
Work Pressures	.39***	.21***
Personal Pressures	.30***	.26***
Personal Satisfaction		−.18***
Work Changes		.13**
Work Satisfaction		−.14*
R^2	.35	.41

$*p < .05.$ $**p < .01.$ $***p < .001.$

has rarely been investigated. As Table 4 shows, Personal Pressures and Work Pressures were the two most important scales in all analyses—furthermore, this was true for both men and women. For men, only one other variable entered any of the analyses: The Work Changes scale was also a predictor of physical symptoms. In spite of these consistencies, the patterning is quite intriguing. Personal pressures were more important predictors of physical problems in men, and work pressures were more predictive of physical problems for women. However, for women, family changes added to the explained variance, and, for men, work changes added to the explained variance.

Behavioral symptomology was very similar for both men and women (see Table 4). For both genders, work pressures were the most important predictors of behavioral symptoms. In addition to the role of personal pressures, additional variance was explained for women by personal satisfactions and work changes. Emotional symptomology was the reverse of physical symptomology, showing that personal pressures for women and work pressures for men were the best predictors of symptoms, respectively. In addition, work changes, work satisfaction, and personal satisfaction increased the explained variance for women. Roughly the same proportion of variance was explained for both men and women for physical symptoms, but more variance (approximately 8%) was explained for the Behavioral and Emotional Symptoms scales for women.

Although the results in Table 4 show that both work and family pressures are important for both men and women, little is known about whether there are specific factors in the work environment that are particularly stressful for one gender or the other. We therefore conducted stepwise multiple regressions separately for each gender and for each symptomology score by using the 28 individual items from the Work Pressures scale.

For the Physical Symptoms scale, all but one item was different for each gender. Only "unfair procedures" was in the equation for both men and women. On the whole, women have more physical distress symptoms if the workplace is physically uncomfortable and if they have a somewhat chaotic or demanding work situation. Men's physical symptomology seems more tied to role ambiguity and a competitive atmosphere. It is notable that *demands* were important for women whereas *pressures* (a subtly different word implying more freedom of choice in the meeting of long-term vs. short-term work tasks) were selected by men.

The predictors of behavioral symptoms were relatively similar for men and women; four items overlap—low job commitment, multiple tasks, conflicts with coworkers, and ethical problems. Women's stressors for behavioral symptomology also seemed to be tied to status (salary) and function (no decision making, high demands), but men showed more symptoms if their skills were not used. For emotional symptomology, low job commitment (which may in itself be a symptom of depression rather than a cause) was the best predictor for both men and women. Again, all other factors were different, with women's pressures relating more to multiple demands and men's relating more to role ambiguity, underuse of skills, ethical issues, and several *pressure* items.

The next question to address was whether there were gender differences in successful strategies used for coping with stress. The six coping resources scales and the six inner world—thoughts and feelings scales were used to address this question. Again, stepwise multiple regressions were done separately for each gender. The physical symptomology equation showed very different patterns for men and women. Self-esteem was the most important predictor of physical symptoms for women, whereas situation mastery (important for both men and women) and time management were the best predictors of physical health for men.

Behavioral symptomology showed similar patterns for each gender, but the rank order of the variables differed somewhat. Time management and connection were more important for men, and self-care and personal power were important for women. Men and women both had the same three variables as the strongest predictors of emotional symptoms, but personal power (e.g., self-efficacy or locus of control) was strongest for women, and situation mastery (Type A behavior pattern) was strongest for men. In contrast with findings from the regression of work pressures items, a substantially greater proportion of the variance for physical symptoms was predicted for women (.39, vs. .22 for men), and on the other two scales, the variance accounted for was roughly the same for men and women (and substantial—40% for behavioral symptoms and about 50% for emotional symptoms).

Coping and dispositional characteristics can be thought of as buffers against the stressors of the environment. To illustrate this, Figure 1 shows the "protective" effects of two important variables—situation mastery (1a) and personal power (1b)—on emotional symptoms. At all levels of work pressures, those who are below the median on situation mastery or personal power show higher levels of emotional symptoms in comparison with those above the median.

Results of final summary analysis, in which we regressed all the different blocks of variables (using forced entry) on each of the three distress symptom scores, are shown in Table 5. We first entered the demographics (age, marital status, and childbearing status) and then the work structural variables (management status, hours worked, income, and occupational level). The coping resources and inner world block was entered next because these were the protective factors (or, if absent, the risk factors), and then the stressors were entered to see if additional variance was accounted for over and above the moderating effect of the coping factors. As we have already observed, the demographic and work status variables were negligible, the coping factors accounted for a substantial portion of the variance, and, then, when the stressors were entered, some additional variance was explained—but much of it was buffered by the preceding block of variables.

Discussion

Several different questions were addressed in this study. The first question— Do women have more environmental stressors and, if so, do they experience more physical, behavioral, and emotional symptoms of distress?—seems to have been supported. The largest differences were on the two pressure scales and the emotional symptomology scale. Surprisingly, there were no differences

a.

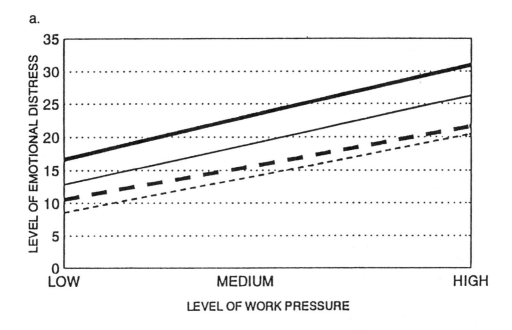

b.

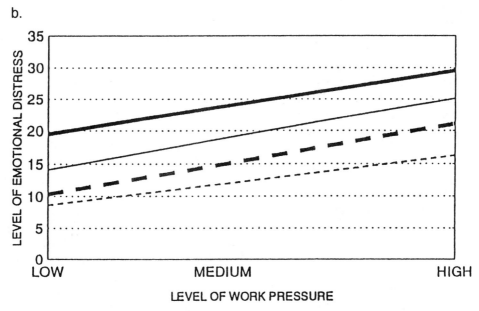

Figure 1. The buffering effect of (a) situation mastery and (b) personal power on levels of emotional distress and work pressure for men and women. Thicker lines show the results for women, and thinner lines show the results for men. Dashed lines indicate those above the median for the coping factor (situation mastery or personal power); solid lines indicate those below the median.

Table 5. Results of Summary Multiple Regression Analyses for Men and Women

Subscale & variable	Cumulative R^2	
	Men	Women
Physical Symptoms		
Demographic variable block	.01	.01
Work status variable block	.01	.05
Coping and inner world variable block	.24	.31
Environmental stressors	.28	.38
Behavioral Symptoms		
Demographic variable block	.01	.02
Work status variable block	.01	.04
Coping and inner world variable block	.39	.42
Environmental stressors	.44	.49
Emotional Symptoms		
Demographic variable block	.01	.03
Work status variable block	.02	.04
Coping and inner world variable block	.48	.50
Environmental stressors	.54	.57

on satisfactions: Men and women seem equally satisfied with personal life and work life. Women tended to have lower scores on many of the coping measures (except for self-care and support seeking, in which they surpassed men), but though this was statistically significant, they differed from men usually by only about 1 point.

The second question thus addressed whether symptom levels are related to personal and work structural factors or to sets of stressors in the work and personal environment. We also tested whether women's symptoms disproportionately arose from occupational factors. Although demographic factors explained little variance, women did have greater explained variance on symptoms measured by the personal scales of the StressMap instrument. In addition, although increments to explained variance for work pressures were virtually identical for women and men on the physical and emotional scales, occupational factors predicted more gender variance on the behavioral scale. Thus women have more symptoms, but some of these are due to family or personal life, a few are due to occupation, and still others result from unexplained factors. Stepwise regressions showed that women seem to react to somewhat different stressors in the environment. Scales measuring more specific personal life and job factors did account for substantial amounts of the variance. Physical wear and tear shows a slight tendency to be linked to gender-incongruent stressors: Men are sicker in response to personal or family pressures first and work pressures second, whereas for women the reverse is true. Emotional symptoms, however, showed higher scores in response to gender-congruent stressors, and for behavioral symptoms, work pressures appeared to be primary for both men and women. It should be noted that in all equations, work pressures and personal pressures accounted for large portions of the variance for both men and women. Neither men nor women are immune from a particular source of stress, and for both, personal and work stress appears to be cumulative.

The third question we addressed was whether specific stressors in the workplace differed for men and women. The analysis of individual items from the Work Pressures scale showed some similarities between men and women, with several notable differences. Overall, women seemed more distressed by job demands, whereas men seemed to react more negatively to role ambiguity and a somewhat competitive atmosphere (e.g., office politics and ethical problems). In an analysis of employed individuals in the Framingham Heart study (Haynes & Feinleib, 1980; Haynes, LaCroix, & Lippin, 1987), coronary heart disease symptoms were higher in women who had high job demands and low clarity from supervisors. Haynes and Feinleib noted that the riskiest combination for women was to be married, to have children, and to be in a clerical occupation. Men in the Framingham study, however, did not show the same risk for coronary heart disease with respect to job demands and, in one category, showed a reduced risk: men whose jobs were both low on demand and low on supervisory clarity. The results reported in this study are consistent with the Framingham pattern for women but inconsistent with the findings for men.

With respect to coping strategies, there are common patterns for men and women but there seem to be somewhat different factors that protect women and men from the effects of stressors. The findings on differences in primary coping styles or differences in personal beliefs are quite interesting. The Personal Power scale is a measure of one's personal feeling of being able to control the world; other, similar constructs measure self-efficacy, locus of control, or learned helplessness (e.g., Bandura, 1977; Seligman, 1975). On the Personal Power scale, some of the strongest items are "I do not think I have control over things in my life" and "I find myself in situations I feel helpless to do anything about." This scale dominates two of the three measures of symptomology for women, whereas situation mastery (Type A behavior pattern) is more central for men. This suggests the possibility of differences in coping style that arise from fundamental societal structural patterns associated with gender.

The results of the coping skills analyses highlight the fact that many of the most common skills emphasized in stress management programs (e.g., self-care and the importance of gaining social support) apparently turn out not to be the most important factors that help individuals deal with stressful environments. Thus, exercise, relaxation, and proper nutrition may not be the only or even the most critical behaviors to modify to reduce the impact of environmental stressors. In our study, self-care was an important predictor for behavioral symptoms for women. As noted earlier, support seeking is the major construct that other researchers have investigated concerning occupational stress for women. However, support seeking was not an important predictor of levels of stress in any of our equations. On the other hand, seeking help from others may not be the same as having a strong social network available when help is needed. It is worthy of note that these two constructs, self-care and support seeking, have been heavily cited in the literature on stress and are the only two constructs on which women in our study had higher scores.

An important implication of this study is that more interventions need to be planned that take gender into account and focus on cognitive and skill-based coping strategies, as well as on relaxation and self-care. Stress management programs in the workplace tend to be short (often lasting only a few hours), tend to focus on physical stress management rather than on cognitive management, and seldom involve any evaluation or long-term follow-up. One more intensive (seven-session) study compared "cognitive" with "relaxation" approaches to stress management among women (Higgins, 1986). Both approaches were found equally effective relative to the approach taken by the control group but their effects were not different from one another. However, posttests were done immediately after the seventh session. Programs that focus on self-care do have an impact—but long-term follow-up may reveal that cognitive and skill-building approaches may have more sustained effects. Women will undoubtedly be helped by programs that teach them how to relax, but they may be even further aided by stress reduction programs that help them perceive themselves as able to influence the environment or as empowered (as illustrated in Figure 1b).

Although we have focused on physical, behavioral, and emotional symptomology as our outcome variables, we should also note that—among those with high work pressures but good coping skills—absenteeism and doctor visits were also lower. This provides a very practical incentive for incorporating stress management programs in the workplace.

Our findings also illustrate that various coping constructs developed by disparate researchers may be additive. That is, if a person feels empowered, engages in few Type A behaviors, and is good at time management, then he or she should be even better able to deal with environmental stressors than someone with only one of these skills. In many previous studies, only one or two coping constructs have been used at a time, leaving the impression that only that single factor was important. Because StressMap permits simultaneous measurement of multiple types of stressors, multiple coping constructs, and different categories of stress symptomology outcome, it offers a more comprehensive perspective.

Several limitations to these findings should be noted. First, these data are from a Canadian population and may not be entirely generalizable to a population in the United States. However, of the several, smaller studies that have been done in the United States with the same instrument, the same general patterns of gender differences have been found. A second limitation is that the questionnaires were distributed to randomly selected individuals within organizations, to be filled out on a voluntary basis. This could have resulted in some undetected but systematic biases in the response patterns of men and women. For instance, more highly stressed women may have been attracted to participating in the survey, whereas more highly stressed men might have seen the study as another demand and ignored it. An additional shortcoming is that the study was cross-sectional. The strong association of stressors and coping factors to symptomology needs to be evaluated in a longitudinal perspective to examine the interaction of worldview and self-perceptions with environmental stressors over time. A chronically stressful work situation can lower self-confidence, produce feelings of lack of control, and make individuals irritable and short-tempered. Although stressors may have "caused" poor coping, it is likely that the solution is still the same: Coping skills need to be built or rebuilt to bring about change in stress symptoms.

In summary, this study has shown that women do have more symptoms of distress than men, that these symptoms arise from both the work and personal environments, and that there are certain coping strategies and cognitive outlooks that appear to act as buffering agents between stressors and symptoms. Although men and women do show considerable overlap in what helps them successfully cope with stress, it is worthwhile to continue experimenting with gender-specific approaches to stress reduction.

References

Anderson, R., & Anderson, O. W. (1979). Trends in the use of health services. In H. E. Freeman, S. Levine, & L. G. Reeder (Eds.), *Handbook of medical sociology* (pp. 371–391). Englewood Cliffs, NJ: Prentice Hall.

Arber, S., Gilbert, G. N., & Dale, N. (1985). Paid employment and women's health: A benefit or a source of strain? *Sociology of Health and Illness, 7,* 375–400.

Bandura, A. (1977). Self-efficacy: Toward a unifying theory of behavioral change. *Psychological Review, 84,* 191–215.

Barnett, R. C., Biener, L., & Baruch, G. K. (Eds.). (1987). *Gender and stress.* New York: Free Press.

Barrera, M. (1988). Models of social support and life stress: Beyond the buffering hypothesis. In L. H. Cohen (Ed.), *Life events and psychological functioning: Theoretical and methodological issues* (pp. 211–236). Newbury Park, CA: Sage.

Baruch, G. K., Biener, L., & Barnett, R. C. (1987). Women and gender in research on work and family stress. *American Psychologist, 42,* 130–136.

Belle, D. (1987). Gender differences in the social moderators of stress. In R. C. Barnett, L. Biener, & G. K. Baruch (Eds.), *Gender and stress* (pp. 257–275). New York: Free Press.

Clarke, J. N. (1983). Sexism, feminism and medicalism: A decade review of literature on gender and illness. *Sociology of Health and Illness, 5,* 62–82.

Crosby, F. (1988). *Spouse, parent, worker: On gender and multiple roles.* New Haven, CT: Yale University Press.

Eckenrode, J., & Gore, S. (1990). *Stress between work and family.* New York: Plenum.

Essi Systems. (1984). *StressMap.* San Francisco: Author.

Essi Systems. (1994). *Technical manual for StressMap (revised).* San Francisco: Author.

Frone, M. R., Russell, M., & Cooper, M. L. (1991). Relationship of work and family stressors to psychological distress: The independent moderating influence of social support, mastery, active coping and self-focused attention. *Journal of Social Behavior and Personality, 6,* 227–250.

Goldberger, L., & Breznitz, S. (Eds.). (1982). *The handbook of stress.* New York: Free Press.

Gove, W. R. (1978). Sex differences in mental illness among adult men and women: An evaluation of four questions raised regarding the evidence on the higher rates of women. *Social Science and Medicine, 12B,* 187–198.

Gove, W. R., & Geerken, M. R. (1979). The effect of children and employment on the mental health of married men and women. *Social Forces, 56,* 66–76.

Gove, W. R., & Tudor, J. F. (1973). Adult sex roles and mental illness. *American Journal of Sociology, 26,* 64–78.

Gove, W. R., & Tudor, J. F. (1984). Adult sex roles and mental illness. *American Journal of Sociology, 98,* 812–835.

Haynes, S. G., & Feinleib, M. (1980). Women, work and coronary heart disease: Prospective findings from the Framingham Study. *American Journal of Public Health, 70,* 133–141.

Haynes, S. G., LaCroix, A. Z., & Lippin, T. (1987). The effect of high job demands and low control on the health of employed women. In J. C. Quick, R. Rasbhagat, J. Dalton, & J. D. Quick (Eds.), *Work stress and health care* (pp. 93–110). New York: Praeger.

Higgins, N. C. (1986). Occupational stress and working women: The effectiveness of two stress reduction programs. *Journal of Vocational Behavior, 29,* 66–78.

Holahan, C. J., & Moos, R. H. (1987). Personal and contextual determinants of coping strategies. *Journal of Personality and Social Psychology, 52,* 946–955.

Holt, R. R. (1982). Occupational stress. In L. Goldberger & S. Breznitz (Eds.), *The handbook of stress* (pp. 419–444). New York: Free Press.

Kessler, R. C., & McRae, J. A. (1981). Trends in sex and psychological distress. *American Sociological Review, 47,* 216–227.

Martin, J., & Roberts, C. (1984). *Women and employment: A lifetime perspective.* London: Her Majesty's Stationery Office.

Martocchio, J. J., & O'Leary, A. M. (1989). Sex differences in occupational stress: A meta-analytic review. *Journal of Applied Psychology, 74,* 495–501.

Maslach, C., & Jackson, S. E. (1981). *Maslach Burnout Inventory.* Palo Alto, CA: Consulting Psychologists Press.

McCue, J. D., & Sachs, C. C. (1991). A stress management workshop improves residents' coping skills. *Archives of Internal Medicine, 151,* 2273–2277.

Nathanson, C. A. (1975). Illness and the feminine role: A theoretical review. *Social Science and Medicine, 9,* 57–62.

Oakley, A. (1974). *The sociology of housework.* New York: Pantheon.

Pearlin, L., & Johnson, J. (1977). Marital status, life strains and depression. *American Sociological Review, 42,* 704–715.

Pleck, J. (1985). *Working wives/working husbands.* Beverly Hills, CA: Sage.

Seligman, M. (1975). *Helplessness.* New York: Freeman.

Statistics Canada. (1989). *1989 National Household Survey.* Ottawa, Ontario, Canada: Special Surveys.

U.S. Bureau of Labor Statistics. (1992). *Work and family: Jobs held and weeks worked by young adults.* Washington, DC: U.S. Government Printing Office.

Verbrugge, L. M., & Madans, J. H. (1985). Social roles and health trends of American women. *Millbank Memorial Fund Quarterly: Health and Society, 63,* 691–735.

Waldron, I., & Herold, J. (1986). Employment, attitudes toward employment, and women's health. *Women and Health, 11,* 79–98.

Warr, P., & Parry, G. (1982). Paid employment and women's psychological well-being. *Psychological Bulletin, 91,* 498–516.

2

Desiring Careers but Loving Families: Period, Cohort, and Gender Effects in Career and Family Orientations

Rebecca A. Parker and Carolyn M. Aldwin

Research on stress in work and family roles has begun to focus on the meaning of roles to individuals (Wiley, 1991). Measures of role meaning have taken many forms, however, making it difficult to compare findings across studies (Komarovsky, 1982). Measurement types can be organized into two general groups. The first includes rewards and costs accruing to roles (sometimes stated as *relative importance for providing life satisfaction*; Faver, 1982; Regan & Roland, 1985; Veroff, Reuman, & Feld, 1984). The second infers role meaning from role aspirations (Fiorentine, 1988; Regan & Roland, 1985) or achievements (Kanter, 1976). This second perspective assumes that values "serve an organizing function in the adolescent-to-young adulthood stage of the life cycle" (Howell, Ohlendorf, & McBroom, 1981, p. 478) and, therefore, that an individual's behavior (e.g., professional aspirations) reflects that person's value hierarchy (e.g., valuing prestige and status). The purpose of our research was to track changes in role meaning among young adults over the past 3 decades by using both measurement approaches. Furthermore, we examined the relationship between each construct and later reports of family or career stress.

The meaning of career and family roles appears to be changing for both men and women, although research has provided conflicting evidence. Analyses performed with measures of benefits and costs have suggested that younger cohorts of men expect less from their careers (Regan & Roland, 1985) but also that they continue to desire the perceived benefits of professional employment (e.g., financial rewards and obtaining recognition; Fiorentine, 1988). These lowered expectations may be associated with weaker attachments to work roles (Korman, 1989). Among women, benefits associated with the work role appear to have greater salience for recent cohorts (Veroff et al., 1984), although for

This research was supported in part by Hatch Act Funds awarded to Carolyn M. Aldwin through the University of California, Davis, and by a grant to both of us from the MacArthur Network on Successful Midlife Development. We thank Paula Schnurr and Avron Spiro III, for counsel on some of the analyses; Leanne Friedman for her help with data management and analyses; and Rael Dornfest, Cory Fitzpatrick, and Tiffany Pfeffers for help with data collection and data entry.

reasons different from men's. Women's interest in professional growth does not replace their traditional orientation toward relationships (Baber & Monaghan, 1988; Gilligan, 1982). Rather, it appears that women either intend to combine traditional with nontraditional activities (Almquist, Angrist, & Mickelsen, 1980; Fiorentine, 1988) or are career motivated by opportunities for social and interpersonal experiences within the work setting (Anselmi & Smith, 1984). Indeed, there is a continuing expectation that men are more willing than women to prioritize work over relationships (Pittman & Orthner, 1988).

This apparent gender difference gained support from Johnson and Jaccard (1980), who reported that men mentioned health strain as a consequence of a career-focused lifestyle whereas women mentioned concerns about raising children. On the other hand, Amatea, Cross, Clark, and Bobby (1986) reported that factor analyses of the rewards associated with work and family roles resulted in substantially identical factors for both men and women, thus providing evidence against gender differences in role meaning.

To further cloud the question of changing role meanings, little is known about men's conceptions of the rewards and benefits of family life. Some would argue, however, that family roles rather than work roles have always been the primary source of satisfaction for men (Cohen, 1987; Pleck, 1985). Nevertheless, despite early evidence that men are increasingly willing to provide full-time care for their children (Russell, 1974), others argue that the "culture of fatherhood" has changed more quickly than men's behavior (LaRossa, 1988) and that even full-time caregiving fathers do not necessarily see their family roles as their primary status (Grbich, 1992).

Evidence gained through measures of role meaning in terms of aspirations and achievement has been more consistent than that reported above. Young men continue to aspire to professional positions, although perhaps at a somewhat lower rate (Regan & Roland, 1985). Career aspirations of young women, however, have increased substantially over the past 2 decades (Komarovsky, 1982; Machung, 1989; Regan & Roland, 1985). It has been suggested, however, that young women may be unaware of the costs of professional career development and, thus, may assert career goals that are inconsistent with their family goals (Machung, 1989).

There is general agreement that values affect appraisals of stress (Amatea et al., 1986), although the particulars of that relationship are not well understood (Aldwin, 1982). For example, it is unclear whether valuing something can lead to increased stress—as threats to a desideratum may be particularly distressing (Lazarus & Folkman, 1984)—or to decreased stress—as strong commitments may provide a sense of meaning or purpose that acts as a buffer to stress (Antonovsky, 1979). Faver (1982) suggested that a discrepancy between roles and values is associated with decreased life satisfaction, especially for women in the prefamily, early motherhood, and late motherhood family stages. That is, women with high career orientations and young children are more likely to be dissatisfied with their lives than are young mothers with low career orientations or high family orientations. On the other hand, multiple-role commitments may be seen as a stress buffer. If performance in one role becomes problematic, an individual may focus more on another role, drawing comfort, satisfaction, and self-esteem from that area. Individuals who place all of their "role eggs" in one basket, as it were, may not have anything else to fall back on if that role becomes problematic, and thus may appraise these situations as extremely stressful (cf. Aldwin & Stokols, 1988).

Present Study

We examined secular trends across 3 decades with two measures of role meaning (perceived primary source of life satisfaction and professional aspirations) in three cohorts of college alumni: 1968–1970, 1979, and 1989. We were particularly interested in the divergence or convergence of these trends and in whether they varied by gender. We were also interested in the extent to which professional aspirations varied as a function of role values. Finally, we especially wanted to examine the relationship between role meaning and the appraisal of stress, defined as "low points" in an individual's life. That is, are individuals with strong commitments to one role more or less likely to experience low points in that role?

Method

Sample and Procedures

The sample consisted of University of California, Davis, alumni who were participants in the Davis Longitudinal Study (Parker & Aldwin, 1993; Regan & Roland, 1985; Yonge & Regan, 1975). Figure 1 shows the design of the study. Members of Cohort A were surveyed first as seniors (1968–1970) and then as alumni, at 10 years (1979) and at 22 years (1991) after graduation (A1–A3, Figure 1). For simplicity's sake, these graduates are hereinafter referred to as *Cohort A*. Members of Cohort B joined the study as seniors in 1979 and were resurveyed 12 years (1991) after graduation (B1–B2, Figure 1). Members of Cohort C entered the study during their senior year (1989) and were resurveyed during the 1991 survey (C1, Figure 1). Analyses for secular trends used data gathered from respondents as seniors (A1, B1, and C1). Analyses of the relationships between role values, role aspirations, and stress used longitudinal data gathered from Cohorts A and B as seniors (A1 and B1) and as 10- and 20-year alumni (A2, A3, and B2).

In any study that draws on longitudinal data, there exists a basic dilemma between maximizing sample size and having a consistent sample across time. Although we initially considered simply using listwise deletion and having a small but consistent sample, we found that we lost too great a proportion of the sample to adequately reflect secular trends. Thus, we opted for a dual strategy. For those analyses in which we examined secular trends in role values and professional aspiration, we retained the maximum sample. However, we used a smaller subsample for the longitudinal analyses. Thus, the sample size varied by analysis.

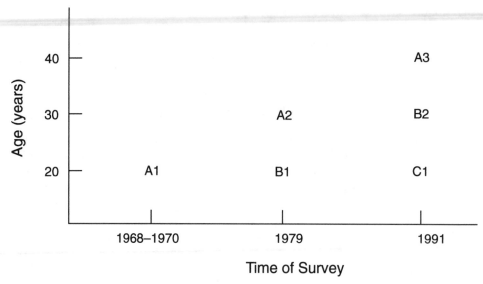

Figure 1. Research design of the Davis Longitudinal Study. A, B, and C designate the three cohorts surveyed. 1, 2, and 3 denote the order of survey time: for example, *B1* denotes the first survey of Cohort B (in 1979).

For the secular trend analyses, the base sample consisted of 4,232 men and women who provided complete surveys as graduating seniors. For Cohort A, 90% of those sampled responded ($n = 1,699$). For Cohort B, the response rate dropped to 61% ($n = 2,019$). For Cohort C, budget limitations necessitated a smaller base population, and, with a response rate of 52%, resulted in a relatively small subsample ($n = 300$). Thus, we supplemented Cohort C with role value data gathered from an additional set of 1989 alumni ($n = 214$) who responded to our 1991 survey 2 years after graduation, creating a cohort of 514 individuals. (The two subsamples of Cohort C did not differ on the dependent variables, using chi-square analysis, thus justifying our combining data sets.) We did not gather professional aspirations data in the 1991 survey; therefore, we had a more limited subsample for those analyses. Although the response rates differed across the cohorts, the relative proportions of men to women remained equal in the samples (i.e., for Cohorts A, B, and C, respectively, 49%, 48%, and 42% were men).

In addition to surveying a new group of seniors (Cohort B), we surveyed Cohort A respondents as 10-year alumni. The response rate was 58%, resulting in a sample size of 847.

In 1991, we resurveyed as many respondents as we could find, adding additional members to Cohort C, as mentioned earlier (see Parker & Aldwin, 1993, for more details). Out of 2,695 surveys sent to current addresses in the summer of 1991, 1,093 returned usable questionnaires, for a 41% response rate. Thus, the longitudinal sample sizes, after listwise deletion, were 464 and 137 for Cohorts A and B, respectively. Again, a roughly equal percentage of men and women responded (percentages of male members were 49% and 50% in Cohorts A and B, respectively). Although the majority of the respondents identified themselves as White (95%, 93%, and 76%, for Cohorts A, B, and C, respectively), the diversity of the sample increased in the younger cohorts. The proportion of each cohort identifying as Asian increased (5%, 4%, and 20%, respectively) at a greater rate than the proportion identifying as Hispanic (1%, .7%, and 3%, respectively). Native Americans made up 2% of Cohorts B and C, whereas African Americans composed less than 1% of all but the most recent (1989) cohort (Cohort C; .2%, .7%, and 1%, for Cohorts A, B, and C, respectively).

Because of the questions being posed, it was important that the sample be varied in terms of marital and career status. At the most recent survey time, the majority of respondents from Cohorts A and B were married, with slightly more men married than women (78% vs. 74% for Cohort A and 77% vs. 73% for Cohort B, men vs. women). Over half (66%) of the sample respondents were working on or had completed postgraduate degree programs. Of those currently employed, 40% were employed at the upper-white-collar level, and an additional 35% were employed at the professional and executive level.

Measures

Role meaning. To measure respondents' perceptions of the benefits and costs associated with roles (our first definition of *role meaning*), we used a question from the Cornell Values Study (Goldsen, Rosenberg, Williams, & Sachman, 1960). Respondents were asked to identify which items, from a list of seven, were primary, secondary, and tertiary sources of life satisfaction. Response options were in seven categories: literature, art or music; career or occupation; family relationships; leisure time, recreational activities; religious activities; participation in community affairs; and participation in activities directed toward national or international betterment. The data were organized in two different ways. Categories 1 and 4–7 were collapsed into a single category labeled *avocation.* For analyses in which the value orientations were dependent variables, we created three dummy variables that indicated the primacy of family, work, and avocation as sources of life satisfaction.

To measure role meaning in terms of aspirations, all senior respondents were asked to identify their long-term occupational goals. Those responses were then categorized into an occupational status and prestige scale with responses ranging from *manual labor* (1) to *executive* (9) (Edwards & Wilson, 1961). The scale then was dichotomized into nonprofessional and professional aspirations; the nonprofessional category was used as the referent for the analyses. This coding system is unusually rigorous in distinguishing professional from white-collar and nonprofessional occupations and considers as professional occupations only those that require lengthy formal preparation, continuous participation, and full-time (or more) involvement. Consequently, by definition, those occupations that are traditionally filled by women (e.g., nursing and teaching) were not coded as professional occupations. This means that any woman in a professional occupation, according to these criteria, was involved in an atypical work role.

Career and family stress. In the 1991 survey, respondents answered the following question: "Most people also have low points in their lives. Please circle the events which have been *major low points* for you." The list of 32 items that followed included marital and relationship problems, problems with children, and career and work problems, as well as other types of problems not examined here. Two dichotomous variables were created from this question: the first identifying those who circled either marital and relationship problems or problems with children, and the second identifying those who circled career and work problems.

Analyses

We used logistic regression with backward stepwise elimination for all analyses. This procedure uses a maximum likelihood method to develop a model predicting the likelihood that an event (coded as a dichotomous variable, 0 or 1) will occur. The impact of each main effect (coded as categorical variables) on the outcome variable is interpreted as the odds that an outcome will occur (Norusis, 1990). We discuss results in terms of the change in the odds (odds ratio, or *OR*) of an event occurring for one category relative to another category (e.g., responses of a woman relative to those of a man). Each set of interactions has an associated *Wald* statistic, which has a chi-square distribution in which the degree of freedom equals $k - 1$ (where k is the number of categories). However, within the set, the individual interaction terms may or may not be significant. Note that in logistic regression, each interaction term singles out a particular group to which everyone else is compared. In our results, we indicate the significance of individual interaction terms by the p value.

Results

Results are divided into three sections. The first addresses secular trends in the two assessments of role meaning, using data collected from the three cohorts of seniors in 1968–1970, 1979, and 1989 (A1, B1, and C1 in Figure 1). In the second section, we used longitudinal data to examine the relationship between the two role-meaning measures: role values and professional aspirations as seniors, and respondents' subsequent professional achievement as 10- and 20-year alumni (A1–A2, B1–B2, and A1–A3). In those analyses, we also examined the effects of gender and cohort. In the third section, we used longitudinal data to evaluate the relationship between two measures of role meaning: endorsed as seniors and career and family stress reported as 10- and 20-year alumni (A1–A3 and B1–B2).

Secular Trends

Role values. Figure 2 presents the secular trends in the three categories of role meaning: (a) family values, (b) career values, and (c) avocation. Contrary

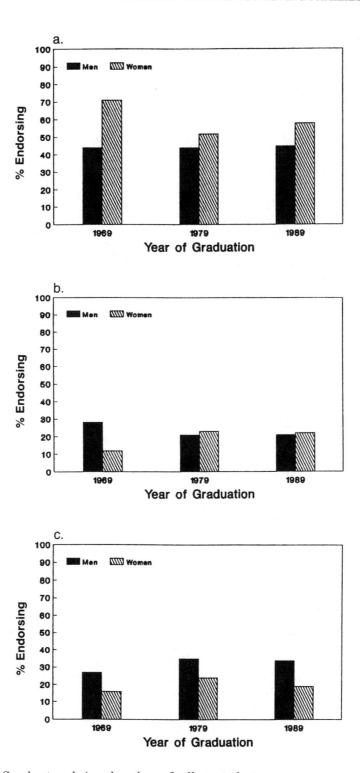

Figure 2. Secular trends in role values of college students.

to popular expectations, men were surprisingly consistent in their valuation of family across cohorts (44%, 44%, 45%, for Cohorts A, B, and C, respectively; see Figure 2a). Furthermore, women in all cohorts chose family well over 50% of the time (71%, 52%, and 58%, respectively).

The full logistical model best predicted the endorsement of family roles, $\chi^2(5, N = 4{,}232) = 186.262, p < .001$, identifying significant gender and cohort differences as well as a significant Gender $\times$ Cohort interaction. In general, men were half as likely as women to endorse family as their primary source of satisfaction ($OR = 0.56, p < .000$), whereas Cohorts B and C endorsed this less frequently ($OR = 0.67, p < .001$) than did Cohort A ($OR = 0.78, p < .05$). Interaction terms showed that the sexes also differed in these secular trends, $Wald(2, N = 4{,}232) = 37.05, p < .001$. Although women's expectations for family roles changed substantially over the 3 decades (decreasing and then increasing slightly), men's expectations were stable. The result of these trends was a decrease in sex difference from Cohort A to Cohorts B and C.

Secular trends in the salience of career roles also showed variability (see Figure 2b). Significant gender effects as well as Gender $\times$ Cohort interactions were identified, $\chi^2(3, N = 4{,}232) = 70.119, p < .001$. Although the overall finding was that men were more likely than women to endorse careers ($OR = 1.64, p < .001$), in fact, that relationship was primarily true for Cohort A. The significant Gender $\times$ Cohort interaction shows that, after 1969, women and men were equally likely to expect primary life satisfaction from careers, $Wald(2, N = 4{,}232) = 51.84, p < .001$. This pattern was a significant departure from what we had expected and suggests that a significant switch had occurred in the meaning of career roles to young adults.

The decreasing salience of career roles among men, without a concomitant increase in family role salience, was unexpected and highlights the need to explore alternative sources of life satisfaction. As shown in Figure 2c, the role of avocations for providing life satisfaction increased substantially between 1969 and 1989, particularly for men. There were significant gender and cohort effects, $\chi^2(3, N = 4{,}232) = 100.864, p < .001$, correctly classifying 74% of the cases. In all cohorts, men were more likely to identify avocational roles as very satisfying ($OR = 1.36, p < .001$). However, the significant cohort effect revealed that, relative to Cohort A, Cohorts B and C were both more likely to anticipate primary life satisfaction from activities that were neither work nor family based (for Cohort B, $OR = 1.50, p < .001$; for Cohort C, $OR = 1.30, p < .05$).

In summary, the belief that family would provide primary life satisfaction remained relatively high for both men and women across the three cohorts. However, men and women showed opposite trends in their expectations about careers. Women were increasingly likely, and men less likely, to endorse careers as salient roles across cohorts. Among men, it appears that avocational interests are replacing careers as significant sources of life satisfaction. In contrast, as women's endorsements of family and career values have increased, their endorsements of avocational values has decreased.

Professional aspirations. If the two measures of role meaning were appraising the same characteristics of an individual, then one would expect that the decrease in reward value of careers for men would be manifested as lower rates of professional aspirations. Similarly, one would expect higher rates of professional aspirations among young women, given their increasing valuation of career-based rewards. These hypotheses were only partially supported. Aspirations for professional employment increased greatly for both men and women (see Figure 3), with significant gender, cohort, and Gender × Cohort effects, $\chi^2(5, N = 2,861) = 746.170, p < .001$. Cohort B and C respondents were 4 times as likely to aspire to professional careers as were Cohort A respondents ($ORs = 3.96$ and 4.21, respectively, $ps < .001$). In addition to this general increase, however, there was a significant Gender × Cohort interaction, $Wald(2, N = 2,861) = 67.273, p < .001$. The substantial gender difference observed in Cohort A, in which men aspired to a career more than women, was significantly diminished among Cohort B and C respondents.

Relationships Between Measures of Role Meaning

Role values and career aspirations of college seniors. To examine the relationships between role salience and career aspirations, we regressed role values (beliefs about the rewards accruing to particular roles) on professional aspirations and cohort. We performed separate analyses for each gender because, in the earlier analyses, gender was always a significant main effect, making the likelihood of three-way interactions (which would be difficult to interpret) very great. In these analyses, Cohort A was the referent for cohort, and family role was the referent for the role-value variable.

For men, professional aspirations were not related to role values. Thus,

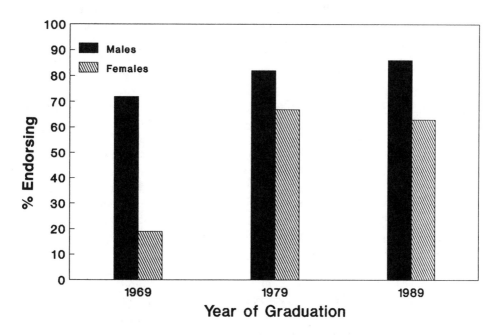

Figure 3.   Secular trends in professional aspirations of college seniors.

only cohort membership was a significant predictor, $\chi^2(2, N = 1,351) = 26.315$, $p < .001$. It appears that aspiring to a professional position, at least for college-educated men, is the norm and therefore is not a reflection of individually held values or expectations about the benefits of professional employment.

In contrast, for women, role values as well as cohort were significant predictors, $\chi^2(4, N = 1,497) = 375.115, p < .001$. Women who anticipated primary life satisfaction from their career roles were twice as likely to aspire to professions as women with salient family roles ($OR = 2.2, p < .05$). Similar trends were seen among women who oriented primarily around avocation activities ($OR = 1.6, p < .01$). Surprisingly, though, there were no significant interactions. As noted above, women who graduated from college in 1979 or 1989 were many times more likely to aspire to professional positions than were women graduating in 1969—respectively, for Cohorts B versus A and C versus A, $ORs = 7.9$ and 6.8 ($ps < .000$)—with the 1979 graduates showing the greatest increase. Thus, Cohort B women were nearly 8 times more likely and Cohort C women were 7 times more likely than Cohort A women to have professional aspirations.

Role meaning and professional aspirations. We next examined the relationship between each measure of role meaning for the college seniors and professional achievement 10 and 20 years after graduation.

Ten years after graduation, employment as a professional in the early 30s, for men, was best predicted by professional aspirations as seniors and by an interaction between cohort and professional aspirations, $\chi^2(2, N = 223) = 29.485, p < .001$. There was no interaction between role values and professional aspirations. In general, men who aspired to a professional career as graduating seniors were many times more likely to be professionally employed in their 30s than were men without those aspirations ($OR = 6.02, p < .001$). Men who graduated in 1979 with professional aspirations, however, were much less likely than similarly oriented 1969 graduates to have achieved professional employment by their early 30s ($OR = 0.31, p < .01$). This interaction effect raises a number of interesting questions. Did criteria for professional employment change between 1970 and 1980? Did economic conditions limit opportunities for professional employment?

For women, professional employment as 10-year alumnae was also associated with main effects of professional aspirations and values, $\chi^2(3, N = 209) = 23.942, p < .001$. Women with professional aspirations were much more likely to be employed in professional positions than those without such aspirations ($OR = 3.83, p < .05$). Interestingly, avocation values were associated with higher rates of professional employment ($OR = 2.87, p < .05$), relative to family values. However, career values were not associated with professional achievement 10 years later.

Twenty years after graduation, men's professional achievement at midlife was predicted by main effects of professional aspirations as college seniors and values, $\chi^2(3, N = 226) = 35.404, p < .001$. Not surprisingly, focusing on avocational roles was associated with lower levels of professional achievement at midlife ($OR = 0.26, p < .001$). Career values, however, were no more likely to predict professional achievement than were family values. As reported above, aspirations were strongly associated with professional employment (OR = 3.99, $p < .001$).

Among women, professional employment at midlife was predicted by professional aspirations as seniors, $\chi^2(1, N = 222) = 16.28, p < .001$. However, value orientations were not associated with achievement as either main effects or in interactions with aspirations. As with the earlier analyses, women who aspired to professions as college seniors were much more likely to be employed as professionals ($OR = 4.01, p < .001$).

In summary, professional achievement occurs more frequently among those who aspire to a professional status as college seniors than among those who do not. Surprisingly, however, successfully meeting those goals was not contingent on beliefs that the professional role would provide primary life satisfaction. Although for women professional aspirations were associated with career values, there was no interaction between these measures in predicting women's professional achievement. Interestingly, the role of avocation values in predicting professional success differed for men and women. Among women, valuing avocational roles was positively associated with professional achievement in their 30s. For men, that value orientation was negatively associated with professional achievement in their 40s.

Longitudinal Analyses on Stress

We next examined the relationship between role meaning (using both measures) and role stress, defined simply as the perception of types of low points in our respondents' lives. For these analyses, we used longitudinal data gathered when the respondents were in their 30s (Cohort B) and their 40s (Cohort A). These data permitted us to analyze the long-term effect of role meaning in the early 20s on midlife perceptions of role stress. If the vulnerability theorists are correct, then role values should correctly predict a greater frequency of low points in that particular role. Thus, strongly valuing family could lead to a higher likelihood of reporting family stressors. In these analyses, we also examined the role consistency versus role complementarity model by examining interaction effects. If the role consistency theorists are correct, then individuals who endorse career values and who have professional aspirations should be less likely to have career-related low points, whereas the opposite would be predicted by the role complementarity theorists. Alternatively, individuals who are committed to multiple roles may experience less stress in any of those roles because of the buffering effects of multiple-role involvement.

We first regressed each low-point variable on gender and cohort. There were significant gender and cohort differences in reports of career low points, $\chi^2(2, N = 601) = 20.739, p < .001$. Women were significantly less likely to report career low points than men ($OR = 0.71, p < .000$), and members of Cohort B reported fewer low points than Cohort A ($OR = 0.66, p < .05$). About 45% and 57% of men and 30% and 38% of women in Cohorts A and B, respectively, reported low points in their careers. (Recall that Cohort A was substantially larger than Cohort B, thus the apparently contradictory results.)

Given these differences, we decided to separate the data for the remaining analyses by gender to avoid the three-way interactions mentioned earlier. Surprisingly, there were no significant differences in the likelihood of reporting family low points by gender or cohort. In general, about 50% of men and women in both cohorts reported having low points in their family roles.

Perceptions of career stress in women were significantly predicted by role values, professional aspirations, and a Cohort × Values interaction, $\chi^2(5, N = 306) = 27.104$, $p < .001$. There was no interaction between values and professional aspirations. Aspiring to professional positions resulted in lower rates of career stress ($OR = 0.44$, $p < .01$). Likewise, expecting primary life satisfaction from one's career appeared to protect women, in general, from experiencing career low points ($OR = 0.33$, $p < .01$), relative to women with high family expectations. There was a significant Cohort × Value interaction, however. Women who graduated in 1979 and who expected much satisfaction from their careers were nearly 4 times as likely to report career low points as were all other women ($OR = 3.9, p < .05$). This cohort effect could be attributed to higher expectations falling on women in the postfeminist cohorts or could be accounted for by the demands of the career-building stage that many women in their 30s would have been responding to.

Similar analyses with men did not result in a model that permitted us to predict career low points as a function of cohort, role values, or career aspirations. Despite the prevalance of reported career problems, none of these characteristics was useful in accounting for those reports.

Similarly, none of the predictor variables—cohort, job aspirations, or role values—significantly predicted reports of family low points for either men or women. Among women, there was a trend for those in Cohort B with primary career values to be about half as likely to report family low points as other women ($OR = 0.4$, $p = .07$). This result provides weak support for the stress-buffering effect of multiple-role incumbency.

Discussion

We examined secular trends in two measures of role meaning—expected satisfaction and professional aspirations—in three cohorts of college seniors (1969, 1979, and 1989 graduates). We examined the interrelationship of the trends as well as their ability to predict subsequent career achievement and low points in family and career in later adulthood.

Surprisingly, the two measures of role meaning showed very different secular trends. Professional aspirations showed marked increases for both sexes across cohorts, although this was especially true for women, undoubtedly reflecting the impact of the women's movement. Although this increase in professional aspirations was paralleled (albeit at a lower level) in the expectation of career as a primary source of life satisfaction for women, an opposite trend was seen for men. Later cohorts of men appeared to expect more satisfaction from their avocations than from their careers, despite the increase in professional aspirations.

More important, nearly 70% of the women and about 50% of the men expected the family to be their primary source of life satisfaction. For men, this was remarkably stable across the three cohorts; however, the 1979 female graduates showed lower rates (similar to the men's) than either the 1969 or 1989 female graduates. It is tempting to speculate that Cohorts A and C reflected mother–daughter similarities and that a cohort graduating in 1999 might more closely resemble Cohort B, but this may be a bit premature. Nonetheless, these findings strongly contradict popular beliefs about decreases in family values in American culture during the past 20 years.

Role-meaning measures also showed different patterns of correlations for men and women. Women who expected careers to be their primary source of life satisfaction were significantly more likely to have professional aspirations than were women with other value orientations, irrespective of cohort membership. In contrast, professional aspirations among men did not reflect expected sources of life satisfaction, perhaps because nearly all college-educated men aspire to professional careers, even if they expect families or avocations to be their primary source of life satisfaction.

In regard to professional achievement, aspiring to a professional career was significantly related to attaining that goal at both the 10- and 20-year points for both men and women. However, career values did not predict professional achievement, either as a main effect or in interaction with aspirations. Women who valued their avocational roles, however, were more likely to have developed their careers by their early 30s. In contrast, men who valued their avocational roles as college seniors were less likely to be in professional positions at midlife.

Among women for whom career was important, career stress was significantly reduced. In contrast with predictions of vulnerability theorists, having high goals for one's career was associated with lower rates of career stress. Similarly then, putting one's eggs in the career basket appears to protect one from perceiving career events as stressful (although there was no interaction between aspirations and values). However, women from Cohort B who expected much from their careers were more vulnerable to career low points than were women from Cohort A. For the latter women, their career values did not protect them from perceiving their careers as stressful. There could be several explanations for this. First, this was the first postfeminist cohort of college seniors in the Davis Longitudinal Study, and it is plausible that these women might have been experiencing impediments in the workplace (e.g., the "glass ceiling") that they might not have anticipated. On the other hand, these women were still at the career-building stage (in their early 30s) and, thus, might have felt particularly vulnerable to frustrations that more experienced career women knew to be temporary and surmountable.

Our analyses provided limited support for role constancy theory. Work and family stress was lower among women who valued careers as sources of life satisfaction and among women who aspired to professional careers. Our analyses on men's career stress did not demonstrate a similar relationship. However, we could not identify any relationships between beliefs about role benefits or professional aspirations as college seniors and later reports of family stress for either men or women.

Several things are notable from this study. The relationship between cost–benefit beliefs about roles and aspirations for those roles varies as a function of gender. The domains of each measure may be relatively independent. Expecting life satisfaction from one life domain (i.e., family) may not predict aspirations in another. Men who anticipate satisfaction from their families are no less likely to have professional aspirations than are men who anticipate satisfaction from their careers. As men increasingly expect primary satisfaction from avocational pursuits, they are increasingly likely to aspire to professional positions. This growing discordance between values and goals is not, however, manifested in either family or career low points, although it may affect professional achievement.

Among women, however, believing that careers will provide significant satisfaction is associated with professional aspirations, which, in turn, is associated with a lower likelihood of career stress. For women, then, there is a relatively direct relationship between role expectations and aspirations as college seniors and later perceptions of stressors.

Finally, there may be cohort differences in the relationship between role meaning and stress. For women in Cohort B (who were the first cohort in this study to experience heightened career aspirations as a function of the women's movement), anticipating satisfaction from a career-focused lifestyle was associated with much greater levels of career stress. It seems less plausible that the stress is a consequence of being in atypical positions, because career-oriented women from Cohort A did not report similar levels of career stress. Rather, perceptions of career stress are either a consequence of being at the height of one's career-building efforts, or social pressure to succeed has increased these young women's stake in their career success.

Some caveats are in order. First, our sample was not representative of the general population. Respondents were all college educated, and many had completed graduate degrees. The differential response rates across cohorts and sampling times suggests that, within our already unrepresentative sample, there might be some additional bias. For instance, it is plausible that individuals who had been unsuccessful at achieving their goals might be less inclined to respond to a survey of this nature. In addition, the measures we used were simple and did not allow our respondents to provide complex pictures of their life goals or life values. Thus, our failure to find strong support for either the role complementarity or role consistency theories may have been due more to the simplicity of our measures than to the inadequacy of those theories. However, the fact that there were gender and cohort differences in the correlates of role meaning suggests that more contextual theories of values and roles may be necessary.

Nevertheless, this study clearly shows that the family is still perceived as the primary source of life satisfaction for men and women. The current cohorts of men and women were equally as likely to value careers, but men are turning more and more to avocation as the primary source of life satisfaction. Regardless, the desire for a professional career is now nearly universal among college graduates, and, as we have shown, aspirations as college seniors provide the best predictor of professional achievement in later adulthood. However, the difficulty in the ability of the younger cohorts to achieve professional status in the 1980s was noteworthy, and the current economic climate suggests that this will only get worse rather than better. Thus, as careers become more stressful, it may be that future cohorts will turn more to family and avocations as sources of life satisfaction.

References

Aldwin, C. (1982). *The role of values in the stress and coping process: A study in person–situation interactions.* Unpublished doctoral thesis, University of California, San Francisco.

Aldwin, C., & Stokols, D. (1988). The effects of environmental change on individuals and groups: Some neglected issues in stress research. *Journal of Environmental Psychology, 8,* 57–75.

Almquist, E. M., Angrist, S. S., & Mickelsen, R. (1980). Women's career aspirations and achievements. *Sociology of Work and Occupations, 7,* 367–384.

Amatea, E. S., Cross, E. G., Clark, J. E., & Bobby, C. L. (1986). Assessing the work and family role expectations of career-oriented men and women: The life role salience scales. *Journal of Marriage and the Family, 48,* 831–833.

Anselmi, D. L., & Smith, K. M. (1984, August). *Gender differences in career, marriage and family expectations of college students.* Paper presented at 92nd Annual Convention of the American Psychological Association, Toronto, Ontario, Canada. (ERIC Document Reproduction Service No. ED 25697)

Antonovsky, A. (1979). *Health, stress, and coping.* San Francisco: Jossey-Bass.

Baber, K. M., & Monaghan, P. (1988). College women's career and motherhood expectations: New options, old dilemmas. *Sex Roles, 19,* 189–203.

Cohen, T. F. (1987). Remaking men. *Journal of Family Issues, 8,* 57–77.

Edwards, T. B., & Wilson, A. B. (1961). *A study of some social and psychological factors influencing educational achievement.* Unpublished manuscript, Department of Education, University of California, Berkeley.

Faver, C. A. (1982). Life satisfaction and the life-cycle: The effects of values and roles on women's well-being. *Sociology and Social Research, 66,* 435–451.

Fiorentine, R. (1988). Increasing similarity in the values and life plans of male and female college students? Evidence and implications. *Sex Roles, 18,* 143–158.

Gilligan, C. (1982). *In a different voice: Psychological theory and women's development.* Cambridge, MA: Harvard University Press.

Goldsen, R. K., Rosenberg, M., Williams, R., Jr., & Sachman, E. (1960). *What college students think.* Princeton, NJ: Van Nostrand Reinhold.

Grbich, C. (1992). Societal response to familial role change in Australia: Marginalization or social change? *Journal of Comparative Family Studies, 23,* 79–94.

Howell, F. M., Ohlendorf, G. W., & McBroom, L. W. (1981). The 'ambition-achievement' complex: Values as organizing determinants. *Rural Sociology, 46,* 465–482.

Johnson, S. J., & Jaccard, J. (1980). Career-marriage orientations in college youth: An analysis of perceived personal consequences and normative pressures. *Journal of Youth and Adolescence, 9,* 419–437.

Kanter, R. M. (1976). The impact of hierarchical structures on the work behavior of women and men. *Social Problems, 23,* 415–430.

Komarovsky, M. (1982). Female freshmen view their future: Career salience and its correlates. *Sex Roles, 8,* 299–314.

Korman, A. K. (1989). Money and self-realization: New trends in western culture. In E. Krau (Ed.), *Self-realization, success, and adjustment* (pp. 26–40). New York: Praeger.

LaRossa, R. (1988). Fatherhood and social change. *Family Relations, 37,* 451–457.

Lazarus, R. S., & Folkman, S. (1984). *Stress, appraisal, and coping.* New York: Springer.

Machung, A. (1989). Talking career, thinking job: Gender differences in career and family ex-
    pectations of Berkeley students. *Feminist Studies, 15*, 35–58.

Norusis, M. J. (1990). *SPSS/PC+ Advanced Statistics 4.0*. Chicago: SPSS.

Parker, R. A., & Aldwin, C. M. (1993). *Does sex-role identity change in adulthood? Differentiating
    between age, cohort and period effects*. Manuscript submitted for publication.

Pittman, J. F., & Orthner, D. K. (1988). Gender differences in the prediction of job commitment.
    Journal of Social Behavior and Personality, 3, 227–248.

Pleck, J. H. (1985). *Working wives/working husbands*. Beverly Hills, CA: Sage.

Regan, M. C., & Roland, H. E. (1985). Rearranging family and career priorities: Professional
    women and men of the eighties. *Journal of Marriage and the Family, 46*, 985–992.

Russell, C. (1974). Transition to parenthood: Problems and gratifications. *Journal of Marriage
    and the Family, 36*, 294–302.

Veroff, J., Reuman, D., & Feld, S. (1984). Motives in American men and women across the adult
    life span. *Developmental Psychology, 20*, 1142–1158.

Wiley, M. G. (1991). Gender, work, and stress: The potential impact of role-identity salience and
    commitment. *Sociological Quarterly, 32*, 495–510.

Yonge, G. D., & Regan, M. C. (1975). A longitudinal study of personality and choice of major.
    Journal of Vocational Behavior, 7, 41–65.

3

Gender, Work, and Mental Distress in an Industrial Labor Force: An Expansion of Karasek's Job Strain Model

Cynthia A. Piltch, Diana Chapman Walsh, Thomas W. Mangione, and Susan E. Jennings

In this chapter, we discuss research that assessed whether gender differences exist in the relationship between work and personal factors associated with mental distress in a sample of male and female workers in New England. Furthermore, we sought to determine whether the Karasek job strain model, which measures the impact of job content on worker health, could be improved to better explain mental distress in men and women.

We began this study intending to do a comparative analysis of job stress and mental distress for men and women inasmuch as most studies have concentrated on male workers, and we had available to us a sample with sufficiently large numbers of women to provide a sound sample. In this chapter, we also describe previous job stress research and assess some of the key sources and moderators of mental distress.

Models of Job Stress and Work

Occupational health research has been expanding in recent years beyond an exclusive focus on physical hazards in the workplace to broader conceptions of health that embrace psychosocial dimensions of work: the "social environment at work, organizational aspects of the job and certain operational aspects of the tasks performed" (Sauter, Murphy, & Hurrell, 1990, p. 1150). Occupa-

The material for this chapter was adapted from a presentation by Cynthia A. Piltch and from her doctoral dissertation conducted at Boston University as a Pew Scholar with a grant from the Pew Memorial Trust. Lois Biener, Jonathan Howland, and Timothy Heeren made helpful contributions to that effort. The New England Worker's Health Study was funded in part by grants to D. C. Walsh from the Commonwealth Fund, the General Electric Foundation, the National Institutes of Health, and the Kellogg National Fellowship Program. Daniel M. Merrigan, Richard Youngstrom, and Susan K. Hamilton made important contributions to the study during its early conceptualization and data collection phases.

tional stress researchers from the United States and Europe (especially Sweden) have examined how specific characteristics of jobs affect mental health (e.g., depression, anxiety, and general mental distress symptoms) and physical outcomes, such as heart disease, ulcers, and chronic pain. (For summaries, see Johnson & Johannson, 1991; Karasek & Theorell, 1990; Sauter, Hurrell, & Cooper, 1989.)

Increasingly, such research has focused on two resources—social support and job control—as potential moderators of the effect of work-related demands and pressures on the mental and physical health of individuals. Social support for work includes help that individuals receive from supervisors, coworkers, spouses, friends, and relatives. Control, in general, is "the ability to exert some influence over one's environment so that the environment becomes more rewarding or less threatening" (Ganster, 1989, p. 3). Job control is the ability to influence the planning and execution of work tasks. Unlike measures of personal control that focus on the individual's personality, job control focuses on how the organization of work may or may not provide the resources necessary for workers to meet the demands of production.

A theoretical model that has increasingly been used to measure the effects of job content on worker health and well-being is the job strain model developed by Robert Karasek (1979, p. 288) and colleagues in Sweden. The two-dimensional model locates the primary source of work stress within the task demands of the job itself. Jobs that simultaneously present heavy psychological demands and restrict the worker's options for responding to those demands (i.e., jobs high in demands and low in decision latitude, or "control") are seen as potentially stressful. Decision latitude includes control over both the use of one's abilities (skill discretion) and the way in which work is accomplished (skill authority). Psychological job demands include such factors as time pressure, deadline stress, heavy workloads, and conflicting demands. Karasek's measures of job demands and control derived originally from the U.S. Quality of Employment Survey (QES), administered in 1969, 1972, and 1977 (Quinn & Staines, 1979). In early analysis, the model was used to test the relationships between self-reported measures of job demands and control and mental strain (exhaustion and depression) in male workers in the United States and Sweden (Karasek, 1979). The U.S. data came from the 1972 and 1977 QES; the Swedish sample came from a 1968 and 1974 longitudinal national survey of workers. The U.S. study showed a fourfold variation in depression between workers in *high-strain jobs* (the high demands and low control group) and those in *low-strain jobs* (high control and low demands). Furthermore, both the U.S. and Swedish samples showed a fourfold variation in exhaustion between the high-strain and low-strain workers.

The job strain model sorts workers into quadrants on the basis of the level of psychological job demands and control they experience. The model is interactive in that the impact of job demands is expected to be moderated by job control. High-strain jobs are expected to produce higher levels of mental and physical distress than low-strain jobs, *active jobs* (high demands and high control), or *passive jobs* (low demands and low control). The interactive model suggests two hypotheses, one each along the major and minor diagonals in the

2 × 2 table: (a) in both cells where demands are relatively greater than control, mental and physical distress will occur (Diagonal A), and (b) when demands and control are both high, active learning should result, whereas when they are both low, skills will atrophy (Diagonal B; Karasek, 1979, p. 288). Virtually all of the research to date using the job strain model has assessed the first hypothesis, not the second.

The job strain model has contributed importantly to the advancement of job strain research (Karasek & Theorell, 1990), but it has limitations, two of which are particularly relevant to our purposes here. First, the model over-simplifies the association between work and mental distress. Second, it has been tested chiefly with samples of men and may not apply as well to female workers. In an effort to address the problem of oversimplification, a few researchers have already expanded the original job strain model to include social support in relationship both to mental health (Hall & Johnson, 1989; Landsbergis, Schnall, Dietz, Friedman, & Pickering, 1990) and to physical outcomes (Johnson & Hall, 1988; Johnson, Hall, & Theorell, 1989; Taylor, 1989). However, research is still needed that will expand the job strain model further to incorporate the demands and control factors with additional environmental and individual factors found in previous research to be related to mental distress. Such factors include career insecurity, environmental hazard exposure, and marital and parental status.

Furthermore, the job strain model needs to be tested more in samples that include women, especially in light of the well-established fact that women have higher prevalence rates of affective disorders than men. The job strain model was originally tested with data from entirely male samples. Although Karasek and his colleagues subsequently analyzed 925 women from the 1972 and 1977 QES data and found patterns among the women that were comparable with those found among men (Karasek & Theorell, 1990, p. 49), only one other published U.S. study has had sufficiently large female and male samples to support meaningful gender comparisons among major occupational groups (Loscocco & Spitze, 1990). Loscocco and Spitze used operational definitions of demands (job strain) and control (autonomy) that were different from the job strain model to study their association with happiness and distress, the latter a measure principally of physical, not psychological, symptoms. The authors found support for an additive effect of demands and control on happiness in both genders, but no support for an interactive effect. Using distress as a dependent variable, they found support for an additive effect of demands and control in men only and no support for an interactive effect in either gender.

To date, the published literature lacks studies using Karasek's measures of demands and control to assess differences between women and men working in similar settings, occupations, or both in the job strain–mental distress relationship. Findings from two studies in Sweden (Hall, 1989) and the United States (Jennings et al., 1989) have suggested that Karasek's job strain model may be less useful for explaining variations in levels of mental distress among working women than it has been among men. In both studies, women generally reported lower levels of job control than men and less occupational variation in control. Note, though, that a relative absence of attention to women appears in job stress studies using the job strain model. As in other areas of biomedical research, men's experiences have implicitly been assumed to suffice as a "gold standard" for women (*Testimony of Mark Nadel*, 1990).

Gender Similarities and Differences Related to Work Stress

Over the past decade, a number of researchers have set out to challenge the assumption that men's experiences can adequately stand in for those of women. Although a substantial and growing body of research has focused on groups of women workers (summarized in Barnett, Biener, & Baruch, 1987), few studies have compared the experiences of women and men working in the same organizational settings, jobs, or both. The limited research actually comparing the impact of work on the mental health of men and women has suggested both similarities and differences. Neil and Snizek (1988) found that within the same jobs, men were more likely to value job status, autonomy, and ability to use their skills, whereas women were more likely to value relationships with others. Although Nelson and Hitt (1992) found no differences between male and female personnel professionals in levels of work–home conflict or social support, they did find that female workers were more likely to report concerns about organizational politics and lack of career opportunities. These factors were associated with greater levels of distress in women.

The most ambitious effort to date to explicate the complex relationships among gender, work, and distress was undertaken by Loscocco and Spitze (1990). In a sample of 1,573 male and 649 female factory workers, they explored how various environmental and individual factors explained the variance in psychophysiological symptoms of distress (frequency of headaches, upset stomach, exhaustion or feeling nervous, fidgety, and tense) and well-being (happiness). More specifically, this study compared the importance of men and women's job demands (overtime and job strain), job deprivations and rewards (substantive complexity, autonomy, income, span of control, and plant size), physical hazards, and work-related social supports in explaining variations in distress and happiness. The authors were able to explain only a modest amount of variance in both distress (8% for men and 9% for women) and happiness (16% in men and 22% in women). However, their findings supported the idea that job demands—especially job strain and physical hazards—contribute to distress whereas job rewards—especially autonomy and good pay—protect against distress, showing similar patterns for men and women. Although marriage played a protective role for both sexes, the presence of children was hazardous for women but not for men.

Loscocco and Spitze (1990) demonstrated the potential value of using a broader framework than that encompassed in Karasek's job strain model to explore the relationship of gender, work, and mental distress. It is important to understand whether women and men working in the same organizational settings, jobs, or both show similar levels of mental distress and what structural and individual factors best explain any variation in levels of distress.

The New England Worker's Health Study

Our own research on sex differences in work stress complements and builds on previous studies. We assessed work and personal factors associated with mental distress in a sample of 2,673 male and female industrial workers in New England. Drawing on previous research, we posed two principal questions in the present study.

First, are there significant gender differences in the important relationships between work and personal factors and mental distress? We expected that women in general would report higher levels of mental distress and that, more than men, women would report greater levels of mental distress if they had less social support, dependent children at home, and more concern about conflicts between work and family obligations. We expected to find higher levels of distress in the absence of job control among men than among women.

Second, can the Karasek job strain model be expanded profitably to incorporate additional structural and personal factors, and will this expanded model provide a more complete explanation of variations in mental distress in the male and female samples?

Our study included 2,004 male and 669 female industrial workers, drawn from a single Fortune 50-sized company. The data were carved out of the larger New England Worker's Health Study, a cross-sectional survey of a probability sample of male and female employees at seven installations of three industrial firms. The survey was administered between March 1985 and June 1986 and has been described more fully by Walsh, Jennings, Mangione, & Merrigan (1991) and by Piltch (1992). The subsample for this study came from four of the participating company's sites in Massachusetts, one in New Hampshire, and one in Vermont. All of the sites were engaged in heavy manufacturing.

Respondents represented all levels of the managerial hierarchy. The random sample was stratified by site, gender, pay status (exempt, nonexempt, or hourly) and work shift (day, evening, or night), so that upper-level management and hourly female workers could be oversampled. The survey was self-administered, by mail for supervisory staff, and in groups on company time for rank-and-file workers. The overall response rate was 63%.

Instruments and Measures

We used a transactional model of mental distress (see Figure 1) to assess gender differences in work and personal factors associated with increased levels of mental distress. The model has five major domains of variables. Adapted from Matteson and Ivancevich's (1987) organizational stress framework, this transactional model assumes a process in which individuals assess the requirements of their work and perceive it as stressful when the demands of the job exceed their coping resources. Perceived stress, in turn, may or may not lead to symptoms of mental distress.

In the transactional model, social and personal coping resources (the equivalent of Kobasa's, 1987, stress-resistance resources of personality and social support) and personal attributes (demographic characteristics that the indi-

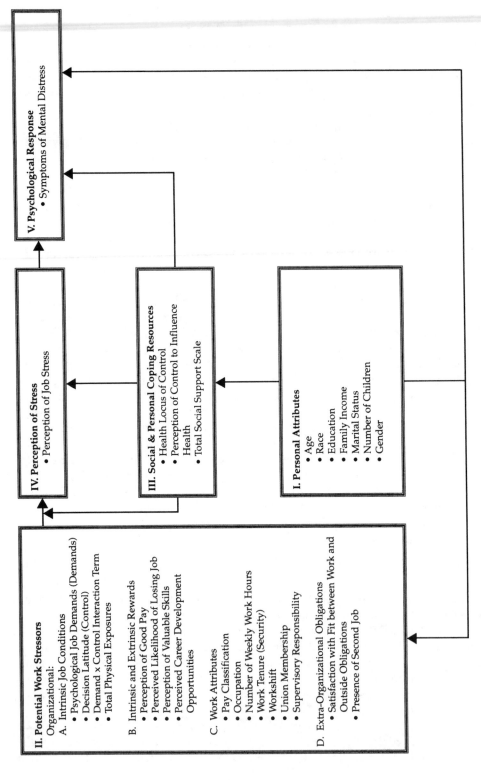

Figure 1. Expanded model of work impact on mental distress.

vidual brings to the job) may have independent effects on each other or on any of the other three domains of variables. The model differentiates components of the work experience in four subcategories: (a) intrinsic job conditions (characteristics inherent to the structure of jobs), (b) intrinsic and extrinsic rewards (elements of compensation associated with jobs), (c) work attributes (objective characteristics associated with occupational position), and (d) extraorganizational obligations (demands outside of work that may affect or be affected by the demands of the job).

A detailed description of all measures within each category of the expanded model is available elsewhere (Piltch, 1992). In this chapter, we summarize major findings concerning differences between women and men. The key variables used in the analysis were constructed as scales and tested for internal consistency by using Cronbach's alpha coefficients (for scales comprising individual items) or reliability of linear combinations (for scales comprising two or more subscales; Nunnally, 1967, pp. 226–230). The variables incorporated in the analysis included certain personal and work factors that had been identified in various studies as having an association with job stress, symptoms of mental distress, or both.

The dependent variable, mental distress, combined three subscales (depression, sleep disturbance, and anxiety) totaling 18 items. It was adapted from physical and psychosomatic strain measures of the QES and from Gurin, Veroff, and Feld's (1960) psychophysiological measures, which were later used by Gore and Mangione (1983). The scale showed a high linear combination reliability of .91 and derived from a question in which respondents assessed the frequency, over the past 12 months, that they had experienced such symptoms as exhaustion, trouble breathing, poor appetite, trouble sleeping, and feeling "blue" or lonely.

Among the key independent variables was a domain tapping potential work stressors, including Karasek's (1979) Job Demands Scale, which consisted of two subgroups of items. The first subgroup included two items that measured the pace and difficulty of the job. The second subgroup included three items that measured time pressures, work overload, and conflicting demands (reliability of linear combination = .81). The Job Control Scale, also from Karasek, combines two subscales with nine items that tap two dimensions of job control. The first subscale includes three items related to the work itself (the degree to which it fostered and rewarded skill and creativity), and the second subscale, including six items, taps the worker's discretion and decision-making authority (reliability of linear combination = .86). A multiplicative interaction term was computed to combine continuous versions of the demands and control variables with the control scale reversed, so that higher values indicated less control.

The measure of total physical exposure incorporated three subscales with 15 items assessing physical effort and activity on the job, exposures to toxic conditions (e.g., solvents, cleaners, degreasers, oiler coolant mist), and hazardous conditions (such as unsafe machinery, inadequate lighting, and loud noise). The reliability of the linear combination was .91. A few items derived from previous research (Karasek, 1985), but most were developed after consultation with a union industrial hygienist at the largest plant.

Perceived likelihood of losing job was a single-item measure in which respondents estimated how likely they felt they were to lose their present job during the next couple of years. Responses were made on a 4-point scale ranging from 1 (*not at all likely*) to 4 (*very likely*).

The work attributes domain included pay classification (*exempt*, e.g., supervisors and managers; *nonexempt*, e.g., clerical, secretarial, and technical; and *hourly*) and workshift (day, evening, night, or rotating shift). For regression analyses, we created dummy variables for these nominal variables.

Fit between work and nonwork obligations was a single-item measure in which respondents indicated their satisfaction with the "conflicts between job demands and outside obligations" along a 4-point response scale ranging from 1 (*not at all satisfied*) to 4 (*very satisfied*).

The social and personal coping resources domain included a measure of health locus of control, which was constructed by reversing and averaging the responses to eight items (with a 7-point response scale), derived from the Self-Control of Health subscale within the Health-Specific Locus of Control Scale (Lau & Ware, 1981). Respondents with high degrees of confidence (i.e., low scores on the scale) had internal locus of control and those with low confidence (i.e., high scores on the scale) had an external orientation. The scale had an alpha of .63.

The total social support scale was constructed by averaging four social support subscales (comprising 17 items) for supervisory support, coworker support, spousal support, and friend and relative support. The items for this scale, which were adapted from previous research (House, 1981), came from five questions asking respondents to assess (a) the degree to which various specific others could be relied on to help with work- or home-related problems, (b) the degree of help specific others provided in getting the job done, and (c) how helpful and concerned their job supervisors were. This scale's reliability of linear combination was .92.

The perception of stress scale was constructed by adding the responses to two questions assessing how serious job stress was for the respondents and the degree to which their jobs created serious stress in their families. The scale had an alpha coefficient of .75.

The personal attributes domain included age, number of children living at home, race, education, family income, and marital status.

Descriptive statistics (*t* tests and chi-squares) were used to assess differences in average levels of mental distress and to identify significant relationships for inclusion in multivariate analyses of the expanded model. We conducted a series of regression analyses on the male and female subsamples separately, using mental distress as the dependent variable and entering each domain of independent variables in stepwise fashion. We constructed final models of mental distress for women and men, including all factors that had remained significant ($p \leq .10$) in the multivariate analyses. For each group, both the job strain model and the expanded model were tested with this analytic approach and the relative explanatory power of the two was established by comparing the amount of variance explained (square of the multiple correlation coefficient) by adding expanded model variables to the core job strain model.

Results

Table 1 shows that, in comparison with men, women in the sample were younger, less educated, had lower family incomes, and were less likely to be White, married, exempt workers, or to have children. Women reported significantly higher levels of mental distress, total physical exposure levels, greater imbalance between work and nonwork obligations, and more external health locus of control orientation than men, as well as lower levels of perceived job stress and job control. Reported levels of social support were similar for women and men.

Results of the regression analyses with the expanded model are summa-

Table 1. Distribution in the Female and Male Subsamples of Demographic Characteristics and Variables in the Final Models

Variable & characteristic	Women ($n = 669$)	Men ($n = 2,004$)	p^a
Dependent			
Mean mental distress level	5.83	5.20	.000
Independent			
Personal			
Mean age (years)	37.9	40.6	.000
% White	93.1	95.0	.001
% with no more than high school education	51.4	27.9	.000
% living in families with annual incomes < $40,000	54.7	46.4	.000
% married	50.1	79.7	.000
% with children	44.0	66.6	.000
Potential work stressors			
Mean psychological job demands level	29.8	31.5	.000
Mean job control level	29.7	35.2	.000
Mean total physical exposure level	3.6	3.3	.000
% with strong perception of likelihood of losing job	9.6	7.4	.001
% with exempt pay status	18.2	49.5	.000
% working day shift	72.6	76.7	.058
% at least somewhat satisfied with fit between work & outside obligations	77.4	80.5	.057
Social and personal coping resources			
Mean health locus of control level	3.0	2.8	.001
Mean total social support level	11.4	11.4	.486
Responses			
Mean perceived job stress level	3.5	3.7	.011

[a]Comparing women and men by using t tests for continuous variables and chi-square tests for nominal variables.

rized separately for men (Table 2) and women (Table 3). In many ways, the two genders were similar. For both, greater mental distress was associated with lower occupational status (nonexempt or hourly pay status in contrast with exempt status), lower levels of total social support, and an imbalance of work–nonwork obligations. Job demands (the Karasek construct) was strongly associated with mental distress for both men and women, and in both models, higher levels of perceived job stress were strongly and independently associated with more reported symptoms of mental distress. Although job demands had a strong positive zero-order association with mental distress for both men (r = .44) and women (r = .42), the regression coefficient shifted to negative as a result of the Demands × Control interaction term in the male model and the perception of job stress variable in the female model.

The analyses also revealed some noteworthy differences by gender. For female workers, but not for men, greater mental distress was associated with perceived likelihood of job loss. The model for men was more complex (with 13 significant independent predictors) than the model for women (with only 6 variables in the final model), and the men's model explained somewhat more of the overall variance (30.2%, in comparison with 26.9% for women).

The most substantive gender difference was that a lack of job control and being in a high-strain job (high demands and low control) were significant factors explaining greater mental distress for men but not for women. In addition, night-shift work, exposure to physical hazards, being unmarried, and having an external locus of control orientation were significant factors ex-

Table 2. Results of Regression Analyses for the Final Expanded Model of Mental Distress for the Male Subsample

Independent variable	β	B	Partial F	p
Job demands (D)	−.039	−.218	−3.21	.0014
Lack of job control (C)	−.028	−.151	−1.98	.0477
D × C	.001	.204	2.42	.0158
Total physical exposure scale	.088	.074	2.67	.0076
Exempt status[a]	−.307	−.102	−3.24	.0012
Day shift[a]	−.290	−.081	−2.64	.0084
Evening shift[a]	−.495	−.109	−3.83	.0001
No. of weekly work hours	−.266	−.101	−4.46	.0000
Satisfaction with fit between work & outside obligations	−.386	−.214	−8.76	.0000
Health locus of control	.154	.086	4.17	.0000
Total social support	−.037	−.054	−2.34	.0194
Married[a]	−.291	−.078	−3.52	.0004
Perceived job stress	.309	.321	12.40	.0000

Note. N = 1,461. All variables were coded from low to high: Higher values represent more of the given factor. For the final model, R^2 = .302; adjusted R^2 = .297; $F(12)$ = 57.42, p = .0000.
[a]Dummy variable.

Table 3. Results of Regression Analyses for the Final Expanded Model of Mental Distress for the Female Subsample

Independent variable	β	B	Partial F	p
Job demands	−.021	−.097	−2.40	.0167
Exempt status[a]	−.417	−.090	−2.43	.0154
Perceived likelihood of job loss	.153	.078	2.15	.0322
Satisfaction with fit between work & outside obligations	−.314	−.155	−3.80	.0002
Total social support	−.142	−.183	−4.85	.0000
Perceived job stress	.366	.338	7.61	.0000

Note. $N = 592$. All variables were coded from low to high: Higher values represent more of the given factor. For the final model, $R^2 = .269$; adjusted $R^2 = .262$; $F(6) = 35.89$, $p = .0000$.
[a]Dummy variable.

plaining mental distress in the male subsample only, whereas perceived likelihood of job loss was significant only for the female subsample.

Furthermore, the strength of some of the associations varied by gender. Lack of social support was more strongly associated with mental distress in women than in men. Further analyses of the support items revealed that the relative importance of different sources of support varied by gender. For men, support from supervisors was more important in mitigating mental distress than were other sources of support, whereas female workers derived greater protection from the support of spouses, other relatives, and friends.

Contrary to expectations, having children at home was not significantly associated with greater mental distress for women. This was the only substantive finding that disconfirmed one of our hypotheses. Two whole-sample regression analyses supported most of what we found in the split-sample analyses. Women reported greater mental distress scores than men did. Almost half (46%) of the gender difference in mental distress was explained by the 14 variables that were significant in the male or female regressions shown in Tables 2 and 3.

Finally, we examined the relative power of Karasek's job strain model, in comparison with the expanded model, to explain the variation in mental distress scores of the male and female subsamples. The job strain model alone performed quite poorly, with squared multiple correlations of .06 for men and .02 for women. Adding other work-related stressors, personal attributes, social and personal coping resources, and perception of job stress to produce the expanded model reported in Tables 2 and 3 yielded another 24% of variance explained in the mental distress scores of the male subsample versus 25% more for the female subsample. The significantly larger squared multiple correlations of the expanded model ($p = .000$ for men and women) suggests that, although the job strain model is helpful in understanding the variance in mental distress symptoms, it overlooks important dimensions that the expanded model incorporates, such as social support, perceived job stress, and fit between work and outside obligations.

Discussion and Conclusions

These analyses confirmed, first, that there are significant gender differences in the important relationships among work, personal factors, and mental distress. As expected, women in general reported higher levels of mental distress and reported greater levels of mental distress if they had less social support or more concern about conflicts between work and family obligations. Among men only we found that higher levels of distress accompanied lower levels of job control. Contrary to expectations, having dependent children at home was not an important factor in mental distress for women.

Second, the analyses showed that the Karasek job strain model provides a less complete picture of variations in mental distress among male and female workers than does an expanded model that incorporates additional structural and personal factors. The expanded model explained a substantial amount of the variance in mental distress for the male (30%) and female (27%) subsamples. This finding highlights the limitations of the job strain model and suggests that future efforts to understand variations in mental distress should operationally define and measure broader constructs than job demands and job control to more fully capture the risks and rewards associated with work. Among the supplementary factors included in our expanded model, perceived job stress and satisfaction with the fit between work and outside obligations contributed substantially to an understanding of the variation in mental distress of both sexes. Perception of stress appeared to function as an intermediate step between other exposure factors in the expanded model and symptoms of mental distress; these perceptions should be examined in future research. The basic similarities in the factors associated with greater mental distress in the male and female models hint at the possibility that women's work lives may not be so different from men's, although without historical or longitudinal data we are not in a position to draw inferences about what the future may hold.

We have left most (54%) of the gender difference in level of mental distress unexplained in this analysis, even when we used the expanded model. The unexplained variance may be a function of something antecedent in the social environment, or it may simply reflect limitations in measurement of the constructs that we did seek to tap. Some of the measures available in this study were necessarily incomplete.

For instance, on the stressor side, we had no measures of sex discrimination or sexual harassment at work, or any that probed specific concerns about support needs of family and friends (such as aging parents). These kinds of issues have been shown to affect the mental well-being of women. Furthermore, our single, crude item touching on the boundary between work and home responsibilities turned out to be important, and we did not have data on flexibility of work hours or time devoted to unpaid work in the home, factors that are more likely to be linked to the experiences of women than men.

On the response side, our scale measuring mental distress focused on self-reported affective measures (depression, anxiety, and sleep disturbance) that men tend to underreport. To assess more fully the meaning of the apparent differences we found in mental distress symptoms among men and women, further research will be needed that includes a greater array of potential stressors and a broader measure of mental distress, perhaps including qualitative as well as quantitative measures (Riessman, 1990). In addition, we are currently testing how well factors in the expanded model explain potential behavioral responses to work stress, such as drinking and drug use, that have been linked more closely to men's experiences.

As expected, job control was more important for understanding the variation in mental distress among men in comparison with women, and social support was more important among women. Given that these were the only important gender differences found to be significant in this sample of industrial workers, further analysis of these differences is warranted. Do gender differences exist in the association between all or only particular components of the job control and social support scales? Do these differences exist between women and men in the same jobs?

One possible framework within which to search for explanations of the differences between men and women in this sample—that is, the fact that social support weighed more heavily for women and job control for men—is the body of research on the psychological and moral development of women (Chodorow, 1980; Gilligan, 1982; Gilligan, Ward, & Taylor, 1988; Miller, 1986). A number of investigators have commented on women's greater comfort with "connection" to others and men's greater comfort with independence and autonomy. It may not be too far-fetched to speculate that the importance of job control for men and social support for women in this study could mean that male and female workers may emphasize different resources (autonomy for men and connection for women) to adjust to the challenges of their work environment. However, it is also possible that our measures of job control and social support reflect different dimensions of a unifying concept—such as "mastery"—that finds different expression in female workers than in their male counterparts. A more focused analysis of job control and social support is needed as a follow-up step in this and other samples of workers.

In addition to lacunae in the measures used in this study, two additional limitations should be kept in mind. First, we used only a single cross-sectional sample and cannot make legitimate claims about causal directions in the associations observed. It is quite possible that workers who reported higher levels of mental distress also reported lower levels of job control because of their generally unhappier frame of mind. The results of this study are therefore exploratory and tentative until they can be confirmed in large-scale longitudinal research.

Second, we had a sample, like most industrial workforces, in which jobs were highly segregated by gender. Even though we oversampled female workers to try to compensate, we were still prevented from pursuing as fully as we would have liked the observation of gender effects or segregation effects. It was not entirely clear whether differences in job control and social support were a function of gender differences in the resources available in particular jobs (i.e., whether women actually had less control or support than men even when they occupied similar jobs) or whether they were a function of variations in how women and men used the resources available in a given job (i.e., if the jobs were basically the same, but the workers were different). Future studies are needed in which larger samples are drawn and reasonably sized subsamples are constructed of men and women in equivalent, if not identical, jobs.

Even with our study's limitations, our results argue forcefully for bringing women more centrally into investigations of work and mental health and point to some potentially fruitful avenues for future research. More research is needed to assess how important risks (such as job demands, job stress, and fit between work and outside obligations) and resources (such as job control and social support) influence workers' mental and physical health. Future studies should use longitudinal designs and incorporate measures of mental health as well as of mental distress because researchers (Barnett & Marshall, 1991) have established that the absence of mental distress is not synonymous with the presence of mental well-being. From a prevention perspective, it would be useful to learn what resources individuals can use to enhance their mental well-being as well as to avoid mental distress.

From the standpoint of policy, the findings reported here lend support to the urgency of learning more about ways in which work experiences produce mental distress. National-level survey data ought to be maintained on the relationship between individuals' work lives and their mental and physical health. The QES, which was last administered in 1977, should be reinstituted by the U.S. Department of Labor and expanded to sample more workers and to collect data on health as well as work. National surveillance would allow researchers and policy makers to track suspected risk factors and identify occupational groups at high risk.

Second, the importance of supervisory social support as a buffer against mental distress for both men and women highlights the need for training to sensitize supervisors to the art of successful communication with employees and the importance of social support. Because social support was especially important among the women workers and because women continue to enter the workforce in large numbers, companies are likely to continue feeling pressure to abandon work structures that tend to isolate workers, foster destructive competition, or both.

Third, for both men and women, the importance of the variable measuring dissatisfaction with the conflict between work and outside obligations underscores that employers will have to find better ways to respond to employees' needs for balance in their lives. Our finding is consistent with reports in the literature and the popular press indicating that increasing numbers of workers of both genders want to decelerate their careers and put in fewer hours on the job so that they can spend more time with their families (Gordon, 1991; Shellenbarger, 1991).

Fourth, because levels of mental distress of women and men in this sample were explained by work-related as well as personal factors, prevention programs should include organizational-level approaches (such as job redesign and more flexible work hours) in addition to more conventional, individually focused strategies, such as training in stress management.

Finally, the small but important gender differences that emerged in this exploration of how work and personal factors affect mental distress reinforce the now-common call for research on women's health as well as for research that adopts a comparative perspective whenever relevant and possible.

References

Barnett, R., Biener, L., & Baruch, G. (Eds.). (1987). *Gender and stress*. New York: Free Press.

Barnett, R., & Marshall, N. (1991). The relationship between women's work and family roles and subjective well-being and psychological distress. In M. Frankenhaeuser, U. Lundberg, & M. Chesney (Eds.), *Women, work and health: Stress and opportunities* (pp. 111–136). New York: Plenum.

Chodorow, N. (1980). Feminism and difference: Gender relations and differences in psychoanalytic perspective. In H. Einstein & A. Jardine (Eds.), *The scholar and the feminist* (Vol. 1, pp. 3–19). New York: G. K. Hall.

Ganster, D. (1989). Worker control and well-being: A review of research in the workplace. In S. Sauter, J. Hurrell, Jr., & C. Cooper (Eds.), *Job control and worker health* (pp. 4–23). New York: Wiley.

Gilligan, C. (1982). *In a different voice*. Cambridge, MA: Harvard University Press.

Gilligan, C., Ward, J. V., & Taylor, J. M. (1988). *Mapping the moral domain*. Cambridge, MA: Harvard University Press.

Gordon, S. (1991, July 28). Men, women and work: Job dissatisfaction knows no gender. *Boston Globe*, p. 68.

Gore, S., & Mangione, T. (1983). Social roles, sex roles and psychological distress: Additive and interactive models of sex differences. *Journal of Health and Social Behavior, 24*, 300–312.

Gurin, G., Veroff, J., & Feld, S. (1960). *Americans view their mental health*. New York: Basic Books.

Hall, E. (1989). Gender, work control and stress: A theoretical discussion and an empirical test. *International Journal of Health Services, 19*, 725–745.

Hall, E., & Johnson, J. (1989). A case study of stress and psychogenic illness in industrial workers. *Journal of Occupational Medicine, 31*, 243–250.

House, J. (1981). *Work, stress and social support*. Reading, MA: Addison-Wesley.

Jennings, S., Piltch, C., Walsh, D., Fung, K., Tracey, L., Gordon, J., & Merrigan, D. (1989, October). *Gender differences in occupational stress*. Paper presented at the American Public Health Association Annual Meeting, Chicago.

Johnson, J., & Hall, E. (1988). Job strain, workplace social support and cardiovascular disease: A cross-sectional study of a random sample of the Swedish working population. *American Journal of Public Health, 78*, 1336–1342.

Johnson, J., Hall, E., & Theorell, T. (1989). Combined effects of job strain and social isolation on cardiovascular disease, morbidity and mortality in a random sample of the Swedish male working population. *Scandinavian Journal of Work and Environmental Health, 15*, 271–279.

Johnson, J., & Johansson, G. (1991). *The psychosocial work environment: Work organization, democratization and health*. Amityville, NY: Baywood.

Karasek, R. (1979). Job demands, job decision latitude and mental strain: Implications for job redesign. *Administrative Science Quarterly, 24*, 285–308.

Karasek, R. (1985). *Job content questionnaire*. Department of Industrial and Systems Engineering, University of Southern California, Los Angeles.

Karasek, R., & Theorell, T. (1990). *Healthy work*. New York: Basic Books.

Kobasa, S. (1987). Stress responses and personality. In R. C. Barnett, L. Biener, & G. K. Baruch (Eds.), *Gender and stress* (pp. 308–329). New York: Free Press.

Landsbergis, P., Schnall, P., Dietz, D., Friedman, R., & Pickering, T. (1990, September). *The patterning of psychological attributes and distress by job strain and social support in a sample of working men*. Paper presented at American Psychological Association and National Institute for Occupational Safety and Health Conference, Washington, DC.

Lau, R., & Ware, J. (1981). Refinements in the measurement of health-specific locus-of-control beliefs. *Medical Care Review, 19*, 1147–1158.

Loscocco, K., & Spitze, G. (1990). Working conditions, social support, and well-being of female and male factory workers. *Journal of Health and Behavior, 31*, 313–327.

Matteson, M., & Ivancevich, J. (1987). *Controlling work stress*. San Francisco: Jossey-Bass.

Miller, J. B. (1986). *Toward a new psychology of women*. Boston: Beacon Press.

National Institutes of Health. *Problems in implementing policy on women in study populations*, 101st Cong., 1st Sess. (1990) (testimony of Mark Nadel) (GAOT-HRD-90-38).

Neil, C., & Snizek, W. (1988). Gender as a moderator of job satisfaction. *Work and Occupations, 15*, 201–219.

Nelson, D. L., & Hitt, M. A. (1992). Employed women and stress: Implications for enhancing women's mental health in the workplace. In J. C. Quick, L. Murphy, & J. Hurrell, Jr. (Eds.), *Stress and well-being at work: Assessments and interventions for occupational mental health* (pp. 164–177). Washington, DC: American Psychological Association.

Nunnally, J. (1967). *Psychometric theory*. New York: McGraw-Hill.

Piltch, C. (1992). *Work and mental distress: A comparative analysis of the experiences of women and men*. Unpublished doctoral dissertation, Boston University, Boston.

Quinn, R., & Staines, G. (1979). *The 1977 Quality of Employment Survey*. Ann Arbor, MI: Survey Research Center.

Riessman, C. (1990). *Divorce talk*. New Brunswick, NJ: Rutgers University Press.

Sauter, S., Hurrell, J., & Cooper, C. (Eds). (1989). *Job control and worker health*. New York: Wiley.

Sauter, S., Murphy, L., & Hurrell, J., Jr. (1990). Prevention of work-related psychological disorders. *American Psychologist, 45*, 1146–1158.

Shellenbarger, S. (1991, November 15). More job seekers put family needs first. *Wall Street Journal*, p. B1.

Taylor, A. (1989). *Psychosocial job characteristics and hypertension: A study of Black women in the Maryland labor force*. Unpublished doctoral dissertation, Johns Hopkins University, Baltimore.

Walsh, D., Jennings, S., Mangione, T., & Merrigan, D. (1991). Health promotion versus health protection? Employees' perceptions and concerns. *Journal of Public Health Policy*, 148–164.

4

The Antecedents and Consequences of Sexual Harassment in Organizations: An Integrated Model

Louise F. Fitzgerald, Charles L. Hulin,
and Fritz Drasgow

In the short time it has been recognized as a serious social and organizational problem, sexual harassment has been shown to have substantial consequences for individuals and organizations alike. Considerable data have accumulated confirming that harassment is widespread in both the public (Culbertson, Rosenfeld, Booth-Kewley, & Magnusson, 1992; Martindale, 1990; U.S. Merit Systems Protection Board [USMS], 1981, 1987) and private sectors (Gutek, 1985; Saunders, 1992; and others) and that it has significant consequences for employee health and psychological well-being. Like other, more familiar, forms of occupational stress, harassment has been linked to psychological distress (Crull, 1982, 1984; Saunders, 1992; Schneider & Swan, 1994, *Testimony of D. G. Kilpatrick*, 1992), to physical symptoms (Gelfand & Drasgow, 1994), and to a wide variety of stress-related illnesses (Gutek & Koss, 1993; Koss, 1990; Koss et al., 1994), as well as to increased use of health care (USMS, 1981, 1987) and use of and need for psychological services. Specific job-related consequences include decreased job satisfaction (Gruber, 1992; Schneider & Swan, 1994), self-reported decrements in job performance (USMS, 1981, 1987), job loss, unemployment, and career interruption (Coles, 1986; Gutek, 1985; Livingston, 1982). Lowered job satisfaction has in turn been causally linked to a variety of organizational withdrawal behaviors (Hanisch & Hulin, 1990, 1991). Given such data, it is not surprising to find that harassment also carries significant organizational costs of both a financial and a less tangible nature. In one recent report (USMS, 1987), it was estimated that sexual harassment cost the federal government more than $250 million in a 2-year period alone, and a study of the Fortune 500 (Wagner, 1992) has indicated that costs per company averaged $6.7 million annually, excluding the cost of litigation.

Despite the abundance of data, harassment is typically ignored in studies of occupational stress, and little coherent theory exists concerning factors that may give rise to it or conditions that may exacerbate or moderate its consequences. In this chapter, we describe an integrated model of the antecedents and outcomes of sexual harassment in organizations. Beginning with a brief overview of legal and behavioral definitions, we highlight the similarity of definitions of harassment to traditional conceptualizations of psychological stress (e.g., Lazarus & Folkman, 1984) and briefly summarize the literature concerning its prevalence, correlates, and outcomes. We then develop a theoretical model that integrates these variables, outline a set of measures designed to assess it, and conclude with a discussion of the practical problems inherent in conducting sexual harassment research in organizations.

Overview of the Literature

Legal Definitions

Despite the recent attention commanded by this topic, considerable misunderstanding persists concerning the definition of harassment, including what behaviors are involved and the circumstances under which each qualifies as harassment. Much of this confusion arises from the fact that harassment is a legal concept as well as a psychological phenomenon (i.e., construct) and that the two are not completely isomorphic (Fitzgerald, Gelfand, & Drasgow, in press; Gelfand, Fitzgerald, & Drasgow, in press). According to the Equal Employment Opportunity Commission (EEOC), *sexual harassment* refers to

> Unwelcome sexual advances, requests for sexual favors, (as well as) other verbal or physical conduct of a sexual nature . . . when (1) submission to such conduct is made either explicitly or implicitly a term or condition of an individual's employment; (2) submission to or rejection of such conduct . . . is used as the basis for employment decisions. . ; or (3) such conduct has the purpose or effect of substantially interfering with an individual's work performance or creating an intimidating, hostile or offensive working environment. (EEOC, 1980, pp. 74676–74677)

Thus, from a legal perspective, harassment includes two broad classes of stimuli: quid pro quo and hostile environment. *Quid pro quo* situations involve instances of coercion in which some job benefit is conditioned on sexual cooperation; *hostile environments*, on the other hand, include a variety of sex-related actions and situations ranging from offensive verbal behavior (e.g., jokes, vulgar comments, or conversation of a derogatory or sexual nature) and unwanted sexual attention to sexual imposition or assault. The EEOC (1993) recently amended its guidelines to emphasize that hostile and derogatory gender-related behavior is prohibited even when no strictly sexual (i.e., erotic) intent is involved.

Legal decisions and accumulated case law have determined that both forms of harassment are illegal under both Title VII and Title IX of the Civil Rights Act (see, e.g., *Alexander et al. v. Yale University*, 1977/1980; *Ellison v. Brady*, 1991; *Franklin v. Gwinnett County School District*, 1992; *Meritor Savings Bank v. Vinson*, 1986; *Robinson v. Jacksonville Shipyards, Inc.*, 1991), although the severity necessary to trigger the legal prohibition (particularly with respect to hostile environment) is a subject of some debate. As a practical matter, a single instance of quid pro quo harassment is frequently considered sufficient to meet the standard, whereas hostile environment situations are generally required not only to be unwanted and offensive but also to be repeated (EEOC, 1990).

The question of whose judgment of offensiveness and severity is to be legally dispositive has also occasioned considerable dispute. Traditionally, courts have invoked the perspective of an abstract "reasonable person" when making such determinations; more recently, some have proposed the substitution of what has come to be known as the "reasonable woman" standard. This standard holds that harassment should be judged from the perspective of the victim, who in most cases will be a woman. For example, in 1991 (*Ellison v. Brady*, 1991), the Sixth Circuit reasoned as follows:

> Conduct that many men consider unobjectionable may offend many women. Because women are disproportionately victims of rape and sexual assault, women have a stronger incentive to be concerned with sexual behavior. . . . Men, who are rarely victims of sexual assault, may view sexual conduct in a vacuum without a full appreciation of the social setting or the underlying threat of violence that a woman may perceive.

The Supreme Court was widely expected to clarify this issue in its most recent harassment decision (*Harris v. Forklift Systems, Inc.*, 1992/1993); the Court, however, contented itself with clarifying the objective severity standard, noting that objectionable behavior did not have to be so severe as to cause serious psychological injury. With respect to the subjective element, the Court retained the "reasonable person" terminology, but added that it was also necessary to consider "the victim's subjective perception that the environment is abusive" (*Harris v. Forklift Systems, Inc.*, 1992/1993, p. 368), thus acknowledging what stress theorists would refer to as the process of *primary appraisal* (Lazarus & Folkman, 1984). Because of the gender-blind nature of this standard, however, there remains considerable ambiguity and the possibility of conflicting decisions at lower judicial levels; thus, many observers expect the Court to revisit this issue at some point in the future.

Behavioral and Psychological Definitions

From a more traditional psychological perspective, harassment can be most appropriately conceptualized as a latent behavioral construct composed of three dimensions: gender harassment, unwanted sexual attention, and sexual coercion (Fitzgerald et al., in press; Gelfand et al., in press). *Gender harassment* is characterized by insulting, misogynistic, and degrading remarks and behavior that are not designed to elicit sexual cooperation but that convey hostility and degrading attitudes about women.[1] *Unwanted sexual attention* con-

---

[1] Women constitute by far the overwhelming majority of sexual harassment victims and are thus the frame of reference for this program of research. The application of the concepts discussed here to male employees is presently unclear.

sists of unwelcome sexual behavior that is unwanted and unreciprocated by the recipient but that is not tied to any job-related reward or punishment. *Sexual coercion* refers to implicit or explicit threats or promises of job-related outcomes conditioned on sexual cooperation. Sexual coercion is thus the behavioral equivalent of the legal concept of quid pro quo, whereas unwanted sexual attention and gender harassment constitute the two aspects of a hostile environment.

In a recent paper, Fitzgerald, Swan, and Fisher (in press) highlighted harassment's role as a psychological stressor by defining it psychologically as follows:

> unwanted sex-related behavior at work that is appraised by the recipient as offensive, exceeding her resources, or threatening her wellbeing. Coping (with harassment) is the process of responding to such unwanted sex-related behavior and includes both practical attempts to solve, manage or alter the situation . . . and attempts to manage cognitive and emotional reactions.

Their definitions, which parallel the classic stress and coping formulations of Lazarus and Folkman (1984), thus locate the phenomenon of harassment clearly within the cognitive behavioral stress research paradigm, providing a rich theoretical framework from which it can be explored.

Prevalence and Correlates

It is by now well documented that harassment is an organizational phenomenon of substantial prevalence.[2] Although truly national figures do not exist, estimates range from 17% of the female labor force, when considering only harassment by supervisors (Saunders, 1992), to more typical figures of 40% (USMS, 1981, 1987) and 50% (Gutek, 1985) when coworker behavior is also included. Such global estimates obscure the differential rates that have been documented for different types of harassment; for example, sexual coercion is estimated to account for only a very small percentage of the problem, despite being the canonical example. In Gutek's (1985) study of the general labor force, unwanted sexual touching was more than twice as common as expectations of sex as "part of the job." Similar ratios of unwanted sexual attention to direct sexual coercion have characterized the federal government studies (USMS, 1981, 1987), Fitzgerald et al.'s (1988) studies of the university environment, and virtually all other incidence and prevalence investigations.

The main organizational factors that have been shown to influence frequency rates include a male-dominated workgroup (e.g., skewed gender ratios, male supervisor, and masculine-typed work activities; Baker, 1989; Gruber & Bjorn, 1982; Gutek, 1985) and an organizational culture tolerant of harass-

---

[2] In epidemiological terms, *prevalence* refers to the estimated percentage of individuals who will experience a particular phenomenon at some point during their lifetime. In contrast, *incidence* refers to the estimated percentage within a particular time period. Sexual harassment studies differ in terms of whether they refer to incidence or prevalence, and this should be kept in mind when interpreting frequency statistics.

ment, as evidenced by lenient management norms (Hulin, 1993; Pryor, LaVite, & Stoller, 1993) or by the weakness or absence of sexual harassment policies, procedures, and remedies (Hesson-McInnis & Fitzgerald, 1992). Although Pryor (1987) has shown that it is possible to identify men who are likely to harass— at least in a laboratory situation—the prevalence of the problem indicates that it cannot be adequately accounted for solely by an individual deviance explanation (cf. Pryor et al., 1993) and that more comprehensive structural and organizational perspectives are required.

With respect to individual-level correlates, most authorities agree that female workers constitute the overwhelming majority of sexual harassment victims, although this assertion is occasionally disputed (see e.g., Vaux, 1993), and the rare suit brought by a male plaintiff receives considerable notoriety in the media. There is some evidence that young, unmarried women are more likely than others to become victims, although, as Koss et al. (1994) pointed out, researchers rarely examine which types of harassment are experienced by which victims. Gender harassment, for example, is not only the most widespread form of harassment, but also likely bears a weaker link to age than do the other categories.

Individual and Organizational Responses to Sexual Harassment

Research on coping responses has until recently been almost exclusively focused on determining whether victims reported the harasser to the organization. Despite the prevalence of harassment, it has been relatively rare for formal complaints to be brought; most evidence suggests that only a small percentage of victims ever discuss their experiences with anyone in authority (Fitzgerald et al., 1988; Gutek, 1985; Livingston, 1982) and that only a small subset of that group file formal complaints with their employers or institutions. In a secondary analysis of the first USMS data set, Livingston (1982) reported that "only 2.5% of the victims made use of formal actions of any kind in response to the harassment incident" (p. 14). Thirty-three percent of those who did take formal action reported that it "made things worse," a finding replicated by Hesson-McInnis and Fitzgerald (1992).

The fear of individual or organizational retaliation that inhibits many victims from responding (Gutek, 1985) thus appears to have some foundation in fact, at least in some organizations. In a reanalysis of the most recent government data set (USMS, 1987), Hesson-McInnis and Fitzgerald (1992) coded victim response on a continuum of assertiveness and found that more assertive responding was associated with more negative outcomes of every sort: job related, psychological, and health related. Although the recent publicity afforded this issue by such high-profile events as the Thomas confirmation hearings and the Navy Tailhook Convention scandal has resulted in substantial increases in agency complaints, the effect on organizational response is unknown.

Little is known in any formal way about how managers in organizations respond to allegations of sexual harassment. Gutek and Koss (1993) suggested that ignoring or downplaying the complaint appears common, possibly because of management inexperience and discomfort when dealing with sexual issues. They also noted the similarity between reporting harassment and whistle-blowing (Miceli & Near, 1988; Near & Miceli, 1987) as an explanation for widespread anecdotal reports and some data (e.g., Coles, 1986; Hesson-McInnis & Fitzgerald, 1992; Livingston, 1982) that victims who report incidents are frequently blamed for causing trouble. "The effects on any workplace caught in the throes of an investigation into an allegation of sexual harassment or divided by a court case of harassment may be more visible to management than the effects of harassment itself" (Gutek & Koss, 1993, p. 36). Formal, organizationally based research on this topic is badly needed.

Individual and Organizational Outcomes of Sexual Harassment

As noted above, considerable evidence exists documenting the negative impact of harassment on individual workers. Such consequences include job loss (Coles, 1986; Crull, 1982; Gutek, 1985; USMS, 1981, 1987), decreased morale and absenteeism (USMS, 1981, 1987), decreased job satisfaction (Baker, 1989; Gruber, 1992), and damage to interpersonal relationships at work (Culbertson et al., 1992; DiTomaso, 1989; Gutek, 1985). Evidence of lowered productivity and decrements in job performance has also been reported (USMS, 1981, 1987). In addition, research has confirmed that harassment can exert a substantial neg-ative impact on psychological well-being as well as have serious health-related consequences (Gutek & Koss, 1993; Koss, 1990; Koss et al., 1994). Psychological reactions include increased fear (Holgate, 1989; Junger, 1987), decreased self-esteem (Gruber & Bjorn, 1982), lowered self-confidence (Benson & Thomson, 1982), increased anxiety, depression, and greater risk of posttraumatic stress disorder (PTSD) (Schneider & Swan, 1994).

With the exception of financial cost—much of it related to negative impact on employees and the costs associated with harassment litigation—there is less agreement on the consequences of harassment for organizations them-selves. Wagner (1992) noted that the nonlegal expenses associated with lower productivity, turnover, and poor morale can be considerable. As reported above, a survey of 160 large manufacturing and service organizations estimated the annual cost of harassment to a typical Fortune 500 company to exceed $6 million, excluding litigation. Such figures are almost surely underestimates; using more sophisticated cost-modeling techniques, Faley, Knapp, Kustis, and Dubois (1994) recently estimated that the cost of harassment to the U.S. Army exceeded $500 million in 1988 alone. Less tangible damages are thought to include lowered morale, reduced loyalty, and a damaged corporate reputa-tion—although formal studies have not been conducted.

A Framework for the Study of Sexual Harassment in Organizations

Sexual harassment was originally cast as an issue of illegal sex-based dis-crimination (MacKinnon, 1979), a formulation that forms the legal basis of contemporary efforts to eradicate it. In addition, feminist writers have framed harassment as an example of the sexual victimization or violence against women that appears to be ubiquitous in contemporary society (Koss et al., 1994)—an issue to which we return below. Attempts to understand harassment from an organizational perspective, however, have been relatively scarce. The work of Gutek (1985) represents probably the most extensive effort, and more recent discussions have been provided by Cleveland and Kerst (1993), Hanisch (1993), and Pryor et al. (1993).

Most recently, Hulin (1993) articulated a rationale for conceptualizing harassment as an example of occupational stress that, like other stressors, has important implications for traditional organizational research as well as for research focusing on occupational safety and health. According to this framework, harassment occurs within a social–technological organizational system defined by, among other things, dimensions of organizational culture and climate. Organizations, in turn, are embedded within external social, political, and economic systems that influence events and processes occurring within the organizational boundaries.

According to this framework, harassment typically takes place within situations defined in large part by the organizational work roles of the victim and the harasser (although harassers may occasionally be clients or customers). The victims, in addition to being victims, are also organizational members with preexisting job attitudes influenced by their work tasks and job characteristics (Hanisch & Hulin, 1991) as well as by their own expectations and dispositions (Judge & Hulin, in press). Such job attitudes are relatively stable and causally related to patterned job behaviors (Hanisch & Hulin, 1991; Roznowski & Hulin, 1992). Additionally, victims—like other, nonvictimized workers—are simultaneously experiencing other work-related stressors, stressors that combine and interact to influence outcomes. Finally, the work roles of victims and harassers frequently overlap in such a way that the two are required to interact on a continuing basis.

These considerations form the background and context for harassment events. They also influence the ways in which victims cope with harassment, their job attitudes, job stress, well-being, and patterns of work-role behaviors in predictable ways. This implies that the study of sexual harassment in the workplace should take place within the framework of a model of organizational behavior that includes provisions for these factors (and possibly others as well) as well as provisions for variables specifically having to do with harassment itself. A similar argument was recently made by Hanisch (1993), who stressed the importance of studying sexual harassment within a comprehensive framework that includes assessment of a variety of job stressors.

The dangers of studying workplace harassment in isolation from other job-related variables are several. Without well-articulated models of organizational attitudes and behaviors, one risks misestimating the importance (and process) of sexual harassment for influencing patterns of organizational behaviors. Similarly, if none of the quotidian work stressors are represented in the models, then estimates of the effects of one particular stressor (in this case, sexual harassment) will be biased because of model misspecification.

There is also risk of error on the output side of any model of organizational behavior that focuses narrowly on one behavior in isolation. For example, Gutek (1993), as well as Koss et al. (1994), have noted that victims engage in many different behaviors in response to harassment. Thus, to focus on only one or two coping strategies (e.g., reporting or filing complaints) may lead one to overlook equally important compensatory or substitute behaviors. In summary, we argue here that it is necessary for researchers to study sexual harassment as they would study other organizational and environmental insults to account for the interdependence of organizational characteristics, occupational stressors, affective and attitudinal responses, and patterns of organizational behaviors. The model we describe below was designed with this perspective in mind.

An Integrated Model of Sexual Harassment in Organizations

Although we do not deny the importance of individual differences (e.g., Pryor, 1987), we propose that sexual harassment in organizations is primarily a function of organizational and job characteristics and, thus, is most appropriately conceptualized and studied in these terms. Like other forms of work-related stress, harassment has been demonstrated to affect individuals' relations to their organizations as well as their physical and emotional well-being. Our model attempts to predict the incidence of organizational harassment and its outcomes for individual workers as well as to describe some of the processes through which these outcomes occur. The model itself is shown in Figure 1.

According to this model, sexual harassment is a function of two exogenous variables: organizational context and job context. *Organizational context* refers to those aspects of organizational climate (Naylor, Pritchard, & Ilgen, 1980) having to do with tolerance of sexual harassment as well as to the presence, accessibility, and effectiveness of harassment remedies. By *job context*, we refer to the factors that constitute the gendered nature of the individual's workgroup, for example, the gender ratio in day-to-day work contacts (Gutek, Cohen, &

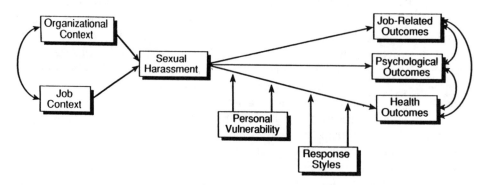

Figure 1. An integrated process model of the antecedents and general outcomes of sexual harassment in organizations.

Konrad, 1990), sex of supervisor, and the gender stereotypes of the job tasks (i.e., traditional or nontraditional).

Sexual harassment includes not only quid pro quo situations but also the two general types of hostile environment behaviors (gender harassment and unwanted sexual attention) that have been identified (Gelfand et al., in press). According to the model we propose, job and organizational context exert direct causal influences on the extent (and possibly, the nature) of sexual harassment in organizations. Harassment is hypothesized, in turn, to affect three sets of outcomes: job-related outcomes, psychological outcomes, and health outcomes. A submodel of job outcomes is shown in Figure 2.

Submodel of Job Outcomes

Consistent with our focus on sexual harassment as an example of occupational stress, we propose a submodel of job outcomes reflecting stress-related cognitions and voluntary behaviors, as opposed to the more frequently cited outcomes of involuntary job loss and career interruption. The submodel depicts the well-documented causal relationship between negative job attitudes and those job-related outcomes termed *organizational withdrawal* by Hanisch and Hulin (1990, 1991). Organizational withdrawal is composed of two classes of behaviors: work withdrawal and job withdrawal. *Work withdrawal* constitutes a cluster of behaviors that reflect attempts to avoid one's work tasks, for example, absenteeism, tardiness, missing meetings, wandering around looking busy, drug or alcohol use before or after work because of things that happen at work, and so forth. *Job withdrawal*, on the other hand, is composed of such factors as turnover intentions, eventual turnover, retirement intentions, subsequent retirement, and related intentions and cognitions.

If one considers only those job outcomes contained in this submodel, then the more general model in Figure 1 can be reconceptualized to reflect the relationships depicted in Figure 3. This version of the model reflects the im-

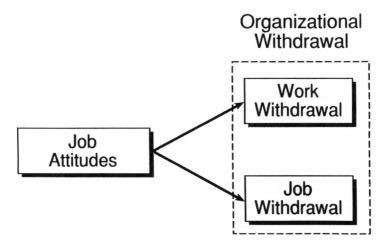

Figure 2.   A submodel of job outcomes.

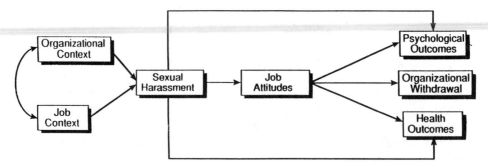

Figure 3. An alternative model of outcomes of sexual harassment.

portance of job attitudes as a mediator of the full range of consequences to individuals in organizations while retaining the direct causal links between harassment and outcomes. (The causal effects of negative job attitudes on health have been established empirically by Hanisch & Hulin, 1991.)

Moderators

The effect of harassment on these endogenous outcome variables is hypothesized to be moderated by the victim's personal vulnerability (indexed by various demographic characteristics, such as age, educational level, and marital and organizational status; previous victimization history; and such cognitive variables as sensitivity to potentially harassing behaviors) and response strategy (i.e., mode of responding to and coping with the harassing situation). Non-harassment-related occupational stressors are not included in the model itself; however, assessments of such stressors are critical because they serve as the baseline against which the effects of harassment can be evaluated when the model is tested. For simplicity's sake, the moderating effects of response style and personal vulnerability are not depicted in Figure 3, although these effects are assumed to be present.

The model is empirically testable through covariance structure modeling (Bentler, 1980; Long, 1983), a technique allowing simultaneous examination of multiple (potentially) causal relationships. Although relationships consistent with the model itself could potentially take a number of forms, we expected certain general relationships to obtain. These are outlined below.

> *Hypothesis 1:* The prevalence of sexual harassment in organizations is a function of a male-dominated job context and an organizational context tolerant of sexual harassment.

> *Hypothesis 2:* Sexual harassment in organizations is associated with more negative outcomes of all types for those who experience it.

> *Hypothesis 3:* Externally focused, assertive response strategies (e.g., reporting the offender or filing a complaint) will exacerbate the psychological and health-related impact of harassment as well as its job-related outcomes.

The first hypothesis is a relatively straightforward derivation from the literature on the organizational correlates of sexual harassment, whereas the second seems reasonable to propose, particularly given the generalized effects of job stress and job attitudes on individuals. The third hypothesis—which may initially strike some as counterintuitive—is also based in the (admittedly sparse) empirical literature on coping with sexual harassment (e.g., Livingston, 1982), including a preliminary test of the present model in an existing archival data set (Hesson-McInnis & Fitzgerald, 1992). In the next section, we outline a program of research designed to produce a rigorous test of the model, with a particular focus on the development of measurement devices for key variables in the model.

Testing the Model: Measurement of Constructs

As Fitzgerald and Hesson-McInnis (1989) have noted, not only has little formal theory emerged in this area, but basic definitional issues remain unresolved: "As with many topics that are both socially important and somewhat controversial, data collection has proceeded rapidly, without benefit of theory, or even the careful formulation of definitions, whether literary or operational" (p. 309). In particular, many key variables—including sexual harassment itself—have generally been only weakly and idiosyncratically operationalized. Here, we briefly describe the development of instruments specifically designed to provide more conceptually and psychometrically sophisticated measures of three key constructs: sexual harassment, organizational climate for sexual harassment, and individual response strategies for coping with harassment.

Sexual Experiences Questionnaire

The study of sexual harassment in organizations has been hampered until recently by the lack of any standard operational definition or measurement strategy. Early studies (e.g., Benson & Thomson, 1982; Gutek, 1985; USMS, 1981) typically presented respondents with a brief checklist of behaviors and asked whether they had experienced them within a particular time frame (generally, 2 years). This methodology has recently been criticized (Gruber, 1990; Koss et al., 1994) on a variety of grounds, as Koss et al. (1994) noted:

> Such lists can be criticized as ad hoc and atheoretical, as little if any rationale is offered for the particular behaviors chosen and many of them are unacceptably vague. . . . Because there has been little agreement on such issues, the target behaviors often vary from study to study, making cross-sample comparisons virtually impossible. (p. 128)

Noting that a sound measurement strategy is a prerequisite for theoretical work, Fitzgerald and her colleagues (Fitzgerald et al., in press; Fitzgerald et al., 1988; Gelfand et al., in press) developed the Sexual Experiences Questionnaire (SEQ), a self-report instrument that assesses the three categories of harassment through a series of behaviorally based items. All items include a standard stem ("Have you ever been in a situation where") and conclude with an explicitly described, behaviorally based example of offensive workplace behavior (e.g., "a supervisor or coworker attempted to establish a romantic or sexual relationship with you despite your efforts to discourage him?"). The words *sexual harassment* do not appear until the end of the inventory, when a final item asks "Have you ever been sexually harassed?"

A variety of studies have confirmed that the SEQ yields reliability and stability estimates in the .80s. Recently, Gelfand et al. (in press) conducted a confirmatory factor analysis of the SEQ in three samples (one of them cross-cultural), and confirmed the three-factor model as well as demonstrating the measurement equivalence of the SEQ across target populations (working women and students) and cultures (United States and Brazil).

The SEQ has recently been revised to address some of the problems associated with assessment of low-frequency behaviors and to provide better coverage of each of the three subtypes of harassing behavior. This 20-item revision uses a 5-point Likert-type frequency response format and a 24-month time frame and provides balanced and comprehensive coverage of each of the three subtypes.

Organizational Tolerance for Sexual Harassment Inventory

Organizations appear to vary widely in their tolerance for sexual harassment of and by their employees, a tolerance that has been related to significant organizational and human costs. As discussed above, such tolerance—as well as related organizational norms—has been implicated in several studies of sexual harassment (Bond, 1988; Hesson-McInnis & Fitzgerald, 1992; Pryor et al., 1993) and plays a prominent predictive role in the present model. As with harassment itself, however, such variables have typically been defined inconsistently, theorized weakly, and measured in a cursory manner.

To assess the construct of tolerance more formally, we proposed a new measure of this important aspect of organizational climate (Hulin, 1993; Hulin, Fitzgerald, & Drasgow, in press), grounded in the theoretical framework proposed by Naylor et al. (1980), who conceptualized climate as shared perceptions of contingencies between behaviors and organizational outcomes (i.e., sanctions or rewards). This scale, the Organizational Tolerance for Sexual Harassment Inventory (OTSHI; Hulin et al., in press), assesses climate by asking participants to report their perceptions of organizational sanctions if specified individuals (coworkers or superiors) engage in specific behaviors reflecting various forms of harassment.

Briefly, the OTSHI consists of a series of 12 vignettes in which organizational status of a male harasser (coworker or superior) is crossed with the three types of harassment (gender harassment, unwanted sexual attention, and sexual coercion), with two replications (i.e., vignettes) per cell of the 2 × 3 design. Participants respond to each vignette on three 5-point scales: the first assesses the degree of risk to a female victim if she were to report the incident, the second assesses the likelihood that she would be taken seriously by the organization, and the third assesses the degree to which the harasser would be punished.

Hulin (1993) reported preliminary data on the OTSHI, based on a sample of 335 graduate students (195 male and 140 female). Coefficient alpha was .96 for the entire inventory and ranged between .90 and .94 for the individual response scales assessing risk, taken seriously, and organizational action. Preliminary substantive findings indicated that the scales behaved according to theoretical expectations. As would be expected, women perceived the organization to be significantly more tolerant of sexual harassment than did men; this was true for all three types of harassing behavior. The women also perceived significantly greater risk to the victim for complaining, significantly less chance that she would be taken seriously, and significantly less chance that the perpetrator would be punished.

In general, the organization was seen as least tolerant of sexual coercion (the traditional quid pro quo situation) and most tolerant of gender harassment. Typically, perceived risk to the victim was greater, and she was also perceived as less likely to be taken seriously, when the perpetrator was a supervisor. Both men and women also perceived that harassers who were supervisors would be dealt with more leniently by the organization; in fact, perpetrator status accounted for 27% of the variance in OTSHI scores, more than twice that of the other main effects combined. A complete account of this research is available from Hulin (1993).

Coping With Harassment Questionnaire

The manner in which individuals respond to and cope with harassment has begun to receive increased attention in the research literature (Fitzgerald, 1990; Gutek, 1993; Gutek & Koss, 1993; Terpstra & Baker, 1989) and, as our model predicts, has been shown to influence victim outcomes in a variety of ways (Hesson-McInnis & Fitzgerald, 1992). Until recently, however, no standard procedure for assessing coping has been proposed, and the methods that do exist—primarily simple checklists of commonsense behaviors—lack both a theoretical framework and known psychometric properties. In addition, most studies have focused on a single class of response variables, that is, whether or not the victim reported the harasser to the organization or filed a formal complaint (e.g., Brooks & Perot, 1991)—admittedly, an important variable but only one of a number of possible responses to harassment.

Fitzgerald (1990) recently reported a series of studies designed to examine harassment coping strategies in a systematic manner. The first of these described the development of a conceptual framework to classify strategies, based on content analysis of actual behaviors reported by participants in the original SEQ study. This analysis identified 10 specific strategies (endurance, denial, detachment, reattribution, illusory control, avoidance, appeasement, assertion, seeking institutional remedies, and seeking social support) that could be classified into two general response categories (internally focused vs. externally focused responses). Although some coping strategies appear to be unique to harassment (e.g., appeasement, which involves attempts to evade the harassment but without confrontation or assertion), the similarity to strategies used in more general coping systems (e.g., Folkman & Lazarus, 1988) is striking.

Following further development and validation of this framework, the final study in the series (Fitzgerald, 1990) described the development of a self-report inventory designed to assess the 10 strategies in an objective manner: the Coping With Harassment Questionnaire, or CHQ. Briefly, the CHQ is a 50-item inventory yielding scores for each of the 10 coping strategies described above. Despite the brevity of the five-item subscales, alpha internal consistencies ranged from .69 to .96 and averaged .84 in the development sample. Initial validity information—derived from an experimental analogue study, factor analytic results, and theoretically expected correlations with other variables (e.g., assertiveness, locus of control, and severity of harassment)—suggested that the scales behaved in theoretically meaningful ways.

Confirmatory factor analysis verified two distinct but related dimensions, with active problem-solving strategies constituting one factor and internal, cognitively oriented strategies the other. Such parallels to more general stress and coping measures (e.g., Folkman & Lazarus, 1988) provide further evidence of the validity of the CHQ. However, the strength of the CHQ is that it allows for the assessment of a variety of strategies, thus recognizing that responding to harassment is not a simple dichotomous process and that victims may use a considerable number of behaviors, either simultaneously or sequentially. An abbreviated version of the CHQ is currently being pilot tested with the goal of constructing a briefer scale more suited to the realities of organizational research.

Testing the Model: Preliminary Results

Hesson-McInnis and Fitzgerald (1992) tested part of the model in an existing archival data set, reporting support for the influence of job context and organizational climate on the prevalence of sexual harassment as well as for the negative effects of harassment of both job- and health-related outcomes. This study was limited, however, by its reliance on an existing data set with relatively poor measurement qualities. Although a complete test of the model is still not available, preliminary results, based on the instruments described above, have recently been reported (Fitzgerald, Hulin, & Drasgow, 1994). In this series of studies, Zickar (1994) confirmed the hypothesized role of climate as an antecedent of sexual harassment, whereas Schneider and Swan (1994) demonstrated the negative effects of harassment on job satisfaction, anxiety, depression, and posttraumatic stress disorder. Finally, Gelfand and Drasgow (1994) tested a reduced version of the model through LISREL analysis and reported an excellent fit to the data, using a traditional measure of occupational stress as a baseline for comparison. These results confirm that the model provides a promising framework for conducting harassment research in organizations, a topic to which we now turn.

Researching Sexual Harassment in Organizations: Delicate Dilemmas and Practical Problems

Researching sexual harassment in organizations presents a considerable challenge to organizational researchers more accustomed to measuring job satisfaction than psychological trauma. The outcomes documented in the sexual harassment literature (e.g., anxiety, depression, and posttraumatic stress disorder) do not fit easily into traditional job-related research frameworks, and even researchers more used to examining occupational stress and health outcomes (e.g., alcohol and drug abuse) may be uncomfortable with the highly personal and emotionally charged issues inherent in the present topic.

Victimization researchers, for their part, are generally unfamiliar with the practicalities of conducting research in organizations. Accustomed to focusing on clinical outcomes of individual victims, trained in a clinical tradition, and usually possessed of a feminist philosophy, such researchers may be frustrated by the need to take organizational practicalities and sensibilities into account. The integration of such distinctly different research traditions, necessary to the theoretical and practical success of projects of this type, represents a challenge of no small magnitude.

In addition to such considerations, a variety of other factors must generally be confronted. Not only are organizations reluctant to allow the collection of data they fear may exacerbate their legal vulnerability, but unions may also object to studies that appear to document employee misbehavior, and workers in general may view the personal nature of such investigations as intrusive or offensive. A complete discussion of such issues is well beyond the scope of this chapter; however, it is possible to offer some general observations and suggestions.

The organizational reluctance to collect data documenting the existence of a problem carrying legal liability may well represent the single most formidable obstacle to conducting research on sexual harassment in organizations. Such concerns—already substantial—were exacerbated by the passage of the 1991 Civil Rights Act, which specified for the first time that victims of illegal work-based harassment are entitled to financial compensation. Although questions concerning the exact nature and conditions of employer liability remain unclear (e.g., *Kauffman v. Allied Signal*, 1992; *Meritor v. Vinson*, 1986), organizations are understandably reluctant to take any action that may—at first glance—appear to increase their liability exposure.

Such concerns are not easily alleviated. At the same time, a variety of benefits accrue to organizations that cooperate with such research. Most obviously, the research can serve as a comprehensive organizational needs assessment—not only identifying the general extent of harassment, but also highlighting areas of the organization in which problems are most likely to occur, as well as the specific nature of the problems. Such participation allows for more precisely targeted interventions, and the demonstration of interest by management that such research signals itself functions as a positive intervention (Fitzgerald, 1992). Finally, organizations can be reminded of court rulings that remedial action can insulate them from liability (*Kauffman v.*

Allied Signal, 1992); thus, actions to improve the work environment (e.g., training) that are based on research findings may well constitute a strength rather than a liability.

The success of research such as we propose depends, of course, on organizational access and management support as well as on employee cooperation. To the degree that employees (both men and women) are convinced that employee confidentiality is completely protected, that data are released only in group form and are suitably disguised, and, particularly, that no actions either against or in support of any individual will arise from the survey, cooperation is considerably more likely. Standard techniques for soliciting worker support—such as the formation and use of focus groups, heterogeneous organizational task forces, and the like—are even more critical than usual to the success of this research.

Finally, the issue of intrusiveness and perceived invasion of privacy, which is difficult to avoid when conducting harassment research, can be addressed through a variety of methods. Data collection instruments can be ordered so that traditional job-related variables appear first and the more clinical outcome instruments and harassment assessments appear at the end, and outcome measures should be selected to ensure that they garner the maximum amount of relevant information from minimally intrusive questions. Although they are not generally used in traditional organizational research, various procedures for protecting participants' sense of privacy have been developed by clinical researchers and may contribute to employees' comfort when responding to sensitive, sex-related material.

In summary, the study of sexual harassment in organizations presents both organizations and researchers with opportunities as well as with a variety of practical problems and delicate dilemmas. To the degree that the insights and experience of organizational and clinical researchers can be integrated and brought to bear on these problems, they stand a much greater chance of successful resolution.

References

Alexander et al. v. Yale University, 459 F. Supp. 1 (D. Connecticut 1977), *aff'd* 631 F.2d 178 (2d Cir. 1980).

Baker, N. L. (1989). *Sexual harassment and job satisfaction in traditional and nontraditional industrial occupations.* Unpublished doctoral dissertation, California School of Professional Psychology, Los Angeles.

Benson, D. J., & Thomson, G. E. (1982). Sexual harassment on a university campus: The confluence of authority relations, sexual interest and gender stratification. *Social Problems, 29,* 236–251.

Bentler, P. M. (1980). Multivariate analysis with latent variables: Causal modeling. *Annual Review of Psychology, 31,* 419–456.

Bond, M. E. (1988). Division 27 sexual harassment survey: Definition, impact and environmental context. *The Community Psychologist, 21,* 7–10.

Brooks, L., & Perot, A. R. (1991). Reporting sexual harassment: Exploring a predictive model. *Psychology of Women Quarterly, 15,* 31–47.

Cleveland, J., & Kerst, M. W. (1993). Sexual harassment and perceptions of power: An under-articulated relationship. *Journal of Vocational Behavior, 42,* 49–67.

Coles, F. S. (1986). Forced to quit: Sexual harassment complaints and agency response. *Sex Roles, 14*, 81–95.

Crull, P. (1982). Stress effects of sexual harassment on the job: Implications for counseling. *American Journal of Orthopsychiatry, 52*, 539–544.

Crull, P. (1984). Sexual harassment and women's health. In W. Chavkin (Ed.), *Double exposure.* New York: Monthly Review Press.

Culbertson, A. L., Rosenfeld, P., Booth-Kewley, S., & Magnusson, P. (1992). *Assessment of sexual harassment in the Navy: Results of the 1989 Navy-wide survey* (TR-92–11). San Diego, CA: Naval Personnel Research and Development Center.

DiTomaso, N. (1989). Sexuality in the workplace: Discrimination and harassment. In J. Hearn, D. L. Sheppard, P. Tancred-Sheriff, & G. Burrell (Eds.), *The sexuality of organizations* (pp. 71–90). Newbury Park, CA: Sage.

Ellison v. Brady, 924 F.2d 871 (9th Cir. 1991).

Faley, R. H., Knapp, D. E., Kustis, G. A., & Dubois, C. L. Z. (1994, April). *Organizational cost of sexual harassment in the workplace.* Paper presented at the 9th Annual Conference of the Society for Industrial and Organizational Psychology, Nashville, TN.

Fitzgerald, L. F. (1990, March). *Assessing strategies for coping with harassment: A theoretical/empirical approach.* Paper presented at the midwinter conference of the Association for Women in Psychology, Tempe, AZ.

Fitzgerald, L. F. (1992). *Sexual harassment in organizations.* Washington, DC: American Society of Association Executives.

Fitzgerald, L. F., Gelfand, M., & Drasgow, F. (in press). Measuring sexual harassment: Theoretical and psychometric advances. *Basic and Applied Social Psychology.*

Fitzgerald, L. F., & Hesson-McInnis, M. (1989). The dimensions of sexual harassment: A structural analysis. *Journal of Vocational Behavior, 35*, 309–326.

Fitzgerald, L. F., Hulin, C. L., & Drasgow, F. (1994, April). *Sexual harassment in the workplace: Instruments, models, and empirical results.* Symposium presented at the 9th annual conference of the Society for Industrial and Organizational Psychology, Nashville, TN.

Fitzgerald, L. F., Shullman, S. L., Bailey, N., Richards, M., Swecker, J., Gold, A., Ormerod, A. J., & Weitzman, L. (1988). The incidence and dimensions of sexual harassment in academia and the workplace. *Journal of Vocational Behavior, 32*, 152–175.

Fitzgerald, L. F., Swan, S., & Fisher, K. (in press). Why didn't she just report him?: The psychological and legal implications of women's responses to sexual harassment. *Journal of Social Issues.*

Folkman, S., & Lazarus, R. (1988). *Manual for Ways of Coping Questionnaire.* Palo Alto, CA: Consulting Psychologists Press.

Franklin v. Gwinnett County School District, 112 S. Ct. 1028 (1992).

Gelfand, M., & Drasgow, F. (1994, April). *Antecedents and consequences of sexual harassment in organizations: A test of an integrated model.* Paper presented at the 9th Annual Meeting of the Society for Industrial and Organizational Psychology, Nashville, TN.

Gelfand, M., Fitzgerald, L. F., & Drasgow, F. (in press). The latent structure of sexual harassment: A cross-cultural confirmatory analysis. *Journal of Vocational Behavior.*

Gruber, J. E. (1990). Methodological problems and policy implications in sexual harassment research. *Population Research and Policy Review, 9*, 235–254.

Gruber, J. E. (1992, March). *The sexual harassment experiences of women in nontraditional jobs: Results from cross-national research.* Proceedings of Sex and Power Issues in the Workplace. Bellevue, WA: Conference on Sex and Power Issues in the Workplace.

Gruber, J. E., & Bjorn, L. (1982). Blue-collar blues: The sexual harassment of women autoworkers. *Work and Occupations, 9*, 271–298.

Gutek, B. (1985). *Sex and the workplace.* San Francisco: Jossey-Bass.

Gutek, B. A. (1993). Responses to sexual harassment. In S. Oskamp & M. Costanzo (Eds.), *Gender issues in contemporary society* (pp. 197–216). Newbury Park, CA: Sage.

Gutek, B. A., Cohen, A. G., & Konrad, A. M. (1990). Predicting social–sexual behavior at work: A contact hypothesis. *Academy of Management Journal, 33*, 560–577.

Gutek, B., & Koss, M. P. (1993). Changed women and changed organizations: Consequences of and coping with sexual harassment. *Journal of Vocational Behavior, 42*, 28–48.

Hanisch, K. A. (1993, April). Sexual harassment as an organizational stressor and its relation to work attitudes and organizational adaptation. In Peg Stockdale (Chair), *Sexual harassment in the workplace: An industrial and organizational research agenda.* Symposium conducted at the conference of the Society for Industrial and Organizational Psychology, San Francisco.

Hanisch, K. A., & Hulin, C. L. (1990). Job attitudes and organizational withdrawal: An examination of retirement and other voluntary withdrawal behaviors. *Journal of Vocational Behavior, 37,* 60–78.

Hanisch, K. A., & Hulin, C. L. (1991). General attitudes and organizational withdrawal: An evaluation of a causal model. *Journal of Vocational Behavior, 39,* 110–128.

Harris v. Forklift Systems, Inc., 976 F.2d 733 (6th Cir. 1992), *cert. granted,* 61 U.S.L.W. 3600 (March 1, 1993).

Hesson-McInnis, M., & Fitzgerald, L. F. (1992, November). *Sexual harassment: A preliminary test of an integrative model.* Paper presented at the 2nd Annual American Psychological Association/National Institute for Organizational Safety and Health Conference on Stress in the Workplace, Washington, DC.

Holgate, A. (1989). Sexual harassment as a determinant of women's fear of rape. *Australian Journal of Sex, Marriage and the Family, 10,* 21–28.

Hulin, C. L. (1993, May). *A framework for the study of sexual harassment in organizations: Climate, stressors and patterned responses.* Paper presented at the annual meeting of the Society for Industrial and Organizational Psychology, San Francisco.

Hulin, C. L., Fitzgerald, L. F., & Drasgow, F. (in press). Organizational influences on sexual harassment. In M. Stockdale & B. Gutek (Eds.), *Women and work* (Vol. 4). Newbury Park, CA: Sage.

Judge, T. R., & Hulin, C. L. (in press). Job satisfaction as a reflection of disposition: A multiple source causal analysis. *Organizational Behavior and Human Decision Processes.*

Junger, M. (1987). Women's experiences of sexual harassment. *British Journal of Criminology, 27,* 358–383.

Kauffman v. Allied Signal, 970 F.2d 178 *cert. denied* 61 USLW 3435 (6th Cir. 1992).

Koss, M. P. (1990). Changed lives: The psychological impact of sexual harassment. In M. Paludi (Ed.), *Ivory power: Sex and gender harassment in the academy* (pp. 73–92). New York: State University of New York Press.

Koss, M. P., Goodman, L. A., Browne, A., Fitzgerald, L. F., Keita, G. P., & Russo, N. F. (1994). *No safe haven: Violence against women at home, at work, and in the community.* Washington, DC: American Psychological Association.

Lazarus, R. S., & Folkman, S. (1984). *Stress, appraisal and coping.* New York: Springer.

Livingston, J. A. (1982). Responses to sexual harassment on the job: Legal, organizational and individual actions. *Journal of Social Issues, 38,* 5–22.

Long, J. S. (1983). *Confirmatory factor analysis: A preface to LISREL.* Newbury Park, CA: Sage.

MacKinnon, C. A. (1979). *Sexual harassment of working women.* New Haven, CT: Yale University Press.

Martindale, M. (1990). *Sexual harassment in the military: 1988.* Arlington, VA: Defense Manpower Data Center.

Meritor Savings Bank v. Vinson, 477 U.S. 57 (1986).

Miceli, M. P., & Near, J. P. (1988). Individual and situational correlates of whistle-blowing. *Personnel Psychology, 41,* 267–281.

Naylor, J. C., Pritchard, R. D., & Ilgen, D. R. (1980). *A theory of behavior in organizations.* San Diego, CA: Academic Press.

Near, J. P., & Miceli, M. P. (1987). Whistle blowers in organizations: Dissidents or reformers? In L. L. Cummings & B. M. Staw (Eds.), *Research in organizational behavior* (Vol. 9, pp. 321–367). Greenwich, CT: JAI Press.

Pryor, J. B. (1987). Sexual harassment proclivities in men. *Sex Roles, 17,* 269–290.

Pryor, J. B., LaVite, C. M., & Stoller, L. M. (1993). A social psychological analysis of sexual harassment: The person/situation interaction. *Journal of Vocational Behavior, 42,* 68–83.

Robinson v. Jacksonville Shipyards, Inc., 59 L Wl 2470 (DC. M. Fla. 1991).

Roznowski, M. A., & Hulin, C. L. (1992). The scientific merit of valid measures of general constructs with special reference to job satisfaction and job withdrawal. In C. J. Cranny, P. C. Smith, & E. F. Stone (Eds.), *Job satisfaction* (pp. 39–85). New York: Free Press.

Saunders, B. E. (1992, October). *Sexual harassment of women in the workplace: Results from the National Women's Study*. Paper presented at the 8th annual North Carolina/South Carolina Labor Law Seminar, Asheville, NC.

Schneider, K. T., & Swan, S. (1994, April). *Job-related, psychological, and health-related outcomes of sexual harassment*. Paper presented at the 9th annual conference of the Society for Industrial and Organizational Psychology, Nashville, TN.

Terpstra, D. E., & Baker, D. D. (1989). The identification and classification of reactions to sexual harassment. *Journal of Organizational Behavior, 10*, 1–14.

Treatment and counseling needs of women veterans who were raped, otherwise sexually assaulted, or sexually harassed during military service, 103rd Cong. (1992) (testimony of D. G. Kilpatrick).

U.S. Equal Employment Opportunity Commission. (1980). Discrimination because of sex under Title VII of the 1964 Civil Rights Act as amended: Adoption of interim guidelines—Sexual harassment. *Federal Register, 45,* 25024–25025.

U.S. Equal Employment Opportunity Commission. (1990). *Policy guidance on sexual harassment*. Washington, DC: Author.

U.S. Equal Employment Opportunity Commission. (1993). Proposed guidelines on harassment based on race, color, religion, gender, national origin, age, or disability (Publication no. 189). *Federal Register, 58,* 51266–51269.

U.S. Merit Systems Protection Board. (1981). *Sexual harassment of federal workers: Is it a problem?* Washington, DC: U.S. Government Printing Office.

U.S. Merit Systems Protection Board. (1987). *Sexual harassment of federal workers: An update.* Washington, DC: U.S. Government Printing Office.

Vaux, A. (1993). Paradigmatic assumptions in sexual harassment research: Being guided without being led. *Journal of Vocational Behavior, 42*, 116–135.

Wagner, E. J. (1992). *Sexual harassment in the workplace: How to prevent, investigate and resolve problems in your organization.* New York: AMACOM.

Zickar, M. (1994, April). *Organizational antecedents of sexual harassment*. Paper presented at the 9th annual conference of the Society for Industrial and Organizational Psychology, Nashville, TN.

5

Unemployment, Social Resources, and Mental and Physical Health: A Three-Wave Study on Men and Women in a Stressful Life Transition

Ralf Schwarzer, André Hahn, and Reinhard Fuchs

In 1989, the East German communist system collapsed. More than 300,000 East German citizens left their country and moved to West Germany. As part of this exodus, more than 50,000 migrants settled in West Berlin. Most of them came via the West German embassies in Warsaw, Prague, or Budapest or fled the country under other dubious and dangerous circumstances, whereas others crossed the border after the fall of the Berlin Wall on November 9, 1989. Our aim in this study was to investigate coping, adaptation processes, and health outcomes of these migrants in their new environment. We focused on the question of whether interindividual health differences can be predicted by personal employment situation and the provision of social support.

The decision to flee one's home and country has far-reaching and severe consequences. This can be considered a nonnormative critical life event (see Montada, Filipp, & Lerner, 1992). As with other critical events (such as accidents, losses, divorce, or illness), the corresponding psychological crisis may have a tremendous impact on an individual's personality development, psychosocial functioning, and health. Migration brings daily hassles—especially cramped living conditions in camps or gyms—as well as the threat of long-term unemployment and the need to build up a new social network. Thus, migrants are disadvantaged not only by higher demands than before migration, but also by heightened individual vulnerability toward stress, because they have to deal with the loss of their jobs and social support from former colleagues, friends, and relatives. According to Lazarus's (1991) cognitive–relational theory of stress, long-term employment and social support, among other factors, can be seen as protective situative resources to be used when facing stressful demands. Material, psychological, social, and health-related resources influence stress appraisals and coping processes; that is, strong resources should invoke more favorable stress experiences and coping behaviors than should a lack of such resources (Hobfoll, 1988, 1989; Hobfoll, Lilly, & Jackson, 1992; Jerusalem & Schwarzer, 1989, 1992).

We discuss employment and social support as resource factors in more detail later. *Employment* is the basis for earning one's living and for being respected in a Western society characterized by high material and economic values. Thus, the impact of unemployment goes beyond direct economic costs. Job loss creates insecurity with respect to one's future life perspective. Although research on unemployment problems has been characterized by inconsistent empirical results, studies have generally reported an impairment of psychological and physical well-being for the majority of the unemployed, especially in the case of long-term unemployment (Dooley & Catalano, 1988; Feather, 1990; Frese & Mohr, 1987; Jahoda, 1982; Mortimer, 1991; Schaufeli & Van Yperen, 1992; Schwefel, Svensson, & Zöllner, 1987; Warr, 1987). The stressing factor of unemployment is mostly attributed to decrements in environmental features, such as weakened control possibilities because of financial hardships or social network disruption, fewer goals and task demands, a larger time budget without time markers to break up and organize each day, or reduced opportunities for social contacts. An enduring status of unemployment requires continuous adaptational efforts—instrumental actions to eliminate the jobless state as well as emotional coping to alleviate the distressing experience (Lazarus, 1991). For migrants, unemployment following relocation appears to be a universal phenomenon hardly under personal control. To these people, problem-focused behaviors, such as searching for or qualifying for a job, are only of limited value. Instead, emotion-focused coping strategies are used more to deal with this problem, particularly in the case of extended unemployment. Long-term psychological consequences of unemployment can be feelings of discouragement, hopelessness, and despondency as well as impairments of self-worth and somatic health. Kelvin and Jarrett (1985) argued that these effects are stabilized through social comparison processes because working people may perceive the long-term unemployed as a negative reference group whose members cope inadequately with life. Moreover, reemployment could be viewed as a necessary condition for reestablishing a personal resource system (Hobfoll, 1989). For these reasons, there must be a very high incentive value attached to reemployment after migration.

A well-established social network is a structural prerequisite of feeling socially integrated and emotionally accepted (Laireiter & Baumann, 1992; Thoits, 1992; Veiel & Baumann, 1992). *Social integration* refers to the mere existence of a quantity of social relationships; it is measured by the size of one's network—the number of one's relatives and friends and the frequency of contact with them. The number of active social ties determines one's degree of embeddedness, with social isolation being the extreme, negative endpoint. *Social support,* on the other hand, refers to the function and quality of beneficial social relationships.

There are different mechanisms through which social relationships may influence the development of health. Support may have a benign effect on health in the normal population, thus appearing as a statistical main effect, or it may alleviate stress and its consequences. In the latter instance, support serves as a buffer or moderator. In the stress-buffering model, support may be influential twice: first when stressful demands are cognitively appraised and again by dampening health-damaging physiological processes (Cohen, 1992;

Henderson, 1992; Monroe & Johnson, 1992; Schwarzer & Leppin, 1991, 1992; Veiel, 1992).

Employment status and social support may confound each other; that is, employment is often connected with social contacts, whereas unemployment may lead to being socially undesirable. In the present sample, the East German migrants needed to strive for both resources in their new environment. A new job is not provided automatically by Western society, and for most newcomers, there is no social network immediately available. For these reasons, looking for an appropriate job as well as trying to establish contact with other people and make friends becomes an essential adaptation problem. Most likely, one's effectiveness in solving these problems will strongly affect one's emotional experiences. Those who are more successful would be expected to feel less stressed and to be better off with respect to psychological well-being.

Following these theoretical considerations, we deal in the present study with the individual health differences of men and women with respect to employment status and social support. We expected that, over time, those who were employed would report better health than unemployed migrants, as would those receiving support as opposed to those lacking support.

Method

In October 1989, before the opening of the Berlin Wall, a study was launched to gain more detailed knowledge about the adaptation and coping processes of refugees and migrants from East Germany. The project was designed as a longitudinal study, with three measurement points during the first 2 years after migration.

The East German migrants were contacted individually in their temporary living quarters (e.g., school gymnasiums, container homes, or other emergency shelters) and were asked to take part in a psychological investigation on their adaptation process in the West. Participation was voluntary and was guaranteed to be anonymous. The standardized written interview took about 1 hour. A numerical code was recorded instead of names or addresses to correctly assign each person to the longitudinal data set. The first wave of data was collected in the fall and winter of 1989–1990, the second in the summer of 1990, and the third in the summer of 1991. A total of 1,036 migrants participated and constituted the first-wave sample. A subsample of 235 completed the questionnaires at all three points in time. Many migrants either refused to participate in the follow-up surveys or could not be tracked down again. We attributed the high attrition rate to (a) lack of incentives for responding, (b) continued mobility of the migrants after their initial arrival in Berlin, and (c) a large number of questionnaire items that took about an hour to answer.

The subjects filled out a questionnaire that measured—among other variables—employment status, received social support, perceived (anticipated) social support, depression, and health complaints. In accordance with theoretical considerations, employment status and social support were taken as

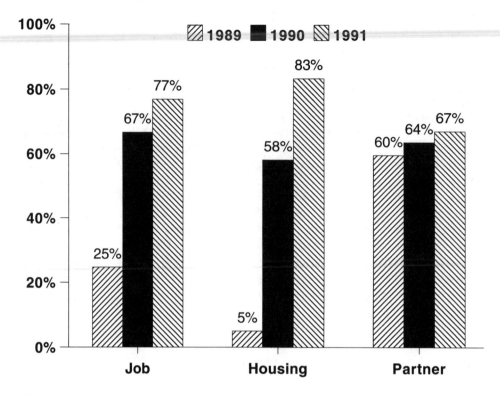

Figure 1. Demographic changes in the sample over time.

independent variables, whereas the experience of depression and physical symptoms served as dependent variables.

Subjects

The present analysis was based on data from 235 migrants who had participated in all three waves of the study. These 126 men (mean age = 31 years, SD = 9.25) and 109 women (M = 32 years, SD = 10.39) had arrived in West Berlin during 1989. At the onset, 63 men and 72 women were either married or had a partner. The majority of the sample consisted of refugees (62%)—defined as those who arrived illegally before the opening of the Berlin Wall on November 9, 1989—whereas the others were considered legal migrants (38%) because they had arrived after this date. Because there were no major psychological differences between refugees and legal migrants in this data set, we combined the groups for further analysis.

Figure 1 shows the reported changes in employment, housing, and partnership for the sample over time. Initially, 28% of the respondents held some kind of a job. Those who had spent several weeks in the West already had a good chance to be employed, whereas those who had just arrived were not yet ready for the job market. Thus, employment at Time 1 mainly reflected the duration of residence and could not be considered a variable worth further exploration. At Time 2, the employment rate had increased to 67%, and at Time 3 it increased to 77%. The sample of those who remained jobless over time was of interest to us.

None of the migrants had housing at the initial interview, because the data were collected in temporary refugee shelters. Only very few were lucky enough to join relatives in the West; they were not part of the present sample. The rate of housing climbed to 58% at Time 2 and to 83% at Time 3. The success rates in employment and housing reflect the conditions for readaptation of the migrants, but they also reveal that 23% did not get jobs and 17% did not find housing after nearly 2 years.

About 60% of the migrants either made their way to the West with their partners or met a new partner during or immediately after their transition. Bonding continued, and the rate of those with intimate partners increased to 67%, but it was not possible to identify whether the participants stayed with their original partners or found new ones. Anecdotal evidence suggested that many migrants separated from their spouses in the stressful context of their critical life transition and built up new personal relationships (see Schwarzer & Hahn, in press).

Measures

The actual employment status (employed vs. not employed) of the subjects was recorded at three points in time. For the longitudinal approach, we determined whether the migrants (a) were jobless at the beginning and the end of the study ("always jobless"; $n = 50$, 15 men and 35 women), (b) were jobless at the beginning but found a job during the 2-year period ("job hunt successful"; $n = 105$, 56 men and 49 women), or (c) were employed at the beginning and at the end ("never jobless"; $n = 54$, 38 men and 16 women). Seven men held jobs at the initial interview but lost them later. These data were discarded from the analyses because of the small cell frequency. For the remaining 19 persons, there were no accurate data available. Evidently, more women than men were unemployed.

The received social support scale consisted of eight items such as "There are people upon whom I can rely when I need help" ($\alpha = .87$). Responses to all items were made on a 4-point Likert-type scale ranging from *not true* (1) to *exactly true* (4). The scores ranged from 8 to 32.

As a measure of depression, we selected a 16-item German depression scale (Zerssen, 1976; $\alpha = .90$). Typical items on this scale are "I feel simply miserable" or "I feel blue and downhearted." The scale anchors were identical to those used for the social support measure.

As indicators of ill health, self-reported physical symptoms were recorded on the basis of a well-known German instrument (Brähler & Scheer, 1983). From this inventory, 24 items ($\alpha = .92$) were taken that were subdivided into four categories: heart complaints, pains in the limbs, stomach complaints, and exhaustion. Responses to all items were made on a 5-point intensity scale ranging from *not* (1) to *strong* (4). Scores ranged from 24 to 96. (Note that, hereinafter, the labels *physical symptoms, health complaints,* and *illness* are used synonymously.)

Results

Unemployment and Depression

We first analyzed the data to determine the relationship between depression and employment status across the three waves. An analysis of variance (ANOVA) was computed with three levels of employment status as one factor and the three points in time as the repeated measures factor. A main effect of employment status resulted, $F(2, 198) = 8.97$, $p < .001$, as did a significant time effect, $F(2, 396) = 5.04$, $p = .007$. There was no significant interaction between employment and time.

Figure 2 depicts the pattern of mean values for the dependent variable depression. The upper line represents those people who remained jobless over 2 years ($n = 46$); they reported the highest level of depression. The middle line represents those who found a job during the 2-year period ($n = 103$). The bottom line ($n = 52$) stands for those who had never been jobless; this last group reported the lowest degree of depression. Figure 2 also shows that there

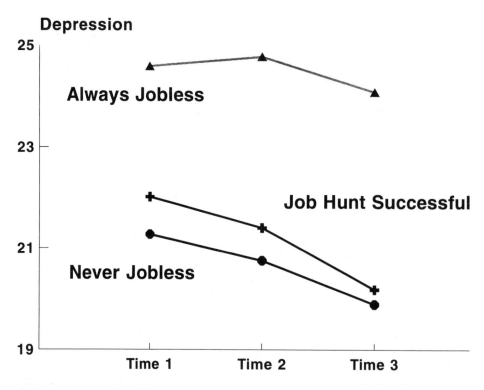

Figure 2. The relationship of employment status and depression over time. Mean scores on the depression scale are given on the vertical axis.

is a stable relationship between one's employment status and depression as well as some improvement of the depression scores over time.

Unemployment and Illness

We next analyzed the relationship between health complaints and employment status across the three waves. We computed an ANOVA with three levels of employment status as one factor and the three points in time as the repeated measures factor. A main effect of employment status resulted, $F(2, 196) = 12.67$, $p < .001$, whereas the time factor was only of borderline significance, $F(2, 392) = 2.75$, $p = .065$. There was no significant Health Complaints $\times$ Employment Status interaction.

Figure 3 depicts the pattern of means for the dependent variable health complaints. The upper line represents those who remained jobless over 2 years ($n = 45$); they reported the highest level of symptoms. In the middle are those who found a job during the 2-year period ($n = 101$). The bottom line ($n = 53$) shows those who had not been jobless. This last group consisted of people investigated several weeks after their arrival who had already found jobs and kept these jobs over the 2-year period; they reported the lowest degree of symptoms. There was a downward trend for all three groups, but, as mentioned

Figure 3. The relationship of employment status and health complaints over time. Mean scores on the indicator of ill-health are given on the vertical axis.

above, this trend did not reach significance. Figure 3 shows a stable relationship between one's employment status and self-reported ill health.

Gender Differences

The relationship between unemployment and health was further elucidated when gender differences were taken into account. Men and women responded differently to the stress of unemployment. At Time 1, women (mean score = 23.6) were more depressed than men ($M = 20.89$), $F(1, 223) = 12.40, p < .001$. At Time 2, there was the same kind of difference ($Ms = 23.24$ vs. 20.63), $F(1, 223) = 10.68$, $p < .001$. But at Time 3, this was no longer significant ($Ms = 21.55$ vs. 20.35), $F(1, 223) = 2.51$, $p < .115$. The relationships appear to be more complex when depression is broken down by gender, employment status, and time (Table 1).

Symptom reporting was much more extreme for men than for women between the three categories of employment status (Table 2). For men, unemployment seemed to be more detrimental, or initial health problems inhibited job search and hiring. At all three time periods, women reported more ill health than men: For Times 1, 2, and 3, respectively, $F(1, 219) = 13.46$, $p < .01$; $F(1, 219) = 14.49$, $p < .01$; and $F(1, 219) = 4.03$, $p < .05$. This effect was caused by the two employed groups, whereas the third group—men who were always jobless—reported more illness.

Social Resources

As a next step, we added social support as a second between-subjects factor. The question was whether support could buffer the negative effect of joblessness. The distribution of the received social support scale was dichotomized at Time 1 and Time 3. Those migrants who scored above the median at both

Table 1. Depression at Three Waves, According to Employment Status, Gender, and Time

Employment status	n	Women			n	Men		
		Time 1	Time 2	Time 3		Time 1	Time 2	Time 3
Always jobless	32				14			
M		24.38	24.00	22.94		25.07	26.57	26.71
SD		7.18	7.01	7.92		7.11	8.24	9.72
Job hunt successful	49				54			
M		23.45	23.16	20.69		20.70	19.80	19.72
SD		6.86	6.94	5.39		4.76	4.31	3.63
Never jobless	15				37			
M		22.80	22.13	20.67		20.65	20.19	19.72
SD		5.02	4.14	3.68		4.02	5.10	3.79
$F(2, 196)$		0.77	0.80	1.79		5.64	10.32	10.20
$p <$		.47	.46	.17		.01	.01	.01

Table 2. Health Complaints at Three Waves, According to Employment Status, Gender, and Time

Employment status	n	Women			n	Men		
		Time 1	Time 2	Time 3		Time 1	Time 2	Time 3
Always jobless	30				15			
M		20.69	17.84	16.68		23.53	26.00	26.67
SD		17.18	15.62	14.84		16.23	15.09	19.01
Job hunt successful	48				53			
M		16.76	16.00	12.75		10.31	8.51	9.53
SD		14.81	13.32	12.56		12.21	9.87	10.07
Never jobless	15				38			
M		14.56	16.07	11.56		8.95	7.16	7.34
SD		9.95	9.55	8.24		11.29	10.93	8.93
$F(2, 194)$		1.81	0.24	1.15		9.76	18.33	15.55
$p <$		.17	.79	.32		.01	.01	.01

times were considered to be benefiting from long-term support, whereas those migrants who scored below the median at both times were considered to be lacking long-term support. Data for all others were discarded for this analysis. To avoid cell frequencies that were too small, we included two levels instead of three in the employment status factor: migrants who remained jobless over 2 years ($n = 39$) and those who either kept a job the whole time or found one during the observation period ($n = 113$). Thus, there were four groups of migrants in this analysis: (a) those who were always jobless and were not supported ($n = 22$), (b) those who were always jobless and received support ($n = 17$), (c) those who were employed and were not supported ($n = 54$), and (d) those who were employed and received support ($n = 59$). We computed a repeated-measures ANOVA with employment status and support as between-subjects factors and time as the within-subjects factor. Because of gender differences, results are presented separately for men and women.

Effects of unemployment and social support on depression. Four analyses are presented that followed the same rationale. First, for women, the joint effects of unemployment and social support on depression were determined, followed by the same procedure for men. Afterward, this pair of computations was repeated with health complaints as the dependent variable.

The analysis of depression for women yielded a main effect for employment status, $F(1, 67) = 4.55, p = .037$; for support, $F(1, 67) = 14.57, p < .001$; and for changes over time, $F(2, 134) = 5.26, p = .006$.

The supported women reported low depression, whether or not they were jobless. For women who were always jobless, support made a difference. Those who suffered jointly from two stressors—that is, being unemployed and having no support—continued to report the highest level of depression at three points in time. Those who remained jobless but received social support showed a decline in depression. Thus, efficient support seems to be able to alleviate depression.

The analysis of depression for men yielded a main effect for employment status, $F(1, 75) = 16.68, p < .001$; a tendency for a main effect of support, $F(1, 75) = 3.10, p = .083$; and a tendency for a Support $\times$ Time interaction, $F(2, 150) = 2.46, p = .089$.

Employed men reported low depression, whether or not they were supported. For the men who were always jobless, support made a difference. Those who suffered jointly from two stressors—that is, being unemployed and experiencing lack of support—continued to report the highest level of depression at all three points in time. When men remained jobless but received social support there was a decline in depression. The marginally significant interaction between support and time was reflected by a scissor effect: Of the unemployed, those with support and those without support experienced a differential development of depression as time went by.

Effects of unemployment and social support on health. The analysis of health complaints for women yielded a tendency of a main effect of employment status, $F(1, 64) = 3.61, p = .062$; a main effect of support, $F(1, 64) = 6.74, p = .012$; and a main effect of changes over time, $F(2, 128) = 3.99, p = .021$. In addition, an Employment $\times$ Support interaction was nearly significant, $F(2, 128) = 2.58, p = .08$, and an Employment $\times$ Support $\times$ Time interaction emerged, $F(2, 128) = 3.11, p = .048$.

At Times 2 and 3, both once employed and unemployed women who were supported reported fewer physical symptoms. For the always jobless women, however, support was critical: Those who lacked support displayed the highest level of ill health. The remarkable decline in ill health over time for jobless women who received support represents impressive evidence of the often-hypothesized buffer effect of social support.

The analysis of health complaints for men yielded a main effect of employment status, $F(1, 75) = 24.64, p < .001$; a tendency of a main effect of support, $F(1, 75) = 3.11, p = .082$; and an Employment $\times$ Support interaction, $F(1, 75) = 4.26, p = .043$.

The employed men enjoyed good health whether they were supported or not. For the jobless men, however, there was a difference between the unsupported, who experienced an increment in ill health, and the supported, who suffered from fewer symptoms.

Discussion

The present study differs from other research on unemployment in terms of the political and socioeconomic background and the transitory context. We examined temporary mass unemployment caused by sudden migration into a wealthy country, where the job market was able to absorb the majority of the unexpected job seekers. Unemployment was an initially universal and normative experience for these migrants but then became more and more personal and nonnormative for those who failed to get a job as time went by.

This study is unique in its long-term assessment of the relationships between unemployment, social resources, and health at three points in time over nearly 2 years. It represents the only available panel study on psychosocial changes in East German migrants of the time. The overall results show that migrants who did not succeed in finding a job suffered from depression and physical symptoms. Although women generally scored somewhat higher in depression and ill health, the detrimental effect of unemployment was stronger for men. Most interesting was that social resources made a difference here: Men and women who received social support reported less depression and symptoms of ill health over time. Thus, support appeared to buffer the stress of unemployment, a phenomenon that has rarely been demonstrated before in longitudinal designs (Cohen & Wills, 1985). This buffer effect illustrates the dynamics of a crisis and, therefore, underscores the hypothesized mechanism by which stress is alleviated through the availability of beneficial social resources.

This study sheds some light on changes of ill health depending on stress and support over a 2-year period, but it also has limitations. It is unfortunate that there was no opportunity to obtain objective health data in this investigation. This was because of the spontaneous nature of the study: It was launched without detailed preparation while the refugees were arriving in great numbers in Berlin and were interviewed, sometimes under very unusual circumstances (e.g., amid suitcases in the waiting hall of the refugee reception center). Another limitation lies in the nature of the sample itself. The findings cannot be generalized to a resident population because they were obtained only in a sample of migrants. Unemployed migrants need not have the same characteristics as long-term unemployed residents. However, the role of resource factors is best examined within a context of high stress (Hobfoll, 1989).

The focus of this study was indeed on the effects of unemployment on health, but the evidence appears to be inconclusive. In particular, it was found that, already at the onset of the study, health differences emerged between the always jobless and the successful job gainers and job holders. The evidence that symptom reporting at the beginning was associated with staying out of a job later on points to the possibility that ill health may be the true independent variable here. Feeling depressed and complaining about various bodily symptoms can be either a justification for not searching for a job or a reason for not being hired. Optimistic and healthy individuals are usually more successful in finding jobs and in staying in them. However, the present study cannot prove any causal directions. Illness and employment can be understood as reciprocal variables, and more data would be required to identify the predominant factor, if there is one.

Another critical issue lies in the definition of *unemployment*. We did not distinguish between unemployment and joblessness, and we implicitly assumed that everyone in the sample wanted to work. One might speculate that, for example, mothers who were raising children did not want a job at the time. However, this critique does not apply here because there were almost no mothers in the sample and because all migrants were eager to make money to rebuild their lives. The East Germans, who had no convertible currency, were without funds, which motivated them to search for any kind of job. Another, similar critique could be that married female participants might feel less inclined to find jobs, being content to be homemakers. This could be true in the future, but at the onset the migrants were very concerned about making their daily living. Nevertheless, the job status of a spouse could be important for one's well-being. Unfortunately, this information was not available. The questionnaire panel study was accompanied by a more qualitative interview study of 44 migrants that provided evidence about their life situation, readjustment efforts, and motives for work. There is no complete information of this kind for the entire sample.

Another limitation is that there were no data about the nature of the available jobs. It is not known whether the jobs were part-time, explicitly temporary, or inadequate in other ways. This, however, would only represent a bias if it were unevenly distributed across the cells of the design, which is unlikely.

The study of health impairment after job loss should, if possible, include a detailed assessment of coping parameters and real opportunities for reemployment. It has been found (Lerner & Somers, 1992) that coping modes and positive illusions may contribute to well-being, job-search intentions, and job-search behavior but that this influence also depends on actual job qualifications and on the dynamics of the crisis. A possible future research question then, would be whether unrealistic optimism would be functional or dysfunctional for job search and well-being. Those who feel well and healthy may do so because they have a positive outlook on life, although their objective reemployment chances might be negligible. In our analysis, it was not possible to further break down the sample in terms of coping modes, living environments, or personality characteristics because the small cell sizes did not allow a more fine-grained examination of the data. Therefore, separate analyses will have to be performed with these variables in the future. In spite of some limitations, these results are among the few that indicate longitudinally a deleterious effect of unemployment and beneficial effects of social support on health. Results of this longitudinal study of cumulative stress add to the understanding of coping with job loss, migration, and stress resource factors.

References

Brähler, E., & Scheer, J. (1983). *Giessener Beschwerdebogen (GBB)* [Giessen catalogue of bodily ailments (GBB)]. Bern, Switzerland: Huber.

Cohen, S. (1992). Stress, social support, and disorder. In H. O. F. Veiel & U. Baumann (Eds.), *The meaning and measurement of social support* (pp. 109–124). Washington, DC: Hemisphere.

Cohen, S., & Wills, T. A. (1985). Stress, social support, and the buffering hypothesis. *Psychological Bulletin, 98,* 310–357.

Dooley, D., & Catalano, R. A. (1988). Recent research on the psychological effects of unemployment. *Journal of Social Issues, 44,* 1–12.

Feather, N. T. (1990). *The psychological impact of unemployment.* New York: Springer.

Frese, M., & Mohr, G. (1987). Prolonged unemployment and depression in older workers: A longitudinal study of intervening variables. *Social Science Medicine, 25,* 173–178.

Henderson, A. S. (1992). Social support and depression. In H. O. F. Veiel & U. Baumann (Eds.), *The meaning and measurement of social support* (pp. 85–92). Washington, DC: Hemisphere.

Hobfoll, S. E. (1988). *The ecology of stress.* Washington, DC: Hemisphere.

Hobfoll, S. E. (1989). Conservation of resources: A new attempt at conceptualizing stress. *American Psychologist, 44*, 513–524.

Hobfoll, S. E., Lilly, R. S., & Jackson, A. P. (1992). Conservation and social resources and the self. In H. O. F. Veiel & U. Baumann (Eds.), *The meaning and measurement of social support* (pp. 125–141). Washington, DC: Hemisphere.

Jahoda, M. (1982). *Employment and unemployment: A social-psychological analysis.* Cambridge, England: Cambridge University Press.

Jerusalem, M., & Schwarzer, R. (1989). Anxiety and self-concept as antecedents of stress and coping: A longitudinal study with German and Turkish adolescents. *Personality and Individual Differences, 10*, 785–792.

Jerusalem, M., & Schwarzer, R. (1992). Self-efficacy as a resource factor in stress appraisal processes. In R. Schwarzer (Ed.), *Self-efficacy: Thought control of action* (pp. 195–213). Washington, DC: Hemisphere.

Kelvin, P., & Jarrett, J. E. (1985). *Unemployment: Its social psychological effects.* Cambridge, England: Cambridge University Press.

Laireiter, A., & Baumann, U. (1992). Network structures and support functions: Theoretical and empirical analyses. In H. O. F. Veiel & U. Baumann (Eds.), *The meaning and measurement of social support* (pp. 33–55). Washington, DC: Hemisphere.

Lazarus, R. S. (1991). *Emotion and adaptation.* London: Oxford University Press.

Lerner, M. J., & Somers, D. G. (1992). Employees' reactions to an anticipated plant closure: The influence of positive illusions. In L. Montada, S.-H. Filipp, & M. J. Lerner (Eds.), *Life crises and experiences of loss in adulthood* (pp. 229–253). Hillsdale, NJ: Erlbaum.

Monroe, S. M., & Johnson, S. L. (1992). Social support, depression, and other mental disorders: In retrospect and toward future prospects. In H. O. F. Veiel & U. Baumann (Eds.), *The meaning and measurement of social support* (pp. 93–105). Washington, DC: Hemisphere.

Montada, L., Filipp, S.-H., & Lerner, M. J. (1992). *Life crises and experiences of loss in adulthood.* Hillsdale, NJ: Erlbaum.

Mortimer, J. T. (1991). Employment. In R. M. Lerner, A. C. Peterson, & J. Brooks-Gunn (Eds.), *Encyclopedia of adolescence* (pp. 311–318). New York: Garland.

Schaufeli, W. B., & Van Yperen, N. W. (1992). Unemployment and psychological distress among graduates: A longitudinal study. *Journal of Occupational and Organizational Psychology, 65*, 291–305.

Schwarzer, R., & Hahn, A. (in press). Reemployment after migration from East to West Germany: A longitudinal study on psychosocial factors. *Applied Psychology: An International Review.*

Schwarzer, R., & Leppin, A. (1991). Social support and health: A theoretical and empirical overview. *Journal of Social and Personal Relationships, 8*, 99–127.

Schwarzer, R., & Leppin, A. (1992). Social support and mental health: A conceptual and empirical overview. In L. Montada, S.-H. Filipp, & M. J. Lerner (Eds.), *Life crises and experiences of loss in adulthood* (pp. 435–458). Hillsdale, NJ: Erlbaum.

Schwefel, D., Svensson, P. G., & Zöllner, H. (Eds.). (1987). *Unemployment, social vulnerability, and health in Europe.* Berlin, Germany: Springer-Verlag.

Thoits, P. A. (1992). Social support functions and network structures: A supplemental view. In H. O. F. Veiel & U. Baumann (Eds.), *The meaning and measurement of social support* (pp. 57–62). Washington, DC: Hemisphere.

Veiel, H. O. F. (1992). Some cautionary notes on buffer effects. In H. O. F. Veiel & U. Baumann (Eds.), *The meaning and measurement of social support* (pp. 273–289). Washington, DC: Hemisphere.

Veiel, H. O. F., & Baumann, U. (1992). The many meanings of social support. In H. O. F. Veiel & U. Baumann (Eds.), *The meaning and measurement of social support* (pp. 1–9). Washington, DC: Hemisphere.

Warr, P. (1987). *Work, unemployment, and mental health.* Oxford, England: Clarendon.

Zerssen, D. V. (1976). *Paranoid-Depressivitäts-Skala (PD-S). Depressivitäts-Skala (D-S)* [Paranoid-Depression Scale (PD-S). Depression Scale (D-S)]. Weinheim, Germany: Beltz Test.

Part II

Culture and Ethnicity

Introduction

Although the workforce is much more culturally and ethnically diverse today than in the past, very little is currently known about the specific impact of this diversity on organizations or about the stress that such diversity imposes on different cultures and ethnic groups. Current U.S. trends show that ethnic minority individuals are entering the workforce at a rate exceeding that for White women. This trend toward faster labor force growth among ethnic minority groups is not limited to women. Such influxes contribute to the evolution of an ethnoculturally pluralized workforce, in which social identities become increasingly more diverse. In this part, the authors provide information on how different cultural and ethnic orientations affect job stress and coping for workers.

First, Bhagat and colleagues examine coping styles, decision latitude, and organizational stress—psychological strain in seven countries. Their primary objective is to compare the relative predictive efficacy of problem- versus emotion-focused coping styles and decision latitude on organizational stress—psychological strain relationships.

Next, Gutierres, Saenz, and Green examine how proportional representation perceptions of perceived discrimination and level of social support affect job stress and self-reported health problems in Hispanic and White workers. They expand their investigation by focusing on how person—environment incongruence affects the stress and health outcomes of these workers.

James continues the examination of workplace factors affecting the health of ethnic minority workers. Like Gutierres et al., he analyzes the relationship among proportion of in-group members in the ethnic minority worker's work unit, perceived levels of prejudice and discrimination, and health. However, James also examines how employee health is affected by individual and group levels of self-esteem, perceived supervisor and peer value differences, and social support.

In the final chapter of this part, Marsella reveals some of the challenges to creating a harmonious workplace with diverse backgrounds and beliefs. He also discusses definitional and methodological issues that need to be addressed in studies of ethnocultural pluralism, including the need to expand the definition of work to include the consequences that work has for personal growth and development.

6

Organizational Stress and Coping in Seven National Contexts: A Cross-Cultural Investigation

Rabi S. Bhagat, Michael P. O'Driscoll, Emin Babakus, Len Frey, Jagdeep Chokkar, B. Habil Ninokumar, Larry E. Pate, Paul A. Ryder, M. Jesus Gonzalez Fernandez, David L. Ford, Jr., and Mohale Mahanyele

The level of stress an individual experiences in his or her organizational context and the extent to which adverse effects (i.e., psychological and other strains) occur depend on how effectively he or she can cope with stressful organizational situations. The empirical literature on organizational stress has grown rather extensively during the past 15 years (Beehr & Bhagat, 1985; Beehr & Newman, 1978; Cooper & Payne, 1980; Jamal, 1984; Parker and DeCotiis, 1983; Schuler, 1980). However, there is still relatively little systematic information (a) on how individuals cope and (b) on the moderating effects of coping styles on organizational stress–psychological strain relationships. Latack (1986) has provided some construct-validity-related evidence for three measures of coping related to job stress: control, escape, and symptom management. She identified some measurement-related issues, particularly with regard to the time-dependent nature of coping. Bhagat and Allie (1989) have found strong support for the moderating role of the sense of competence (White, 1959) in organizational stress–life strain relationships.

In continuing their interest in exploring the moderating role of coping, Bhagat, Allie, and Ford (1991) also completed a recent investigation into the relevance of Lazarus and Folkman's (1984; Folkman & Lazarus, 1980) conceptualization of coping as being situation specific. According to Lazarus and Folkman, coping-related activities come into play in specific situations, such as being confronted with an excessive overload at work. These authors defined *problem-focused coping* as attempts to alter or manage the situation (e.g., "Got the person responsible for creating the excessive workload to change his or her mind" or "Made a plan of action and worked on it"). *Emotion-focused coping* was defined as attempts to reduce or manage distress associated with the

Partial support for this study came from a summer grant to Rabi S. Bhagat by the Fogelman College of Business and Economics, University of Memphis, Memphis, Tennessee.

experience of stress (e.g., "Looked for the 'silver lining in the cloud'" or "Tried to look on the brighter side of things"). Their results show that problem-focused coping acts as a superior moderator in comparison with the moderating effects of emotion-focused coping.

Bhagat et al. (1991) were interested in exploring the relative efficacies of these two styles of coping in an organizational context. On the basis of Folkman and Lazarus's (1980) pioneering investigation of coping in a middle-aged community—showing that individuals cope by using either a problem-focused or an emotion-focused mode of coping—Bhagat et al. argued and found support for the proposition that problem-focused coping is a superior moderator. However, they also noted that, although this was the case in a majority of the stress-outcome relationships, emotion-focused coping did emerge as a moderator in some situations and that emotion-focused coping would be of considerable significance in exploring the nature of such relationships in other organizational contexts, where it could indeed be an important moderator. Lazarus and Folkman (1984)—in their well-known volume entitled *Stress, Appraisal, and Coping*—discussed the relevance of both conceptual and empirical factors for differentiating between these two styles of coping.

Menaghan (1984) observed that coping styles, like personal resources, are considered to be general and relatively enduring personal qualities of individuals that they activate in response to situational demands. In addition, the effectiveness of these coping styles depends on their relative suitability or match to a given context. Evidence of the effectiveness of these styles can be found in the literature dealing with cancer patients. For example, Worden and Sobel (1978) showed that emotional distress is inversely related to a tendency to redefine problems and positively related to tendencies to blame others and accept problems in a fatalistic or helpless mode. In a related vein, Rosensteil and Roth (1981), studying respondents who had experienced massive spinal-cord injuries and subsequent paralysis, found that rationalization and denial were predictive of such positive outcomes as subsequent life satisfaction, higher productivity, and greater maintenance of optimal physical health and that extensive preoccupation and catastrophizing had the opposite effect.

In her review, Menaghan (1984) carefully distinguished between coping resources, coping styles, and coping efforts, urging that future research efforts be directed at assessing the effectiveness of coping styles in different situational contexts. On the basis of this history of work on coping, we developed the following conceptual framework to guide the present investigation.

A Conceptual Framework

The definition of organizational stress as it was used in this investigation followed from House, Schuler, and Levanoni's (1983) constructs of role ambiguity and role conflict and from Beehr, Walsh, and Taber's (1976) constructs of role overload. Basically, we defined *organizational stress* as a problematic level of environmental demand that emerges when the amount of ambiguity present in one's work role, the degree of conflict that it fosters, and the extent of overload that it creates for the role occupant are relatively high. Organizational stress interacts with the individual to change (i.e., to disrupt or to enhance) his or her psychological or physiological condition such that the person is forced to deviate from normal functioning.

Coping was defined as efforts that help individuals manage (i.e., master, tolerate, or reduce) the internal demands and conflicts that emerge from stressful experiences in the organization and tax or exceed their resources (Bhagat et al., 1991; Lazarus & DeLongis, 1983; Lazarus & Folkman, 1984; Lazarus & Launier, 1978). These efforts may be either of a problem-focused type or intrapsychic in nature. Problem-focused coping centers around cognitive and problem-solving efforts, information-seeking efforts, and behavioral efforts made to decrease or manage emotional distress (Bhagat et al., 1991; Folkman & Lazarus, 1980). Strategies such as intellectualization, social isolation, suppression (Folkman & Lazarus, 1980; Lazarus & Launier, 1978), optimistic comparison and restricted expectations (Menaghan & Merves, 1984) are examples of emotion-focused coping mechanisms.

In addition to these two coping styles, we also decided to examine the significance of decision latitude in ameliorating the experience of stress. *Decision latitude* was defined as the discretion or control that an individual is permitted in deciding to meet his or her job demands (Karasek, 1979). Karasek's research on job decision latitude is well established in the literature. However, there has been no empirical investigation into direct or main effects or into the potential moderating role of decision latitude in the organizational stress–psychological strain relationship. Karasek noted that if organizations are careful to redesign work processes in such a way as to allow increases in decision latitude, then they will also succeed in reducing mental strain without necessarily changing job demands (Karasek, 1979, p. 285). His job strain model postulated that psychological strain results not from a single aspect of the work environment but from the joint effects of organizational stress and the range of decision-making freedom (i.e., discretion) available to the individual in his or her work role. He clearly stated that if an individual can take either no action or very little action or if he or she must forgo other desires because of low job decision latitude (Henry & Cassel, 1969, p. 179), then the unreleased energy is likely to be internally transformed into mental or psychological strain.

The conceptual framework for our study, depicted in Figure 1, shows our two basic propositions. First, we expected both problem-focused coping and emotion-focused coping to act as moderators in the organizational stress–psychological strain relationship. Second, job decision latitude, a variable that is strictly under organizational control and is not under any kind of predispositional control of the individual employee, was expected to reduce psychological strain directly as well as to moderate the organizational stress–psychological strain relationship much like problem-focused and emotion-focused coping.

Our main objective was to compare the relative predictive efficacies of

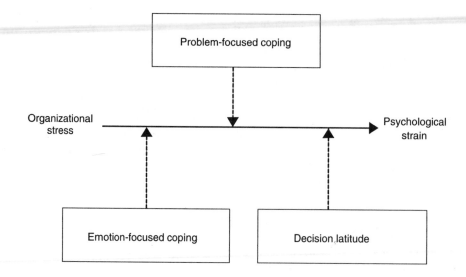

Figure 1. A conceptual model of the moderating effects of problem-focused coping, emotion-focused coping, and decision latitude on the relationship between organizational stress and psychological strain. The solid line indicates a direct relationship, whereas dashed lines indicate moderating relationships.

these three moderating influences on organizational stress−experienced strain relationships in seven different cultural contexts. One question we were trying to answer in this cross-national investigation dealt with the relevance of Hofstede's (1980, 1983, 1991) dimensions of cultural variations for providing a context for explaining our results.

Method

Data Collection

Data were gathered from managers and staff members of participating financial service and high-technology organizations in seven countries: the United States, India, West Germany, Spain, New Zealand, Australia, and South Africa. One academic research team member from each country managed the data collection process in that country. The overall data-collecting strategy was managed by Rabi S. Bhagat from the United States and by Michael P. O'Driscoll from New Zealand. In line with the recommendations pertaining to data collection strategies made by Bhagat, Kedia, Crawford, and Kaplan (1990), we took several steps.

First, the researchers in these seven countries (all of whom met and discussed the nature of the investigation during two international conferences) examined the face validity of the measures. Second, these measures were appropriately translated and back translated for two of the countries, Germany and Spain; in all other countries, the English-language versions were used.

Finally, to minimize problems of response consistency and priming, the data were collected in two separate administrations in all of the seven countries. Overall, much care was taken to ensure that the data collection strategy was identical in all of the countries.

Measures

Organizational stress. Organizational stress was measured with the combined scales for assessing role ambiguity and role conflict (House et al., 1983) and work overload (Beehr et al., 1976). The measure elicited responses to 25 items, which were made on 5-point Likert-type scales (1 = *not at all* and 5 = *a great deal*). Sample items include "To what extent do you work under policies and guidelines which are unclear?" and "To what extent do you get involved in situations where there are conflicting requirements?"

Coping styles. A 15-item adaptation of Pearlin and Schooler's (1978) instrument was used to measure coping mechanisms. This scale was consistent with the coping scale used by Bhagat et al. (1991). Respondents rated the degree to which they used each of the 15 coping mechanisms on 6-point Likert-type scales (1 = *never* and 6 = *all the time*). The coping scale is composed of two distinct dimensions of coping styles. Five items are intended to measure the problem-focused coping dimension, and the rest of the items are intended to capture the emotion-focused coping style. Items measuring the problem-focused coping style included "seeking advice from someone who could help," "trying to stay on top of things by planning and organizing," and "talking with others to find solutions to the problems." Items measuring emotion-focused coping included such interpsychic actions as "trying to ignore the difficulties by looking for the good things in one's job," "telling one's self [*sic*] that problems or difficulties are not worth getting upset about," and "comparing one's self [*sic*] with others who are worse off than he/she is." These two coping styles are similar to those identified by Ilfeld (1980) in a reanalysis of Pearlin and Schooler's (1978) data.

Decision latitude. Decision latitude was measured with four items developed by Karasek (1979) and by Ivancevich and Smith (1982). The scale items were presented to determine the degree to which respondents had the freedom to decide how to organize their work, had control over what happened in their jobs, had sufficient resources to make and implement decisions regarding their jobs, and had input into decisions that affected their work. Responses to the items were made on 5-point Likert-type scales (1 = *not at all* and 5 = *a great deal*).

Psychological strain. The psychological strain measure was adapted from a scale used by Banks (1980). The 12-item scale was designed to measure negative affective outcomes associated with the experience of organizational stress. Participants were asked to indicate to what extent they had experienced various reactions to their work situations in the past 4 to 6 weeks. A 4-point response format (1 = *not at all* and 4 = *very often*) was used to record the frequency of such occurrences as "losing sleep over worry," "feeling unhappy," or "depressed."

Analytical Procedures

Two sets of analyses were conducted. First, the measurement properties of the scales were examined. This was followed by tests of the research hypotheses through moderated regression analysis. We interpreted interactions in accordance with suggestions made by Cohen (1978) and by Peters and Champoux (1979). In accordance with their procedure, the organizational stress and moderating variable (i.e., problem-focused coping, emotion-focused coping, or decision latitude) interaction term was added to the regression equation, which already contained the organizational stress variable and the designated moderators. The increment in the variance explained above and beyond the additive effects of the organizational stress and the potential moderator was then tested for significance. Separate analyses were performed for each of the potential moderators.

Results

The measurement scales were subjected to reliability analyses for each of the countries. Internal consistency reliability coefficients (coefficient alphas) for each scale and descriptive statistics of the summed scale scores are presented in Table 1.

An examination of Table 1 reveals that the organizational stress measure showed adequate internal consistency reliability across the seven study groups. The coefficient alpha values ranged from .77 (New Zealand) to .86 (United States). The reliability coefficients for the problem-focused coping style ranged from .55 (India) to .75 (Australia and South Africa). For the measure of emotion-focused coping style, reliabilities ranged from .52 (Australia) to .78 (Spain). The decision latitude scale had reliabilities from .67 (Spain) to .83 (United States) across all seven samples. Finally, the measure of the dependent variable—experienced (psychological) strain—proved to be reliable across countries, with alphas ranging from .80 (India) to .89 (New Zealand). Although the reliabilities of some scales were below the desirable .70 cutoff value (Nunnally, 1978) for some samples, the scales exhibited adequate reliabilities on the average.

Table 2 contains sample correlation matrixes for study variables for all seven countries. A number of statistically significant correlations between study variables occurred consistently across study groups. Organizational stress consistently correlated positively with experienced strain beyond a significance level of .01. The magnitude of the correlation ranged between .41 (New Zealand) and .68 (South Africa).

Experienced strain was negatively correlated with decision latitude, with correlations ranging from −.28 to −.50 ($p < .01$). This finding suggests that

Table 1. Means, Standard Deviations, and Reliabilities for the Variables Across Study Groups

Group	n	Organizational stress (25)	Problem-focused coping (5)	Emotion-focused coping (10)	Decision latitude (4)	Psycho-logical strain (12)
		Variable				
United States	147					
M		72.6	20.6	31.7	13.8	20.5
SD		12.2	3.3	5.8	3.1	5.4
α		.86	.66	.70	.83	.85
India	224					
M		66.5	18.8	31.8	12.9	21.8
SD		10.7	3.4	6.5	3.0	5.3
α		.78	.55	.68	.68	.80
West Germany	88					
M		61.6	17.7	27.9	14.8	22.1
SD		10.5	3.3	5.3	2.7	4.7
α		.81	.71	.72	.71	.81
Spain	168					
M		74.6	18.6	26.6	13.7	23.4
SD		11.0	3.6	6.6	2.7	4.8
α		.81	.70	.78	.67	.81
New Zealand	86					
M		62.9	19.9	29.5	14.8	22.5
SD		9.6	3.3	5.6	2.5	6.3
α		.77	.68	.74	.75	.89
Australia	127					
M		62.9	20.3	28.8	14.5	22.4
SD		10.7	4.0	5.4	3.1	6.1
α		.80	.75	.52	.72	.83
South Africa	124					
M		69.4	20.5	27.5	14.2	23.6
SD		12.0	4.0	6.8	3.0	5.7
α		.81	.75	.72	.77	.82

Note. Sample sizes differed slightly from variable to variable because of missing values. The number of items in the measures are given in parentheses after each variable.

those who have little job-related decision latitude experience greater psychological strain. A similar pattern of correlations was also observed between organizational stress and decision latitude. There was a significant negative correlation between organizational stress and decision latitude in all data but those from West Germany. In the West German data, the correlation was negative but was not significant. Finally, there was a consistent pattern of negative relations between experienced strain and problem-focused coping style. However, this relationship was not statistically significant across the study groups. Findings from the correlation analysis were consistent with findings from earlier studies (e.g., Bhagat & Allie, 1989).

The results of the moderated regression analyses are summarized in Table 3. A separate moderated regression model was tested for each designated mod-

Table 2. Intercorrelation Matrixes for All Variables by Cross-National Study Group

Variable	1	2	3	4	5	6	7	8
United States								
Independent								
1. Role ambiguity	—							
2. Role conflict	.40**	—						
3. Work overload	.12	.56**	—					
4. Organizational stress	.69**	.88**	.69**	—				
Moderator								
5. Problem-focused coping	−.07	−.03	−.03	−.05	—			
6. Emotion-focused coping	.26**	.18*	−.03	.22**	.05	—		
7. Decision latitude	−.59**	−.30**	.07	−.40**	−.04	−.19*	—	
Dependent								
8. Psychological strain	.50**	.34**	.23**	.47**	−.18*	.13	−.36**	—
India								
Independent								
1. Role ambiguity	—							
2. Role conflict	.33**	—						
3. Work overload	.06	.39**	—					
4. Organizational stress	.66**	.81**	.64**	—				
Moderator								
5. Problem-focused coping	−.15*	.18**	.15	.07	—			
6. Emotion-focused coping	.09	.12	.08	.08	.07	—		
7. Decision latitude	−.58**	−.20**	.02	−.37**	.16*	−.11	—	
Dependent								
8. Psychological strain	.59**	.34**	.12	.48**	−.15*	.08	−.50**	—
West Germany								
Independent								
1. Role ambiguity	—							
2. Role conflict	.29**	—						
3. Work overload	.09	.51**	—					
4. Organizational stress	.65**	.84**	.72**	—				
Moderator								
5. Problem-focused coping	−.08	.23*	.13	.11	—			
6. Emotion-focused coping	.00	.15	.15	.15	−.10	—		
7. Decision latitude	−.29**	−.02	.12	−.08	.23*	−.07	—	
Dependent								
8. Psychological strain	.43**	.32**	.34**	.49**	−.18	.14	−.42**	—
Spain								
Independent								
1. Role ambiguity	—							
2. Role conflict	.47**	—						
3. Work overload	−.08	.32**	—					
4. Organizational stress	.67**	.87**	.55**	—				
Moderator								
5. Problem-focused coping	−.04	.07	.10	.08	—			
6. Emotion-focused coping	.03	.00	.02	.04	−.02	—		
7. Decision latitude	−.57**	−.39**	.12	−.43**	.15*	−.06	—	
Dependent								
8. Psychological strain	.52**	.42**	.03	.47**	−.12	.00	−.28**	—

Table 2. *(Continued)*

Variable	1	2	3	4	5	6	7	8
New Zealand								
Independent								
1. Role ambiguity	—							
2. Role conflict	.24*	—						
3. Work overload	−.11	.36**	—					
4. Organizational stress	.62**	.76**	.59**	—				
Moderator								
5. Problem-focused coping	−.30**	.17	.05	−.06	—			
6. Emotion-focused coping	.12	.08	.18	.16	.31**	—		
7. Decision latitude	−.28**	−.14	−.01	−.21*	.24*	−.09	—	
Dependent								
8. Psychological strain	.41**	.15	.10	.37**	−.25*	.22*	−.38**	—
Australia								
Independent								
1. Role ambiguity	—							
2. Role conflict	.49**	—						
3. Work overload	.08	.52**	—					
4. Organizational stress	.65**	.90**	.71**	—				
Moderator								
5. Problem-focused coping	−.05	.01	−.13	−.09	—			
6. Emotion-focused coping	−.03	.15	.08	.09	−.16	—		
7. Decision latitude	−.48**	−.22*	−.05	−.27**	.17*	.06	—	
Dependent								
8. Psychological strain	.58**	.52**	.22**	.56**	−.32**	.05	−.41**	—
South Africa								
Independent								
1. Role ambiguity	—							
2. Role conflict	.50**	—						
3. Work overload	.27**	.46**	—					
4. Organizational stress	.74**	.85**	.72*	—				
Moderator								
5. Problem-focused coping	−.26**	−.10	−.04	−.15	—			
6. Emotion-focused coping	.18*	.09	−.03	.04	−.02	—		
7. Decision latitude	−.64**	−.47**	−.18*	−.58**	.22**	−.20	—	
Dependent								
8. Psychological strain	.67**	.50**	.27**	.64**	−.15	.17*	−.50**	—

*$p < .05$.   **$p < .01$.

erator. In each analysis, the dependent variable was psychological strain and the first independent variable was the organizational stress variable. The top portion of Table 3 shows the results of using problem-focused coping style as a potential moderator. The middle and bottom portions provide results of using emotion-focused coping style and decision latitude as the moderators, respectively.

Of the 21 moderated regression analyses (7 samples × 3 moderators), the interaction term was significant in only two instances. First, in the case of data from Spain, problem-focused coping moderated the relationship between

Table 3. Results of Analyses Assessing Possible Moderators of the Organizational Stress–Psychological Strain Relationship

Independent variable & moderator	United States				India				West Germany				Spain				New Zealand				Australia				South Africa			
	R	R²	β	ΔF	R	R²	β	ΔF	R	R²	β	ΔF	R	R²	β	ΔF	R	R²	β	ΔF	R	R²	β	ΔF	R	R²	β	ΔF
OS	.47	.22	.47	40.6**	.52	.27	.52	77.5**	.51	.26	.51	27.7**	.52	.27	.52	57.6**	.40	.16	.40	15.9**	.60	.36	.60	69.7**	.68	.46	.68	95.0**
PFC	.51	.26	-.18	6.1*	.56	.31	-.20	12.1**	.57	.32	-.25	7.1**	.55	.30	-.18	6.9**	.45	.20	-.19	3.6	.67	.45	-.29	17.9**	.69	.47	-.08	1.2
OS × PFC	.51	.26	-.47	0.6	.37	.32	-.51	1.0	.57	.32	.03	0.1	.58	.33	-1.45	5.9*	.47	.22	-1.17	1.9	.67	.45	.02	0.0	.69	.47	-.63	1.7
EFC	.47	.22	.06	0.5	.52	.27	.02	0.1	.51	.26	.07	0.6	.52	.27	.01	0.0	.43	.18	.15	2.2	.60	.36	.00	0.0	.69	.47	.10	2.5
OS × EFC	.48	.23	-.33	0.3	.53	.28	.19	0.2	.51	.26	-.05	0.0	.53	.28	.38	0.4	.43	.18	-.07	0.0	.61	.37	-.84	1.9	.70	.49	-.98	4.5*
DL	.49	.24	-.16	3.6	.60	.36	-.33	28.4**	.64	.41	-.40	20.8**	.54	.29	-.16	4.3*	.49	.24	-.30	8.7**	.63	.39	-.18	5.8*	.70	.49	-.20	5.1*
OS × DL	.50	.25	-.36	0.6	.60	.36	.10	0.1	.65	.42	.27	0.1	.54	.29	-.23	0.3	.50	.25	-.57	0.8	.63	.39	-.15	0.1	.70	.49	.02	0.0

Note. In all regression equations, psychological strain was the dependent variable. OS = organizational stress; PFC = problem-focused coping; EFC = emotion-focused coping; DL = decision latitute.

*p < .05. **p < .01.

organizational stress and strain. The explained variance increased significantly (from 30% to 33%) with the addition of the Organizational Stress × Problem-Focused Coping Style interaction term, $\Delta F(1, 164) = 5.9$, $p < .05$. Second, for South Africa, emotion-focused coping style moderated the relationship between organizational stress and psychological strain. The addition of the Organizational Stress × Emotion-Focused Coping interaction term increased the explanatory power of the model significantly, $\Delta F(1, 120) = 4.5$, $p < .05$. Therefore, the overall findings from the moderated regression analyses did not support the hypothesized moderating roles of coping styles and decision latitude.

The results of the moderated regression analyses can be summarized as follows. First, organizational stress was significantly correlated with experienced strain in all of the seven countries. The magnitude of correlations was fairly high. Second, problem-focused coping, which has been found to be an important moderator in the United States in past studies, had significant independent effects in five countries: the United States, India, Germany, Spain, and Australia. Third, emotion-focused coping, which has been found to be a relatively weak moderator in the United States in past studies, did not have either an independent effect or a moderating effect in any of the seven countries. Finally, decision latitude had an independent effect in all of the seven countries studied. Once again, however, no moderating effect was observed.

Discussion

In this investigation, we were interested in examining direct as well as moderating effects of three different types of variables on the organizational stress–psychological strain relationship. Given our pattern of results, it seems clear that organizational stress is indeed a predictor of experienced strain in all seven countries. In addition, the magnitude of correlations in all of these cases was fairly high. The failure of problem-focused coping to moderate the stress–strain relationship in these seven countries is also interesting and stands in sharp contrast to what Bhagat et al. (1991) found. The measures used by Bhagat et al. were only slightly longer than those used in the present investigation. Both measures were adapted from Pearlin and Schooler's (1978) instrument for examining the structure of coping. We were not surprised, however, that emotion-focused coping failed to moderate the relationship between organizational stress and psychological strain, because we found a similar pattern in earlier studies (Bhagat et al., 1991).

It seems clear that both problem-focused coping and decision latitude acted independently on organizational stress to reduce the level of experienced psychological strain in six out of the seven countries we studied. This finding provides further support to the notion that individuals who view stressful circumstances as opportunities for exercising personal and social resources and gaining mastery are able to reduce their levels of psychological strain as experienced in the organizational context. Furthermore, this pattern seems to be true both cross-culturally and cross-nationally. Countries like India, Spain, and South Africa are collectivistic in their orientations. There seems to be a tendency in all of these countries to focus on problem-focused coping as opposed to emotion-focused coping in ameliorating the effects of stress on experienced strain. However, one must remember that these data were collected from white-collar employees, who are likely to be higher than blue-collar employees in the ability to successfully deal with organizationally relevant stressful encounters by using a problem-solving orientation.

Perhaps the most interesting explanation is to be found in Lazarus and Folkman's (1984) work on coping and appraisal processes. Coping is an idiosyncratic and situational process. The measures that normally are used to capture the nature of coping are simply not comprehensive enough to capture the whole range of coping strategies and situationally specific skills that one might use in these different national contexts. Menaghan (1984) provided a compelling case for examining the relevance of different types of conditions that might foster the significance of various types of coping variables in moderating such relationships. We believe that an emic (Bhagat & McQuaid, 1982, p. 356) approach to understanding stress and coping is likely to be more fruitful in future research endeavors. Different work environments clearly impose different demands, especially when one is attempting to understand stress and coping in a cross-national sense. Researchers would be well advised to examine the adaptational demands of each of the country-specific organizations they study in an emic sense.

Our findings lead us to recommend a paradigm of research that explicitly recognizes society as a shaper of individuals and of the groups in which they are immersed. Coping is a transactional process whose true effectiveness is captured through process-oriented research combining the effectiveness of problem-focused coping and emotion-focused coping in a comprehensive manner and using an emic perspective.

References

Banks, R. L. (1980). A scale for measuring psychological strain. *Journal of Occupational Psychology, 53*, 187–194.

Beehr, T. A., & Bhagat, R. S. (Eds.). (1985). *Human stress and cognition in organizations: An integrated perspective.* New York: Wiley.

Beehr, T. A., & Newman, J. E. (1978). Job stress, employee health, and organizational effectiveness: A facet analysis. *Personnel Psychology, 31*, 665–700.

Beehr, T. A., Walsh, J. T., & Taber, T. D. (1976). Relationship of stress to individually and organizationally valued states: Higher order needs as a moderator. *Journal of Applied Psychology, 61*, 41–47.

Bhagat, R. S., & Allie, S. M. (1989). Organizational stress, personal life stress and symptoms of life strains: An examination of the moderating role of sense of competence. *Journal of Vocational Behavior, 35*, 231–253.

Bhagat, R. S., Allie, S. M., & Ford, D. L. (1991). Organizational stress, personal life stress and life strains: An inquiry into the moderating role of coping. *Journal of Personality and Social Behavior, 6*, 163–184.

Bhagat, R. S., Kedia, B. L., Crawford, S. E., & Kaplan, M. (1990). Cross-cultural and cross-national research in organizational psychology: Emergent trends and directions for research in the 1990's. In C. L. Cooper & I. Robertson (Eds.), *International review of industrial and organizational psychology* (Vol. 5, pp. 59–99). New York: Wiley.

Bhagat, R. S., & McQuaid, S. J. (1982). The role of subjective culture in organizations: A review and directions for future research. *Journal of Applied Psychology Monographs, 5,* 355–389.

Cohen, J. (1978). Partial products are interactions: Partial powers are curve components. *Psychological Bulletin, 85,* 858–866.

Cooper, C. L., & Payne, R. (Eds.). (1980). *Current concerns in occupational stress.* New York: Wiley.

Folkman, S., & Lazarus, R. S. (1980). An analysis of coping in a middle-aged community sample. *Journal of Health and Social Behavior, 21,* 219–239.

Henry, J., & Cassel, J. (1969). Psychological factors in essential hypertension, recent epidemiological evidence and animal experimental evidence. *American Journal of Epidemiology, 90,* 171–200.

Hofstede, G. (1980). *Culture's consequences: International differences in work-related values.* Beverly Hills, CA: Sage.

Hofstede, G. (1983). The cultural relativity of organizational practices and theories. *Journal of International Business Studies, 14,* 75–89.

Hofstede, G. (1991). *Cultures and organizations.* New York: McGraw-Hill.

House, R. J., Schuler, R. S., & Levanoni, E. (1983). Role conflict and ambiguity scales: Reality or artifacts? *Journal of Applied Psychology, 68,* 334–337.

Ilfeld, F. W. (1980). Coping styles of Chicago adults. *Journal of Human Stress, 6,* 2–10.

Ivancevich, J. M., & Smith, S. V. (1982). Job difficulty as interpreted by incumbents: A study of nurses and engineers. *Human Relations, 35,* 391–412.

Jamal, M. (1984). Job stress and job performance controversy: An empirical assessment. *Organizational Behavior and Human Performance, 33,* 1–21.

Karasek, R. A. (1979). Job demands, job decision latitude, and mental strain: Implications for job design. *Administrative Science Quarterly, 24,* 285–311.

Latack, J. C. (1986). Coping with job stress: Measures and future directions for scale development. *Journal of Applied Psychology, 71,* 377–385.

Lazarus, R. S., & Delongis, A. (1983). Psychological stress and coping in aging. *American Psychologist, 38,* 245–254.

Lazarus, R. S., & Folkman, S. (1984). *Stress, appraisal, and coping.* New York: Springer.

Lazarus, R. S., & Launier, R. (1978). Stress-related transactions between person and environment. In L. A. Perrin & M. Lewis (Eds.), *Perspectives in interactional psychology* (pp. 287–327). New York: Plenum.

Menaghan, E. A. (1984). Individual coping efforts: Moderators of the relationship between life stress and mental health outcomes. In H. B. Kaplan (Ed.), *Psychosocial stress: Trends in theory and research* (pp. 154–191). San Diego, CA: Academic Press.

Menaghan, E. G., & Merves, E. S. (1984). Coping with occupational problems: The limits of individual efforts. *Journal of Health and Social Behavior, 25,* 406–423.

Nunnally, J. C. (1978). *Psychometric theory.* New York: McGraw Hill.

Parker, D. F., & DeCotiis, T. A. (1983). Organizational determinants of job stress. *Organizational Behavior and Human Performance, 32,* 160–177.

Pearlin, L. I., & Schooler, C. (1978). The structure of coping. *Journal of Health and Social Behavior, 19,* 2–21.

Peters, W. S., & Champoux, J. E. (1979). The role and analysis of moderator variables in organizational research. In R. T. Mowday & R. M. Steers (Eds.), *Research in organizations: Issues and controversies* (pp. 239–253). Santa Monica, CA: Goodyear.

Rosensteil, A. K., & Roth, S. (1981). Relationship between cognitive activity and adjustment in four spinal-cord-injured individuals: A longitudinal investigation. *Journal of Human Stress, 7,* 35–43.

Schuler, R. S. (1980). Definition and conceptualization of stress in organizations. *Organizational Behavior and Human Performance, 25,* 184–215.

White, R. W. (1959). Motivation reconsidered: The concept of competence. *Psychological Review, 5,* 297–333.

Worden, W. J., & Sobel, H. J. (1978). Ego strength and psychosocial adaptation to cancer. *Psychosomatic Medicine, 40,* 585–592.

7

Job Stress and Health Outcomes Among White and Hispanic Employees: A Test of the Person–Environment Fit Model

Sara E. Gutierres, Delia S. Saenz, and Beth L. Green

The link between occupational stress and poor health outcomes among employees has been documented in a vast and rapidly expanding literature (see Beehr & Bhagat, 1985, for a review). These detrimental health outcomes have been related to employee absenteeism, escalating health care costs, and lowered organizational productivity (e.g., Kizer, 1987; Matteson & Ivancevich, 1988). In response to the magnitude of these problems, researchers have attempted to (a) identify major stressors in the workplace, (b) develop theoretical models that can integrate disparate research findings, and (c) provide direction in the development of interventions aimed at reducing the impact of occupational stress on employees' health.

One framework that has proven useful in understanding the causes of occupational stress is the Person–Environment Fit (PEF) model (e.g., Caplan, 1983; Van Harrison, 1985). The PEF model posits that stress ensues from situations in which incongruence exists between the person's attributes and the environmental configuration. In particular, lack of fit between the person and the environment occurs along either of two dimensions. One type of misfit is that between the individual's needs or preferences and the organization's ability to provide rewards or resources to fulfill those needs. Inadequate pay or hostile work environments wherein employees may come to doubt that they can attain important outcomes are examples of this type of incongruence (Chemars, Hays, Rhodewalt, & Wysocki, 1985). The second type of incongruence is reflected by misfit between the individual's work style or ability level and the organizational requirements or job demands. Poor management skills or

Sara E. Gutierres and Delia S. Saenz contributed equally to this work; order of authorship was determined by flip of a coin. We thank Barbara Mawhiney and her staff in the Affirmative Action Office at Arizona State University for their invaluable help in the identification and recruitment of study participants. We also thank Stephen G. West for helpful comments on a draft of the chapter. Support for this research was provided by grants to Sara E. Gutierres and Delia S. Saenz from the Hispanic Research Center, Arizona State University; additional support was provided by a Faculty Research Grant from Arizona State University—West to Sara E. Gutierres.

inadequate employee training that prevent the individual from fulfilling job responsibilities are representative of this type of incongruence.

According to the PEF model, both types of incongruence create stress by placing the person in a situation in which he or she is personally motivated to attain important outcomes while being faced with high levels and long durations of uncertainty about whether those outcomes can be achieved (Beehr & Bhagat, 1985). Three central elements—important outcomes, uncertainty in achieving those outcomes, and long duration of uncertainty—act multiplicatively in producing stress.

There is an abundance of research supporting the basic premises of the PEF model in which both types of incongruence have been tested (Curbow, 1990; Gerstein, Topp, & Correll, 1987). Some of this work has focused on incongruence between the organization's and employee's expected levels of output (e.g., French, Caplan, & Harrison, 1982). Other work has focused on the fit between the individual's personality style (e.g., locus of control, Type As, and tolerance for ambiguity) and occupational environments (e.g., Arney, 1988; House & Rizzo, 1972; Ivancevich & Matteson, 1984). The general finding from this body of research is that the incongruence between the person and the environment that results in long-term, uncertain goal attainment creates stress. Furthermore, among employees, stress may produce negative consequences, including (a) psychological strain, such as job dissatisfaction, depression, and tension (e.g., Beehr, 1976); (b) physiological health problems such as hypertension and ulcers (e.g., Cobb & Kasl, 1972; House, 1974); and (c) such behavioral outcomes as substance abuse and absenteeism (e.g., Newman & Beehr, 1979).

Despite the large number of investigations conducted to test the link between stress and these negative outcomes however, there are significant limitations that prevent one from drawing broad generalizations from this work. In particular, many of the investigations examining the link between stress and health within a PEF framework have focused on employees in management positions (e.g., Glowinkowski & Cooper, 1986). With few exceptions (e.g., Fernandez, 1981; Ford, 1981; S. A. James, Lacroix, Kleinbaum, & Strogatz, 1984; Ramos, 1975), the primary targets of investigation have been White men.

One underlying assumption in this previous research may have been that employees of different ranks, racial and ethnic backgrounds, and genders respond similarly to incongruence in the workplace. To date, the empirical literature has not provided sufficient data to support this assertion. Moreover, even if employees of different cultural backgrounds display similar response patterns to incongruity as White male managers, it is likely that certain groups—such as ethnic minority members—face additional sources of stress because of their category membership.

Stressors Unique to Ethnic Minority Workers

Both structural and social contextual factors in the workplace may affect adversely the health outcomes of ethnic minority employees. For example, proportional representation of one's ethnic group may influence the degree to which the employee feels accepted by coworkers and supervisors. In addition to structural features, direct social contextual elements such as level of perceived discrimination on the job might increase levels of stress for minority workers.

To the extent that such stressors are prevalent, it is doubtful that interventions developed on the basis of research conducted with White male managers will show parallel benefits for ethnic minority workers. In the sections that follow, we elaborate on two stressors that are putatively unique to ethnic minority employees. In addition, we briefly discuss the moderating role of social support on stress. Finally, we present findings from a survey we conducted to examine stress and health outcomes in ethnic minority and nonminority employees who hold different jobs.

In-group–Out-group Proportions

As mentioned previously, small proportions of one's in-group in the work setting may result in negative, stressful consequences for an individual of that group. Research has shown that solo status (being the only one or one of a few people of a given sex, race, or ethnicity in a larger group in which the majority are of a different category membership) engenders disproportionate scrutiny, extreme evaluations, and highly stereotyped impressions of the minority on the part of majority members (Kanter, 1977; Taylor, Fiske, Close, Anderson, & Ruderman, 1977). Relative to Whites, minority employees may be more noticeable to their coworkers, may be evaluated more critically in terms of job performance, and may be perceived in terms of racial stereotypes.

Negative outcomes associated with numerical distinctiveness also have been found in laboratory research by Saenz and her colleagues (Lord & Saenz, 1985; Saenz, 1994; Saenz & Lord, 1989). They showed that numerically distinctive people who were aware that they were different from majority group members displayed performance deficits on both memory and problem-solving tasks, even in the absence of differential treatment from majority members.

The additional stigma of "token" status may be ascribed to minority employees in the work setting. Often, the underlying assumption of coworkers is that minority group members were hired only to reach affirmative action (AA) quotas. This leads to the further assumption that these individuals are likely to be incompetent at their jobs (Morland, 1965). Individuals with tokens status are often viewed as test cases, and their failures can be used to reinforce the idea that members of a certain minority group are not well suited for the job (Yoder, 1985). In one study conducted in the corporate world, for example, Fernandez (1981) asked White and ethnic minority managers to indicate whether they agreed with this statement: "Minorities are made to feel they got their jobs not on ability, but quotas" (p. 51). He reported that 46% of the respondents believed that most White managers convey the message that minority managers got their jobs because of AA and Equal Employment Opportunity targets, rather than because of their ability. This perception might prompt minority managers to question their own abilities, which in turn may influence their self-concept and, ultimately, their job performances. Employees are also likely to be less cooperative with a manager that they perceive to be incompetent. These circumstances may set up a self-fulfilling prophecy that could eventually lead to the minority manager's isolation and failure.

The negative effects of being in a numerical minority may represent incongruence between the employee's expected and actual levels of evaluation, performance, and outcomes. This incongruence may serve to exacerbate stress and, consequently, to impair health. Given that ethnic minority members are more likely than Whites to be numerically distinctive, it is likely that they will experience negative outcomes more frequently as a function of this factor. One study by K. James (1994) has illustrated the link between numerical representation and health among minority workers. James reported significant negative correlations between perceived proportion of one's in-group in the work unit and self-reported health problems. He also reported a negative relationship between proportional representation of the in-group and employee blood pressure levels. Hence, disproportionately low in-group representation was associated with cardiovascular distress. Further work is needed to assess the range of negative health outcomes related to in-group representation.

Prejudice and Discrimination

Along with disproportionate representation, prejudice and discrimination in the workplace are often mentioned as sources of stress for minority workers (Martin, 1987). There is some evidence that racist attitudes are prevalent in the workplace; there is less empirical work, however, linking these attitudes to psychological and physical health outcomes.

In one investigation, Fernandez (1981) measured racist tendencies in corporations by asking minority and White managers how much they agreed with five statements representing these tendencies. Of the African American managers surveyed, 48% agreed that four or five of the conditions existed in their work settings. In contrast, only 9.5% of White managers and 20% of Hispanic managers expressed agreement with several statements reflecting differential treatment of minority managers. Analysis of responses to one of the five items was particularly revealing: 65% of African American managers agreed that minority managers are excluded from informal work groups, in comparison with 29% of White managers and 30% of Hispanic managers. These data suggest that racist practices are interfering with minority managers' equal participation in their work environments.

Perceived discrimination among minorities is not limited to management. Results from the 1989 national survey by the National Career Development Association (NCDA) showed that African Americans and Asian Pacific Islanders were significantly more likely than Whites and Hispanics to report that both women and minorities were discriminated against in their work settings (Brown, Minor, & Jepsen, 1991). These findings mirror those from the NCDA survey in 1987 (Gallup Organization, 1989). Brown et al. concluded that discrimination in the workplace remains an unsolved problem.

The few studies that have investigated the consequences for the person experiencing prejudice and discrimination in the workplace have suggested that the psychological and physical costs for minority workers may be very high (Frone, Russell, & Cooper, 1990). S. A. James et al. (1984) found that discrimination on the job significantly contributed to perceived stress among African Americans. In another study on minority employees, K. James (1994) found a relationship between perceived prejudice and discrimination on the job and self-reported health problems. His results indicated that prejudice and discrimination scores were positively related to higher blood pressure levels.

In general, there is evidence that prejudice and discrimination play a role in contributing to stress among African American employees. Less evidence exists to show that prejudice and discrimination also promote poor health outcomes. It is possible that for minority workers discrimination represents incongruence between their expected and actual outcomes. If this is the case, then incongruence may result in frustration or stress as well as in reduced productivity over time.

Moderators of Stress in the Workplace

In addition to the limited attention that has been directed at documenting stressors specific to minority employees, there has also been a paucity of research examining potential moderators of stress in these populations. One primary moderator of occupational stress that has been identified in the general literature is social support. This variable has been found to have both direct effects (Barling, Bluen, & Fain, 1987; Ganster, Fusilier, & Mayes, 1986) and moderating effects (Beehr, King, & King, 1990; Kirmeyer & Dougherty, 1988) on reported stress and health problems in the workplace. As with the research on stress in the workplace, most of the work examining the influence of social support has been based on investigations of White workers.

In two investigations of African American workers, however, similar results regarding social support emerged. Ford (1981) found that job stress, burnout, and frustration were negatively related to work support among African American professionals (men and women). He also reported that emotional support was more important than other types of support in the prediction of work outcomes. Similarly, Edwards (1980) reported that job stress was negatively correlated with both structural support and satisfaction with work among African American female professionals.

Level of social support may be particularly crucial for minority employees whose stressful work situations are exacerbated by the presence of prejudice and discrimination and isolation from supervisors and peers. Some evidence exists from studies of African American participants to corroborate this assertion. Whether this relationship holds for ethnic minority employees other than African Americans, however, is unknown.

In summary, only a small body of research exists that has examined stress among ethnic minority employees. Some of this work has suggested that there are parallel effects of stress on Whites and ethnic minority workers; other results have indicated that minority employees are subject to unique sources of stress. There is clearly a need for additional work in this area. The few studies that have addressed the issues raised in the previous sections have been limited methodologically in terms of subject samples and variables tested. Most studies have focused on African American samples, and few have made comparisons with White employees. Although much has been written regarding the unique sources of stress for minority employees, little empirical work has accompanied this discussion. Also, given the importance of social support in the stress–health relationship, little attention has been paid to the influence of this factor on outcomes for minority workers. It is therefore important to investigate the link between stress and health in populations across the broad spectrum of groups that represent the American workforce.

Overview

In the present investigation, we examined the impact of person–environment incongruence on the psychological and physical health outcomes of minority and White employees in different job categories within a university setting. In particular, we examined the influence of proportional representation of the in-group, employees' perceptions of perceived discrimination, and level of social support on job-related tension and self-reported health problems. We primarily focused on whether person–environment incongruence on relevant dimensions yielded parallel or divergent patterns among Hispanic[1] and White employees.

We expected the following relationships among the variables of interest:

Hypothesis 1: Proportional representation of the in-group will affect outcome measures for employees, especially Hispanic workers. (a) Numerical minority status will be associated with higher levels of stress, and (b) numerical minority status will be associated with increased self-reported health problems.

Hypothesis 2: Perceived discrimination in the workplace will be associated with negative outcomes for minority employees. (a) Higher levels of perceived discrimination will be related to higher levels of stress among Hispanic employees, and (b) higher levels of perceived discrimination will be related to higher levels of self-reported health problems among Hispanic employees.

Hypothesis 3: Job-related stress will produce increased health problems among all employees.

Hypothesis 4: The presence of social support will moderate the relationships between these stressors and increased health problems.

---

[1] The majority of Hispanics in this institutional setting were Mexican American. We adopted the term *Hispanic*, primarily because it reflects the self-identification used by the participants.

Method

Sample

The data reported here represent a subsample from a larger survey conducted at a large southwestern state university. The general sample included 1,456 employees: 306 each of minority and White men, and 422 each of minority and White women. All minority employees (i.e., African Americans, Hispanics, Asians, and Native Americans) in the institutional workforce were selected to receive the survey and White employees were matched to these individuals on the basis of gender, job title, and salary. Response rate to the survey was 63%.

From this general sample, we delineated a subset of 463 White respondents (133 men and 330 women) and 224 Hispanic respondents (62 men and 162 women). The samples representing the two groups were comparable in a number of ways. In particular, there were no significant differences between Hispanics and Whites on marital status. For both groups, approximately 62% were married, 16% were single, 16% were divorced or separated, 4% were living with a partner, and 2% were widowed. Job category breakdown for both groups included 21% faculty, 25% academic professionals, 36% clerical staff, 5% technicians, and approximately 12% other. Similarly, no differences were found between the two groups on educational attainment. For both groups, approximately 10% reported they had a high school education or less, 37% had completed some college, 21% had a college degree, and 32% had graduate degrees. Salary distributions across the two groups also showed no differences, with 43% reporting incomes of less than $20,000, 40% earning $20,000–$40,000, and 17% earning more than $40,000. The lack of differences across education and salary were not surprising given the matching procedure we used. One index, age, did reveal a significant difference across the two groups. An analysis of variance (ANOVA) with ethnicity and sex as independent variables showed a main effect for ethnicity, such that the Hispanic sample was younger ($M = 37.8$ years) than the White sample ($M = 42.1$ years), $F(1, 666) = 27.4$, $p < .001$. There was no theoretical reason, however, to expect that a 4-year difference in age would affect relationships among the variables of interest.

Procedure

Surveys were sent to the sample of minority and White employees through campus mail. Accompanying the questionnaire was a letter explaining that the purpose of the study was to facilitate better understanding of the factors contributing to employee stress in the workplace. Respondents were assured that completion of the survey was voluntary and that responses would be anonymous and confidential. To increase the response rate, a lottery ticket was included with the questionnaire and letter. All those who returned the questionnaire with their ticket would be included in a drawing for $300 that would be held 3 months later. The winner's name was subsequently published in the university faculty and staff monthly publication.

Questionnaire

In addition to demographic information (age, occupation, ethnicity, marital status, number of children, and education) the following measures were included in the survey.

The Job-Related Tension Index (JRTI; Kahn, 1964) comprises 15 items assessing the extent to which individuals are bothered by various job-related problems (e.g., "How frequently are you bothered by feeling that you're not fully qualified to handle your job?"). Each item is scored on a Likert-type scale ranging from 1 (*never*) to 5 (*nearly all the time*). Reliability for this scale (alpha) was calculated at .86.

The Perceived Discrimination Scale (PDS; Fernandez, 1981) comprises 16 items designed to assess discrimination against women and minorities in the workplace (e.g., "Women are excluded from informal work networks by men" and "Minorities must be better performers than Anglos to get ahead"). Items are scored on a Likert-type scale ranging from 1 (*strongly disagree*) to 5 (*strongly agree*). Reliability for this scale was .93 for the minority subscale and .92 for the gender subscale. Our focus in the present investigation was on the minority subscale.

The Social Support Index—Work and Family (SSI–W and SSI–F; House, 1981) comprises 12 items: 6 assessing social support in the workplace and 6 assessing family-based social support. Items tap the individual's perceptions of supervisors, work peers, spouse or partner, relatives, and friends as being helpful and reliable in solving work-related problems (e.g., "How much can other people at work be relied on when things get tough?"). Items are scored on a scale ranging from 0 (*not at all*) to 3 (*very much*). Respondents can also indicate if a response is not applicable (e.g., if they have no spouse or partner). The alpha reliability coefficients were .81 for the work subscale and .78 for the family subscale.

The Health Problems Checklist (HPC; Boaz, 1982) is a 62-item checklist of various health problems, including such items as sore throat, diarrhea, change in blood pressure, depression, and headaches. Participants are asked to indicate how often they experienced each problem in the past year, such that 0 = *did not experience this problem*, 1 = *experienced this problem a little*, and 2 = *experienced this problem quite a bit*. Coefficient alpha for this scale was calculated to be .91.

In addition to these four measures, we included a series of questions designed to assess the structure of the workplace in terms of gender and ethnic makeup. Respondents were asked to indicate the relative proportion of employees in their unit or department who were male, female, African American, Hispanic, Asian American, Native American, or White. The following response options were provided: "none," "very few," "about a third," "about half," and "the majority."

Results

Our primary focus was on stress and health outcomes among employees. We investigated the influence of both in-group representation and perceived discrimination on these two central outcomes. Within each relevant group of analyses, we also examined the moderating role of social support.

Numerical Minorities in the Workplace

The first set of analyses examined the effect of having one's in-group in a numerical minority in the workplace. We predicted that being in a numerical minority would have detrimental stress and health consequences, especially for Hispanic workers. Because of the relative infrequency with which Hispanic workers were actually a numerical majority, we considered Hispanics to be in the minority if there were very few or no other Hispanics in the work setting. A "majority" of Hispanics, therefore, existed if about a third or more people in the work environment were Hispanic. Whites were designated to be in the majority if one half or more of the workers in a particular unit or department were White and were said to be in the minority if one third or fewer of the workers were White.

Job-related stress. We conducted a 2 × 2 (Numerical Proportion × Ethnicity) ANOVA, using mean scores for the JRTI as the dependent variable. This analysis revealed an unexpected main effect for ethnicity, such that Hispanics experienced less stress ($M = 2.26$) than Whites ($M = 2.41$), $F(1, 672) = 6.71, p < .01$. This effect, however, was qualified by a significant Numerical Proportion × Ethnicity interaction, $F(1, 672) = 5.00, p < .05$. The pattern of means indicated that although there was little difference in the amount of job-related stress experienced by Hispanics ($M = 2.38$) and Whites ($M = 2.39$) when their in-group constituted the majority, Whites reported greater job-related tension ($M = 2.53$) relative to Hispanics ($M = 2.23$) when their in-group was in the minority (see Table 1).

Health. We then performed the same 2 × 2 ANOVA, using the summed scores HPC as the dependent variable. There were no significant effects. However, although the Numerical Proportion × Ethnicity interaction was not conventionally significant, $F(1, 677) = 2.99, p = .08$, the pattern of means did mirror the results found for job-related stress (see Table 1). That is, when either Hispanics or Whites were in the majority, there was little difference between their respective health scores (for Hispanics, $M = 18.63$; for Whites,

Table 1. Job-Related Stress and Number of Self-Reported Health Problems as a Function of Proportional Representation of In-Group and Subject Ethnicity

In-group representation	Stress				Health			
	Hispanic	n	White	n	Hispanic	n	White	n
Minority	2.23	172	2.53	62	17.82	173	21.71	62
Majority	2.38	46	2.39	396	18.63	48	17.75	398
Marginal M	2.26	NA	2.41	NA	18.00	NA	18.28	NA

Note. NA = not applicable.

M = 17.75). However, when they were in the minority, Whites reported greater health problems (M = 21.71) than did Hispanics (M = 17.82).

Social support. We originally hypothesized that social support would moderate the effect of being a member of a numerical minority on stress and health problems. We therefore repeated the analyses already described, using social support from the family (high vs. low, by median split) and then social support at work (high vs. low, by median split) as additional variables in the design. The results indicated that level of social support (family and workplace) did not qualify the effects already reported (all Fs < 1, ns).

The Effect of Perceived Discrimination

To examine the effect of perceived discrimination[2] in the workplace on job-related stress and health, we conducted a median split on the PDS—Minority (PDS–M) scores. We then calculated separate 2 (Perceived Discrimination) × 2 (Ethnicity) ANOVAs, using job-related stress and health as dependent variables.

Job-related stress. We predicted a two-way interaction such that the presence of discrimination was expected to produce higher levels of stress for Hispanic employees but not for Whites. Contrary to this prediction, only a significant main effect for perceived discrimination emerged: Subjects reporting greater discrimination against minorities in their work unit experienced greater job-related stress (M = 2.42) than did subjects reporting less discrimination (M = 2.33), $F(1, 669)$ = 10.34, p < .001. Thus, both White and Hispanic employees experienced heightened stress when they perceived higher levels of discrimination against minorities in their work unit (see Table 2).

Health. Perceived discrimination and ethnicity produced no independent or interactive effects on health (all Fs < 2.5, ns); however, these variables were implicated in a three-way interaction involving social support.

Social support. As with analyses on numerical representation, we examined the moderating influence of family and work social support (median splits: high vs. low) on the relationship between perceived discrimination and stress and discrimination and health, respectively.

Social support did not moderate the relationship between perceived discrimination and stress, but it did have an independent effect on stress. That is, people receiving more social support experienced less job-related tension (for work, M = 2.16; for family, M = 2.31) than those receiving less social support (for work, M = 2.65; for family, M = 2.47): for SSI–W, $F(1, 646)$ =

---

[2] In examining participants' general perceptions of the level of discrimination against minorities in the work unit, we found a pattern consistent with previous work: Hispanic employees reported higher levels of discrimination (M = 2.99) than White employees (M = 2.08), $F(1, 670)$ = 110.05, p < .001.

Table 2. Job-Related Stress as a Function of Level of Perceived Discrimination Against Minorities in the Workplace and Subject Ethnicity

Perceived discrimination	Ethnicity			
	Hispanic	n	White	n
Low	2.12	73	2.37	338
High	2.34	144	2.51	118

124.37, $p < .001$; for SSI–F, $F(1, 413) = 7.51$, $p < .01$.[3] These effects were not qualified by subject ethnicity.

In addition, work social support played a role in the relationship between perceived discrimination and health. In particular, the three-way ANOVA (Perceived Discrimination [high, low]) × Ethnicity [Hispanic, White]) × SSI–W [high, low]) yielded a marginal triple interaction, $F(1, 648) = 3.62$, $p < .06$. The pattern of means suggested that Whites and Hispanics were affected differentially as a function of the presence of discrimination and social support in the workplace.

Among Whites, health was not affected by level of perceived discrimination, but, rather, by level of social support. Specifically, Whites incurred fewer health problems when they had high levels of social support (for low PDS–M, $M = 16.23$; for high PDS–M, $M = 17.75$) and greater health problems when they received low levels of social support (for low PDS–M, $M = 21.12$; for high PDS–M, $M = 19.70$). The pattern of means indicated that level of discrimination did not make a difference in the health outcomes of White employees. The pattern of reported health problems among Hispanic employees was similar to that of Whites when work social support was high but differed when social support was low. That is, with high levels of social support, Hispanic employees also reported fewer health problems, irrespective of whether perceived discrimination was high ($M = 16.44$) or low ($M = 17.05$). However, when social support among Hispanics was low, differing levels of perceived discrimination influenced their health outcomes in expected ways. In particular, Hispanics incurred the greatest number of health problems when perceived discrimination was high ($M = 21.19$) and far fewer health problems when perceived discrimination was low ($M = 14.50$). Thus, the health outcomes of Hispanic employees were influenced by the interaction of perceived discrimination and social support.

The Effect of Job-Related Stress on Health

The final set of analyses investigated the relationship between work-related stress and health problems. We performed an ANOVA, using the HPC scores as the dependent variable and mean scores on the JRTI (high vs. low by median split) and ethnicity (Hispanic vs. White) as independent variables. In line with our prediction, a significant main effect of stress emerged: Employees expe-

---

[3] Analyses involving social support from the family were performed with a reduced sample size because people who did not have a spouse or other partner were excluded from the sample.

Table 3. Number of Self-Reported Health Problems as a Function of Stress and Subject Ethnicity

Job-related stress	Ethnicity			
	Hispanic	n	White	n
Low	15.27	115	14.75	211
High	20.20	103	21.18	250

riencing higher levels of stress reported greater health problems ($M = 20.90$) than those experiencing less stress ($M = 14.94$), $F(1, 677) = 37.89$, $p < .001$. No other effects were significant (all Fs < 1.00; see Table 3).

In examining the effects of social support on health, we found that people receiving more work-based social support reported fewer health problems ($M = 16.64$) than those reporting lower levels of social support ($M = 20.41$), $F(1, 649) = 13.18$, $p < .001$. Contrary to our predictions, there was no significant main effect of family social support on health. Moreover, neither family nor work social support moderated the relationship between stress and health.

Discussion

Our investigation produced both expected and unexpected results. Within the category of expected outcomes was the relationship found between stress and health. In general, higher levels of job-related stress were associated with more numerous health problems. This finding is consistent with previous work based on the PEF model. Given that many of the items on the job-related tension index reflect incongruence between the employee and his or her environment (e.g., feeling unqualified to handle the job, having too little authority to carry out responsibilities, and having to do things on the job that are against one's better judgment), it is not surprising to find negative health outcomes among employees as a function of higher stress levels. It is important to highlight the fact that this relationship between stress and health emerged among both Hispanic and White employees. This finding supports the idea that incongruence leads to parallel outcomes across groups of different backgrounds.

Other findings—which were not unexpected—were the positive effects associated with social support. For all employees (White and Hispanic) there were direct ameliorative effects of both work social support and family social support on stress; similarly, work social support resulted in better health outcomes. In terms of the PEF model, these results suggest that the negative costs associated with incongruence will be minimized in environments that are supportive and that provide the employee with either avenues for acknowledging difficulty in completing their jobs or access to people from whom they can seek help or both. These resources are likely to ensure that important outcomes are not perceived as permanently unattainable.

In addition to the expected findings, there were results that were not explicitly predicted. Many of the results in this category implicated subject ethnicity. For example, disproportionately low in-group representation was expected to adversely affect both stress and health. These relationships did emerge, but they were limited to White employees. Being in a numerical minority resulted in both higher levels of stress and more numerous health problems for White workers. Hispanic employees, by comparison, did not show pronounced levels of stress and health problems when their in-group was in a numerical minority. In fact, their mean scores on these measures were in the opposite direction. This latter pattern was not predicted, nor was it consistent with findings from previous work (cf. K. James, 1994).

One possible explanation for these results is that being in a numerical minority may have represented a normative situation for the Hispanics in our sample, but not for the Whites. Hence, Hispanics may have adapted more readily to their numerically distinctive status and incurred fewer psychological and physical costs than did their White counterparts. For Whites, in contrast, minority status might represent an atypical experience (except in cases in which they occupy supervisory roles). Thus, the White participants in our sample whose in-group representation was disproportionately low might have experienced anxiety and discomfort, along with disruptive self-presentational concern (cf. Saenz, 1994). This explanation is, of course, merely suggestive, given that no data were collected to assess subjects' evaluations of their minority status. Nonetheless, if minority status represents an incongruence between expected and actual working conditions for White employees, then the manifestation of negative consequences is not surprising.

Another unexpected finding—and perhaps the most interesting and important result—was the general effect that perceived discrimination against minorities produced. We predicted that Hispanic employees would evince higher levels of stress when they worked in units where they perceived a significant amount of discrimination against minorities. The presence of discrimination (e.g., exclusion from informal networks, having to work harder to get ahead, and being placed in dead-end jobs) would clearly contribute to the perception that important outcomes cannot be attained. Thus, increased levels of stress were both expected from and displayed by targets of discrimination. We did not predict, however, that similar costs would be incurred by Whites. After all, Whites are not the direct recipients of behaviors reflecting prejudice and discrimination against minorities. Nevertheless, White employees reported heightened stress when the level of perceived discrimination against minorities in their work unit was high.

This finding may reflect the interdependence that exists across employees in many organizational settings. That is, achieving institutional goals often requires the joint efforts of all employees. If workers in one group are hindered by discriminatory treatment, then their job performances may suffer. This outcome, in turn, may adversely affect others who are in an interdependent relationship with the hindered employees. In the present case, discrimination in the workplace may have represented incongruence between expected and actual working conditions—not just for Hispanics, but also for Whites. Specifically, White employees might experience general discomfort in response to their awareness of unfair practices. Alternatively, majority employees might feel resentment at the need to compensate for hindered coworkers' diminished performance. Either of these putative incongruences between expected and actual working conditions would likely produce dissatisfaction among majority members and serve to magnify their stress levels, especially if the detrimental working conditions were perceived to be long-term.

Perceived discrimination against minorities was also predictive of health problems. As expected, however, differential outcomes in this domain were specific to Hispanic employees. Unlike the pattern that emerged for stress, Whites reported no difference in the number of health problems they experienced as a function of level of perceived discrimination. Instead, social support was more predictive of their health outcomes. By comparison, Hispanic workers incurred a greater number of health problems when faced with discrimination in the workplace and in the absence of social support, relative to when discrimination was low.

Theoretical Implications for the PEF Model

The present study provided a test of the PEF model, using a sample of Hispanic and White university employees. Unlike some previous studies, this investigation included workers representing numerous job categories (i.e., professional, technical, and clerical staff). Our results provided some corroboration for previous findings derived from samples composed primarily of White male managers.

The obtained pattern of results, for example, indicated that stress levels were predictive of health outcomes. This finding expands the scope of previous work by demonstrating that the relationship occurs for both majority and minority group employees. The present work also demonstrated that both Hispanic and White employees exhibit parallel effects on stress levels as a consequence of social support. This finding, too, is consistent with previous work conducted with primarily White samples and suggests that employees from different ethnic backgrounds and from varying job categories reap benefits when their work environments provide resources that counteract incongruence.

In addition to showing comparable response patterns to stress and social support, Hispanics and Whites also demonstrated similar response patterns in their reaction to the presence of perceived discrimination in their work unit. Although not expected, both groups reported higher levels of stress when they perceived that discriminatory practices against minorities were present. To our knowledge, this finding is novel. Previous work on the effects of discrimination has focused primarily on the costs incurred by ethnic minority members (e.g., K. James, 1994; S. A. James et al., 1984). Moreover, empirical investigations that have explicitly compared minority with majority members have failed to go beyond a simple measurement of the differential perceptions of members in the two groups. That is, comparative studies have demonstrated that minority group members are more likely to report higher levels of discrimination in the workplace than majority members (Brown et al., 1991; Fernandez, 1981; Gallup Organization, 1989). Our approach not only assessed differential perceptions of discrimination as a function of ethnic background, but also looked at the consequences associated with perceived discrimination for both minority and majority members. Our findings suggest that incongruence in the workplace need not involve direct linkages to oneself to produce negative outcomes: White employees who were not the targets of differential treatment showed comparable effects with Hispanic employees on the stress measure.

The set of relationships discussed in this study (the deleterious effects of stress on health, the ameliorative effects of social support, and the detrimental effect of discrimination) suggests that in some arenas, person–environment incongruence can yield similar outcomes for both majority and minority group employees. However, there was also evidence in our data indicating that certain environmental factors can have differential effects on minority and majority workers. Incongruence stemming from one factor—the employee's in-group representation—influenced the stress and health outcomes of Whites, but not Hispanics. As mentioned previously, this difference might be due to the normative expectations for in-group representation held by members of the respective groups. Incongruence because of a different factor—perceived discrimination—produced negative health outcomes for Hispanics, but not for Whites. This finding was intriguing given that stress outcomes as a function of perceived discrimination were comparable for the two groups. One plausible explanation for these disparate patterns is that perceiving and experiencing the direct brunt of discrimination may produce more negative outcomes than does simply being aware of the incongruence. Thus, Whites exhibited heightened stress levels from their perception of discriminatory practices, and Hispanic employees, in comparison, manifested both heightened stress and impaired health as a function of bearing the discrimination directed at them.

One implication of these different sets of findings is that greater specificity may be required in the development of predictive models linking incongruence in the work setting to negative stress and health outcomes. Our work suggests that the confluence of important elements, such as employees' racial and ethnic backgrounds and structural environmental factors, needs to be considered. This is not to say that the present conceptualization of the relationship between incongruence and negative outcomes is entirely inadequate but, rather, that interpretations of the PEF model need to include more of the different person–environment interactions that comprise organizational behavior (cf. Caplan, 1983). This may present a major challenge to contemporary and future investigators of occupational stress.

Practical Applications

A second challenge that faces researchers is the design and implementation of interventions directed at either eliminating person–environment misfit altogether or at attenuating its negative effects when it is not feasible to remove incongruence. Our findings, as well as recent discussions in the literature (Copeland, 1988), suggest that one important area of intervention that might yield benefits for a broad category of employees is the reduction of discrimination in the workplace. The general workforce is currently undergoing a change in its demographic composition. Hence, many work settings are becoming increasingly diverse in terms of their employees' racial and ethnic backgrounds. Given the pattern of outcomes related to discriminatory practices that emerged in our investigation, it may be valuable to focus on interventions that curtail the incongruences associated with the differential treatment of minority and majority group members. Our data suggest that interventions designed to minimize the effects of incongruence along this dimension may be beneficial to all employees, regardless of their category membership.

An initial step in this direction would be to alert managers about the institutional costs of prejudice and discrimination in the workplace. Additionally, it may be helpful to provide them with information regarding the potential effect of structural features in their organizations. This recognition might then promote educational programs for employees regarding (a) the costs to the individual and the institution of prejudice and discrimination and (b) the cultural and value differences of the various ethnic groups with whom interaction will become increasingly frequent in the future.

A more assertive approach would call for introducing interdependent activities into the workplace more directly; that is, companies could adopt a "team" approach in their organizational structure. Work assignments that involve the direct cooperation of employees from different backgrounds might yield numerous benefits. Sharing of information and task responsibility, for example, might serve to counteract majority members' assumptions of incompetence on the part of minority members (cf. Desforges et al., 1991). Interaction of this nature could also foster acknowledgment of common interests and goals among individuals of different groups (cf. Gaertner, Mann, Dovidio, Murrell, & Pomare, 1990). Furthermore, by having employees acknowledge that their behavior is facilitating the performance of an out-group member, they may develop more favorable views of the out-group (cf. Saenz & Lewis, 1993). These outcomes, in turn, might yield work environments that are characterized by greater levels of social support. By modifying the structural and social contextual features in the work environment, organizations would not only be reducing the stress levels and health problems among employees, but might also increase productivity in general. Hence, adopting an interdependent or team approach might result in broad-ranging benefits.

It should be kept in mind that the suggestions we make are based in part on the pattern of results we obtained and also on interpretation of principles derived from social psychology. Before our recommendations are implemented, however, it will first be necessary to establish whether the relationships that emerged among the variables in our study are representative of those in other work settings. Hence, we recommend that additional research be conducted to assess whether structural and social contextual incongruences produce similar effects in other organizational settings and with other populations.

We also recommend that a variety of stress and health measures be used. One limitation of our study was its reliance on self-reported health outcomes. Research conducted by other investigators (e.g., K. James, 1994) has provided more direct evidence of physiological distress (e.g., blood pressure levels). Research measuring direct health outcomes and monitoring health changes over time, rather than at a given point in time, would be valuable.

In addition, we recommend that the role of other employee characteristics, such as gender, be examined. In our investigation, we focused primarily on ethnicity. Although we conducted analyses to examine the effect of gender on the relationships described here, none of the effects we reported were qualified by employee gender. In some respects, this is not surprising, given that the structural and social contextual factors we examined dealt strictly with subject ethnicity (e.g., discrimination against minorities). We believe that similar effects might emerge in future investigations that focus on employee gender, and we encourage researchers to pursue this possibility.

In general, we urge investigators of occupational stress to broaden their focus and examine the variety of person–environment interactions that are predictive of both stress and health outcomes among diverse groups of employees. Such comprehensive research approaches will expand the understanding of occupational stress and provide guidance for the development of effective interventions.

References

Arney, L. K. (1988). Effects of personality–environment fit on job stress. *Educational and Psychological research, 8*, 1–18.

Barling, J., Bluen, S. D., & Fain, R. (1987). Psychological functioning following an acute disaster. *Journal of Applied Psychology, 72*, 683–690.

Beehr, T. A. (1976). Perceived situational moderators of the relationship between subjective role ambiguity and role strain. *Journal of Applied Psychology, 61*, 35–40.

Beehr, T. A., & Bhagat, R. S. (1985). Introduction to human stress and cognition in organizations. In T. A. Beehr & R. S. Bhagat (Eds.), *Human stress and cognition in organizations: An integrated perspective* (pp. 3–19). New York: Wiley.

Beehr, T. A., King, L. A., & King, D. W. (1990). Social support and occupational stress: Talking to supervisors. *Journal of Vocational Behavior, 36*, 61–81.

Boaz, T. L. (1982). *Sensation seeking, locus of control, and self-control as moderator variables in the relationship between life stress and physical and mental disorders.* Unpublished master's thesis, University of Kansas, Lawrence.

Brown, D., Minor, C. W., & Jepsen, D. A. (1991). The opinions of minorities about preparing for work: Report of the Second NCDA national survey. *Career Development Quarterly, 40*, 5–19.

Caplan, R. D. (1983). Person–environment fit: Past, present, and future. In C. L. Copper (Ed.), *Stress research: Where do we go from here?* (pp. 35–77). New York: Wiley.

Chemars, M. M., Hays, R. B., Rhodewalt, F., & Wysocki, J. (1985). A person–environment analysis of job stress: A contingency model explanation. *Journal of Personality and Social Psychology, 49*, 628–635.

Cobb, S., & Kasl, S. V. (1972). Some medical aspects of unemployment. *Industrial Gerontology, 12*, 87–96.

Copeland, L. (1988, June). Making the most of cultural differences at the workplace. *Personnel,* 52–60.

Curbow, B. (1990). Job stress in child care workers: A framework for research. *Child and Youth Care Quarterly, 19*, 211.

Desforges, D. M., Lord, C. G., Ramsey, S. L., Mason, J. A., Van Leeuwen, M. D., & West, S. C. (1991). Effects of structured cooperative contact on changing negative attitudes toward stigmatized social groups. *Journal of Personality and Social Psychology, 60*, 531–544.

Edwards, K. L. (1980). *The influence of management function and perceived environmental support on perceived stress and job satisfaction of black females in managerial and professional positions in industry.* Unpublished doctoral dissertation, University of Cincinnati, OH.

Fernandez, J. P. (1981). *Racism and sexism in corporate life.* Lexington, MA: Lexington Books.

Ford, D. L. (1981, October). *The relative contributions of facets of work support in the prediction of stress-related work outcomes for Black professions.* Paper presented at the Conference on Black Stress/Distress and Coping Strategies, University of Alabama, Tuscaloosa.

French, J. R. P., Caplan, R. D., & Harrison, R. V. (1982). *The mechanisms of job stress and strain.* New York: Wiley.

Frone, M. R., Russell, M., & Cooper, M. L. (1990, August). *Occupational stressors, psychosocial resources, and psychological distress: A comparison of Black and White workers.* Paper presented at the Annual Meeting of the Academy of Management, San Francisco.

Gaertner, S. L., Mann, J. A., Dovidio, J. F., Murrell, A. J., & Pomare, M. (1990). How does cooperation reduce intergroup bias? *Journal of Personality and Social Psychology, 59,* 692–704.

Gallup Organization. (1989). *A Gallup survey regarding career development.* Princeton, NJ: Author.

Ganster, D. C., Fusilier, M. R., & Mayes, B. T. (1986). Role of social support in the experience of stress at work. *Journal of Applied Psychology, 71,* 102–110.

Gerstein, L. H., Topp, C. G., & Correll, G. (1987). The role of the environment and person when predicting burnout among correctional personnel. *Criminal Justice and Behavior, 14,* 352–369.

Glowinkowski, S. P., & Cooper, C. L. (1986). Managers and professionals in business/industrial settings: The research evidence [Special issue: Job stress: From theory to suggestion]. *Journal of Organizational Behavior Management, 8,* 177–193.

House, J. S. (1974). Occupational stress and coronary heart disease: A review and theoretical integration. *Journal of Health and Social Behavior, 15,* 12–27.

House, J. S. (1981). *Work stress and social support.* Reading, MA: Addison-Wesley.

House, J. S., & Rizzo, J. R. (1972). Role conflict and ambiguity as critical variables in a model of organizational behavior. *Organizational Behavior and Human Performance, 7,* 467–505.

Ivancevich, J. M., & Matteson, M. T. (1984). A Type A–B person–work environment interaction model for examining occupational stress and outcomes. *Human Relations, 37,* 491–531.

James, K. (1994). Social identity, work stress, and minority workers' health. In G. P. Keita & J. J. Hurrell, Jr. (Eds.), *Job stress in a changing workforce: Investigating gender, diversity, and family* (pp. 127–145). Washington, DC: American Psychological Association.

James, S. A., Lacroix, A. Z., Kleinbaum, D. G., & Strogatz, D. S. (1984). John Henryism and blood pressure differences among Black men: II. The role of occupational stressors. *Journal of Behavioral Medicine, 7,* 259–275.

Kahn, R. L. (1964). *Organizational stress: Studies in role conflict and ambiguity.* New York: Wiley.

Kanter, R. M. (1977). Some effects of proportions on group life: Skewed sex ratios and responses to token women. *American Journal of Sociology, 82,* 965–991.

Kirmeyer, S. L., & Dougherty, T. W. (1988). Work load, tension and coping: Moderating effects of supervisor support. *Personnel Psychology, 41,* 125–139.

Kizer, W. M. (1987). *The healthy workplace: A blueprint for corporate action.* New York: Wiley.

Lord, C. G., & Saenz, D. S. (1985). Memory deficits and memory surfeits: Differential cognitive consequences of tokenism for tokens and observers. *Journal of Personality and Social Psychology, 49,* 918–926.

Martin, E. V. (1987). Worker stress: A practitioner's perspective. In L. R. Murphy & T. F. Schoenborn (Eds.), *Stress management in work settings* (pp. 149–172). Cincinnati, OH: National Institute for Occupational Safety and Health.

Matteson, M. T., & Ivancevich, J. M. (1988). Health promotion at work. In C. L. Cooper & I. Robertson (Eds.), *International review of industrial organizational psychology* (pp. 279–306). New York: Wiley.

Morland, J. K. (1965). Token desegregation and beyond. In M. Rose & C. B. Rose (Eds.), *Minority problems* (pp. 229–238). New York: Harper & Row.

Newman, J. E., & Beehr, T. A. (1979). Personal and organizational strategies for handling job stress: A review of research and opinion. *Personnel Psychology, 32,* 1–43.

Ramos, A. A. (1975). The relationship of sex and ethnic background to job related stress of research and development professionals. *Dissertation Abstracts International, 9*, 1862A.

Saenz, D. S. (1994). Token status and problem-solving capability deficits: Detrimental effects of distinctiveness and performance monitoring. *Social Cognition, 12*, 61–74.

Saenz, D. S., & Lewis, B. P. (1993). *Changes in interpersonal perceptions of ingroup and outgroup members: The role of counternormative behavior in intergroup interactions.* Manuscript submitted for publication.

Saenz, D. S., & Lord, C. G. (1989). Reversing roles: A cognitive strategy for undoing memory deficits associated with token status. *Journal of Personality and Social Psychology, 56*, 698–708.

Taylor, S. E., Fiske, S. T., Close, M., Anderson, C., & Ruderman, A. J. (1977). *Solo status as a psychological variable: The power of being distinctive.* Unpublished manuscript, Harvard University, Cambridge, MA.

Van Harrison, R. (1985). The person–environment fit model and the study of job stress. In T. A. Beehr & R. S. Bhagat (Eds.), *Human stress and cognition in organization: An integrated perspective* (pp. 23–55). New York: Wiley.

Yoder, J. D. (1985). An academic woman as a token: A case study. *Journal of Social Issues, 41*, 61–72.

8

Social Identity, Work Stress, and Minority Workers' Health

Keith James

Costs for organizations associated with workers' health problems are substantial. Kizer (1987) reported that U.S. companies spent more on health insurance premiums in 1985 than they paid in dividends to all of their shareholders. Partly in response to this problem, in recent years a significant amount of research on work-stress effects on health outcomes has been done. Little of this research, however, has examined work stress among minority employees (Ford, 1985; Frone, Russell, & Cooper, 1990; K. James & Khoo, 1991; S. A. James, 1985).

This is true despite the fact that the percentage of minority group members in the total workforce of the United States is increasing and is projected to increase even further in coming years (Johnson & Packer, 1989) and despite evidence (to be discussed) that some organizational and individual precursors of health problems may differ for minority and nonminority individuals. It is clearly important for organizational researchers and theorists to directly examine the question of how organizational and individual factors affect the health of minority workers.

The purpose of the studies reported in this chapter was to help fill some of the gaps in existing knowledge of stress processes and outcomes among minority workers. I argue that social identity is a central issue to consider in studies of work stress among minorities. Social identity is proposed to exert a major influence both on behaviors directed toward minority workers by nonminority colleagues that can be stressors and on minority individuals' own perceptions of stress and their ability to cope with it. In the sections that follow, I first outline the social, situational, and cognitive dynamics of social identity by using Tajfel and Turner's (Tajfel & Turner, 1979; Turner, 1985; Turner & Associates, 1986) social identity theory (SIT) as a framework. Many of the variables targeted in this conceptual framework were then tested in three studies. One of these studies (Study 2) has been described in greater detail elsewhere (K. James, Lovato, & Khoo, 1994). The others have not been previously published.

Social Identity Theory

In SIT, a desire to maintain a positive identity (i.e., a sense of esteem) is seen as a major force driving individuals' cognitions, emotions, and behaviors. Because group memberships contribute substantially to identity and esteem, they are capable of influencing virtually all types of behaviors, cognitions, and emotions. Race is a membership category that typically has strong identity influences for minority individuals in the United States across a variety of situations for historical, cultural, social–structural, and perceptual reasons (Allport, 1954; Tajfel & Turner, 1979). More specifically, because most minority individuals work for majority-dominated companies, race becomes an acutely prominent component of their workplace social identities because of strong contrast effects (K. James & Khoo, 1991; Pettigrew & Martin, 1987).

Social Identity Influences on Minority Workers' Stress Levels

Individual–in-group and in-group–out-group relations are interrelated, according to Tajfel and Turner (1979). Individuals' evaluations of important in-groups on (culturally and personally) valued characteristics and, thus, much of their ability to maintain a positive sense of personal worth, are possible only through in-group–out-group comparisons. This sets the stage for prejudice and discrimination against individuals who are classified as being part of an out-group, especially when the characteristic or characteristics on which that grouping is based are normatively associated with low status and negative stereotypes. This is the case with most minority groups, the exception being perhaps Asian Americans, for whom stereotypes may tend to be a complex mixture of positives and negatives (Fernandez, 1991).

Perceptions by members of the majority that minority individuals differ from them in normative behavior, values, or other major aspects of culture may also help promote prejudice and discrimination (Becker, 1973; Greenberg, Pyszczynski, & Solomon, 1986; Turner, 1985). In organizations, specifically, both case and quantitative field studies have provided evidence that real or apparent cultural differences can help trigger majority denigration of and discrimination against minority individuals (see K. James & Khoo, 1991, for a review).

Prejudice, Discrimination, and Stress

The limited empirical evidence available supports the idea that discrimination and prejudice on the job contribute to minority stress and stress-related disturbances. S. A. James and his colleagues (James, LaCroix, Kleinbaum, & Strogatz, 1984) found that rated discrimination on the job significantly contributed to blood pressure levels among some African Americans. In another study of discrimination on the job, Frone, Russell, and Cooper (1990) studied samples of 439 African Americans and 349 White workers and found that discrimination scores added significantly to the prediction of work distress, depression, and physiological symptoms among the African American workers. Similarly, Erlich and Larcom (1992), in a survey of a stratified national sample, found that individuals who reported having experienced group-membership-based verbal or physical harassment at work also reported higher levels of symptoms of psychological and physical disorder than those who had not experienced race-based harassment. Even those who had experienced abuse (verbal or psychological) for reasons other than ethnicity exhibited fewer indirect psychological or physical problems than those abused because of their ethnic background. Moreover, for the latter group, the more extreme the ethnic harassment experienced, the higher the level of subsequent psychophysical disorder suffered.

Data somewhat discrepant from this pattern have been reported by Gutierres, Saenz, and Green (1994). The Hispanic participants in their study reported perceiving higher levels of discrimination against minorities on the job than did their White counterparts. However, both minority and nonminority workers who perceived that discrimination against minorities occurred in their work units had higher levels of stress than those who did not. These authors also found that minority individuals who thought that antiminority bias occurred in their work units did not have higher stress levels than nonminority individuals with the same perception. Gutierres et al. asked about prejudice and discrimination in one's work unit in general, however, whereas other researchers discussed above asked about personal prejudice and discrimination experiences at work. This difference may account for the fact that Gutierres et al. obtained somewhat different results from other researchers who have examined prejudice and discrimination as a stressor.

Cultural Conflict and Marginality for Minority Workers

There are indications that members of the major U.S. minority groups generally differ from the majority on such things as linearity of presentation style (Khoo, 1988), decision-making strategies (Badwound & Tierney, 1988), inclination toward social cooperation versus competition (Triandis, Bontempo, Villareal, Asai, & Lucca, 1988), and integration of work with other phases of life (Bopp et al., 1989).

Real or perceived cultural differences may affect the health of minority individuals in majority-dominated organizations through the process of acculturative stress or marginality. Phinney (1991) defined *marginality* as weak identification with both a minority in-group and the majority. Others (e.g., Stonequist, 1937) have defined it more broadly as the necessity to adapt to or interact with a culture or social group other than one's own. SIT integrates both positions by positing that individuals have the greatest trouble coping when they are unable to view their in-group positively and are prevented by in-group or out-group pressures from transferring their loyalties to the out-group, but must interact with both groups (Tajfel & Turner, 1979; see also Starr, 1977). This may often be the case for minority workers in majority-dominated organizations (Denton, 1990; K. James & Khoo, 1991; K. James, Lovato, & Khoo, 1994).

Minority Social Identity and Coping With Stress

In addition to serving as a trigger of some unique sources of work stress, membership in a minority group may also impair one's ability to cope effectively with high levels of work stress. One major reason for this is that social support at work may be less likely when one is a member of a minority group and most of one's colleagues, especially one's supervisor, are not. Another is that a positive sense of identity can enhance resilience in the face of tribulations in life. Frequent exposure to normatively higher status groups, culturally different others, and group-based prejudice can inhibit or erode such feelings.

Social Support at Work

Social support on the job has been shown repeatedly to reduce the negative effects of work stressors when they do exist and to sometimes help individuals reduce or eliminate some stressors (e.g., coworker assistance with heavy work demands; see Cohen & Wills, 1985, for a review). The two major categories of social support at work that have been examined are support from peers and support from supervisors. Both types may be problematic for minority employees, although little research has been done directly on social support processes and outcomes for minorities (S. A. James, 1985).

Because of the social identity effects on in-group–out-group relations already outlined, minority workers may not obtain sufficient social support from either a nonminority supervisor or from nonminority coworkers. Nonminority organization members may not willingly provide such support, and minority workers may not seek it from majority employees or may be skeptical if it is offered (Ford, 1985). Ford argued that supervisory support is particularly important for minimizing work-stress effects. Amick and Celentano (1991) produced some evidence that this is true among nonminority workers. They found that both socioemotional and instrumental (i.e., assistance in completing tasks) aid from supervisors helped to significantly reduce the negative health effects of work stress but that peer support was unrelated to health outcomes.

Ford (1985) also argued that relationships with supervisors may be particularly important to the work-stress outcomes of minority individuals. Indirect evidence supporting this view also came from a study by Cummins (1990), in which it was found that supervisory support in particular has more value for reducing stress effects for individuals with a high relationship orientation than for individuals with a low relationship orientation (i.e., degree to which social relationships are viewed as highly important). Because members of the major U.S. minority groups seem to be generally more collectivistic and relationship oriented than members of the majority (K. James & Khoo, 1991; Triandis et al., 1988), it makes sense that supervisory support would generally be more valuable in buffering health from stress effects for the former than for the latter.

The present studies explored some of these issues. The first study focused on prejudice and discrimination on the job and an organizational factor that may promote prejudice as correlates with minority workers' health outcomes. The second study retained these variables but also assessed value conflicts between minority and majority workers as well as minority workers' own perceptions of personal and ethnic-collective esteem. The third study focused on value conflicts, esteem, and workplace social support as predictors of minority workers' health.

Study 1

Group Proportions as a Situational Influence on Prejudice and Discrimination

In SIT, individual focus (on self or others) and group focus (on in-group or out-group) are viewed as two ends of a continuum (see Turner, 1985). Available empirical evidence indicates that the ratio of in-group to out-group in a setting may be the most powerful situational factor in influencing which is the unit of focus. The basic effect of in-group–out-group proportions is that the greater the discrepancy in size between two groups in a setting, the more attention is paid to group membership and perceived group characteristics and the less attention is paid to individual uniqueness (Kanter, 1977; Kanter & Stein, 1979; Mullen & Baumeister, 1987; Taylor & Fiske, 1978). The closer minority individuals approach being unique in a setting, the greater the likelihood that majority individuals will (a) exaggerate whichever characteristics, behaviors, or values are seen as defining their own group; (b) hold stereotypical conceptions of the minority individuals (Kanter, 1977; Pettigrew & Martin, 1987); (c) focus on and exaggerate intergroup differences (Fernandez, 1974; Kanter, 1977); and (d) scrutinize minority individuals intently (Kanter & Stein, 1979; Mullen & Baumeister, 1987).

In addition to these effects, solo status also makes minority group members more likely to be seen as "tokens"—that is, as owing their positions solely to affirmative action policies. Categorization of someone as a token tends to lead to an assumption that he or she is incompetent (Fernandez, 1974, 1981; Pettigrew & Martin, 1987). Tokens are thus placed in double jeopardy: They are subject to the same pressures, stereotypes, and prejudices as those with solo status, but have the additional stigma of being categorized as incompetent.

By way of these solo and token effects, group proportions in organizations have been argued to influence how likely and how extreme prejudice and discrimination experiences will be for minority workers. This was examined in Study 1, along with how these variables would be related to minority workers' health outcomes.

Hypotheses

The following three hypotheses were tested, on the basis of the ideas outlined above:

> *Hypothesis 1:* Minority workers' perceptions of levels of prejudice and discrimination engaged in by nonminority organization members will be significantly and positively associated with health problems.

Hypothesis 2: Proportions of in-group members in organizations will be significantly but negatively associated with health problems.

Hypothesis 3: The effect of in-group proportions on health will be at least partially mediated by experienced organizational prejudice and discrimination.

Method

Subjects

All participants were professional- and managerial-level minority employees, who were paid for completing the materials. Of the 58 participants, 35 were Hispanic, 15 were Asian American, 5 were Native American, and 3 were African American. Thirty-one were men, and 27 were women. Participants' average tenure in their current jobs was 7.23 years. Their average age was 41.8 years.

Measures

I developed two items to assess perceived prejudice and discrimination at work. These two items correlated at .65, which indicates reasonable agreement in the two ratings. They were therefore combined into one score reflecting perceived prejudice and discrimination at work. In-group proportions were measured by asking subjects to calculate and report the percentage of the members of their work units (i.e., those who they directly interacted with on a more-or-less daily basis) who were from their own ethnic group.

Finally, physical health problems were assessed with a modified version of the Seriousness of Illness Rating Scale developed by Wyler, Masuda, and Holmes (1968). I used 35 of a larger number of illnesses included on Wyler et al.'s original scale that a panel of physicians in a study by Kriek (1988) selected as clearly possessing an important psychosomatic component. Participants were asked to mark any illnesses that they had experienced in the two years prior to the study. Severity scores (ranging from 81 to 855, as determined by Wyler et al., 1968) for all illnesses checked by each participant were summed to produce a score for the seriousness of his or her health problems. This score was the dependent measure of this study. Wyler et al. (1968); K. James et al. (1994), and Kriek (1988) have presented evidence indicating that this scale is reliable and valid as a measure of health.

Results

Possible main effects of gender were tested in all three studies, but no such effects were found. Physical health problems correlated significantly and positively with the prejudice and discrimination scores. Thus, Hypothesis 1, which predicted that higher levels of prejudice and discrimination would be associated with higher levels of health problems, was supported. The percentages of minority group members in the respondents' work units were significantly and negatively related to health problems, a finding that supported Hypothesis 2.

To test Hypothesis 3, I used a procedure detailed by Baron and Kenny (1986) to test for mediation. This required that work-unit minority percentages be significantly related to rated prejudice and discrimination; however, this relationship was not significant. Thus, the expected mediation by prejudice and discrimination of the in-group percentage–health relationship was not supported, although in-group percentages were significantly related to health-problem scores.

To assess the combined effects of the predictors, I included in-group percentages and prejudice and discrimination ratings in a multiple regression analysis, with health-problem scores as the dependent measure. This regression yielded significant effects (at the .05 level) of both predictors. For the variable of the percentage of minority group members making up respondents' work units, $F(2, 56) = 3.92$, $p < .05$ ($\Delta R^2 = .06$). As in the bivariate correlations, this relationship was negative. For rated prejudice and discrimination, $F(2, 56) = 3.40$, $p < .05$ ($\Delta R^2 = .05$). The full equation was significant and accounted for 11% of the variance in illness-checklist scores.

Study 2

An objective measure of health outcomes was used in this study, rather than self-reports. Some other predictors thought likely to interrelate with those used in Study 1 were also added. Perceived value differences from nonminority organization members were assessed (separately for supervisor and for peers) for the reasons described in the introduction of this chapter. That is, the perceived value differences and their possible impact on minority workers' experiences of prejudice and discrimination and on their sense of ethnic group pride and self-worth were evaluated. Inventories for self- and collective- (i.e., ethnic-group) esteem levels were also added to Study 2 as measures of the latter two constructs.

Self- and Collective-Esteem

A positive sense of identity, or esteem, has been found to be associated with good health in majority individuals (Harter, 1983; Whitley, 1985), including samples of majority workers (Ivancevich & Matteson, 1980; Mossholder, Bedeian, & Armenakis, 1981). Esteem seems to be a general, enduring cognitive resource that provides individuals with a buffer against acute threats and stressors (Brockner, 1988). Thus, higher levels of esteem should help minority workers tolerate negative organizational events and situations so that these will be less likely to have negative health effects. This had not, however, been directly tested before.

Self-esteem is based on personal characteristics and achievements and evaluations of these by the individual and the individual's social contacts (Luhtanen & Crocker, 1992; Whitley, 1985). Collective-esteem is based on in-group characteristics and achievements and evaluations of these by the individual and by society (Luhtanen & Crocker, 1992; Tajfel & Turner, 1979). Group conceptions may be more central to the identities of individuals from various minority groups than to the identities of nonminority persons (see reviews by K. James & Khoo, 1991; Triandis, 1989), a finding that makes inclusion of collective-esteem scores important when researching social identity influences on minority health.

Prejudice and discrimination, as negative reactions to an individual based on his or her group identity, may influence levels of self- and collective-esteem (Phinney, 1991; Tajfel & Turner, 1979). Group proportions may also have implications for self- and collective-esteem. With smaller in-group proportions, existing in-group stereotypes may be more likely to influence minority individuals' self-perceptions, including their self-esteem (Crocker & Major, 1989; Mullen & Baumeister, 1987; Pettigrew & Martin, 1987). Negative impacts on collective-esteem may also be more likely when in-group numbers are low (Kanter, 1977; Pettigrew & Martin, 1987; Tajfel & Turner, 1979). In addition, Crocker and Major stated that psychological and social defenses that normally help buffer esteem from the effects of "social stigma" become more difficult to use in cases of solo status. Thus, proportions of minorities in an organization might influence levels of prejudice and discrimination experienced from out-group members as well as minority individuals' sense of collective- or self-esteem.

Perceived Value Differences

Minority workers' perceived value differences from their nonminority organization colleagues were measured and examined both for potential direct relationships to health and for possible indirect effects on health mediated by esteem or prejudice and discrimination. In-group values may provide individuals with a sense of esteem by giving purpose and meaning to their lives (Greenberg et al., 1986; Phinney, 1991; Tajfel & Turner, 1979). Out-group contact can be threatening to this function of in-group values (Greenberg et al., 1986; K. James & Khoo, 1991). Prejudice and discrimination levels may also be influenced by majority and minority value differences (Greenberg et al., 1986; Katz & Hass, 1988). Perceptions by members of the majority that minority groups differ in values have been shown to trigger prejudice and discrimination toward minority individuals in both organizations (Fernandez, 1974, 1981) and society at large (e.g., Katz & Hass, 1988). Thus, value differences between minority and majority organization members may exert some effects on health indirectly by way of either collective-esteem or experienced prejudice and discrimination.

Measure of Health

Critics of work-stress research (e.g., Watson, Pennebaker, & Folger, 1986) have argued that self-reports of health may not be valid and that their frequent use weakens the believability and value of the work-stress literature. Therefore, in the present investigations, I used an objective measure of one aspect of health: blood pressure levels.

Cardiovascular illnesses are a major source of health-related costs for organizations (e.g., Felton & Cole, 1963). Even "mild" elevations of blood pressure levels (i.e., elevations that have traditionally not been considered abnormal) seem to be a major precursor of cardiovascular disease (Julius et al., 1990). For the minority group for whom the most data are available, African Americans, high blood pressure has been found to be more common and to produce more health damage than is seen in White Americans with the same levels of hypertension (Saunders, 1987). Thus, even factors that have only moderate associations with minority blood pressure levels are of potential concern. Evidence has linked minority blood pressure levels to a variety of psychosocial factors, but the social identity variables targeted here have largely not been studied for effects on blood pressure.

Hypotheses

On the basis of theoretical possibilities discussed above, the following hypotheses were developed:

> *Hypothesis 1:* Higher levels of perceived prejudice and discrimination experienced at the hands of other organization members will be related to higher health-problem scores (i.e., higher scores on the illness checklist and elevated blood pressure scores) among minority workers.

> *Hypothesis 2:* Perceived differences in values from supervisory and nonminority colleagues will be related to higher levels of health problems among minority workers. On the basis of Ford's (1985) research and theory, value differences from supervisors should have a stronger relationship to health-problem scores than value differences from nonminority colleagues.

> *Hypothesis 3:* The proportion of in-group members in the participants' organizations will have significant negative associations with scores indicating health problems.

> *Hypothesis 4:* Levels of self- and collective-esteem will have significant negative associations with scores indicating health problems.

In addition to the main-effect predictions stated in Hypotheses 1–4, some tentative mediational hypotheses were investigated:

> *Hypothesis 5:* Perceived prejudice and discrimination will at least partially mediate (a) the relationship between in-group proportions and health-problem scores and (b) the relationships between the two types of value

differences (i.e., value differences from supervisors and value differences from peers) and health-problem scores.

Hypothesis 6: Collective-esteem and self-esteem will at least partially mediate (a) the relationship between experienced prejudice and discrimination and health-problem scores, (b) the relationship between in-group proportions and health-problem scores, and (c) the relationships between the two types of value differences and health-problem scores.

Method

Subjects

The participants were 89 working minority volunteers (60 women and 28 men) from four organizations. Sixty-four percent were Mexican American, 18% were African American, 10% were Asian American, 3% were Native American, and 5% were individuals who indicated mixed heritage. Participants' mean tenure in their current jobs was 2.5 years.

Measures

Prejudice and discrimination. A 16-item scale developed and validated by K. James, Lovato, and Cropanzano (in press) was used in place of the ad hoc, unvalidated scale used in Study 1. Participants indicated their level of agreement with each item on a 7-point Likert-type scale, ranging from 1 (*totally disagree*) to 7 (*totally agree*). The internal consistency (Cronbach's alpha) of this scale was .90.

Self-esteem. I used the revised Janis–Field Self-Esteem Inventory (Robinson & Shaver, 1973) to measure self-esteem. This 17-item inventory uses a 5-point scale and has been extensively validated (some of the validity data are discussed by Robinson & Shaver, 1973). It is widely used by self-esteem researchers, including those interested in self-esteem and organizational phenomena (see Brockner, 1988). The survey's internal consistency for this sample was .66.

Collective-esteem. I used a slightly modified four-item inventory developed and validated by Crocker and Luhtanen (1990; Luhtanen & Crocker, 1992) to measure racial-group membership esteem (i.e., group pride). This inventory used a 7-point Likert-type scale. Its internal consistency was .87.

Value differences from supervisor and nonminority peers. Two sets of three items developed and validated by K. James (1994) were used to measure value differences from supervisors and from nonminority peers. All were rated by respondents on a 7-point Likert-type scale. Internal consistencies were .91 and .84 for the supervisory and peer scales, respectively.

Proportions of in-group in the organization. Participants were asked "What percentage of the members of your organization are from your minority group?" A check against actual ethnic proportions obtained from the records of the organization for which the largest subset of subjects worked yielded significant and substantial agreement with self-reported in-group proportions.

Control Variables

Both age and weight have sometimes been found to influence blood pressure levels. Therefore, information about both of these variables was obtained, and the effects of the main predictors were tested with these variables statistically controlled.

Dependent Measure

Two blood pressure measurements were taken for each participant, both while the person was seated. One measurement was done after the general purpose of the study had been reviewed (participants had approximately 5 minutes to relax before the measurement was taken). The second measurement was taken after all other measures had been completed. Readouts of systolic and diastolic blood pressure were double-checked and recorded after each measurement. The two systolic and the two diastolic scores correlated highly and were averaged for each subject.

Results

Main-Effect Hypotheses

Prejudice and discrimination scores were significantly positively related to blood pressure levels. Thus, Hypothesis 1 was supported. Both the relationships between perceived differences with supervisors' values and blood pressure levels and between perceived differences with peers' values and blood pressure levels were significant, but they were not in the predicted direction. That is, for both variables, higher levels of perceived differences were associated with lower blood pressure levels. Thus, the correlations did not support the hypothesized relationship of perceived value differences to blood pressure levels.

The posited positive effects (i.e., positive in the sense of being associated with lower blood pressure scores) of higher in-group percentages on blood pressure were supported (Hypothesis 3). Self-esteem scores had the predicted negative relationship to both blood pressure scores, supporting Hypothesis 4. Collective-esteem was significantly related only to diastolic blood pressure. Thus, the predictions for collective-esteem were only partially supported.

Mediational Hypotheses

In mediated regressions (see Baron & Kenny, 1986), no part of Hypothesis 5 was supported. However, evidence supportive of Hypotheses 6a, 6b, and 6c was found. The direction of the relationships of collective-esteem to perceived prejudice and discrimination and value differences were, however, the opposite of those expected.

Regression Analyses

Separate multiple regression analyses were conducted in which systolic and diastolic blood pressure scores were regressed on all predictors. Results were essentially the same for the two types of blood pressure. Prejudice and discrimination (positive relationship), self-esteem, collective-esteem, percentage of own ethnic group coworkers, and rated value differences from supervisor were the significant predictors of blood pressure levels (the latter three all with negative relationships). The squared multiple correlation for self-esteem was .09; for collective-esteem the change in squared multiple correlation was .03; for value differences from supervisor, it was .03; for prejudice and discrimination, .02; and for percentage of own-group coworkers, .01. Together they accounted for 18% of the blood pressure variance ($p < .05$).

Discussion

The main-effect hypotheses were largely supported. Posited mediational effects of collective- and self-esteem were somewhat supported; however, those of prejudice and discrimination were not. This indicates that other mediational mechanisms need to be examined. One discussed in the introduction of this chapter but not tested in either Study 1 or Study 2 was the level of social support at work. This particular variable was targeted in Study 3.

Contrary to expectations, higher levels of value differences were actually associated with lower blood pressure levels. One possible explanation for this result that is congruent with SIT is provided by a positive relationship of rated differences in values from both peers and from supervisor to collective-esteem. The idea of differences as a threat comes primarily from White writers analyzing the circumstances of the majority. Differences from the majority, being expected, may not by themselves be a cause for concern or a source of threat for minority individuals. Instead, perceptions of value differences from nonminority colleagues may actually help to validate the ethnic identity of minority workers, yielding greater collective-esteem (cf. Phinney, 1991).

Study 3

I have argued that social identity variables are likely to be unique influences on the health of minority, relative to majority, workers. In the first two studies, however, only minority employees were included so that no direct evidence of this was produced. In Study 3, the stress-coping resources of self- and collective-esteem and social support at work were the focus of a comparative investigation that included both minority and nonminority workers. The value-conflict construct from Study 2 was also retained in an attempt to replicate its association with collective-esteem and to test whether social support levels mediate the effects of value conflicts on health outcomes.

In addition, I used a health-outcome measure that assessed health effects likely to be directly and immediately costly to an employer. This was done to bring this program of research more closely in line with the idea that social identity effects on minority workers' health have important negative implications for their organizations as well as for themselves.

The following hypotheses were examined:

> *Hypothesis 1:* Minority workers will report greater value conflict, greater collective-esteem, and lower social support at work than their nonminority colleagues. Self-esteem will not differ for the two groups (see Crocker & Major, 1989).

> *Hypothesis 2:* Value-conflict and social support levels will be significantly and negatively correlated.

> *Hypothesis 3:* Collective-esteem, self-esteem, and social support levels will be negatively correlated with health-problem scores.

> *Hypothesis 4:* Value-conflict levels will be positively correlated with health-problem scores.

> *Hypothesis 5:* Value-conflict levels will be negatively correlated with social support levels, with social support levels mediating the effect of value conflict on health.

Method

Subjects

The participants were 102 technical and professional employees of a large university in the Eastern United States. Sixty-four of them were White; 38 were African American. Men made up 69% of the White group and 53% of the African American group. Members of both groups were identified through personnel office records.

Materials

A booklet of questionnaires was put together that contained three of the measures used in Study 2: the Janis–Field Self-Esteem Inventory (Robinson & Shaver, 1973), the Luhtanen & Crocker (1992) Collective-Esteem Inventory, and the Value Difference Questionnaire. Value differences in this study were assessed for coworkers generally. No separate categories existed for peers or supervisor. This was done for consistency with the social support-at-work questionnaire used, an instrument that combined support from all sources into a single score. A demographic information form, on which race was the relevant question, and a five-item inventory of social support at work developed and validated by Unden, Orth-Gomer, and Elofsson (1991) were included in the booklet. Finally, three items that directly asked about the incidence of health outcomes directly affecting organizational success were used to obtain a dependent measure. These items asked how many days the individual had missed from work in the previous 2 years because of sickness (respondents were instructed not to count sick days taken for reasons other than their own illness), how many visits had been made to the doctor or to emergency rooms in that same 2-year period, and how many prescriptions (for the individual's own conditions) had been filled and paid for or partially paid for by the organization's health insurance carrier.

Procedures

All listed full-time professional and technical staff members who had identified themselves as African American and who had been in their current positions for at least 4 years were sent a copy of the study booklet along with a cover letter. The minimum 4-year tenure cutoff was selected so that there would have been time for conditions of the current job to have affected the health outcomes assessed. A 45% response rate was achieved with this group.

Questionnaires were also sent to 150 randomly selected full-time professional and technical staff members who had identified themselves as White and who had also been employed in their current positions for at least 4 years. A response rate of 43% was attained with this second group.

Results

Analyses of Variance for Race Effects

The self-esteem, collective-esteem, value-conflict, social-support, and health-outcome scores were each tested separately for differences between the two racial groups. The results showed no significant effects for self-esteem, $F(4, 100) = 1.06$, $p > .05$; a significant effect for collective-esteem, $F(4, 100) = 4.05$, $p < .05$; a significant effect on value-conflict levels, $F(4, 100) = 4.93$, $p < .05$; a marginally significant effect on social support, $F(4, 100) = 3.44$, $p < .10$; and a significant effect on health-problem scores, $F(4, 100) = 4.73$, $p < .05$. The African American employees had higher mean collective-esteem scores (17.2, vs. 16.1 for Whites), value-conflict scores (22.6 vs. 16.5), and health-problem scores (12.4 vs. 5.5) than the White workers. White respondents had higher mean social support scores than the African American respondents (23 vs. 19.5).

Regression Analyses of Health Outcomes

An initial multiple regression was performed in which the participant's race, self-esteem, collective-esteem, value conflict, and social support were entered in a single step. Race ($\beta = .32$, $R^2 = .07$), $F(4, 98) = 8.07$, $p < .05$); self-esteem ($\beta = -.16$, $R^2 = .02$), $F(4, 98) = 2.69$, $p < .05$); collective-esteem ($\beta = -.25$, $R^2 = .05$), $F(4, 98) = 5.76$, $p < .05$); and value conflict ($\beta = .18$, $R^2 = .05$, $F(4, 98) = 5.30$, $p < .05$) entered as significant predictors of health outcomes. Social support was not significant. The squared multiple correlation value was .16, which was significant, $F(4, 98) = 5.80$, $p < .05$.

Next, a mediated regression equation was done in which social support was forced into the equation before the other predictors, and the two esteem variables and value conflict scores were entered in a single step before race. Again, race, self-esteem, collective-esteem, and value conflicts were significant predictors; however, social support was also significant, $\beta = -.40$, $R^2 = .04$, $F(4, 98) = 4.18)$, $p < .05$. The change in the squared multiple correlation value for race dropped substantially in magnitude, from .05 to .01, a finding that supports mediation of race effects primarily by social support, with which it was significantly correlated. Separate regressions for African American and White participants indicated that social support was a significant predictor of health outcomes for Whites, such that greater social support on the job was associated with fewer behaviors reflecting health costs for them. Social support was not, however, related to health outcomes among African Americans.

Discussion

The results of Study 3 replicated, for the common variables, the pattern of results observed among the minority participants of Study 2. That is, value-conflict scores were positively associated with collective-esteem and negatively related to health outcomes, whereas both self- and collective-esteem had positive effects on health. In addition, the comparative component of Study 3 provided evidence that the group-based components of social identity (collective-esteem and values) are more important to the identity of minority individuals and distinctly relevant to their outcomes.

As expected, African Americans reported having lower levels of social support at work than did White Americans. In addition, social support levels were negatively associated with value-conflict levels, as hypothesized. Along with the fact that African Americans reported significantly higher levels of value conflict and significantly lower levels of social support than their White colleagues, this correlation points toward the possibility that the existence of value conflicts with other organization members mitigates against access to social support on the job. Social support also had ameliorative effects on health outcomes only for Whites. These results all fit well with the tenets of SIT.

In contrast, the one individual-level element of social identity assessed (self-esteem) did not differ significantly between the groups and was equally relevant to health outcomes for both. This provides further support for the importance of cultural and ethnic identity in the health outcomes of minority workers. Because of the nature of the health-outcome measure used, Study 3 also provides direct evidence of how social-identity-related work-stress effects on the health of minorities can be costly to organizations.

One reason why social support might not have been a predictor for minorities in this study is that the inventory I used assessed only global support on the job. It did not distinguish between support from supervisor and support from peers (see Ford, 1985), nor did it independently assess the different types of social support (e.g., emotional, informational, and resource; see Cohen & Wills, 1985) that have been identified in the literature. It may be that greater precision in measurement of support is necessary to detect its health effects for minorities. This would fit with the findings in Study 2 that value conflicts with supervisors had a stronger relationship to negative health outcomes for minority workers. In addition, better matching of support type with stressor type (e.g., emotional support for identity-related stressors) might increase the likelihood of detecting support and health relations (see Cohen & Wills, 1985).

Conclusions

The data presented here demonstrate that substantial proportions of the variance in several measures of health outcomes are associated with social identity processes. In future studies, I hope to examine simultaneously both social identity influences and other types of work influences (e.g., time pressures and task ambiguity) on health among both minority and nonminority workers to see how the two classes of influence compare and interact. Studies comparing across minority groups and examining ethnicity by gender interactions are also needed.

No main effects of gender were observed in the studies reported here; however, because of the limited number of individuals of at least one gender in each study, statistical power for testing gender effects was poor. In fact, the possibility of an Ethnicity × Gender interaction in Study 3 was not examined because, given the small sample size for African Americans, power would have been very poor. There are, however, good reasons to suspect that the variables examined here might have different patterns and effects across various ethnicity and gender combinations (see Ford, 1985; K. James & Khoo, 1991; K. James & Levi, 1994; Shumaker & Hill, 1991).

A methodological issue that cannot be addressed in the type of cross-sectional studies reported here is whether variations in the elements of social identity are actually causal to, or simply concomitant with, physiological disturbance. Data from longitudinal studies (e.g., Tessier, Fillion, Muckle, & Gendron, 1990) are beginning to appear, however, that indicate that antecedent psychosocial stressors and individual difference factors do seem to be associated with subsequent physical illness. Similar longitudinal studies that include minority individuals are needed; such studies should examine social identity influences on health as well as more traditional work stressors.

The present studies contribute to the knowledge of factors relevant to the health of minority organization members. With enough such information, programs of intervention could be developed and aimed either at altering those factors (e.g., by training individuals to understand the cultures of out-groups in their organization in an attempt to minimize value conflicts; see K. James & Khoo, 1991; K. James & Levi, 1994) or at teaching individuals how to cope with these factors in ways that would minimize their negative effects. Research of this sort thus promises to help reduce negative outcomes for minority workers and the organizations to which they belong.

References

Allport, G. (1954). *The nature of prejudice.* Reading, MA: Addison-Wesley.

Amick, B. C., & Celentano, D. D. (1991). Structural determinants of the psychosocial work environment: Introducing technology in the work stress framework. *Ergonomics, 34,* 625–646.

Badwound, E., & Tierney, W. G. (1988). Leadership and American Indian values: The tribal college dilemma. *Journal of American Indian Education, 28,* 9–15.

Baron, R. M., & Kenny, D. A. (1986). The moderator–mediator variable distinction in social psychological research: Conceptual, strategic, and statistical considerations. *Journal of Personality and Social Psychology, 51,* 1173–1182.

Becker, E. (1973). *The denial of death.* New York: Free Press.

Bopp, M., Fritz, G., McNeil, D., Lucas-Morris, P., Strikes-With-A-Gun, G., Strikes-With-A-Gun, P., Waboose, S., & Warrior, E. L. (1989). A wholistic approach and how we used to work. *Four Worlds Exchange, 1,* 18–20.

Brockner, J. (1988). *Self-esteem at work.* Lexington, MA: Lexington Books.

Cohen, S., & Wills, T. A. (1985). Stress, social support, and the buffering hypothesis. *Psychological Bulletin, 98,* 310–357.

Crocker, J., & Luhtanen, R. (1990). Collective self-esteem and in-group bias. *Journal of Personality and Social Psychology, 58,* 60–67.

Crocker, J., & Major, B. (1989). Social stigma and self-esteem: The self-protective properties of stigma. *Psychological Review, 96,* 608–630.

Cummins, R. C. (1990). Job stress and the buffering effect of supervisory support. *Group and Organizational Studies, 15,* 92–104.

Denton, T. (1990, August). *When social support matters: Life structures, stress, and biculturalism among Black professional women.* Paper presented at the meeting of the Academy of Management, San Francisco, CA.

Erlich, H. J., & Larcom, B. E. K. (1992, November). *The effects of prejudice and ethnoviolence on workers' health.* Paper presented at the 2nd American Psychological Association and National Institute of Occupational Safety and Health Conference on Work Stress and Health, Washington, DC.

Felton, J. S., & Cole, R. (1963). The high cost of heart disease. *Circulation, 27,* 957–962.

Fernandez, J. P. (1974). *Black managers in White corporations* (U.S. Department of Labor Tech. Rep. DLMA 92-11-72-36-1). Springfield, VA: National Technical Information Service.

Fernandez, J. P. (1981). *Racism and sexism in corporate life.* Lexington, MA: Lexington Books.

Fernandez, J. P. (1991). *Managing a diverse work force: Regaining the competitive edge.* Lexington, MA: Lexington Books.

Ford, D. L. (1985). Job-related stress of the minority professional. In T. A. Beehr & R. S. Bhagat (Eds.), *Human stress and cognition in organizations* (pp. 287–323). New York: Wiley.

Frone, M. R., Russell, M., & Cooper, M. L. (1990, August). *Occupational stressors, psychosocial resources, and psychological distress: A comparison of Black and White workers.* Paper presented at the annual meeting of the Academy of Management, San Francisco.

Greenberg, J., Pyszczynski, T., & Solomon, S. (1986). The causes and consequences of need for self-esteem: A terror management theory. In R. F. Baumeister (Ed.), *Public self and private self* (pp. 189–212). New York: Springer-Verlag.

Gutierres, S. E., Saenz, D., & Green, B. L. (1994). *Occupational stress and health among White and ethnic minority university employees: A test of the person–environment fit model.* In G. Puryear Keita & J. J. Hurrell, Jr. (Eds.), *Job stress in a changing workforce: Investigating gender, diversity, and family* (pp. 107–125). Washington, DC: American Psychological Association.

Harter, S. (1983). Developmental perspectives on the self system. In E. M. Heatherington (Ed.), *Handbook of child psychology* (Vol. 4, pp. 275–385). New York: Wiley.

Ivancevich, J. M., & Matteson, M. T. (1980). *Stress at work: A managerial perspective.* Glenview, IL: Scott, Foresman.

James, K. (1994). Contrasting levels of value conflicts at work among Anglo Americans and Mexican-born and U.S.-born Mexican Americans. Manuscript in preparation.

James, K., & Khoo, G. (1991). Identity-related influences on the success of minority workers in primarily non-minority organizations. *Hispanic Journal of Behavioral Sciences, 13,* 169–192.

James, K., & Levi, D. (1994). Diversity in high technology organizations. Manuscript submitted for publication.

James, K., Lovato, C., & Cropanzano, R. (in press). Correlational and known-group comparison validation of a workplace prejudice/discrimination inventory. *Journal of Applied Social Psychology.*

James, K., Lovato, C., & Khoo, G. (1994). Social correlates of minority workers' blood pressure. *Academy of Management Journal, 37,* 383–396.

James, S. A. (1985). Psychosocial and environmental factors in Black hypertension. In W. D. Hall, E. Saunders, & N. B. Shulman (Eds.), *Hypertension in Blacks: Epidemiology, pathophysiology, and treatment* (pp. 132–143). Chicago: Year Book Medical Publications.

James, S. A., Lacroix, A. Z., Kleinbaum, D. G., & Strogatz, D. S. (1984). John Henryism and blood pressure differences among Black men: II. The role of occupational stressors. *Journal of Behavioral Medicine, 7,* 259–275.

Johnson, W., & Packer, A. (1989). *Workforce 2000: Work and workers for the 21st century.* Indianapolis, IN: Hudson Institute.

Julius, S., Jamerson, K., Mejia, A., Drause, L., Schork, N., & Jones, K. (1990). The association of borderline hypertension with target organ changes and higher coronary risk. *Journal of the American Medical Association, 264,* 354–358.

Kanter, R. M. (1977). Some effects of group proportions on group life: Skewed sex ratios and responses to token women. *American Journal of Sociology, 82,* 965–991.

Kanter, R. M., & Stein, B. (1979). *Life in organizations.* New York: Basic Books.

Katz, I., & Hass, R. G. (1988). Racial ambivalence and American value conflict: Correlational and priming studies of dual cognitive structure. *Journal of Personality and Social Psychology, 55,* 893–905.

Khoo, G. P. S. (1988). *Asian Americans with power and authority in the corporate world.* Unpublished senior thesis, University of California, Santa Cruz.

Kizer, W. M. (1987). *The healthy workplace: A blueprint for corporate action.* New York: Wiley.

Kriek, H. (1988). *Time utilization and physiological disturbance.* Unpublished doctoral dissertation, University of South Africa, Cape Town.

Luhtanen, R., & Crocker, J. (1992). A collective self-esteem scale: Self-evaluation of one's social identity. *Personality and Social Psychology Bulletin, 18,* 302–318.

Mossholder, K. W., Bedeian, A. G., & Armenakis, A. A. (1981). Role perceptions, satisfaction, and performance: Moderating effects of self-esteem and organizational level. *Organizational Behavior and Human Performance, 28,* 224–234.

Mullen, B., & Baumeister, R. F. (1987). Social loafing, social facilitation, and social impairment. In C. Hendrick (Ed.), *Group processes and intergroup relations* [Review of *Personality and Social Psychology, 9,* (pp. 189–206). Newbury Park, CA: Sage.

Pettigrew, T. F., & Martin, J. (1987). Shaping the organizational context for Black American inclusion. *Journal of Social Issues, 43,* 41–78.

Phinney, J. S. (1991). Ethnic identity and self-esteem: A review and integration. *Hispanic Journal of the Behavioral Sciences, 13,* 193–208.

Robinson, J. R., & Shaver, P. R. (1973). *Measures of social psychological attitudes*. Ann Arbor, MI: Institute for Social Research.

Saunders, E. (1987). Hypertension in Blacks. *Medical Clinics of North America, 71*, 1013–1029.

Shumaker, S. A., & Hill, D. R. (1991). Gender differences in social support and physical health. *Health Psychology, 10*, 102–111.

Starr, P. D. (1977). Marginality, role conflict, and status inconsistency as forms of stressful interaction. *Human Relations, 30*, 949–961.

Stonequist, E. V. (1937). *The marginal man*. New York: Scribner.

Tajfel, H., & Turner, J. C. (1979). An integrative theory of intergroup conflict. In W. G. Austin & S. Worchel (Eds.), *The social psychology of intergroup relations* (pp. 33–47). Pacific Grove, CA: Brooks/Cole.

Taylor, S. E., & Fiske, S. T. (1978). Salience, attention, and attribution: Top of the head phenomena. In L. Berkowitz (Ed.), *Advances in experimental social psychology* (Vol. 11, pp. 249–288). San Diego, CA: Academic Press.

Tessier, R., Fillion, L., Muckle, G., & Gendron, M. (1990). Quelques mesures-critères de stress et la prédiction de l'état de santé physique: Une étude longitudinale [Prior measurement of stress and the prediction of the state of physical disturbance: A longitudinal study]. *Canadian Journal of the Behavior Sciences, 22*, 271–281.

Triandis, H. C. (1989). The self and social behavior in differing cultural contexts. *Psychological Review, 96*, 506–520.

Triandis, H. C., Bontempo, R., Villareal, M. J., Asai, M., & Lucca, N. (1988). Individualism and collectivism: Cross-cultural perspectives on self-ingroup relationships. *Journal of Personality and Social Psychology, 54*, 323–338.

Turner, J. C. (1985). Social categorization and the self-concept: A social cognitive theory of group behavior. In E. J. Lawler (Ed.), *Advances in group processes: Theory and research* (Vol. 2, pp. 77–122). Greenwich, CT: JAI Press.

Turner, J. C., & Associates. (1986). *Rediscovering the social group: A self categorization theory*. Oxford, England: Basil Blackwell.

Unden, A.-L., Orth-Gomer, K., & Elofsson, S. (1991). Cardiovascular effects of social support in the workplace: Twenty-four hour ECG monitoring of men and women. *Psychosomatic Medicine, 53*, 50–60.

Watson, D., Pennebaker, J. W., & Folger, R. (1986). Beyond negative affectivity: Measuring stress and satisfaction in the workplace. *Journal of Organizational Behavior Management, 8*, 141–157.

Whitley, B. (1985). Sex role orientation and psychological well-being: Two meta-analyses. *Sex Roles, 12*, 209–225.

Wyler, A. R., Masuda, M., & Holmes, T. H. (1968). Seriousness of illness rating scale. *Journal of Psychosomatic Research, 11*, 363–374.

9

Work and Well-Being in an Ethnoculturally Pluralistic Society: Conceptual and Methodological Issues

Anthony J. Marsella

As a new century and a new millenium draw near, America can be characterized as a place of struggle, opportunity, and change. Americans are laboring to gain an economic foothold and to assume a comfortable existence as fully contributing citizens. To appreciate what this means for such a rich blend of ethnically diverse individuals, one must first understand how ethnocultural factors shape and determine human behavior and social institutions as well as what ethnocultural pluralism means for individual and societal well-being.

Perhaps the most powerful "battlefield" for this struggle is the workplace, where economic and social gains are won and lost daily. In this chapter, I discuss the challenges of creating a harmonious workplace for individuals with diverse backgrounds and beliefs. Although research on the role of workplace stress among ethnic groups has been rare, there are definitional and methodological issues that require careful thought for the sound study of ethnocultural pluralism. I discuss these issues and then consider the workplace itself as a critical agent for shaping a healthy and fully functional society. Finally, I urge readers to join me in expanding the definition of work to include the consequences of work for personal growth and development. Only by acknowledging the consequences of work will people learn to value the unique strengths and offerings of each individual in the thriving ethnocultural workplace.

Ethnocultural Diversity as a Sociopolitical Reality

The United States is among the world's most ethnoculturally diverse nations. According to recent national census figures, of its population of approximately 240 million people, 12% are African Americans, 9% are Hispanic Americans, and 5% are Asian Americans or Native Americans, with the remainder consisting of hundreds of other Western and non-Western nationality groups and various racial and cultural mixtures. The extent of this society's ethnocultural diversity is evident in many public arenas. For example, it has been reported that the Dade County Public School System in Florida (the fourth largest school system in the United States) includes students from 123 countries (Gray, 1991, p. 15).

Ethnocultural pluralism is also reflected in the workplace, which is becoming increasingly diverse. An analysis conducted by Gannett News Service (1993) revealed that, although in 1993 participation in the total workforce in the United States increased across all groups by 11.8% for men and 26.9% for women, the increases for ethnocultural minorities exceeded these figures dramatically. During the same time period, among African Americans, men increased 16.2% and women 29.8%; among Hispanics, men increased 63.9% and women 72.3%; among Asians, men increased 105.2% and women 107.2%; and among Native Americans, men increased 36.7% and women 56%. At present, 77.9% of the U.S. workforce are Whites, 10.4% are African Americans, 8.1% are Hispanics, 2.8% are Asians, and .6% are Native Americans.

It is clear from these figures that ethnocultural pluralism is a sociopolitical reality. Many companies and businesses are now actively seeking to improve relations among different racial and ethnocultural groups through cross-cultural communication programs. Mercer (1993) reported that, among 55 corporations surveyed (employing 1.5 million people), 32% had cross-cultural communication programs and 31% were developing them. In addition, 3 corporations provided multilingual training programs.

But although diversity in the workplace may be a matter of pure demographics, ethnocultural harmony among workers is not. Iwata and Rowe (1993) discussed some reasons for this:

> In the headlong rush to create America's rainbow workforce, companies large and small are finding agony and challenge in a seemingly simple task—melding a staff reflective of the mix of races and backgrounds in the United States. As with every rainbow, the pot of gold at the end looks easy to reach. Hire a diverse workforce, comply with the law, and reap the benefits of increased creativity, productivity, and profitability that comes from a richer talent pool. Yet the reward has proved elusive, mostly because companies that have tried to hire a good mix of workers often have no idea how to get them to work together. (p. D2)

Cultural Bias in the Workplace

There are many success stories of contemporary ethnocultural minorities achieving personal and economic successes in the workplace (e.g., in regard to Asian Americans, see Borjas, 1986; Caplan, Whitemore, & Choy, 1989; Weyl, 1989), but it remains important to understand the burden that work stress imposes on the members of minority populations. A number of employment and work-related factors are sources of stress for all workers, but these are particularly stressful for members of ethnocultural minority groups. For example, ethnocultural minorities are much more likely than the majority culture to face unemployment as well as underemployment. Those who do find jobs are much more likely to occupy low-status positions in the service industry or civil service or to be part of the manual labor force. This is compounded by the fact that minority workers often lack the benefits of a quality education and receive substandard skill and technical training, which limits opportunities for advancement and the development of special talents. Often, minority workers are forced to take high-risk jobs that may expose them to hazards, toxins, or pollution because these are the only jobs available to them. Furthermore, many minority workers find themselves in jobs that pay poorly and offer few if any benefits (Goldsmith & Blakely, 1992).

Cultural bias in the work setting is also apparent in expressed insensitivity to the values, language, dress, food, and personal styles of different ethnocultural groups. Bias is most blatantly displayed when minority workers are exposed to prejudice and racism in the work setting, expressed in the form of humor directed at minorities, jokes made at their expense, and, in some instances, physical violence.

The range of psychosocial stressors that can occur in the workplace for ethnocultural minorities (Marsella, 1987) is illustrated in Figure 1. As is indicated, the sources of work stress can be generated from conflict, confusion, deprivation, denigration, or discrepancies across five critical psychosocial behavior patterns: needs, values, roles, status, and identity.

Yet another way to look at the problem of work stress for ethnocultural minorities is to consider the endless cycle that continues to sustain the problem. The cycle begins at the ideological level with racism and ethnocentrism. This is transformed to the attitudinal level in the form of prejudice, which in turn evidences itself at the behavioral level in the form of discrimination. Discrimination then finds itself represented at the expressive level through such avenues as oppression, exploitation, stereotyping, abuse of power, and forced acculturation. The ethnocultural minority worker may find himself or herself underrepresented, outvoted, and manipulated and may experience resulting destructive consequences at the biopsychological level involving problems of

PSYCHOSOCIAL BEHAVIORS

		NEEDS	VALUES	ROLES	STATUS	IDENTITY
	CLARITY					
	CONFLICTS					
PARAMETERS	DEPRIVATION					
	DENIGRATION					
	DISCREPANCY					

Figure 1. Matrix of psychosocial stressors for ethnocultural minorities in the workplace.

inferiority, depression, anger, fear, and low self-concept levels (see Lum, 1992). The cycle from ideology to destructive consequences is illustrated in Figure 2.

Constant exposure to stress from these problems eventually erodes the coping skills of ethnocultural minorities and results in increased risks for illness and disease as well as increased problems in marital and family relationships and social functioning (Pinderhughes, 1989). Ultimately, many ethnocultural minority members find themselves relying on defensive behaviors that serve neither the purposes of the workplace nor the worker (Goldsmith & Blakely, 1992). The failure of the workplace to prize and support ethnocultural pluralism has pernicious consequences for all of society because the stressors and failures engendered in the workplace are often expressed as frustration, anger, and illness in the nonwork environment. The angry, bitter, and frustrated worker may well manifest his or her discontent through family abuse, alcoholism, substance abuse, and physical violence. Kasl (1992); Quick, Murphy, and Hurrell (1992); Marsella (1993); and Landy (1992) have provided literature reviews and updates of the many mental health consequences of work stress.

The Challenges of Ethnocultural Research

There has been proportionately little comparative research on the role of work stress among ethnocultural minorities in the United States. Although anecdotal commentaries abound, the majority of studies either have focused on members of majority cultures or have failed to consider ethnocultural minority status as a research variable. This is true for much of the psychological research literature. For example, Graham (1992) observed that the psychological lit-

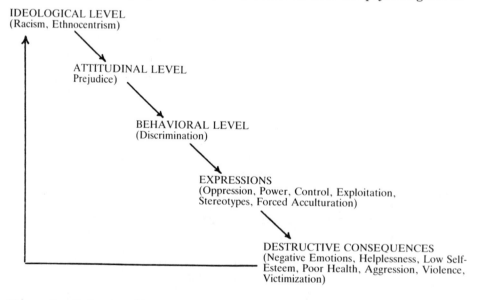

Figure 2. Cycle of problems in the ethnocultural minority workplace. From *Social Work Practice and People of Color: A Process-Stage Approach* (2nd ed., p. 155), by D. Lum, 1992, Pacific Grove, CA: Brooks/Cole. Copyright 1992 by Brooks/Cole. Adapted by permission.

erature is "in danger of becoming raceless" because it has given only limited attention to research on African Americans and, implicitly, other minority groups. She did note that, among the few studies that were conducted between 1970 and 1990, the emphasis was placed on job training, occupational attitudes, test bias, and managerial styles. In contrast, as previously noted, the international research literature on work and work stress and satisfaction has been rapidly growing (e.g., Hui, 1990; Tannenbaum, 1980; Triandis, 1991), revealing numerous differences in worker attitudes, satisfaction, and performance patterns.

Defining Diversity

To respond to the sociopolitical realities of ethnocultural pluralism, it is essential to become more informed regarding the foundations of ethnocultural research. To this end, an understanding of certain terms is needed. Specifically, these terms are *ethnocentrism, culture, ethnocultural identity*, and *equivalency*.

Ethnocentricity. One of the major reasons that ethnocultural factors are often ignored or denigrated is because of ethnocentrism. *Ethnocentrism* has been defined as "a habitual, and often unconscious, tendency or disposition to evaluate foreign people or cultures by the standards and practices of one's own ethnocultural group [and an] inclination to view one's own way of life as the only proper or moral way with a resulting sense of personal and cultural superiority" (Websters Third New International Dictionary, 1981).

Brewer and Campbell (1976) and Triandis (1990) have pointed out that all people have the following tendencies: (a) to define what goes on in their own cultures as "natural" and "correct" and other cultural practices as "unnatural" and "incorrect"; (b) to perceive in-group customs as universally valid, that is, "what is good for us is good for everybody"; (c) to think that in-group norms, roles, and values are obviously correct; (d) to believe that it is natural to help and cooperate with members of one's in-group; (e) to act in ways that favor the in-group; (f) to feel proud of the in-group; and (g) to feel hostility, suspicion, and distrust toward out-groups.

It is likely that ethnocentrism has its roots in primitive behavior patterns that may have been conditioned in the ancient past. Clearly, there is survival value inherent in familiarity. In primordial days, strangers were most likely a source of danger. But modern society requires that "primitive" responses to differences be altered by more reasoned approaches. People can no longer accept the idea that because ethnocentrism may be "natural" it can be tolerated in an ethnoculturally pluralistic society. Rather, efforts must be made to raise public consciousness and expand information about the dangers of ethnocentrism.

Culture. Marsella and Kameoka (1989) offered the following definition of *culture*:

> Shared learned behavior which is transmitted from one generation to an-
> other for purposes of promoting individual and societal survival and ad-
> aptation. Culture has both external representations (e.g., artifacts, roles,
> institutions) and internal representations (e.g., values/attitudes/beliefs, cog-
> nitive/affective styles, consciousness patterns, epistemologies). (p. 233)

It should be noted that because culture helps shape people's values, attitudes, beliefs, lifestyles, epistemologies, consciousness, and even their sense
of causality, time, and space, individuals from different cultural groups differ
from one another in numerous and profound ways. One should not assume
that because some universals exist in human behavior people are all the same.
To be Japanese is to experience the world very differently from someone who
is European. Around the world, the thousands of diverse cultures and sub-
cultures offer people contrasting ways of life that have adapted to distinct
historical, geographical, and biophysical variations. Because of the "blindness"
encouraged by ethnocentrism, it is difficult for people to understand, appreciate, and acknowledge cultural differences and the implications that these
differences have for everyday life.

Although researchers have been interested in ethnocultural differences in
work, the topic has often been ignored by employers, managers, and supervisors. As a result, ethnocultural variations in worker behavior have not been
considered important to productivity and to worker well-being. Many companies simply assume that all workers will perform all tasks with equal motivation, interest, dedication, and skill because individual differences among
workers are expected to yield to productivity concerns. Of course, this is not
the case. With the growing cultural diversity in the workforce that is occurring
throughout the Western world, it will be necessary to give increased attention
to ethnocultural variations among workers.

In combination with biological, psychological, and environmental factors,
culture helps to shape human behavior. Culture influences human behavior
by shaping (a) values, attitudes, beliefs, and standards of normality and ab-
normality; (b) notions of time, space, and causality; (c) patterns of human
communications and interaction, including verbal, nonverbal, and paraverbal
communications; (d) expressive styles in clothing, food preferences, and rec-
reation; (e) familial, marital, and child-rearing practices and preferences; (f)
preferred cognitive styles and coping and problem-solving styles; (g) interpersonal relationship patterns, especially regarding authorities, gender, and the
elderly; and (h) the structure and dynamics of institutions, such as the family,
schools, military, government, religion, the socioeconomic system, and the
workplace. If one considers the impact of these influences for the workplace,
it is immediately obvious that virtually all aspects of work reflect cultural
variation, including attitudes toward work, employer–employee relationships,
worker relationships, communications, human–machine relationships, work
effort, energy expenditures, and so forth.

Ethnocultural identity. A third concept important for an informed understanding of ethnocultural pluralism is ethnocultural identity. Marsella (1990)
defined *ethnocultural identity* as "the extent to which an individual or group

is committed to both endorsing and practicing a set of values, beliefs, and behaviors which are associated with a particular ethnocultural tradition" (pp. 7–8).

Among ethnocultural minorities, the variations in behavior within a given ethnocultural group are dramatic and profound, and any effort to group people together for research on the basis of the largest possible ethnocultural dimension (e.g., as Arabs, Asians, Blacks, or Hispanics) contributes to the likelihood of errors. Even within these larger categories, shared culture may be minimal because of geographical, genetic, and psychocultural variations. In brief, researchers must emphasize the variations and patterns within an ethnocultural tradition and heritage and must not simply group subjects into general categories when conducting research.

The acknowledgment of ethnocultural variation has also challenged old models of acculturation. Scholars are no longer content with views of ethnocultural identity that expect to find a linear progression toward acculturation and assimilation (i.e., that each new generation becomes progressively more American). Such views considered the dominant ethnocultural majority as being the end point toward which all ethnocultural minorities were striving. As a result, the failure to acculturate to the majority could result in being negatively labeled *bicultural, marginal, anomic, deviant, multicultural,* or *traditional.* The ideal of the past—full linguistic and social acculturation—is being questioned in research into today's widely varied workplace.

Greenfield (1991) had the following comments about people's ambivalent views of ethnocultural identity:

> Our main problem with the idea of ethnicity . . . is that we spend half our time embracing the idea and the other half repudiating it. When we are not thanking our lucky stars that we have assimilated ourselves into ethnicity-free Americanness, we are organizing ourselves into ethnic extraction lobbies and/or singing the praises of newly rediscovered ethnic consciousness. The fundamental contradiction extends to our attitude toward people and countries abroad. (p. 70)

Measuring Diversity

Ethnocultural Identity

If research on ethnocultural identity is to progress and replace or complement current reliance on broader ethnic categories (i.e., Arab, Asian, Black, or Hispanic), it is critical that efforts be made to develop valid and reliable methods for assessing ethnocultural identity. Marsella (1990) has noted a number of different ways to assess ethnocultural identity. First, one could use attitude questionnaires to determine the extent to which respondents endorse attitudes that are consistent with traditional cultural views and positions. Second, behavior checklists might be used to measure the extent to which respondents endorse a series of specific behaviors (e.g., speaks the language, eats the food, or reads ethnic newspapers). The Multiple Identity Profile Scale offers a third option for assessing the extent to which respondents affirm their affiliation with and support for different ethnocultural traditions (e.g., with such items as "To what extent do you consider yourself to be Japanese, Hawaiian, Chinese, Filipino, Samoan?"). Finally, semantic and behavioral differential scales could be developed from bipolar adjective and behavioral intention scales to measure the extent to which respondents' descriptions of themselves parallel descriptions of baseline ethnocultural groups.

Equivalency

If measurement concepts and methods are to be valid when they are applied across cultures, then they should meet certain requirements regarding equivalency in language, concepts, scales, and norms. By *equivalency*, I am referring to the extent to which these topics are similar or equivalent for the different cultural groups under study (see Marsella & Kameoka, 1989).

Four types of equivalency are important for accurate measurement and assessment in the workplace:

1. Linguistic equivalency: Is there an accurate and valid language translation of measures?
2. Conceptual equivalency: Are concepts from one culture equivalent to concepts in another (e.g., dependency, loyalty, or anger)? What does work mean across cultures?
3. Scale equivalency: Are the scales used to measure a concept equivalent in meaning and scalar implication (e.g., true–false, Likert scales, or scaling in general)?
4. Normative equivalency: Are the norms for tests derived from appropriate population samples? Should Eurocentric norms be applied in tests of African Americans, American Indians, Asian Americans, Hispanic Americans, and so on?

Ethnosemantics

If the measures being used in a study do not meet the equivalency challenges, then a researcher may want to consider developing instruments specifically for the culture under study. This can be done through the use of ethnosemantic methods, a series of techniques that have long been established in anthropology to reduce ethnocentricity and bias (see Marsella, 1987). For example, it cannot be assumed that "work" as it is defined and measured in the Western world is relevant to the world of non-Western people. It is not simply a question of translation but a question of worldview and of the implications that different worldviews may have for understanding human behavior.

A good example of this is the Japanese phenomenon called *karoshi*, or "death from overwork." Recent newspaper articles (see Jones, 1993; Nickerson, 1991) have described Japan's concern with the growing number of Japanese businessmen who have died from overwork because of the "perverse pride in the extraordinary sacrifices of time, energy, family life, and health that company loyalty demands" (Nickerson, 1991, p. D1). This loyalty emerges from Japanese socialization practices that encourage collective identity and well-being at the expense of individual identity and well-being. According to Jones (1993), "karoshi occurs most commonly in workplaces where jobs require strenuous effort and where people work without the help of other employees. It usually refers to acute heart failure following high blood pressure, arteriosclerosis or cerebral hemorrhage" (p. A11).

As is well known, the Japanese company or corporation mimics the family. It offers group identity and economic security, and it expects in return extraordinary effort, diligence, devotion, and loyalty. The price is high. Hiroshi Kawahito, the head of Japan's National Council for Victims of Karoshi, has stated that "Japanese workers are sacrificing their health, and all too often their lives for the sake of their companies" (Nickerson, 1991, p. D1). He claimed that nearly 10,000 Japanese die each year because of overwork. In response to this problem, the Japanese Ministry of Labor has initiated a $2 million study of job-related illness.

Work Values

In addition to differences in race, gender, skills, education, ages, lifestyles, and ability levels (Jamieson & O'Mara, 1991), individuals vary in their attitudes toward work. When researchers measure occupational stress, they must acknowledge that different cultures view work in different ways and that the contextual nature of work varies widely among cultures. Some of the dimensions on which cultures differ include (a) the importance of work; (b) work-related values, attitudes, beliefs, and needs; (c) perceptions of work and the workplace; (d) expectations regarding work roles; (e) commitment to work responsibilities and role patterns; (f) the nature of job satisfaction and job satisfaction levels; (g) managerial–worker relationships; (h) workplace communication patterns; (i) decision latitude and personal control preferences and patterns; (j) workplace impact on psychological needs; (k) design of the workplace; (l) patterns of organizational loyalty and alienation; (m) preferences for certain approaches for conflict and dispute resolution; and (n) patterns of health and well-being, especially as these are expressed in emotional communications.

Clearly, the ethnocultural background of a worker has a profound impact on the entire spectrum of his or her work-related behaviors. For example, workers from a Chinese cultural tradition may well be imbued with a Confucian work ethic that emphasizes sobriety, educational achievement, family obligations, respect for authority, and hierarchical social status (e.g., Kahn, 1979; Kahn & Byosiere, 1991). In contrast, a Polynesian's behavior in the workplace may be driven more by a group orientation toward productivity without reference to personal achievement (Marsella, Oliviera, Plummer, & Crabbe, in press). Hui (1990) has suggested that cultural values constitute the basic foundation for job satisfaction because they determine worker values.

The worker's values, in turn, mediate job outcomes and job expectations, both of which influence job satisfaction.

Tannenbaum (1980), Hui (1990), and Triandis (1991) have provided excellent overviews of the cross-cultural literature on organizational psychology and work-related behaviors, especially with reference to work attitudes, managerial patterns, leadership styles, and communication styles. Hofstede's (1980) important book on cultural differences in work values among collectivistic and individualistic cultures has become a landmark cross-cultural study.

For many non-Western ethnocultural groups, an orientation that emphasizes self and individual decision making is in direct opposition to their sociocentric and collectivistic traditions. This creates added stress for them within the workplace because such opposition brings many of the individualistic–collectivistic conflicts to the forefront of daily behavior. In some instances, a bizarre accommodation strategy is played out in which the ethnocultural minority member must learn one set of behaviors for the workplace and another for home life. This is sometimes called *biculturalism*, and, although it may be a virtue, it may also result in stress.

The Power of the Workplace

Many of the conflicts and debates regarding the ambivalence toward ethnocultural pluralism are played out in the workplace. For contemporary American society, the workplace is a critical location for addressing and resolving the issues associated with ethnocultural pluralism because it is where people from different races and cultures must work together for personal and economic productivity and growth. In fact, it is in the workplace that cultural learning, cultural suppression, or both occur the most frequently and intensely, with the possible exception of in schools. In the workplace, society's long legacy of ethnocentric bias and racial and cultural hatred is most often vented and continued. Therefore, the workplace is one of the most important locations in which to raise consciousness about ethnocultural pluralism.

Quite simply, the workplace must be recognized as a socialization context that is as important as the family and the school in shaping society's well-being and future. To the extent that organizations abandon this responsibility in favor of a pure "profit motive," without respect for the larger social functions and responsibilities of the work setting, the workplace may survive commercially, but only at the expense of the well-being of the worker and the larger society of which he or she is a member. The research long has been clear in pointing out the close relationship between quality of life and work satisfaction (e.g., Rice, Near, & Hunt, 1980). Recently, in fact, Galinsky (1992) reported that work stress spills over into family life more than family-life problems affect work.

It is within the context of the workplace that ethnocultural pluralism—as a value, an ideology, a historical truism, and a biosocial and evolutionary principle—may assume its greatest meaning and importance. The workplace is a powerful arena for shaping ideas, values, and normative behavioral patterns. If the workplace is to be a resource, however, ideas regarding the nature of its responsibilities toward workers and toward larger society will need to be changed.

Work as a True Human Resource

As long as people choose to limit their definition of *work* to the expenditure of energy (i.e., labor) for purposes of financial compensation (i.e., wages), the economic, political, and spiritual growth and development of American society will be limited. Marsella (1993), offered a human resources definition of work that considers the consequences of work for personal growth, development, and well-being. He concluded by defining *work* in the following way:

> Those activities (i.e., labor) which an individual engages in for purposes of (1) financial reward and compensation, (2) personal satisfaction and development, and (3) the promotion of psychosocial wellbeing and survival. These activities result in the production of a particular product (i.e., material goods, services, ideas and/or knowledge and wisdom) which have individual and/or societal value and worth for which there is often compensation in the form of wages. These activities have far reaching consequences for an individual's sense of self worth, dignity, and physical and mental wellbeing. (Marsella, 1993, p. 196).

The ethnoculturally sensitive workplace proactively addresses the challenges of salutogenesis and pathogenesis for workers and the organization through the implementation of enlightened policies and programs. Such policies and programs must include the following basics: (a) strong commitment to Equal Employment Opportunity and Affirmative Action philosophies and programs; (b) vigorous on-the-job training opportunities; (c) race and cultural relations programs; (d) multilingual communications; (e) public relations programs that communicate a commitment to ethnocultural pluralism; (f) frequent worker evaluation of the workplace climate and culture with regard to pluralism and diversity; (g) attention to elements of job satisfaction for ethnocultural minority workers; and (h) sensitivity to and awareness of ethnocultural differences in human behavior and the role that these differences play in work.

Social psychologists have long understood that racial and ethnic prejudices can be increased or decreased by creating certain contexts that reduce competition and promote cooperation across racial and ethnic lines. For example, Amir (1969; see also Lum, 1992) noted that prejudice can be reduced when four conditions are present: (a) when there is equal-status contact and power distribution between members of various ethnic groups, (b) when an authority favorably promotes intergroup contact, (c) when intergroup contact is rewarded, and (d) when members of both groups interact functionally in important activities, developing common goals or superordinate goals that rank higher than the goals of each group.

Ethnocultural Pluralism in the Enlightened Workplace

The value of ethnocultural pluralism for American society and the American workplace has been gaining increasing credence in recent years. Portes and Rumbaut (1990) have described the historical basis for such an appreciation:

> Immigrants and refugees will continue to come, giving rise to energetic communities, infusing new blood in local labor markets, filling positions at different levels of the economy, and adding to the diversity of sounds, sights, and tastes in our cities. The history of America has been to a large extent, the history of its immigrants—their progress reflecting and simultaneously giving impulse to the nation's expansion. Although problems and struggles are inevitable along the way, in the long run, the diverse talents and energies of newcomers will reinforce the vitality of American society and the richness of its culture. (p. 246)

Ethnocultural diversity can be promoted without the destruction of the larger social fabric of society. Such diversity can be used as an expression of the self-assertive tendencies of a group of people, helping them to define and refine their nature and identity while still promoting the group's linkages with the larger society. But the key to this pathway is equality. Ethnocultural diversity is not the source of the many national and international conflicts people face. Rather, the source of the problem resides in the prejudice, intolerance, bias, and hostility that are generated when people fail to cope with ethnocultural diversity. A society can tolerate extensive ethnocultural diversity if it is willing to provide members from different ethnocultural traditions with equal opportunity and freedom. Within this kind of society, diversity will thrive, as will a commitment to national unity.

How much ethnocultural diversity can a society take before it ceases to function as a whole? The answer to this is simple: Ethnocultural diversity can exist in proportion to the society's commitment to guarantee equality, justice, and opportunity to all citizens, regardless of ethnocultural differences. The citizens will then act to preserve the unity of the society (Marsella, 1994).

The Nobel Prize Winner Octavio Paz recognized the importance of diversity for cultural survival. He wrote:

> What sets worlds in motion is the interplay of differences, their attractions and repulsions. Life is plurality, death is uniformity. By suppressing differences and peculiarities, by eliminating different civilizations and cultures, progress weakens life and favors death. The idea of single civilization for everyone, implicit in the cult of progress and technique, impoverishes and mutilates us. Every view of the world that becomes extinct, every culture that disappears, diminishes a possibility of life. (in Highwater, 1981, p.vii)

Paz understood that ethnocultural variability, like biological variability, promotes and sustains life. To the extent that people insist on homogeneity, they are closing themselves to needed options and alternatives. Successful evolution requires variability, because variability creates the differences necessary for adaptation to changing environmental demands. The "unenlightened" society will continue to insist on "cultural homogeneity" and, in doing so, will foster its own demise. The enlightened society, and the enlightened workplace, will acknowledge and promote the diversity that will encourage its survival.

References

Amir, Y. (1969). Contact hypothesis in ethnic relations. *Psychological Bulletin, 71*, 319–342.

Borjas, G. (1986). The self-employment experience of immigrants. *Journal of Human Resources, 21*, 485–506.

Brewer, M., & Campbell, D. (1976). Ethnocentrism and intergroup attitudes. New York: Wiley.

Caplan, N., Whitemore, J., & Choy, M. (1989). *The boat people and achievement in America*. Ann Arbor: University of Michigan Press.

Galinsky, E. (1992, December). Work stress: A survey of 2,399 employees of a large corporation. In N. Youngstrom, Juggling jobs and family? Sensitive employer helps. *APA Monitor*, p. 33.

Gannett News Service. (1993, September 26). The changing face of corporate America. *Honolulu Advertiser*, p. D2.

Goldsmith, W. W., & Blakely, E. J. (1992). *Separate societies: Poverty and inequality in U.S. cities*. Philadelphia: Temple University Press.

Graham, S. (1992). Most of the subjects were White and middle class. *American Psychologist, 47*, 629–639.

Gray, P. (1991, July 8). Whose America? *Time*, pp. 12, 15.

Greenfield, M. (1991, April 1). A messy new world order. *Newsweek*, p. 70.

Highwater, J. (1981). *The primal mind: Vision and reality in Indian America*. New York: New American Library.

Hofstede, G. (1980). *Culture's consequences: International differences in work-related values*. Beverly Hills, CA: Sage.

Hui, H. (1990). *Applied cross-cultural psychology*. Newbury Park, CA: Sage.

Iwata, E., & Rowe, J. (1993, September 26). In reality, diversity is tough. *Honolulu Advertiser*, p. D2.

Jamieson, D., & O'Mara, J. (1991). *Managing workforce 2000: Gaining the diversity advantage*. San Francisco: Jossey-Bass.

Jones, G. (1993, August 12). Too much work, no play killing some Japanese. *Honolulu Star Bulletin*, p. A11.

Kahn, H. (1979). *World economic development: 1979 and beyond*. Boulder, CO: Westview Press.

Kahn, R. L., & Byosiere, P. (1991). Stress in organizations. In M. Dunnette & L. Hough (Eds.), *Handbook of industrial and organizational psychology* (Vol. 3, 2nd ed., pp. 571–650). Palo Alto, CA: Consulting Psychologists Press.

Kasl, S. (1992). Surveillance of psychological disorders in the workplace. In G. Keita & S. Sauter (Eds.), *Work and well-being: An agenda for the 1990s* (pp. 73–95). Washington, DC: American Psychological Association.

Landy, F. (1992). Work design and stress. In G. Keita & S. Sauter (Eds.), *Work and well-being: An agenda for the 1990s* (pp. 119–167). Washington, DC: American Psychological Association.

Lum, D. (1992). *Social work practice and people of color*. Belmont, CA: Brooks/Cole.

Marsella, A. J. (1987). The measurement of depressive experience and disorders across cultures. In A. J. Marsella, R. Hirschfeld, & M. Katz (Eds.), *The measurement of depression* (pp. 376–398). New York: Guilford Press.

Marsella, A. J. (1990, June). Ethnocultural identity: The "new" independent variable in cross-cultural research. *Focus: Newsletter of The American Psychological Association Division on Minorities*, 7–8.

Marsella, A. J. (1993). The measurement of emotion in the workplace. In F. LaFerla & L. Levi (Eds.), *Towards a healthier work environment: Basic concepts and methods of measurement* (pp. 169–198). Copenhagen, Denmark: World Health Organization.

Marsella, A. J. (1994). Ethnocultural diversity and international refugees: Challenges for the global community. In A. J. Marsella, T. Bornemann, S. Ekblad, & J. Orley (Eds.), *Amidst peril and pain: The mental health and well-being of the world's refugees* (pp. 341–364). Washington, DC: American Psychological Association.

Marsella, A. J., & Kameoka, V. (1989). Ethnocultural issues in the assessment of psychopathology. In S. Wetzler (Ed.), *Measuring mental illness: Psychometric assessment for clinicians* (pp. 229–256). Washington, DC: American Psychiatric Press.

Marsella, A. J., Oliviera, J., Plummer, M., & Crabbe, K. (in press). Native Hawaiian concepts of culture, mind, and well-being. In H. McCubbin, A. Thompson, & E. Thompson (Eds.), *Stress and resiliency in racial minority families in the United States*. Madison: University of Wisconsin Press.

Mercer, W. (1993, September 26). Survey of diversity training in corporations. *Honolulu Advertiser*, p. D2.

Nickerson, C. (1991, May 5). Overwork, or "Karoshi," is killing thousands. *Akron Beacon Journal*, p. D1.

Pinderhughes, E. (1989). *Understanding race, ethnicity, and power*. New York: Free Press.

Portes, A., & Rumbaut, R. (1990). *Immigrant America: A portrait*. Los Angeles: University of California Press.

Quick, J. C., Murphy, L. R., & Hurrell, J. J., Jr. (Eds.). (1992). *Stress and well-being at work: Assessments and interventions for occupational mental health*. Washington, DC: American Psychological Association.

Rice, R., Near, J., & Hunt, R. (1980). The job satisfaction/life satisfaction relationship: A review of empirical research. *Basic and Applied Social Psychology, 1*, 37–64.

Tannenbaum, A. (1980). Organizational psychology. In H. Triandis & R. Brislin (Eds.), *Handbook of cross-cultural psychology* (Vol. 5). Boston: Allyn & Bacon.

Triandis, H. (1990). Theoretical concepts that are applicable to the analyses of ethnocentrism. In R. Brislin (Ed.), *Applied cross-cultural psychology* (pp. 34–35). Newbury Park, CA: Sage.

Triandis, H. (1991). Cross-cultural industrial and organizational psychology. In M. Dunnette (Ed.), *Handbook of industrial and organizational psychology*. Chicago: Rand McNally.

Webster's Third New International Dictionary. (1981). Springfield, MA: Merriam-Webster.

Weyl, N. (1989). *The geography of American achievement*. Washington, DC: Scott-Townsend.

Part III

Age

Introduction

The labor force is not only changing with respect to gender, ethnicity, and culture, but in the age of workers as well. Labor force projections indicate that between now and the year 2005, the participation rate of U.S. workers between 45 and 65 years of age will grow most rapidly. The research presented in this part of the book examines how work-related stress affects this expanding older group of workers.

First, Wooten, Sulzer, and Cornwell investigate the effects of career and employment expectancies resulting from job loss as well as the effects of age and financial strain on the stress-related anxiety of adults who have lost their jobs.

Next, Staats, Partlo, Armstrong-Stassen, and Plimpton examine experiences of job stress and quality of life in an often overlooked population: older working widows. They explore similarities and differences between this population and older married women, examining both future expectations and present experiences of quality of life.

The issue of the aging workforce has been the focus of a major initiative in Finland. The Finnish Institute of Occupational Health's multidisciplinary program, "Respect for the Aging," is described in the final chapter of this part. In this chapter, Huuhtanen discusses the methodology and results of the attitude surveys of this project, which assessed attitudes toward work and retirement and differences and similarities between work-motivated and retirement-motivated groups with respect to health, physical capacity, stress, and mental resources.

10

The Effects of Age, Financial Strain, and Vocational Expectancies on the Stress-Related Affect of Adult Job Losers

Kevin C. Wooten, Jefferson L. Sulzer, and John M. Cornwell

Increasingly, individual employees across vocations and industries have become susceptible to unemployment possibilities. As society in general, and the workforce specifically, becomes increasingly older and less financially secure, the psychological trauma resulting from mergers, acquisitions, plant closings, and corporate restructuring becomes increasingly more alarming. Although considerable research on the effects of job loss has been conducted, a much more rigorous and comprehensive approach needs to be taken, especially with regard to the role of age and financial resources. In reviewing the research agenda for involuntary job loss, Leana and Ivancevich (1987) observed that "more information is needed about how the negative effects of job loss are incurred, what demographic, financial, and psychological factors moderate these effects, and what factors exacerbate them" (pp. 308–309).

The purpose of this study was, therefore, to investigate two variables known to be related to or to moderate job-loss reactions. Specifically, we examined the effects of age and financial strain in regard to their impact on the stress-related anxiety of adults who have lost their jobs (hereinafter referred to as *adult job losers*). More important, however, we sought to investigate the effects of career and employment expectancies resulting from job loss. Although such effects have been suggested in numerous models (Catalano & Dooley, 1977; DeFrank & Ivancevich, 1986; Fineman, 1979; Kaufman, 1982; Leana & Feldman, 1988) and in literature reviews (Archer & Rhodes, 1987; Dooley & Catalano, 1986; Horwitz, 1984; Jahoda, 1988; Leana & Ivancevich, 1987; Warr, 1984), to date no one has systematically explored such expectancies among adults. This is particularly true in the context of a causal model with variables (i.e., age and financial strain) known to moderate job-loss reactions.

Age and Job Loss

Numerous studies have linked the age of unemployed people to depressive affect (Daniel, 1974; Dressler, 1986; Hepworth, 1980b; Fryer & Warr, 1984;

Jackson & Warr, 1984; Leventman, 1981; Warr, 1982; Warr & Jackson, 1984, 1985), to time use (Hepworth, 1980a), to fulfilling the expectations of others (Warr & Jackson, 1985), to employment commitment and job seeking (Jackson & Warr, 1984), and to ability to concentrate (Fryer & Warr, 1984). In general, these studies have found middle-aged job searchers to be most susceptible to poor psychological health, with older job losers having greater difficulty thinking clearly, living up to the expectations of others, and engaging in job search as well as experiencing lower employment commitment. However, no studies have reported links between age and career or job expectancies in an adult population.

Financial Strain

Interest in the effects of financial strain on attitudes of the unemployed can be traced back to the early work of Eisenburg and Lazarsfeld (1938). More recently, studies examining links between financial strain and affective variables have yielded high clarity. Wilcox and Franke (1963), as well as Estes and Willensky (1978), found that those with the highest financial strain were couples with school-age dependent children. Warr and Jackson (1984) and Payne and Jones (1981) have reported that unemployed men with financial worries and strain experienced poorer psychological health, in comparison with unemployed men without such worries. Financial strain also has been found to be predictive of family strain (Klandermans, 1980).

Vocational Expectancies

Studies involving career and job expectancies of unemployed youth have produced several trends applicable to this study. Confidence in finding a job has been positively related to job need, search efforts, and job-search attitudes and negatively related to depression, hopelessness, and self-esteem (Feather, 1983; Feather & Barber, 1983; Feather & Davenport, 1981; Feather & O'Brien, 1986; Singer, Stacey, & Ritchie, 1987; Vinokur, Caplan, & Willliams, 1987). Kanfer and Hulin (1985) found search expectancies—such as confidence in sourcing job opportunities, filling out applications, and properly investigating job leads—to be related to age, length of unemployment, job performance, attitude, and educational level of outplaced hospital employees.

On the basis of this wealth of literature, we made four predictions. First, we hypothesized that age would be negatively related to career and employment expectancies. Second, we predicted that lower career expectancies would be associated with poorer mental health. (However, because the scales we used to measure expectancies were purely developmental, we did not propose specific linkages.) Third, we hypothesized that financial strain would be negatively related to anxiety. Here, financial strain was operationalized as weeks following job loss until onset of distress and lack of economic resources. Thus, the higher the number of weeks, the lower the strain experienced. Finally, we expected that feelings of anxiety would be predictive of depressive affect.

Method

Respondents

The participants in this study were 426 individuals who had recently lost their jobs. All participants were corporate-sponsored clients of a nationwide out-placement firm. The research sample was geographically diverse, representing residents of over 40 major U.S. cities and metropolitan areas. Over 69% of the sample was composed of executives, administrators, or managers, with 16.87% being specialty professionals. The sample was heterogeneous with respect to industry sector, with the largest groups being composed of former employees in the manufacturing industry (12.49%); communications and public utilities (5.10%); retail trades (5.18%); and the financial, insurance, and real estate sectors (24.28%).

The sample was 71.8% male, and 28.2% female; 91.6% of respondents were White, 4.5% were Black, 1.9% were Hispanic, 1.2% were Asian, and .7% were from other minority groups. The average age was 42.40 years. Respondents had earned an average salary of $59,310 and had average job tenure of 9.23 years. Thirty-four percent of respondents had lost a job at least once before. The average number of dependents for respondents was 1.73, with 70.3% of the sample married, 17.9% single, 10.8% separated or divorced, and 1% widowed.

Measures

We used a pencil-and-paper survey that was administered as part of a larger study.

Employment expectancies. On the basis of work by Feather (1983), Feather and Bond (1983), and Feather and Davenport (1981), eight items were developed to measure employment expectancies. The area of employment expectancy involved confidence in reemployment, belief in chances relative to others with similar abilities and skills, chances relative to others with similar education, chances relative to others the same age, chances relative to others with similar experience, confidence relative to others at a similar salary level, confidence in getting a job at a better salary, and confidence in getting a job using one's skills and abilities. Responses to each item were made on Likert-type scales ranging from 1 (*not confident*) to 5 (*very confident*).

Career expectancies. Five items were used to assess career expectancies. The first three items asked subjects to rate the degree to which they were confident that their remaining work years would provide opportunities for growth, be personally satisfying, and meet their financial needs. Responses were made on Likert-type scales ranging from 1 (*not confident*) to 5 (*very confident*). The last two items asked subjects to rate their chances during the remainder of their work years concerning change of career or having to move to another industry. Responses to these items were made on scales ranging from 1 (*very low*) to 5 (*very high*).

Financial resources. Four items were used to ascertain the financial resources of job losers. First, subjects were asked whether or not members of their household were currently employed. The second item asked subjects to what extent they were able to rely on a spouse or other family members to assist them financially during their job search. The third item asked respondents to assess the extent to which they could rely on savings and other sources of income during their job search. Items 2 and 3 were scaled such that each subject could respond in one of four ways: *to a great extent* (3), *to some extent* (2), *to a little extent* (1), or *none* (0). The fourth item asked subjects how many weeks they could go before becoming financially distressed.

Affective reactions. Affective reactions of job losers was measured with the Positive and Negative Affect Schedule (PANAS-X; Watson & Clark, 1989a). The PANAS-X is a 44-item inventory measuring the mood states of fear and anxiety, anger and hostility, guilt, sadness and depression, shyness, fatigue, surprise, general positive affect, and general negative affect. This instrument is based on the cumulative efforts of researchers to derive a factor theory of dispositions and affect (Watson & Clark, 1984; Watson, Clark, & Tellegen, 1988).

Each item was scaled to reflect the affect of the respondent since receiving news of their job loss. In accordance with the PANAS-X manual, each respondent was asked to rate descriptions of their different feelings and emotions on a 5-point scale, ranging from 1 (*very slightly*) to 5 (*extremely*). For this study, only the scales involving fear, hostility, guilt, and depression were used.

Procedure

Individual and group outplacement clients were given preaddressed research packets. Clients were administered research packets when they first entered the outplacement program, typically when they completed other psychological tests for assessing interest and personality.

Results

Descriptive Statistics and Correlations

All statistical tests performed in this study involved over 390 subjects. Table 1 shows the descriptive characteristics for the items and scales. Among the 13 items used to measure vocational expectancies, expectations about obtaining a better salary were rated the lowest, and job chances in general were rated the highest. Among affective variables, anxiety and fear were rated the highest and guilt was rated the lowest. The means and standard deviations for affective

Table 1. Means and Standard Deviations for Items and Scales

Measure	n	M	SD
Financial resources			
Household	420	1.25	0.70
Reliance	419	1.19	1.06
Resource	421	1.87	0.91
Strain	409	39.54	89.00
Employment expectancies			
Job chances	419	4.26	0.90
Chances—ability	419	4.00	0.75
Chances—education	420	4.10	0.77
Chances—age	419	4.14	0.76
Chances—experience	410	3.97	0.72
Confidence—job salary	419	3.45	1.24
Confidence—better salary	420	2.98	1.32
Confidence—skill use	420	4.09	0.86
Career expectancies			
Confidence—career growth	420	3.91	1.04
Confidence—career satisfaction	420	3.97	0.93
Confidence—financial needs	420	3.92	0.97
Field change	420	3.26	1.16
Industry change	419	3.49	1.10
Affective reactions			
Anxiety	405	15.20	5.95
Depression	405	11.61	4.56
Hostility	404	13.12	5.56
Guilt	404	9.27	4.46

variables were similar to those reported by the developers of the PANAS-X (Watson & Clark, 1989a, 1989b).

As shown in Table 2, a variety of significant relationships were found between various demographic variables and vocational expectancies. Age was a significant predictor of 7 of the 13 items, organizational tenure was significantly related to 6 items, education was significantly related to 4 items, and number of dependents was significantly related to concerns about salary. However, gender, marital status, previous job loss, and job classification were not found to be good predictors of career and employment expectations. Examination of Table 3 illustrates that demographic variables and affect were not particularly related, with the exception of anxiety. Here, the higher the previous salary and job classification, the higher the anxiety.

Table 4 shows that approximately half of the relationships between financial data and affect reached significance. Again, financial resources (i.e., savings) was found to be the best predictor of affect. Table 5 shows that 43 of 52 vocational expectancies–affect relationships reached significance. In general, lowered employment and career expectancies were related to heightened anxiety, depression, hostility, and guilt. Items measuring anticipated changes in occupational fields and changes in industries were not particularly related

Table 2. Correlations Between Demographic Variables and Vocational Expectancies

Expectancy	Age	Sex	Marital status	Dependents	Organizational tenure	Job class	Salary	Previous job loss	Education
Job chances	-.127**	.044	-.051	-.036	-.099	.018	-.106*	.059	-.055
Chances—ability	-.079	-.023	.039	.013	-.123*	.079	.051	.013	.000
Chances—education	-.072	-.021	.000	-.040	-.006	.006	.000	-.001	-.110*
Chances—age	.043	.000	.051	-.031	.039	.055	.036	-.010	.019
Chances—experience	-.016	-.058	-.015	.000	-.047	.047	.012	-.019	.030
Job salary	-.187**	.032	-.089	-.112*	-.221**	.012	-.057	-.005	.109*
Better salary	-.215**	.056	-.008	-.120*	.201**	-.008	-.096	-.018	.090
Use skill	.003	.037	.029	.007	-.161**	.122*	.055	.074	.055
Career growth	-.308**	.079	.085	-.088	-.226**	.046	-.012	.058	.011
Career satisfaction	-.031	.058	-.002	-.042	-.100	.036	.057	.053	.094
Financial stability	-.116*	.034	-.050	-.076	.078	.035	.060	.071	-.132**
Field change	-.208**	.024	-.027	.031	.062	-.103	-.122*	-.013	.071
Industry change	-.180**	.001	.002	.028	.109*	-.020	.070	.026	-.138**

*p < .05. **p < .01.

Table 3. Correlations Between Demographic Variables and Measures of Affect

Measure	Age	Sex[a]	Marital status[b]	Dependents	Organiza-tional tenure	Job class[c]	Salary	Previous job loss[d]	Education[e]
Anxiety	-.055	.060	-.053	.049	-.015	-.105*	-.123*	-.023	-.058
Depression	.003	.025	.023	.020	.015	-.012	-.033	.036	.035
Hostility	-.021	-.090	.002	.076	.037	.012	-.024	.045	-.010
Guilt	.028	.005	-.056	.042	-.018	-.038	-.018	-.004	-.065

[a]Coded 1 = *male* and 2 = *female*. [b]Coded 1 = *single*, 2 = *married*, 3 = *separated/divorced*, and 4 = *widowed*. [c]Coded 1 = *hourly production*, 2 = *support staff*, 3 = *technical professional*, 4 = *supervisory*, 5 = *managerial*, and 6 = *executive*. [d]Coded 1 = *yes and* 2 = *no*. [e]Coded 1 = *less than high school*, 2 = *high school graduate*, 3 = *some college*, 4 = *college graduate*, 5 = *postgraduate work*, and 6 = *graduate degree*.
*p < .05.

Table 4. Correlations Between Financial Data and Measures of Affect

Measure	Household	Reliance	Resources	Financial strain
Anxiety	.026	−.065	−.251**	−.125**
Depression	.069	−.113*	−.177**	−.034
Hostility	.120*	−.038	−.084	−.029
Guilt	.069	.084	−.147**	−.080

*p < .05. **p < .01.

to anxiety, depression, or hostility. However, these items were significantly and positively related to guilt.

Exploratory and Confirmatory Analyses

Because many of the items were developed specifically for the purposes of this study, we performed both exploratory and confirmatory factor analyses. We subjected 13 items involving career and employment expectancies to a principal-components analysis, using both orthogonal and oblique methods. In both cases, four factors were extracted: two involving career issues and two involving reemployment. We used the criterion of loadings above .60 to identify separate factors.

The first factor, career stability, was composed of items involving career growth, career satisfaction, and financial stability. The second factor reflected issues of career change and was composed of expectancies involving changing fields and industries during the remainder of one's career. Comparison to a referent for reemployment was the third factor extracted, involving chances for reemployment in comparison with others with similar abilities, education, age, and experience. The last factor, employment salary, involved job salary

Table 5. Correlations Between Vocational Expectancies and Measures of Affect

Expectancy	Anxiety	Depression	Hostility	Guilt
Job chances	−.207**	−.222**	−.099*	−.194**
Chances—ability	−.220**	−.189**	−.134**	−.215**
Chances—education	−.155**	−.204**	−.127*	−.162**
Chances—age	−.160*	−.192*	−.075	−.073
Chances—experience	−.111*	−.110*	−.026	−.057*
Job salary	−.217**	−.212**	−.194**	−.203**
Better salary	−.276**	−.197**	−.154**	−.168**
Use skill	−.107*	−.167**	−.137**	−.218**
Career growth	−.125*	−.191**	−.211**	−.190**
Career satisfaction	−.125**	−.144**	−.221**	−.164**
Financial stability	−.227**	−.249**	−.250**	−.222**
Field change	.003	−.032	.029	.131**
Industry change	.030	.029	.032	.170**

*p < .05. **p < .01.

and a better salary. Coefficient alphas of .78, .83, .84, and .89 were obtained for scales measuring career change, career stability, employment referent, and employment salary, respectively. One item, measuring a general expectancy for reemployment, loaded across most of the factors, but had lower overall loadings.

On the basis of the pattern of factor loadings and the number of factors extracted, we conducted a confirmatory factor analysis, using EQS (Bentler, 1989). A second-order factor model was tested, with each of the four factors extracted from principal components composing a global factor called *vocational expectancy*. The general item of job chances was the sole item not hypothesized to be part of a separate factor but, nevertheless, it was hypothesized to be a component of the higher order factor.

We used the Wald Test (Bentler, 1989) to determine which parameters to remove from the model. The LaGrange Multiplier Test (Bentler, 1989) was used to determine which parameters should be added to the model. The analysis suggested no parameters for removal, and the parameter addition suggested by the LaGrange Multiplier Test did not enhance the fit of the model. Although the chi-square for the first model was significant, $\chi^2(50, N = 413) = 98.032$, $p < .001$, the comparative fit index was .978, with a Bentler–Bonett index of .972. This model is shown in Figure 1. These data suggested that the hypothesized second-order-factor structure fit the covariance matrix reasonably well.

Exploratory and confirmatory analyses were also conducted on the affective variables to ensure the validity of their factorial structure in an adult population. As for the previous model, we performed a principal-components analysis, using both orthogonal and oblique methods. In total, 23 items were used. The analysis revealed patterns of factor loadings quite similar to those reported by Watson and Clark (1989a, 1989b). Two exceptions were notable, however. First, items involving anxiety and depression loaded fairly heavily together, although they remained distinct. Second, items measuring depression—although identifiable as a separate factor—had smaller factor loadings in comparison with those previously reported by Watson and Clark (1989b). Two items—feeling downhearted and feeling blue—had loadings lower than .40.

Figure 2 illustrates the results of the confirmatory analysis, in which EQS was used. The Wald Test indicated that there were no parameters to remove. The LaGrange Multiplier Test indicated that a large number of items covaried with one another. As shown, the intercorrelations between the scales were quite high; in fact, they were somewhat higher than those reported by Watson and Clark (1989a). This was particularly pronounced for the relationships of anxiety to depression and of hostility to depression. The chi-square for the model was significant, $\chi^2(222, N = 396) = 837.512$, $p < .001$, with a comparative fit index of .899 (Bentler–Bonett index = .888). The results of the exploratory and confirmatory factor analyses were interpreted as sufficient evidence, along with the results reported by Watson and Clark (1989a, 1989b), to indicate the independence of the four factors of emotional affect. Reliability of these four scales was also relatively high, with coefficient alphas of .91, .84,

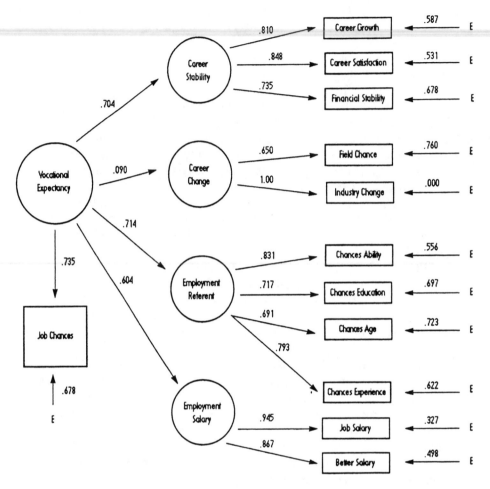

Figure 1. The latent factor structure of vocational expectancies. E = error.

.87, and .90 reported for anxiety, depression, hostility, and guilt, respectively.

Test of Structural Model

On the basis of the hypothesized relationships, we tested a structural model, using age as a predictor of vocational expectancy, vocational expectancy as a predictor of anxiety, financial strain directly in relation to anxiety, and depressive affect predicted by anxiety. When the model was subjected to EQS, several parameter changes were recommended. The Wald Test indicated that the parameter of career change and the relationship between career stability and anxiety should be dropped. As a result, the following prediction equations were found to be significant:

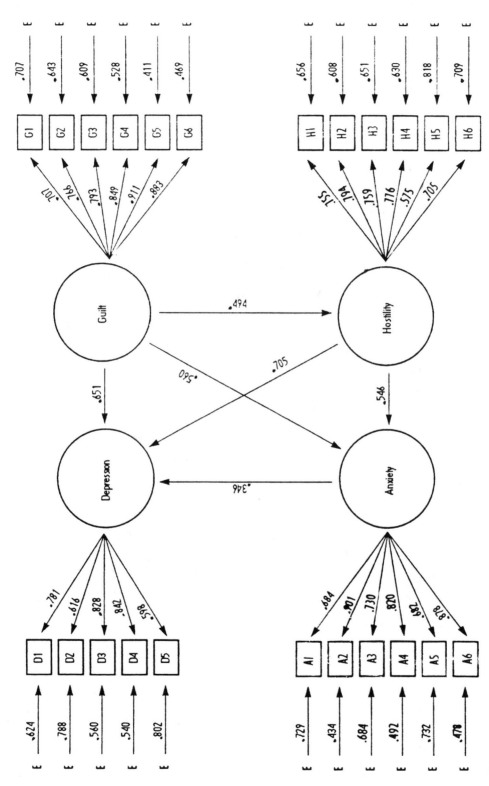

Figure 2. The latent factor structure of emotional affect. E = error.

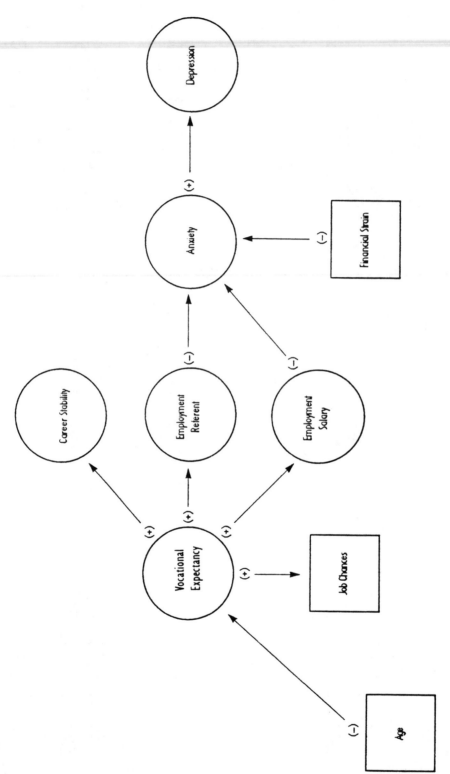

Figure 3. The structural model of the interaction between age, vocational expectancies, financial strain, and affect.

Vocational expectancy = $-.163$ Age $+ .987$ Error

Career stability = $.704$ Vocational expectancy $+ .710$ Error

Employment referent = $.738$ Vocational expectancy $+ .675$ Error

Employment salary = $.626$ Vocational expectancy $+ .780$ Error

Job chance = $.716$ Vocational expectancy $+ -.698$ error

Anxiety = $-.138$ employment referent $+ -.256$ Employment salary $+ -.140$ Financial strain $+ .929$ Error

Depression = $.854$ Anxiety $+ .521$ Error

In this model, age accounted for 2.6% of the vocational expectancy variance, with 97.4% of the variance attributed to error. Vocational expectancies accounted for 49.5% of the variance in career stability, 54.5% of the variance in employment referent, 39.1% of the variance in employment salary, and 51.2% of the variance in chances for reemployment. Employment referent accounted for 1.9% of anxiety variance, whereas employment salary accounted for 6.5% of the anxiety variance and financial strain accounted for 1.9% of the variance; 86.3% of the anxiety variance was attributed to error. Anxiety accounted for 72% of the depression variance, and error accounted for over 27% of the depression variance. The chi-square for this revised model was significant, $\chi^2(268, N = 374) = 580.186$, $p < .001$, with a comparative fit index of .938 and a Bentler–Bonett index of .930. This resulting model is shown in Figure 3.

Discussion

Although the chi-square for the final model tested was significant, it should be noted that in a recent review (James & Jones, 1989) of the causal modeling literature in organizational research, over 80% of the models tested were disconfirmed. The comparative fit index of our final model was .93; therefore this model can be considered viable. However, our findings were achieved after a specification search that resulted in theory trimming and parameter changes. Although the covariance matrix was significantly different from the sample matrix used, this difference may have been mainly attributable to the large sample size (Gerbing & Anderson, 1992).

Our results have several important theoretical and practical implications. First, they suggest that age is predictive of a variety of career and employment expectancies, specifically, expectations about reemployment, obtaining the same or a better salary, opportunities for career growth, financial stability, and chances of moving to a different industry or career field. This is not a surprising finding given the wealth of previous research linking age to depressive affect, to the expectations of others about the job loser, and to the willingness to job seek. The results of our study also extend the work of Kanfer and Hulin (1985), who found that age was related to expectancies about ability to source opportunities, fill out applications, and investigate job leads. Taken together, this evidence suggests that older employees whose jobs have been terminated constitute an at-risk population from a mental health perspective.

Second, the finding that vocational expectancies may act as moderators between age and stress-related affect of job losers is most important. The potential for constructing more predictive models of job-loss reactions may rest on the examination of how job losers cognitively frame their futures (i.e., expectancies). Of specific importance is the fact that previous research by Shamir (1985) has shown anxiety to be highly predictive of job search behavior, including completing job applications, networking, telephoning potential employers, interviewing, and so on. Our results suggest that anxiety may be predicted by many forms of career and employment expectancy and, in turn, may predict other forms of affect. Thus, the finding that age predicts vocational expectancies—specifically, reemployment expectancies—is particularly noteworthy.

On a practical level, our results suggest that for those who are older, have lower employment expectancies, and experience financial strain, some form of cognitive–perceptual reappraisal may be necessary to negate the effects of anxiety and subsequent depressive affect after job loss. Specific counseling interventions for older workers, both before and after job loss, are indicated by this and previous research. In addressing the anxiety of older workers, it would be adaptive to create a new meaning of work, to reframe the circumstances surrounding job loss, and to engage in reattribution for the job loss. Thus, in accordance with an approach articulated by Lazarus and Folkman (1984), potential or actual job loss for older workers could potentially be experienced more as a challenge than as a loss or harm. This suggests that organizational and vocational counselors alike need to provide increased services to older job losers to improve cognitive interventions aimed at reducing their anxiety and, ultimately, to enhance their palliative and active coping abilities.

Results concerning the influence of financial variables on the anxiety of job losers were also important. For this relationship, the number of weeks after job loss until financial distress significantly predicted feelings of anxiety. These findings further extend the small number of studies (Payne & Jones, 1981; Warr & Jackson, 1984) to have investigated this critical variable. Future investigations concerning the impact of monetary concerns on the unemployed should operationalize this variable differently than in the present study. Specifically, future researchers should use a multifaceted approach, including existing and potential financial resources. We compared resource availability (other income, savings, etc.) with financial strain (weeks after job loss until financial distress) and found resource availability to be clearly superior as a predictor. The lack of alternative resources was not only predictive of anxiety, but was also predictive of depression and guilt.

References

Archer, I., & Rhodes, V. (1987). Bereavement and reactions to job loss: A comparative review. *British Journal of Social Psychology, 26*, 211–224.

Bentler, P. M. (1989). *EQS: Structural equation program manual.* Los Angeles: BMDP Statistical Software.

Catalano, R., & Dooley, D. (1977). Economic predictors of depressed mood and stressful life events. *Journal of Health and Social Behavior, 24,* 292–307.

Daniel, W. W. (1974). *A national survey of the unemployed.* London: Political and Economic Planning Institute.

DeFrank, R. S., & Ivancevich, J. M. (1986). Job loss: An individual level review and model. *Journal of Vocational Behavior, 28,* 1–20.

Dooley, D., & Catalano, R. (1986). Do economic variables generate psychological problems? Different methods, different answers. In A. J. MacFayden & H. W. MacFayden (Eds.), *Economic psychology: Intersections in theory and application* (pp. 503–546). Amsterdam: North Holland.

Dressler, W. W. (1986). Unemployment and depressive symptoms in a southern Black community. *Journal of Nervous and Mental Disease, 174,* 639–645.

Eisenburg, P., & Lazarsfeld, P. F. (1938). The psychological effects of unemployment. *Psychological Bulletin, 35,* 358–390.

Estes, R. J., & Willensky, H. L. (1978). Life-cycle squeeze and the morale curve. *Social Problems, 25,* 277–292.

Feather, N. T. (1983). Causal attributions and beliefs about work and unemployment among adolescents in state and independent secondary schools. *Australian Journal of Psychology, 35,* 211–232.

Feather, N. T., & Barber, J. C. (1983). Depressive reactions and unemployment. *Journal of Abnormal Psychology, 92,* 185–195.

Feather, N. T., & Bond, M. J. (1983). Time structure and purposive activity among employed and unemployed university students. *Journal of Occupational Psychology, 56,* 241–254.

Feather, N. T., & Davenport, P. R. (1981). Unemployment and depressive affect: A motivational and attributional analysis. *Journal of Personality and Social Psychology, 41,* 422–436.

Feather, N. T., & O'Brien, G. E. (1986). A longitudinal analysis of the effects of different patterns of employment and unemployment on school leavers. *British Journal of Psychology, 77,* 459–479.

Fineman, S. (1979). A psychosocial model of stress and its application to managerial unemployment. *Human Relations, 32,* 323–345.

Fryer, D. R., & Warr, P. B. (1984). Unemployment and cognitive difficulties. *British Journal of Clinical Psychology, 23,* 67–68.

Gerbing, D. W., & Anderson, J. C. (1992). Monte Carlo evaluation of goodness of fit for structural evaluation models. *Sociological Methods and Research, 21,* 132–160.

Hepworth, S. J. (1980a). The impact of unemployment upon the self-esteem of managers. *Journal of Occupational Psychology, 53,* 147–155.

Hepworth, S. J. (1980b). Moderating factors of the psychological impact of unemployment. *Journal of Occupational Psychology, 53,* 139–145.

Horwitz, A. V. (1984). The economy and social pathology. *Annual Review of Sociology, 10,* 95–119.

Jackson, P. R., & Warr, P. B. (1984). Unemployment and psychological ill health: The moderating role of duration and age. *Psychological Medicine, 14,* 605–615.

Jahoda, M. (1988). Economic recession and mental health: Some conceptual issues. *Journal of Social Issues, 44,* 13–24.

James, L. R., & Jones, L. A. (1989). Causal modeling in organizational research. In C. L. Cooper & I. Robertson (Eds.), *International review of industrial and organizational psychology* (pp. 371–401). New York: Wiley.

Kanfer, R., & Hulin, C. L. (1985). Individual differences in successful job searches following layoff. *Personnel Psychology, 38,* 835–847.

Kaufman, H. (1982). *Professionals in search of work.* New York: Wiley.

Klandermans, B. (1980). *Unemployment and the unemployment movement.* Unpublished manuscript, Department of Social Psychology, Free University, Amsterdam, Holland.

Lazarus, R. S., & Folkman, S. (1984). *Stress, appraisal, and coping.* New York: Springer.

Leana, C. R., & Feldman, D. C. (1988). Individual responses to job loss: Perceptions, reactions, and coping behavior. *Journal of Management, 14,* 375–389.

Leana, C. R., & Ivancevich, J. M. (1987). Involuntary job loss: Institutional interventions and research agenda. *Academy of Management Review, 12,* 301–312.

Leventman, P. G. (1981). *Professionals out of work.* New York: Free Press.

Payne, R. L., & Jones, J. G. (1981). Social class and re-employment: Changes in health and perceived financial circumstances. *Journal of Occupational Behavior, 8*, 175–184.

Shamir, B. (1985). Sex differences in the psychological adjustment to unemployment and reemployment: A question of commitment alternatives or finance? *Social Problems, 31*, 67–79.

Singer, M. S., Stacey, B. G., & Ritchie, G. (1987). Causal attributions for unemployment: Personal consequences of unemployment and perceptions of employment prospects for young university students in New Zealand. *Journal of Genetic Psychology, 41*, 507–517.

Vinokur, A., Caplan, D. R., & Williams, C. C. (1987). Effects of recent and past stress on mental health: Coping with unemployment among Vietnam veterans and nonveterans. *Journal of Applied Social Psychology, 17*, 710–730.

Warr, P. B. (1978). The study of psychological well-being. *British Journal of Psychology, 69*, 111–121.

Warr, P. B. (1982). Psychological aspects of employment and unemployment. *Psychological Medicine, 12*, 7–11.

Warr, P. B. (1984). Work and unemployment. In P. J. D. Drenth, H. Thierry, P. J. Williams, & C. J. deWolf (Eds.), *Handbook of work and organizational psychology* (pp. 413–443). New York: Wiley.

Warr, P., & Jackson, P. (1984). Men without jobs: Some correlates of age and length of unemployment. *Journal of Occupational Psychology, 57*, 77–85.

Warr, P. B., & Jackson, P. R. (1985). Factors influencing the psychological impact of prolonged unemployment and re-employment. *Psychological Medicine, 15*, 795–807.

Watson, D., & Clark, L. A. (1984). Negative affectivity: The disposition to experience aversive affect in strokes. *Psychological Bulletin, 96*, 465–490.

Watson, D., & Clark, L. A. (1989a). Development and validation of the Positive and Negative Affect Schedule (expanded form): A preliminary manual. Unpublished manuscript.

Watson, D., & Clark, L. A. (1989b, August). General affective dimensions versus discrete emotional factors: A hierarchical model. In C. Smith (Chair), *The emotional basis of personality*. Symposium conducted at the 97th Annual Convention of the American Psychological Association, New Orleans, LA.

Watson, D., Clark, L. A., & Tellegen, A. (1988). Development and validation of brief measures of positive and negative affect: The PANAS Scales. *Journal of Personality and Social Psychology, 54*, 1063–1070.

Wilcox, R. C., & Franke, W. H. (1963). *Unwanted workers: Permanent layoffs and long term unemployment*. New York: Free Press of Glencoe.

11

Older Working Widows: Present and Expected Experiences of Stress and Quality of Life in Comparison With Married Workers

Sara Staats, Christie Partlo,
Marjorie Armstrong-Stassen, and
Lovinia Plimpton

There are 11.3 million widows in the United States, and demographics indicate that their numbers will increase in the future. Despite being a well-represented group, older working widows are underrepresented in studies of quality of life (QOL), quality of work life (QWL), job stress, and job satisfaction. The older working widow is at the center of a concentric set of underresearched populations. Moving out from the older working widow, one may consider the older working woman and then older workers in general. In this chapter, we present preliminary data that compare the work experiences of older working widows with older married workers. We begin to address our target group, older working widows, by briefly commenting on the state of research in the parent populations of older workers and older women in the workforce.

Older Workers

The proportion of older persons in the population has increased markedly because of greater longevity and a declining birthrate. In spite of uncertainty and organizational change in the workplace and a decline in rate of workforce participation by older workers, an overall "graying" of the workforce is expected to continue (Doeringer, 1990, 1991; Fontana & Frey, 1990; Kacmar & Ferris, 1989; Wittwer, 1990). Residual negative stereotypes of older workers (e.g., as "crotchety" and "unable to learn new tricks") are gradually being countered by data indicating that older as well as younger workers benefit from training (Salthouse, 1991; Sparrow & Davies, 1988) and by higher-than-

This research was supported in part by a grant from the American Association of Retired Persons, Andrus Foundation, and by an Academic Challenge Grant from the State of Ohio.

average ratings of older workers' job performance. Older workers are often seen as people to count on in a crisis (see Hayslip & Panek, 1993). The aging nature of the workforce is not without some benefits.

The present cohort of older workers is in better health, is better educated, and is more politically active than previous cohorts. They will have a continuing and increasing effect on the workplace. Until quite recently, older persons were typically retiring at earlier and earlier ages (Herzog, House, & Morgan, 1991). The state of the economy—the current recession with a predicted slow recovery—and uncertainties about health care add to an increased reluctance among older workers, both women and men, to retire. Therefore, the QOL and QWL of older workers is and will continue to be a salient issue.

Older Working Women

An obvious but underresearched corollary of the increase in older workers is an increase in the proportion of women in the workplace. Most women work outside the home, and it has been estimated that 90% of women aged 25 to 64 years will be in the workforce by the year 2000 (Matthews & Rodin, 1989). However, studies of work stress and work satisfaction generally underrepresent women, particularly older women (Kline & Snow, 1992). Older women are often the unnoticed and unsupported infrastructure of the workforce. For example, recent years have seen increased awareness of child-care issues, a need of younger women, rather than awareness of the need for elder care, a task typically left to the middle-aged or older woman. There is a paucity of research on mediators of employment–health relationships for women in general, and again, especially for older women. However, even given the additional and unique stressors that women experience at work, the effects of paid employment seem beneficial for unmarried women and for women who have favorable attitudes toward employment (see Nelson & Hitt, 1992, and Repetti, Matthews, & Waldron, 1989, for a recent review of this literature).

Older Working Widows

Of the 13.7 million widowed workers in the United States, 11.3 million are women (U.S. Bureau of the Census, 1992). Widowhood is an increasingly likely future for a majority of married women, given the increased proportion of older persons in the population and the fact that women often marry men older than themselves and typically have greater longevity than men (Kinderknecht & Hodges, 1990).

Furthermore, widows are less likely to remarry than are widowers. Kinderknecht and Hodges (1990) noted that the average age of widowhood for women is 56 and that only 7 of every 100 women 56 years of age or older will remarry. The proportion of widows increases with increasing age groups and is contributing to the feminization of the older workforce (Rix, 1990). Older divorced women and older never-married women are also significant constituencies in the workforce; however, the widow is the prototype for the current older population.

Most of the women widowed today are currently working and will continue to do so for many years. Employment trends lead one to expect that the proportion of working widows will increase with future cohorts. Today, most women work outside the home, even during their child-rearing years, and have considerable work experience. Widows today generally have a work history, were enculturated into the women's movement during their early adulthood, and are expected to have more commitment to remaining in the workforce than previous cohorts of widows.

In contrast with their strong representation in the workforce, women—especially older widows—are poorly represented in the research literature (Doeringer, 1991; Lund, 1989). The young to middle-aged male worker is not only a popular stereotype but also a popular source of research data. A recent literature review revealed no matches for widows and job satisfaction and very few for women and work. The time is long past for a concentrated study of the stress experiences and QWL of the older, working widow. In this study, we explored differences between working widows and older, married workers, with older working widows as the focus of interest.

In this chapter, we present data on the daily work experiences, both positive and negative, of older workers and suggest directions for future research. Because older as well as younger people are planful and future oriented (Staats & Stassen, 1987), we considered the future expectations as well as present experience of QOL of the older workers in this study.

The present sample was drawn from a minilongitudinal study (Staats, 1991) of older people funded by the American Association of Retired Persons. The primary purpose of the present study was to explore differences between older working widows and other older workers. We considered the well-being of the older working widow with respect to QOL, work uplifts, work hassles, hopefulness, and self-assessment of functional age. The lack of previous research did not encourage theoretically based hypotheses. However, because measures of well-being are positively correlated, we expected that work uplifts, a youthful bias in functional age, and hopefulness would be significant predictors of present and anticipated QOL for older workers.

Method

Subjects

Questionnaire and interview data were collected from people over 50 years of age during five different sessions. Volunteers over 50 years of age were solicited through newspaper advertisements and at a major nonresidential senior citizens' center. Participants were paid a $10 honorarium. Some selective sampling was done at the end of the study to match the diversity of the sample to that of the catchment area (e.g., data were collected at a predominately Black Baptist Church to match the 2% Black population of the area).

We selected 217 workers over 50 years of age (mean age = 64.4 years) from the data set. This set included 51 widows, 51 married men, and 81 married women, as well as 34 persons who did not indicate their marital status. Thirty-two of the participants were employed part time and 185 were employed full time. The most typical income bracket of the group was $11,000 to $20,000 annually. Of the sample, 11% had finished grade school, 47% had finished high school, and the remainder had completed 2 or more years of postsecondary instruction.

The present data were collected during the first interview and survey session, with the exception of questions pertaining to functional age, which were added at the final session that occurred approximately 6 months after the initial interview data were collected.

Measures

QOL was measured with two interview items. Participants' reports of present and future QOL were obtained during the interview using nine-rung Cantril Ladders that were anchored at the bottom with the *Worst life that I could expect* (1) and at the top with the *Best life that I could expect* (9).

The questionnaire packet included the Daily Events Scale, the Hope Index (Staats, 1989), and Functional Age items from Kastenbaum, Derbin, Sabatini, and Artt's, (1972) study. QWL was examined by using work-related hassle and uplift items abstracted from the Daily Events Scale (DeLongis, Coyne, Dakof, Folkman, & Lazarus, 1982). *Hassles* are microstressors, such as irritating demands, troubled relationships, or frustrations, that are perceived as distressing or annoying. An *uplift* is an event that makes one feel good, glad, joyful, or satisfied. We extracted work-related items from Delongis et al.'s scale for separate analysis. These items were used to construct new scales that provided an indication of work uplifts as well as work hassles. Items referred to fellow workers, clients or customers, supervisors, the nature of work, workload, job security, and several items related to finance.

On the basis of an exploratory factor analysis of the uplift and hassle items, four scales were constructed: work uplifts, work hassles, money hassles, and money uplifts. For this sample, these four new scales yielded coefficient alphas of .82, .89, .85, and .82, respectively, indicating acceptable scale reliability.

The Hope Index (see Staats, 1989, 1991; Staats & Partlo, 1993, for psychometric information) is a future-oriented measure that presents 16 desirable events, such as "to be happy," "to be competent," "our nation to be more productive," "peace in the world," and "resources for all." The coefficient alpha for the Hope Index for the present sample was .88, and similar values were obtained for individual Hope Index items. Participants indicated the degree to which they wished for each item on a scale ranging from 0 (*not at all*) to 5 (*very much*). They then indicated the degree to which they expected that circumstance would occur on the same point scale. The total hope score was obtained by multiplying Wish × Expect scores and summing across the 16 positive hope items. Total hope scores were expected to relate positively to expected QOL, as well as to present QOL and uplifts.

An early interest in functional age, in opposition to chronological age, was driven by labor shortages in World War II (McFarland, 1973; Welford, 1977). Future labor shortages may renew interest in the concept. The idea is that one's ability to work or one's general status is not solely determined by chronological age.

Functional age items (Kastenbaum et al., 1972) ask people to compare their looks, activities, and interests with people of different ages. For example, one item reads "Most of the time I feel" and includes these responses: *quite a bit older than people my age* (5), *a little bit older than people my age* (4), *neither younger nor older than people my age* (3), *a little younger than most people my age* (2), and *quite a bit younger than most people my age* (1). People choosing the midpoint of this scale are indicating a match between their functional age and chronological age. We used functional age in the present study because in some contexts functional age has been found to be more predictive of well-being than objective measures (Barnes & Piotrowski, 1989).

Results

Typically, older workers in this sample (measured in 1988 and 1989) presented a positive image. They reported functional ages less than their chronological ages (i.e., showed a "youthful bias"). Total uplifts exceeded total hassles, $t(179)$ = 6.87, $p < .0001$, and this pattern was consistent across individual items. Their 5-year expected QOL marginally exceeded their present QOL, $t(214) = -1.86, p < .06$. Such positive expectations concerning the future are generally taken to indicate well-being in older as well as younger adults (Hooker, 1992; Staats & Skowronski, 1992; Staats & Stassen, 1987).

Daily work uplifts and daily work hassles provide one window on QWL. Although most researchers in this area have focused on hassles as sources of stress (Lazarus, 1991), uplifts can be considered not only as stress-coping resources or as buffers but also as legitimate sources of happiness, hope, and well-being (a view that we take in the present research). We therefore analyzed uplifts as well as hassles. For the total group of older workers, the Work Uplifts Scale scores were much greater than the Work Hassles Scale scores, $t(191)$ = 7.78, $p < .0001$. The Financial Uplift scores exceeded the Financial Hassles scores, $t(192) = 3.59, p < .001$. If one considers QWL as a preponderance of work-related uplifts in relation to work-related hassles, then the total sample of older workers in the present study experienced a highly positive level of QWL.

Present QOL was positively correlated with income bracket, the Financial Uplifts Scale, and a youthful functional age (rs = .25, .25, and .24, respectively; $ps < .01$). Present QOL was negatively correlated with financial hassles ($r = -.21, p < .01$). A similar pattern for these variables was observed for future QOL. Income was related to education ($r = .40, p < .001$). Hope was related to present QOL ($r = .31, p < .01$) and to future QOL ($r = .34, p < .01$). Hope was also related to financial uplifts ($r = .18$, $p < .05$). Uplift measures were positively related and hassle measures were negatively related to QOL and to hope.

Comparison means and probability statistics for the sample are presented in Table 1. Analyses of variance (ANOVAs), using a general linear model, revealed significant differences among widows, married women, and married men for the demographic variables of age and income. Widows were older and had less income than married persons. Total work hassles did not differ among the groups but total work uplifts did, with widows experiencing fewer work-related uplifts than did other older workers. An examination of individual Financial Uplifts Scale items revealed a consistent pattern across all items, with widows having lower means. The greatest individual uplifts for all groups were associated with fellow workers, the nature of work, and workload. These data suggested a lower QWL for widows than for married workers. Before attributing this decreased positive affect of widows to generalized depression or low affect associated with age (Diener, Sandvik, & Larsen, 1985), one must note that there were no significant differences between the groups on present QOL or on Hope Index scores. In fact, Hope Index scores tended to be higher for widows in general and were significantly higher for those who had been widows for more than 10 years. Widows and married men were similar in their expectations for future QOL; both had lower scores than married women.

Groups constructed on the basis of marital status often have age as a natural confound. This occurs because women usually marry older men and because of the greater longevity of women (Lewis, 1978). The means presented in Table 1 are the best description of the real world that includes this ecologically imbedded interaction. Arguably, they are the best data from which to plan interventions and evaluations because they represent the real-world interactions of age and marital status.

Table 1. Mean Comparison of Study Variables for Sample of Older Workers

| | | Married workers | | | | |
Variable	Widows	Women	Men	F	p	dfs
Age (years)	68.55	61.38	64.75	13.84	.0001	2,180
Functional age[a]	2.23	2.25	2.11	1.58	ns	2,159
Income	2.35	3.34	3.06	10.29	.0001	2,167
HS money	3.19	2.65	2.35	0.84	ns	2,170
UP money	2.93	4.73	4.69	4.80	.01	2,166
HS work	1.18	1.73	1.82	0.73	ns	2,165
UP work	2.54	4.48	4.90	2.78	.07	2,158
QOL present	7.06	7.25	6.96	0.65	ns	2,180
Hope	269.69	254.37	236.68	2.19	.12	2,132
QOL future	6.78	7.76	6.80	8.14	.0004	2,177

Note. HS money = financial hassles; UP money = financial uplifts; HS work = work hassles; UP work = work uplifts; QOL present = present quality of life; QOL future = future quality of life; Hope = hope for others and self.

[a]Score of 3 represented functional–chronological age equivalency. Lower scores indicate lower functional age.

However, one may wonder what the data would look like if they were not confounded by age. This concern becomes more relevant when we note that the Daily Events Scale (from which the uplift and hassle items were derived) is basically an affective scale and that affect intensity does decrease with increasing age (Diener, Sandvik, & Larsen, 1985; Staats & Stassen, 1987). Because of these concerns, we performed an analysis of covariance (ANCOVA) with age as a covariate. No substantive changes were found for the present QOL, functional age, or for hope (see Table 2). The results of the ANCOVA in general produced a less favorable result for the widows. Hassles with money became significant, with widows experiencing more hassles than the other two groups. Work hassles became significant, with married women showing fewer hassles, and widows and married men experiencing similar levels. Finally, work uplifts that had been marginally significant in the previous analysis achieved the traditional level of significance while retaining the same pattern of differences. In the ANCOVA analysis, widows had significantly fewer work uplifts.

To examine the amount of variance that daily hassles and uplifts accounted for in present and future QOL, we conducted hierarchical regression analyses. In the first step, age and functional age were entered as control variables. In the second step, four variables—hassles with work, uplifts with work, hassles with money, and uplifts with money—were entered. For widows, a second hierarchical regression was run, with length of widowhood entered as a third step. The results of these analyses are presented in Tables 3 and 4.

In regard to present QOL, age and functional age made a significant contribution for married men only. Entering the hassle and uplifts scales increased squared multiple correlations for married men and women, but not for widows. Finally, entering length of widowhood produced an increase in squared multiple correlations for widows. A negative beta, relating uplifts from work with present QOL for married men, was obtained.

Table 2. Results of Analyses of Covariance With Age as the Covariate: Mean Comparison by Groups

| Variable | Widows | Married workers | | F | p | dfs |
		Women	Men			
Functional age[a]	2.30	2.24	2.11	0.98	ns	2,145
HS money	4.15	2.44	2.36	2.72	.02	2,167
UP money	2.82	4.76	4.71	1.94	.05	2,168
HS work	1.91	1.38	1.90	3.73	.003	2,162
UP work	3.94	4.18	5.01	3.09	.01	2,155
QOL present	6.96	7.36	6.98	2.04	.08	2,177
Hope	251.59	252.70	236.30	1.69	.14	2,129
QOL future	6.72	7.70	6.87	8.88	.0001	2,174

Note. HS money = financial hassles; UP money = financial uplifts; HS work = work hassles; UP work = work uplifts; QOL present = present quality of life; QOL future = future quality of life; Hope = hope for others and self.

[a]Score of 3 represented functional–chronological age equivalency. Lower scores indicated lower functional age.

Table 3. Results of Hierarchical Regression Analyses for Present Quality of Life With Unstandardized Beta Weights for Three Groups of Older Workers

Variable	Widows		Married women		Married men	
Age	−.03		.03		−.05*	
Functional age	−.10		.01		−.11*	
R^2		.17		.06		.20
F		2.81		1.64		4.51*
HS work	−.25		−.04		−.08	
HS money	−.08		−.16*		.06	
UP work	.02		.02		−.12*	
UP money	.14		.04		.20**	
R^2		.32		.18		.45
ΔR^2		.15		.12		.25
F		1.33		2.01*		3.46*
No. of years widowed	.06					
R^2		.43				
ΔR^2		.11				
F		4.38*				

Note. HS work = work hassles, HS money = financial hassles; UP work = work uplifts, UP Money = financial uplifts.

*$p \le .05$. **$p \le .01$

In regard to future QOL, age and functional age were significant contributors for both widows and married men. The addition of the hassle and uplift scales provided a significant increase in squared multiple correlations for married women and married men, but not for widows. Length of widowhood was a significant contributor to future QOL as well as to present QOL. Again, the anomalous negative relationship between work uplifts and future QOL was present for married men. For both present and future QOL, the F value for change in squared multiple correlations when hassles and uplifts were entered was significant for married women and married men but not for widows. For the widows, length of widowhood contributed significantly to both present and future QOL.

With the exception of length of widowhood, none of the individual predictors of present QOL were significant for widows. Fewer hassles with money was the only significant predictor for married women. Lower chronological age, a youthful functional age, and uplifts associated with money, but few uplifts associated with work, were predictive for married men.

A youthful functional age and length of widowhood were significant individual predictors of future QOL for widows. Younger chronological age, fewer hassles with work and uplifts associated with money were predictive for married women. Finally, younger chronological age, younger functional age, uplifts with money, and few uplifts with work were predictive of future QOL for married men.

Thus, there were different patterns of predictors for older workers who differed in marital status. The present scales provided better prediction for

Table 4. Results of Hierarchical Regression Analyses for Future Quality of Life With Unstandardized Beta Weights for Three Groups of Older Workers

Variable	Widows		Married women		Married men	
Age	−.01		−.03*		−.11**	
Functional age	−.18**		−.03		−.03	
R^2		.35		.06		.19
F		7.55**		1.74		4.23*
HS work	−.06		−.13*		−.12	
HS money	−.06		.02		.02	
UP work	.03		.04		−.13*	
UP money	.11		.08*		.18*	
R^2		.41		.25		.42
ΔR^2		.06		.19		.22
F		0.61		3.25*		2.97*
No. of years widowed	.07*					
R^2		.56				
ΔR^2		.14				
F		7.00**				

Note. HS work = work hassles; HS money = financial hassles; UP work = work uplifts; UP money = financial uplifts.
$*p \leq .05.$ $**p \leq .01.$

men than for women. The importance of length of widowhood for women and the curious negative relation between QOL measures and work uplifts for men are relationships in need of future verification. All older workers are not alike, as evidenced by the variations within the group of older workers that we studied. Specifically, the present data clearly showed differences not only in gender groups but also between women when marital status was considered.

Discussion

The negative side of Daily Events, a Hassle subscale, has been widely used as a measure of stress, and it has typically yielded acceptable reliability estimates. Lazarus and others have viewed hassles as measures of stress (Kanner, Coyne, Schaefer, & Lazarus, 1981; Lazarus, 1990). We assumed that work-related items that have content validity relate to QWL. We expected that work uplifts, in contrast with work hassles, would bear a positive relationship to present QWL. Conceptually, work uplifts should map onto job satisfaction and work hassles should map onto job dissatisfaction.

Uplift and hassle items from the Daily Events subscale provide a reliable measure for examining some affective features of the work experience. We are not debating the relative virtue of hassles and uplifts versus major life changes (Holmes & Rahe, 1967) as measures of stress (see Lazarus, 1990, and following commentaries for differing views on this issue). We chose items from the Daily Events subscale because the content of several items are work related, because this permits one to assess uplifts with the same methodology as hassles (thereby facilitating comparative estimates of the influence of hassles and uplifts on QOL and QWL perceptions), and because of their availability in the data set we used. We have used these scales and other measures to provide a glimpse of the QWL of older workers, and of older working widows in particular. Older workers who obtain uplifts from work were expected to report comparatively high job satisfaction. Such workers are organizational assets, in terms of knowledge, skills and ability as well as in disinclination to quit or undercut organizational goals. Such workers are at an advantage in coping with work stress.

Considering all of our older workers, the preponderance of work uplifts over work hassles suggests that these workers might have reported being satisfied with their work. Relations of age and job satisfaction are often considered to be unreliable for workers over age 60, but most researchers have found an increase in job satisfaction from middle age to the older years (Schultz & Schultz, 1990; Warr, 1992).

The QWL of older working widows, here operationalized in terms of work uplifts and work hassles, is lower than that of other older workers. Income of the working widow is also lower. Because income is a key job characteristic, the significantly lower income of widows and the lower total work-related uplifts of widows in comparison with other older workers highlights a particular area of concern. The lower income of widows is certainly not news (Herzog, Holden, & Seltzer, 1989; Lopata, 1987; Lund, 1989); however, we have not found previous documentation of low work-related uplifts in widows. This sort of information is not readily available in the literature. Indeed, some employers may speculate that widows compensate for spousal loss by becoming "married to their jobs" and need not have material rewards because of the great intrinsic rewards that they reap from working. That was not the case for this sample.

Herzberg (1966) identified salary as a unique variable with the capability of contributing to both job satisfaction and dissatisfaction. The present data provide support for this role of salary and indicate that uplifts associated with money act as contributors to present and future QOL whereas hassles associated with money are negatively related to present QOL. In addition, financial assessments are more strongly related to QWL than are other work-related assessments.

The typically lower income of widows is a grave practical concern for the older population and is both logically and theoretically related to the relative lack of work uplifts for our sample of widows. Unwarranted lower incomes for older working widows must be identified and corrected. Equitable educational and retraining opportunities should be provided for older working widows as well as for other populations.

The ANCOVA controlling for age suggested that a widow's degree of dissatisfaction with income is masked by an age-related decline in the reporting of affect. It is possible that widows and other older workers complain less about low income and hassles related to money than do younger persons in the same circumstances. In other words, uplifts associated with money may be even lower than are commonly reported by widows. This lack of reporting low income as a hassle could contribute to the lower income that widows generally receive. Other bad news is that work-related uplifts other than financial ones also tend to be lower for widows than for married workers. The good news for widows is that age is not significantly related to QOL variables, that the functional age of widows does not differ from other older workers in spite of their greater chronological age, and that there is a tendency for a widow's hope for the future to be greater than that of other older workers.

Clearly, longitudinal studies using diverse measures would be a welcome addition to knowledge of the widow's affective job experience and would provide a clearer picture than the present secondary analysis. We expect and hope that other researchers will develop better measures and methods for understanding the work experiences of older individuals, especially widows.

Our hierarchical regression analyses also revealed different patterns for different marital groupings of older workers. For men, youthfulness, money, and few work uplifts were associated with present QOL. The negative relation of work uplifts and QOL for men was not expected. One might speculate that this signifies the beginning of a disengagement phenomenon for men; that men with unsatisfactory supervisory or client relationships at work compensate by having better nonwork relationships, or vice versa; or that other complex relationships are involved. It is notable that neither age nor functional age were significant predictors of present QOL for women.

The regression patterns for future QOL showed an increased importance of age for married women and functional age for widows. Number of years of widowhood also significantly contributed to expected QOL for the widows. We have previously noted that people who have been widowed for many years show an increase in hope (Plimpton, Staats, & Partlo, 1992). Women who have been widowed 10 or more years are survivors and, as such, have achieved numerous goals. We believe that these past achievements provide reasonable expectations of future goal achievement.

One's chronological age cannot be changed. However, interventions can be devised to decrease the small daily hassles and, especially, to increase the small daily uplifts in the work environment. These small, frequent pleasures are important sources of happiness and well-being (Diener, 1984). Certainly, it is easier to manipulate small daily hassles and uplifts than it is to alter major life events or to make major organizational changes.

The other good news is that uplifts, daily hassles, hope, and the perceptions of one's functional age are amenable to training (Fordyce, 1976; Staats, 1991; Staats et al., 1992). Older workers are good candidates for training, and, although it may require more time (Rix, 1990), training to increase daily uplifts could be incorporated into existing QWL or work-wellness programs with minimum expense. Such an enhanced program has the potential to greatly strengthen mental health at the work site.

Herzberg (1966), Kobasa (1979), Lazarus (1991), and, indeed, the *DSM-III-R* (American Psychiatric Association, 1987) have explained the roles of satisfaction, happiness, and well-being in addition to the role of stress in personal adjustment and satisfaction. In spite of all of the above voices, uplifts and positive affects are still underresearched in comparison with hassles and other negative affects. We will not have a complete picture of well-being at work or at home until the uplifts, joys, and satisfactions are fully considered.

Uplifts and positive expectations are key characteristics of well-being on the job as well as off the job. Increasing daily work uplifts is a promising route to the improvement of job satisfaction, stress reduction, and stress management. The nature of daily work uplifts may need to be tailored to different groups of workers.

Health promotion in the workplace faces new challenges and has new opportunities to improve the internal working environment, QWL, and QOL for the changing, aging, and feminized workforce of the year 2000 (Quick, Murphy, & Hurrell, 1992). Widowhood is one of the most traumatic events that occurs in a person's life (Holmes & Rahe, 1967). Numerous indicators of decreased QOL and positive affect have been associated with widowhood in previous studies (Cohen, 1988; Wilson, 1967). However, in the majority of these studies showing negative effects of widowhood, effects have been measured early in bereavement or within the first few months or years of widowhood (Lund, 1989). The average length of widowhood of the women in this study was more than 12 years.

Although only a small minority of older widows remarry, few studies have looked at long-term widowhood. Even a fewer of these studies have considered length of widowhood or "state of widowhood." Length of widowhood does not consistently relate to measures of present QOL (Barrett & Schneweis, 1980– 1981; Lowenstein & Rosen, 1989). Researchers have rarely considered the work domain of widows or the future expectations of widows. However, a study by Plimpton et al. (1992) showed that as length of widowhood increases, some indicators of future or expected QOL, such as hope, increase. Because future expectations lead to intentions that in turn lead to behavior, these attitudes toward the future are a salient aspect of human functioning (Staats, Atha, & Isham, 1990; Staats & Stassen, 1987). Clearly, longitudinal studies are needed to see if future expectations, as well as the experiences of uplifts, hassles, job satisfaction, job stress, and QWL, change over the course of widowhood.

Older working widows are present in the workplace in increasing numbers. Without too much exaggeration, one may say that "to be old is to be female, and to be an old female is to be a widow." But widows remain a nonentity in a couple and male-oriented society (Bankoff, 1983). Widows have often entered or reentered the workforce because of sudden necessity and may be underplaced because of this fact, and widows may elicit avoidance behavior in other women as well as men (Heineman, 1982). Because of the number of widows in the workforce, their present and future QOL is the proper concern of business organizations as well as of psychologists. One should not assume that the experience of the older widow is the same as for other older workers but, rather, should determine what, if any, differences in their experiences do exist. The present study suggests an area in which industrial and organizational psychologists have ample room to improve the QWL of a significant portion of the workforce and thereby increase positive outcomes associated with perceptions of high QWL. New directions in QOL and QWL research should consider accentuating the positive as well as eliminating the negative for all older workers. To do this, one needs to know more about the experience of different older workers. The present pilot investigation suggests some directions and argues for increasing work uplifts as well as decreasing work hassles. Future research should be devoted to identifying those work factors responsible for fewer work uplifts in older working widows and to searching for remedies.

Relatively little is known about the QWL of widows, who are at the center of an expanding older workforce. Using an existing data set, we have only begun to examine such crucial variables as QOL, future expectations, and QWL of older working widows in comparison with older married workers. Our sample participants, who were primarily volunteers solicited through newspaper advertisements and measured in nonwork settings, may not have provided the best representation of older workers. Additional research is need to test the generalizability of the present results. The present pattern of lower uplifts and lower income of widows indicates a lower QWL of widows in comparison with other older workers. Because the workforce is increasingly composed of older workers—especially, of older widows—research concerning their work experiences is long overdue.

The role of positive work experiences in QOL for older workers, especially for widows, is poorly understood. Training to increase positive experiences on the job and small work modifications aimed at increasing small but frequent pleasures is possible and should commence. In addition to such practical applications, future research concerning the positive and negative experiences of older working widows should be pursued to increase the generality of theories of job satisfaction and dissatisfaction.

References

American Psychiatric Association. (1987). *Diagnostic and statistical manual of mental disorders* (3rd ed., revised). Washington, DC: Author.

Bankoff, E. A. (1983). Social support and adaptation to widowhood. *Journal of Marriage and the Family, 45,* 827–839.

Barnes, J. H., & Piotrowski, M. (1989). Workers' perceptions of discrepancies between chronological age and personal age: You're only as old as you feel. *Psychology and Aging, 4,* 376–377.

Barrett, C. J., & Schneweis, K. M. (1980–1981). An empirical search for stages of widowhood. *Omega, 11,* 97–104.

Cohen, L. H. (Ed.). (1988). *Life events and psychological functioning: Theoretical and methodological issues.* Newbury Park, CA: Sage.

DeLongis, A., Coyne, J. C., Dakof, G., Folkman, S., & Lazarus, R. S. (1982). Relationships of daily hassles, uplifts, and major life events to health status. *Health Psychology, 1,* 119–136.

Diener, E. (1984). Subjective well-being. *Psychological Bulletin, 95,* 542–575.

Diener, E., Sandvik, E., & Larsen, R. (1985). Age and sex effects for emotional intensity. *Developmental Psychology, 21,* 542–546.

Doeringer, P. B. (Ed.). (1990). *Bridges to retirement: Older workers in a changing labor market.* Cornell, NY: ILR Press.

Doeringer, P. B. (1991). *Turbulence in the American workplace.* New York: Oxford University Press.

Fontana, A., & Frey, J. H. (1990). Postretirement workers in the labor force. *Work and Occupations, 17,* 355–361.

Fordyce, M. W. (1976). Development of a program to increase personal happiness. *Journal of Counseling Psychology, 24,* 511–521.

Hayslip, B., & Panek, P. (1993). *Adult development and aging.* New York: Harper & Row.

Heineman, G. (1982). Why study widowed women? A rationale. *Women and Health, 7,* 17–29.

Herzberg, F. (1966). *Work and the nature of man.* Cleveland, OH: World.

Herzog, A. R., Holden, K. C., & Seltzer, M. (Eds.). (1989). *Health and economic status of older women.* Amityville, NY: Baywood.

Herzog, A. R., House, J. S., & Morgan, J. N. (1991). Relation of work and retirement to health and well-being in older age. *Psychology and Aging, 6,* 202–211.

Holmes, T. H., & Rahe, R. H. (1967). The social readjustment rating scale. *Journal of Psychosomatic Research, 11,* 213–218.

Hooker, K. (1992). Possible selves and perceived health in older adults and college students. *Journal of Gerontology: Psychological Sciences, 47,* 85–95.

Kacmar, K. M., & Ferris, G. R. (1989). Theoretical and methodological considerations in the age–job satisfaction relationship. *Journal of Applied Psychology, 74,* 201–207.

Kanner, A. D., Coyne, J. C., Schaefer, C., & Lazarus, R. S. (1981). Comparison of two models of stress measurement: Daily hassles and uplifts versus major life events. *Journal of Behavioral Medicine, 4,* 1–39.

Kastenbaum, R., Derbin, B., Sabatini, P., & Artt, S. (1972). "The ages of me": Toward personal in interpersonal definitions of functional age. *International Journal of Aging and Human Development, 3,* 197–212.

Kinderknecht, C. H., & Hodges, L. (1990). Facilitating productive bereavement of widows: An overview of the efficacy of widow's support groups. *Journal of Women and Aging, 2,* 39–54.

Kline, M. L., & Snow, D. L. (1992, November). Longitudinal effects of a worksite coping skills intervention on women's psychological adjustment and substance use. Paper presented at the APA/NIOSH conference "Stress in the 1990s: A changing workforce in a changing workplace," Washington, DC.

Kobasa, S. C. (1979). Stressful life events, personality and health: An inquiry into hardiness. *Personality and Social Psychology, 37,* 1–11.

Lazarus, R. S. (1990). Theory-based stress measurement. *Psychological Inquiry, 1,* 3–13.

Lazarus, R. S. (1991). *Emotion and adaptation.* New York: Oxford University Press.

Lewis, G. L. (1978). Changes in women's role participation. In I. H. Frieze, J. E. Parsons, P. B. Johnson, D. N. Ruble, & G. L. Zellman (Eds.), *Women and sex roles: A social psychological perspective* (pp. 137–156). New York: W. W. Norton.

Lopata, H. Z. (1987). *Widows* (Vol. 2). Durham, NC: Duke University Press.

Lowenstein, A., & Rosen, A. (1989). The relation of widows' needs and resources to perceived health and depression. *Social Science Medicine, 5,* 659–667.

Lund, D. (1989). *Older bereaved spouses: Research with practical application.* New York: Hemisphere.

Matthews, K. A., & Rodin, J. (1989). Women's changing work roles. *American Psychologist, 44,* 1389–1393.

McFarland, R. A. (1973). The need for functional age measurements in industrial gerontology. *Journal of Gerontology, 1,* 1–9.

Nelson, D. L., & Hitt, M. A. (1992). Employed women and stress: Implications for enhancing women's mental health in the workplace. In J. C. Quick, L. R. Murphy, & J. J. Hurrell (Eds.), *Stress and well-being at work: Assessments and interventions for occupational mental health* (pp. 164–177). Washington, DC: American Psychological Association.

Plimpton, L., Staats, S., & Partlo, C. (1992, May). *Comparison of hope and social functioning in widows and married women: Widowhood (the long of it).* Paper presented at the 64th annual meeting of the Midwestern Psychological Association, Chicago.

Quick, J. C., Murphy, L. R., & Hurrell, J. J. (Eds.). (1992). *Stress and well-being at work: Assessments and interventions for occupational mental health.* Washington, DC: American Psychological Association.

Repetti, R. L., Matthews, K. A., & Waldron, I. (1989). Employment and women's health. *American Psychologist, 44,* 1394–1401.

Rix, S. E. (1990). *Older workers: Choices & challenges.* Santa Barbara, CA: ABC-CLIO.

Salthouse, T. A. (1991). *Theoretical perspectives on cognitive aging.* Hillsdale, NJ: Erlbaum.

Schultz, D. P., & Schultz, S. E. (1990). *Psychology and industry today.* New York: Macmillan.

Sparrow, P. R., & Davies, D. R. (1988). Effects of age, tenure, training, and job complexity on technical performance. *Psychology and Aging, 3,* 307–314.

Staats, S. R. (1989). Hope: A comparison of two self-report measures for adults. *Journal of Personality Assessment, 53,* 366–375.

Staats, S. R. (1991). Quality of life and affect in older persons: Hope, time frames, and training effects. *Current Psychology, 10*, 21–30.

Staats, S. R., Atha, G., & Isham, J. (1990). Variations in expected affect in young and middle-aged adults. *Journal of Genetic Psychology, 151*, 419–429.

Staats, S. R., Heaphey, K., Miller, D., Partlo, C., Romine, N., & Stubbs, K. (1992). Biases in functional age and in perceptions of health for older persons with differential health status. *International Journal of Aging and Human Development, 37*, 191–203.

Staats, S. R., & Partlo, C. (1993). A brief report on hope in peace and war, and in good times and bad. *Social Indicators Research, 29*, 229–243.

Staats, S. R., & Skowronski, J. (1992). Perceptions of self-affect: Now and in the future. *Social Cognition, 10*, 415–431.

Staats, S., & Stassen, M. (1987). Age and present and future perceived quality of life. *International Journal of Aging and Human Development, 25*, 167–176.

U.S. Bureau of the Census. (1992). *Marital status of the population by sex, race, and Hispanic origin: 1970–1991* (No. 49, Statistical Abstracts of the United States, 1992). Washington, DC: U.S. Government Printing Office.

Warr, P. (1992). Age and occupational well-being. *Psychology and Aging, 7*, 37–45.

Welford, A. T. (1977). Motor performance. In J. E. Birren & K. W. Schaie (Eds.), *Handbook of the psychology of aging* (pp. 450–490). New York: Van Nostrand Reinhold.

Wilson, W. (1967). Correlates of avowed happiness. *Psychological Bulletin, 67*, 294–306.

Wittwer, J. (1990). Shades of Grey—The demographic timebomb. *International Journal of Physical Distribution and Logistics Management, 20*, 9–12.

12 ―――――――――――――――――――

Improving the Working Conditions of Older People: An Analysis of Attitudes Toward Early Retirement

Pekka Huuhtanen

The increasing average age of the population will challenge social, health, and human resource policies in most industrialized countries in the near future. In 1980, 32% of the entire working population was older than 45 years in countries belonging to the Organization for Economic Cooperation and Development (OECD). This proportion is expected to increase to 35.5% by the year 2000 and to 41.3% by the year 2025 (World Health Organization, 1993). By about 2020, nearly 40% of the workforce in OECD countries will be between 45 and 65 years of age.

The issue of aging and work capacity is increasing in importance because of these demographic trends. The work capacity of older people is often incompatible with work demands, and this situation can lead to stress, health problems, and high mortality. Age-related changes occur in human physiological and psychological functions, in attitudes and ways of learning, and in the acquisition of new skills (McEvoy & Cascio, 1989; Rhodes, 1983). Such changes may have negative impacts on stress and well-being, depending on the way changes and learning possibilities are arranged (e.g., Czaja, 1988; Huuhtanen & Leino, 1992; Huuhtanen, Nygård, Tuomi, Eskelinen, & Toikkanen, 1991).

Early exit from work and early retirement have been increasing. Pensions accounted for more than 33% of total social expenditures throughout the 1960s and 1970s in many West European countries and for more than 40% of social budgets at the end of the 1980s in Scandinavian countries (Salminen, 1993). It has been estimated that the ratio of people working to those retired will increase from 5:2 to 2:5 between 1990 and 2030 in Finland.

These trends clearly suggest that issues surrounding work, work capacity, and aging will become increasingly important. Between 50 and 65 years of age, individuals make decisions concerning the continuation of work and going into retirement. These decisions have an impact on human resource, social, and productivity issues at the societal and company levels. So far, little thought and planning have been directed to the later stages of working life. Most studies on physical and mental capabilities have been based on comparisons of people over 60 with 20 year olds, neglecting middle-aged people (e.g., see "Aging at work," 1993).

To meet the challenge of the near future described above, the Finnish Institute of Occupational Health has been carrying out a multidisciplinary program called "Respect for the Aging," or the FinnAge program (Ilmarinen, 1991). The program has two primary objectives: (a) creating optimal working conditions for aging workers and (b) promoting health, work ability, and well-being of aging workers. The emphasis is on workers over 45 years of age. The program consists of about 20 projects in industry, the municipal sector, and private service sectors. The University of Jyväskylä and the Swedish School of Economics and Business Administration, Helsinki, Finland, are taking part in the program, which is supported by the Finnish Work Environment Fund.

The basic methodology combines research, job design, interventions, and training in different organizations and occupational groups. Psychological, physiological, economic, and medical data are being gathered. The psychological part of the program consists of repeated surveys on work and retirement attitudes and on the motivation of workers and pensioners at 2-year intervals (Huuhtanen & Piispa, 1992a; Tikkanen & Kuusinen, 1992), on development of tasks and cooperation between young and old workers, on training in computer applications, on user design of data systems suitable for aging workers (Hukki & Seppälä, 1992), on group work in the clothing industry, and on work and health among aging teachers (Kinnunen, Rasku, & Parkatti, 1992).

In this article, I describe results and methodology of the attitude surveys. The focus is on the first phase of the retirement process—that of preference or anticipation. Thoughts of retirement are seen as attitudinal antecedents of retirement that provide a basis for better understanding how to address the aging working population.

Work and Retirement Attitudes

Research Questions

As the starting point for the Respect for the Aging program, an interview study was carried out in 1990 dealing with the attitudes of people toward work and retirement. The following five questions from the interviews are discussed in this article: (a) How frequently do you have thoughts of early retirement? (b) What are the grounds for these thoughts? (c) How many persons in the workforce and on pension are interested in still working after retirement? (d) How do work-motivated groups and retirement-motivated groups differ with respect to health, physical capacity, stress, and mental resources? and (e) What, in general, are the prerequisites for continuing to work up until retirement age, and what are the personal prerequisites for taking part in work life after early retirement? The data presented in this article are descriptive, being the first step in addressing the emerging issue of improving work conditions for aging workers.

Materials and Method

The study was conducted with two samples, each with 1,000 Finnish workers. Sample 1 contained workers over 35 years of age, and Sample 2 consisted of workers who were already retired. The samples were selected from the Labor Force Survey compiled by the Central Statistical Office of Finland, which is based on a sample of the total Finnish population aged 15 to 74. Samples of the Labor Force Survey number 36,000 per quarter and are divided into three monthly samples of 12,000. The data I used were collected in September 1990.

Sample 1 consisted of 879 persons (51% women and 49% men) over the age of 35 years who were in the Finnish labor force. Sample 2 comprised 836 persons (56% women and 44% men) who were already retired. The data were collected through telephone interviews in connection with the Labor Force Survey.

Interviewers asked questions concerning thoughts of early retirement, offering four response categories: "has not thought," "has thought sometimes," "is thinking continuously," and "has applied for a pension." Occupation was classified on the basis of a respondent's socioeconomic status.

Grounds for thoughts of early retirement were classified into five categories, which were formed on the basis of information first gathered with an open-ended question. The categories were health and work capacity (loss of these or fear of losing them or wants to retire while still in good health), attraction of the life sphere outside work (e.g., family or hobbies), aging as such and factors connected with it (i.e., "I have already been working for 20–30 years and think it is enough"), the contents of work and work stress, and other reasons.

A list of 10 items of possible improvement was given to those still working, and they were asked to state whether they thought the presented issue would be an important factor in reducing unnecessary early retirement. For those who were already retired and had thought of working, researchers asked about personal prerequisites for taking part in work life. Retirees responded with one of the following alternatives for each item: 1 = *is important as a prerequisite to taking part in work life* and 2 = *is not important as a prerequisite to taking part in the work life.*

Mental resources were measured with standardized scales used in earlier studies by the Finnish Institute of Occupational Health. A scale of mental resources was based on the following three questions: "Have you enjoyed your daily routines recently?" "Have you been active and energetic recently?" and "Have you felt yourself optimistic as regards the future recently?" Responses were made on a 5-point scale ranging from 4 = *very often* to 0 = *never*. The reliability of the scale was .67 (Cronbach's alpha), and scores ranged from 0 to 12.

Physical capacity was measured on a 5-point scale on which the subjects evaluated their physical capacity in comparison with that of others in the same age group. The scale of work capacity ranged from 0 (*cannot work*) to 10 (*best ever*). For this measure, respondents compared their current work capacity with their "best ever" capacity, on a scale ranging from 1 (*much better*) to 5 (*much worse*) than others.

The statistical analyses for this study were based on frequency distributions, tables, and means. The significance of the differences between the two samples was tested with chi-square tests and *t* tests.

Results

Thoughts of retirement. Two thirds of both men and women had at least sometimes thought of retirement before their normal old-age pension age (normally 63 or 65 years in Finland). Serious thoughts ("is thinking continuously" or "has applied for retirement") increased with age, from 7% in the age group of 35–39 years to 31% in the age group of 55–59 years (see Table 1; Huuhtanen & Piispa, 1992a). However, the prevalence of thoughts of early retirement (62%) was at the same level in the three youngest groups.

Grounds for thoughts of retirement. The most common reason for considering early retirement was the fear of losing, or the loss of, one's health and work capacity (34%; see Table 2). This was followed by work content and work stress (22%), attraction of the life sphere outside work (21%), aging per se and factors connected to it (18%), and other reasons (5%). Women expressed fear of loss of health and work capacity and work content reasons slightly more frequently than did men. Age as such was mentioned more often by men.

Health and work capacity was a more common ground in the two oldest age groups (38% and 52%, for 50–54 years and 55–59 years, respectively), whereas attraction of other life spheres was most cited by workers in the three youngest groups (26%, 26%, and 23%, respectively). Aging per se was more common for 45 to 49 year olds (20%) and for 50 to 54 year olds (25%). Work was mentioned slightly more often by the youngest groups (Huuhtanen & Piispa, 1992a).

Table 3 shows the data organized by occupational category. Health and work capacity was a significantly more frequent reason for thoughts of retirement among manual workers, and life sphere outside work was emphasized by both upper- and lower-level employees. Work content and stress were men-

Table 1. Number and Percentage of People With Thoughts of Early Retirement

Age (years)	n	Has not thought (%)	Has thought sometimes (%)	Is considering continuously or has applied for retirement (%)
35–39	217	38	55	7
40–44	247	38	53	9
45–49	172	38	47	15
50–54	119	27	45	28
55–59	98	24	45	31
All	853	35	50	15

Table 2. Percentage of Men and Women Citing the Most Important Grounds for Thoughts of Early Retirement

Gender	n	Health and work capacity (%)	Attraction of the life sphere outside work (%)	Aging as such and factors connected to it (%)	Content of work and work stress (%)	Other reasons (%)
Men	265	31	20	21	19	9
Women	276	37	22	14	24	3
Both	541	34	21	18	22	5

Note. Between men and women, $\chi^2 = 16.97$, $p < .005$.

tioned relatively often by senior officials, health and social service personnel, and industrial workers.

Work and retirement orientation. Intentions to continue working (paid work) after retirement were determined by responses to the following question: "What do you think your attitude toward work might be when you reach retirement age?" The responses were as follows: "I would stop paid work immediately," "I would accept some nonpermanent work," "I would like to have a permanent part-time job," "I would like to continue in a permanent full-time job after retirement," "I am probably going to retire early," or "Cannot say." Thirty-two percent of the respondents said that they would stop working, women (36%) more often than men (28%). Temporary work would be accepted by 45% (women, 40% and men, 50%), a regular part-time job by 7%, and a regular full-time job by 3% of the respondents. Thirteen percent had no opinion about the issue. Women were slightly less motivated to continue working than men ($p = .005$). White-collar workers were more likely to indicate plans to work after retirement than were blue-collar workers.

On the basis of their thoughts about early retirement, respondents were classified into two categories: work oriented (35%, $n = 312$) and retirement oriented (65%, $n = 565$). These groups differed with respect to their subjective

Table 3. Percentages of the Total Sample Citing the Most Important Reasons for Thoughts of Early Retirement, by Occupational Category

Reason	Upper-level employees		Lower-level employees			Workers	
	A	B	C	D	E	F	G
Health and work capacity	17	27	27	31	25	36	46
Life sphere outside work	34	27	17	25	27	16	15
Aging	17	15	29	23	17	16	11
Work	26	24	20	16	27	29	19
Other reason	6	7	7	5	4	3	9

Note. $N = 541$. A = managers and employees in research and planning; B = employees in education, training, and others; C = supervisors; D = office and sales workers; E = health care and social workers; F = industrial workers; G = other workers.

evaluation of physical capacity (in comparison with others of the same age), psychological resources, psychological stress symptoms, and the number of diagnosed diseases. In all these issues, those in the work-oriented group evaluated their situation to be better than did those in the retirement-oriented group.

Preconditions for continuing work. A list of 10 items of possible improvements at work was presented to all respondents, and each respondent was asked to evaluate whether he or she considered the issue as important in limiting unnecessary early retirement. The percentages of total respondents reacting positively to these items were as follows: the amount and haste of work, 80%; flexible working hours, 76%; improvement of the work environment, 76%; possibilities for rehabilitation, 76%; wages, 67%; work content, 66%; occupational health services, 64%; leadership styles, 63%; training possibilities, 57%; and a sabbatical year, 59%.

Women put more emphasis on improvements at work, especially for such issues as occupational health care, wages, and sabbatical year. In general, the youngest groups emphasized improvements more than the oldest ones.

The preconditions differed by occupational category (see Table 4). Managers emphasized work content more often than did others. Possibilities for rehabilitation were an important precondition for lower-level employees. Improvements in leadership styles were emphasized by supervisors more than by others. Only wages were a more pronounced precondition for workers in comparison with the other occupational groups.

Comparision of workers and pensioners. The participation of retired persons in work life was determined by responses to this question: "Have you thought of the possibility of somehow still taking part in work life?" The group's

Table 4. Percentages of Respondents Choosing Various Preconditions for Continuing Work, by Occupational Category

Precondition	Upper-level employees		Lower-level employees			Workers	
	A	B	C	D	E	F	G
Amount and haste of work	76	87	79	86	88	75	83
Flexible work hours	77	85	77	76	86	69	74
Work environment	81	82	84	74	78	77	73
Rehabilitation	69	71	84	86	80	77	77
Wages	39	57	61	73	79	76	81
Work content	84	71	75	66	76	59	58
Occupational health services	52	51	61	65	73	67	74
Leadership style	76	74	84	71	64	58	55
Sabbatical year	66	76	52	67	79	55	54
Training	58	66	64	54	73	54	45

Note. $N = 715$. A = managers and employees in research and planning; B = employees in education, training, and others; C = supervisors; D = office and sales workers; E = health care and social workers; F = industrial workers; G = other workers.

responses were as follows (n = 836): "I have not thought about it," 82%; "I have thought about it sometimes," 12%; "I am thinking continuously about it," 2%; and "I am already working within the limits of regulations (e.g., right to pension, taxation, amount of pension)," 4%.

Physical capacity and work capacity were connected with work and retirement motivation in the retirement sample, as was expected. When work-motivated subgroups of workers and pensioners were compared, those already retired reported having a significantly lower physical and work capacity. However, the differences between the retirement-motivated subgroups were also significant with regard to mental resources (Huuhtanen & Piispa, 1992b).

Positive ratings given by the retirement group with respect to the personal prerequisites for taking part in work life were as follows (n = 113): good health, 83%; changes in the regulations of pension systems and taxation, 74%; suitable job locally available, 71%; part-time job, 66%; autonomous work schedule, 61%; better wages, 43%; possibilities to influence one's work, 34%; improvement in work content, 26%; improvement in the work environment, 24%; improvement in leadership style, 21%; and change in family situation, 14%.

Those still working generally emphasized wanting more improvements in work environment and in leadership styles. They also placed more stress on wages and work content.

Discussion

Retirement Attitudes

Surveys in 1990 revealed that two thirds of both men and women over 35 years of age had at least sometimes thought of retiring before the normal pension age (63 years or 65 years in Finland). These thoughts were even relatively common among younger workers. Health and work conditions and work content were important grounds for thoughts of early retirement. Health and work capacity were also reasons for such thoughts, especially among blue-collar workers. The data showed a relationship between work and retirement attitudes and subjective evaluations of mental and physical well-being.

It must be emphasized that thoughts of early retirement are not the same as the decision to start the process of retirement or actual retirement. Instead, thoughts represent the first, anticipatory phase in the transition from work to retirement (e.g., Beehr, 1986; Hanisch & Hulin, 1990). In addition, the five categories of grounds for retirement formed from responses to the open-ended question are not totally separate; for example, health and work can be strongly related to each other.

Women and health and social care employees put more emphasis on improvements at work, especially such issues as occupational health care, wages, and a sabbatical year. This might reflect gender differences both in work conditions and in the sensitivity to problems at work. The oldest groups emphasized improvements less than did the younger groups. A plausible explanation could be that the older respondents felt that the suggested improvements, however important, were not rapid enough to exert positive effects on work near their retirement age. They may also have been more skeptical than the younger respondents about getting real improvements in working conditions.

The interviews revealed that interest in taking part in work life after retirement was much higher in the group that was still working than among those already retired. The comparision of mental resources and physical and mental work capacity of the groups indicated that individual resources and capacity influence work and retirement motivation more when people are on early retirement than when they are still working. Aspects other than health or the loss of health were more important for those still working. The prerequisites for continuing to work after retirement were very personal issues for the pensioners. It should be noted, however, that interviewers did not ask workers for their own personal prerequisites.

One should keep in mind that people who are still working near the old-age pension age represent the "healthy worker effect." Most of those who have already retired at these ages are on disability pensions and have done so because of poor health or low work capacity, as was clearly demonstrated by the results of the retirement sample. In Finland, only a fraction of those on early pension have retired voluntarily, without any loss of health.

Developmental Needs

To enhance the possibilities that aging people will continue to work until the normal retirement age, surveys on both attitudes and work-site interventions are needed. Relevant psychological research data would help to change attitudes and negative stereotypical beliefs about aging workers. Human resource planning and counseling should reflect the attitudinal antecedents of individuals' retirement intentions in addition to their year of birth. The use of standardized attitude measurement scales would also prove useful at the company level by providing a basis for resource planning for aging workers.

To ensure a more individualistic choice between work and other life activities for people nearing retirement age, working conditions, regulations, and individual capabilities and personal resources must be developed. This is a challenge for both researchers and practitioners in the field of work psychology. To start with, measures should be better adapted to the type of work and to the increased individual variability among aging workers.

The situation of having older people at work depends heavily on the labor policy of firms. The integration of older workers into the labor force also varies with the supply and demand of labor, on both societal and company levels. The current recession has led governments and companies to reduce benefits and protection for workers and pensioners. Pressed by global competition, companies are trying to develop measures to lower monthly retirement payments and to raise retirement ages and the years that must be worked to get full retirement benefits. Because social and environmental factors vary considerably from country to country and between companies, programs designed for older workers will need to vary accordingly (Kohli & Rein, 1991; Laczko

& Phillipson, 1991). On the company level, ongoing longitudinal studies and developmental projects in the FinnAge program will add to knowledge about the temporal changes of attitudes and behavior of the aging workforce.

One ongoing project is aimed at the development of tasks and cooperation between young and old workers. The goals of the project are as follows: first, to combine different capabilities, knowledge and experience of age and cohort groups at work; second, to enhance the individual choices of aging workers about continuing to work until normal retirement age; and third, to minimize harmful competition between age groups. These goals will be reached by increasing the knowledge and changing the attitudes of supervisors and workers, by developing a division of tasks, by developing social support and learning, and by creating methods for personnel administration and occupational health and safety personnel.

More detailed multivariate statistical analyses will be done with the Labor Force Survey data in the future. New data were collected in the same size study populations of workers and pensioners in Finland in 1992 and in 1994. To develop psychological theories on adult development and on aging in connection with work and stress, international comparative studies and theoretical discussion are needed from researchers and from industrial and occupational psychologists in different countries.

References

Aging at work: Consequences for industry and individual [Editorial]. (1993, January 9). *The Lancet*, p. 340.

Beehr, T. A. (1986). The process of retirement: A review and recommendations for future investigations. *Personnel Psychology, 9*, 31–55.

Czaja, S. J. (1988). Microcomputers and the elderly. In M. Helander (Ed.), *Handbook of human–computer interaction* (pp. 581–598). Amsterdam: Elsevier.

Hanisch, K. A., & Hulin, C. L. (1990). Job attitudes and organizational withdrawal: An examination of retirement and other voluntary withdrawal behaviors. *Journal of Vocational Behavior, 37*, 60–78.

Hukki, K., & Seppälä, P. (1992). Utilization of users' experiences in the introduction of information technology: A study in a large municipal organization. In J. Ilmarinen (Ed.), *Proceedings of an international scientific symposium on aging and work* (Vol. 4, pp. 170–176). Helsinki, Finland: Finnish Institute of Occupational Health.

Huuhtanen, P., & Leino, T. (1992). The impact of new technology by occupation and age on work in financial firms: A 2-year follow-up. *International Journal of Human–Computer Interaction, 4*, 123–142.

Huuhtanen, P., Nygård, C.-H., Tuomi, K., Eskelinen, L., & Toikkanen, J. (1991). Changes in the content of Finnish municipal occupations over a four-year period. *Scandinavian Journal of Work and Environment Health, 17*(Suppl. 1), 48–57.

Huuhtanen, P., & Piispa, M. (1992a). Work or retirement: Alternatives of elderly people in the 1990s. *Arbete och Hälsa, 29*, 60–66.

Huuhtanen, P., & Piispa, M. (1992b). Work and retirement attitudes of 50- to 64-year-old people at work and on pension. *Scandinavian Journal of Work and Environment Health, 2*(Suppl. 18), 21–23.

Ilmarinen, J. (1991, August 2). FinnAge: Action program on health, work ability, and well-being of the aging worker. In *Työterveiset*. Helsinki, Finland: Finnish Institute of Occupational Health.

Kinnunen, U., Rasku, A., & Parkatti, T. (1992). Aging among the teaching profession: Work, well-being and health among aging teachers. In J. Ilmarinen (Ed.), *Proceedings of an international scientific symposium on aging and work* (Vol. 4, pp. 157–161). Helsinski, Finland: Finnish Institute of Occupational Health.

Kohli, M., & Rein, M. (1991). The changing balance of work and retirement. In M. Kohli, M. Rein, A.-M. Guillemard, & H. van Gunsteren (Eds.), *Time for retirement: Comparative studies of early exit from the labor force* (pp. 1–35). Cambridge, England: Cambridge University Press.

Laczko, F., & Phillipson, C. (1991). *Changing work and retirement: Social policy and the older workers.* Philadelphia: Open University Press.

McEvoy, G. M., & Cascio, W. F. (1989). Cumulative evidence of the relationship between employee age and job performance. *Journal of Applied Psychology, 74,* 11–17.

Rhodes, S. R. (1983). Age-related differences in work attitudes and behavior: A review and conceptual analysis. *Psychological Bulletin, 93,* 328–367.

Salminen, K. (1993). *Pension schemes in the making: A comparative study of the Scandinavian countries* (Studies, No. 2). Helsinki, Finland: Central Pension Security Institute.

Tikkanen, T., & Kuusinen, J. (1992). Retirement and retirement preparation. In J. Ilmarinen (Ed.), *Proceedings of an international scientific symposium on aging and work* (Vol. 4, pp. 188–194). Helsinki, Finland: Finnish Institute of Occupational Health.

World Health Organization. (1993). *Aging and working capacity* (WHO Tech. Rep. Series, 835). Geneva, Switzerland: Author.

WORK AND
NONWORK

Part IV

Work and Family Functioning

Introduction

It is clear that when people arrive at work they do not forget family-related difficulties, nor do they forget work-related problems when they return home. The four chapters in this part deal with the broad topic of stress as it relates to work and family functioning. Two of the chapters examine the consequences of family-related problems for organizations, whereas the remaining two discuss the spillover effects of job stress on family life.

First, Dompierre and Lavoie address the relationship between job-related stress and violence. They report the results of a survey study in which they evaluated the contribution of work stress to employees' violence toward their partners and children.

Next, Tetrick, Miles, Marcil, and Van Dosen survey working parents and their colleagues to evaluate problems associated with working and child care. Specifically, Tetrick et al. examine how child-care difficulties affect productivity-related outcomes among working mothers and fathers as well as their coworkers.

Kelloway and Barling present the results of a three-wave panel study of the impact of job demands and the worker's sense of job control on marital functioning. They specifically examine both direct and indirect linkages between work, stress, and marital functioning.

Finally, Marshall and Barnett describe their study of the effects of family-friendly work policies. Using data obtained from nearly 300 couples, they examine how giving employees the flexibility at work to respond to nonwork situations affects job satisfaction, interference with family life, and mental health.

13

Subjective Work Stress and Family Violence

Johanne Dompierre and Francine Lavoie

Models explaining family violence have often included stress as a determining variable (e.g., Dutton, 1988; Garbarino, 1977; Gelles, 1973; Straus, 1973). However, only a few empirical studies have recently been conducted. These studies have been conducted within the classical paradigm based on the number of stressful life events. Only a few recent studies have looked at the subjective perception of stress. Browne (1986); Garbarino (1976); Justice, Calvert, and Justice (1985); Seltzer and Kalmuss (1988); and Straus (1980a, 1980b) have considered the number of life events of varied origin and concluded that there is a link between stressful life events and family violence. Other work has reported a link between life events and coercive behavior toward children (Desfossés & Bouchard, 1987). Farrington (1986) and Howze and Kotch (1984) criticized the use of only objective measures of stress and stated a preference for research on violence that draws on more recent theoretical models (e.g., Lazarus & Folkman, 1984) that are better articulated and integrate not only objective stressors but also perceptions of these stressors and coping strategies. As it is known that not everyone reacts to stress with family violence, consideration of perception of stressors would make it easier to understand the role of risk or protective factors in the link between stressors and violence. Note also that lists of life events refer to a great variety of contexts—such as family life, work life, and life as a citizen—and so, lead to confusion. Although there was early interest in the more detailed study of work and its influence on family violence, as yet, researchers have provided only secondary data analysis.

For violence between partners, Straus (1980a) has shown that there is a link between life events and the occurrence of violence toward partners among both men and women. Furthermore, he reported that the link was even stronger when he used only occupational and financial events from the previous year— namely, misunderstandings with colleagues or superiors, increased workload, job loss, loans falling due, and increased financial problems. It would thus seem impossible to look only at the influence of job-related stressors. Finn (1985) looked more at the subjective aspect of stress. When questioning people involved in violent spousal relationships, he found that work was at the origin of difficulties with the spouse for 47% of violent men and for 57% of female victims. Unfortunately, no further details were given on the precise source of the problem. Thus, the early research on domestic violence indicated some leads without specifying the origin of job-related stress. For violence against women by their male partners, Barling and Rosenbaum (1986) added two dimensions of perceived stress to the number of typical job-related stressors: the negative perception of the impact of job-related stressful events and a measure of job involvement. Using the Conflict Tactics Scales (Straus, 1979) to measure violence between partners, they compared groups of abusive men, men satisfied with their relationships, and men who were dissatisfied with their relationships. They concluded that abusive men had experienced a greater number of stressful events at work and also had a more negative perception of these events. On the other hand, no link was found between job involvement and violence toward their partners.

In the case of violence toward children, the analysis of survey data by Straus (1980b) showed that the number of stressful events of all types was associated with a greater occurrence of violence by fathers. However, this relation was weaker for mothers; the level of violence was quite high at all levels of stress. No details were given about job-related stressors. Furthermore, the fact that many mothers in the sample were not in the workforce must also be taken into account.

Despite recommendations by Farrington (1986) to study the link between stress and violence, both in the context of violence toward children and toward partners, few comparative research studies have been conducted. Finkelhor (1983) reported that acts of violence against a child or partner seem to be committed to compensate for a perceived lack or loss of power. The study of certain workplace variables might contribute to this discussion. Furthermore, abusive partners or parents are often found in the same family (Straus, Gelles, & Steinmetz, 1980). It is thus the simultaneous study of partner and child abuse that will contribute to the clarification of these points.

The present research conducted among workers thus serves to identify how the perception of work stressors contributes to the explanation of violent behavior. As recommended by Greenhaus and Parasuraman (1986), we have integrated the perceived job stressors into a model with economic and family stressors. Furthermore, this investigation simultaneously considers violence toward children and violence toward a partner to enhance the understanding of common and individual factors.

In this study, we evaluated the possibility of discriminating between violent and nonviolent workers who direct violence toward their families (i.e., children or partner) by using variables linked to the workplace, the family, finances, and health status.

Method

Participants

Participants were French Canadian and were recruited from four types of organizations: insurance, catering, government, and education. Agreements were made with the department of human resources or the union in each organization. Selection criteria were full-time employment (30 hr per week) on a permanent basis, with at least 3 months in the same position. Overall, 854 out of 1,938 possible participants answered the questionnaires. This represents a participation rate of 44% (schools, 34%; insurance, 45%; catering, 23%; and government, 63%). From this sample, two subsamples were formed for this study: participants with children (Sample 1, $n = 367$) and participants cohabiting with a partner (Sample 2, $n = 529$).

Sample 1 was distributed as follows in the occupational fields: insurance (9.5%), catering (12.8%), school (4.9%), and government (72.8%). In addition, 13.7% were in management positions, 35.2% were professionals, and 51.1% were neither in management nor were professionals. Twenty-eight percent of the sample were women, and 72% were men. The mean age was 40 years, and the mean completed educational level was junior college. Mean occupation of the current position was 6 years and 6 months. Mean income was Can$693 per week.

Sample 2 came from the following fields: insurance (7.2%), catering (16.1%), school (10.0%), and government (66.7%). There were 12.3% in management positions, 30.9% were professionals, and 56.8% were neither managers nor professionals. Thirty-five percent were women, and 65% were men. Their mean age was 38 years, and the mean completed education level was junior college. Mean occupation of the current position was 5 years and 11 months. Mean income was Can$623 per week.

Procedure

A self-administered questionnaire was distributed in the workplace with a reply envelope and two letters of introduction, one from the department of human resources or the union and another explaining the research aims. The completed questionnaires were returned in sealed envelopes either to the department of human resources or to the union. Three reminders were sent to the employees. The study was conducted in 1987.

Instruments

Workplace variables. Work-related stressors were measured with indexes developed by Dolan and Arsenault (1983). Quantitative overload, role conflict, and role ambiguity subscales were used, with some modifications. The final overload subscale had five items and adequate internal consistency ($\alpha = .63$). The role conflict and role ambiguity subscales each had two items and so were merged to make a role difficulties subscale ($\alpha = .61$). Responses to these measures were made on 5-point Likert scales and resulted in high scores indicating high perceived exposure to these stressors. The scales ranged from 1 (*almost always*) to 5 (*almost never*). We hypothesized that greater work demands may be an important factor in discriminating between violent and nonviolent individuals because such demands generate the perception of being overwhelmed or not being in control of the work situation.

Three indexes developed by Dolan and Arsenault (1983) were merged to measure decision latitude, namely, participation in decision making, restricted autonomy, and underutilization of abilities. (The restricted autonomy and underutilization of skills indexes were recoded and are hereinafter referred to as *autonomy* and *utilization of abilities*.) Some modifications were made. The total scale (15 items) had very good internal consistency (α = .87). The response format was identical to the format used for the stressors. The higher the score, the more the participant reported exercising latitude. Decision latitude corresponds to the opportunities at work that allow responses to job demands. The absence of latitude may prove to be a source of stress in that what could have been an opportunity may become a constraint.

Under the heading *interpersonal stressors* were variables associated with the presence of work conflicts with coworkers or superiors (two items), the presence of aggressive colleagues (one item), and a lack of communication with superiors (one item). These three variables may constitute sources of stress and were analyzed separately. We merged the Supervisor Support subscale (eight items, excluding the item about salary increases) and the Peer Cohesion subscale (nine items) of the Work Environment Scale (Insel & Moos, 1974) to form a perceived support at work scale (α = .84). The relational aspect was also involved here: The lack of support could also be considered to be a source of stress.

We postulated that being exposed to sources of stress at work would distinguish the groups of violent and nonviolent participants. We further hypothesized that violent (potentially or actively) participants would be distinguished from nonviolent participants according to the following profile: work demands—more overload and more role difficulties; work constraints—less latitude; and interpersonal stressors—more work conflict, more aggressive colleagues, less communication, and less support at work.

Family variables. There were two variables in this category: domestic load and nonfinancial stressful events. Domestic load consisted of two items: "Normally, on work days, how much time do you spend all together [*sic*] on the following tasks: meal preparation, dishes, and housework?" and "Normally, on work days, how much time do you spend looking after your children?" For both of these items, participants responded on a 7-point Likert-type scale ranging from 1 (*none*) to 7 (*more than 3 hr per day*). The nonfinancial stressful events variable drew heavily on the scale used in the Québec-Health Survey (Kovess, 1982). It involved 17 events that may have happened over the previous year (the greater the score, the more there were stressful events). These two variables correspond to demands by the family. We postulated that violent participants would differ from nonviolent participants in their exposure to family demands (e.g., showing more domestic burden and more nonfinancial stressful events) because excessive family demands induce a perception of being overwhelmed or not having control over the home situation or because the demands lead to a state of fatigue.

Economic variables. This category was represented by two variables. The stressful financial events variable was a dichotomous variable (yes–no) measuring the presence of financial difficulties in the previous year. The other variable was income. We postulated that being exposed to sources of economic stress distinguishes violent from nonviolent participants. More precisely, violent participants were expected to report more financial demands and constraints (i.e., more economic difficulties and less income).

Health status. Three indicators were used to measure health status. Emotional distress was measured with the Psychiatric Symptom Index (Ilfeld, 1976), a 29-item scale translated by the Quebec-Health Survey research team (Kovess, 1982). A validation study conducted by Vézina (1988) among 134 Quebec widows (French-speaking population) showed that the scale was homogeneous (Cronbach's $\alpha = .96$, split-half reliability $= .95$, $p < .001$) and showed good convergent validity with the General Health Questionnaire (Goldberg, 1972; $r = .81$, $n = 120$, $p < .001$). The scale was also sensitive to change. The instrument measures general symptomatology and not specific pathology. In the present study, the internal consistency was excellent ($\alpha = .94$). Respondents indicated to what extent a symptom was felt or experienced during the last week on a 3-point Likert-type scale ($0 = never$ and $3 = very\ often$). The greater the score, the more the respondent reported feeling distressed. Two further indicators were the consumption of medication in the previous 2 days (time-limited situation) and consumption during the previous year (chronic situation). For both indicators, the greater the score, the greater the variation in consumption. We hypothesized that violent participants would differ from nonviolent participants in their state of health (the greater the emotional distress, the greater the consumption of medication during the two time periods).

Family violence. Violence was measured on two axes—potential versus expressed and children versus partner—thus leading to four items. The reference period was the previous week. Potential violence toward children was measured by the question "Have you been on the point of losing control of your words or your actions toward your child?" Expressed violence toward children was measured by the question "Have you been on the point of losing control of yourself to the point of being physically violent with your child?" Potential and expressed violence toward partner were measured in the same way. Participants responded on a 4-point Likert-type scale for each of the four questions ($0 = never$ and $3 = very\ often$). Given difficulties with the frequency distribution of these variables, the ordinal scale was dichotomized ($0 = never$ and $1 = at\ least\ from\ time\ to\ time$).

Control variables. The following sociodemographic variables were also measured: gender ($1 = woman$ and $2 = man$) and cohabitation ($0 = not\ cohabiting\ with\ a\ partner$ and $1 = cohabiting\ with\ a\ partner$). When participants with children indicated that they were not living with a partner, they were considered to be a single-parent family.

Results

In the present study, we tried to answer two questions: First, is it possible to distinguish workers who report being potentially violent from workers who do not on a number of variables associated with work, family, finances, and health? Second, is it possible to distinguish workers who report being violent from workers who do not with the same variables? These two questions were examined for both violence toward children and violence toward partners.

A first series of analyses was conducted to identify variables associated with violence toward children or toward partners. We conducted chi-square tests or t tests on all variables. Following these analyses, all variables were retained for further analyses because they were associated with one or other of the types of violence.

We conducted the second series of analyses while controlling for Type I error by using discriminant analysis. The objective of the discriminant analysis is to find a classifying function or to identify a subset or linear combination of variables that best distinguishes among the groups. Using SAS software (SAS Institute, 1985), we conducted four standard discriminant analyses, one for each of the four dependent variables (potential violence–child, expressed violence–child, potential violence–partner, and expressed violence–partner). The same independent variables were used in all cases to simplify and standardize the analyses. The variables retained for the model were work demands (overload and role difficulties), work constraints (lack of decision latitude), interpersonal stressors (work conflicts, aggressive colleagues, lack of communication with the superior, and perceived support at work), family demands (domestic load and nonfinancial stressful events), financial demands and constraints (stressful financial events and income), health status (consumption of medication in the previous 2 days and over the previous year and emotional distress), and sociodemographics (gender and cohabitation).

Potential Violence Toward Children

In Sample 1, as many workers described themselves as potentially violent (n = 153) as described themselves as nonviolent (n = 149). The discriminant function was significant, indicating that the linear combination of the variables distinguished between the groups, $F(16, 283) = 5.20, p < .0001$. Examination of the univariate tests indicated that almost all of the variables were significant; in order of decreasing importance, results were as follows: emotional distress, $F(16, 283) = 63.68, p = .0001$; lack of communication with superior, $F(16, 283) = 17.16, p = .0001$; stressful financial events, $F(16, 283) = 9.59, p = .01$; role difficulties, $F(16, 283) = 6.71, p = .01$; decisional latitude, $F(16, 283) = 6.69, p = .01$; aggressive colleagues, $F(16, 283) = 6.00, p = .01$; gender, $F(16, 283) = 5.50, p = .05$; work overload, $F(16, 283) = 4.51, p = .05$; domestic load, $F(16, 283) = 5.504, p = .05$; work conflict, $F(16, 283) = 4.27, p = .05$; and the consumption of medication in the previous 2 days, $F(16, 283) = 4.03, p = .05$).

Variables of all classes discriminated significantly between potentially violent and nonviolent workers: work (demands, constraints, and interpersonal stressors), family (family demands), finances (financial demands), and health. Emotional distress and lack of communication with superior were the most significant variables. Five variables were not significant, namely, perceived support at work, income, nonfinancial stressors, cohabitation, and consumption of medication over the previous year. Classification with the discriminant function showed that 85.8% of nonviolent participants were correctly classified but that only 69.7% of potentially violent participants were correctly classified.

Expressed Violence Toward Children

For expressed violence toward children, the groups identifying themselves as violent ($n = 21$) and nonviolent ($n = 281$) were very unequal in size. However, the proportion reporting violence is not surprising and probably accurately reflects reality, because it has been estimated that about 10% of parents abuse their children. The discriminant function was highly significant and distinguished between the groups, $F(16, 283) = 2.88, p < .001$. Examination of the univariate tests indicated that only five variables were significant: domestic load, $F(16, 283) = 17.29, p = .0001$; emotional distress, $F(16, 283) = 13.91$, $p = .001$; role difficulties, $F(16, 283) = 7.88, p = .01$; work overload, $F(16, 283) = 5.66, p = .05$; gender, $F(16, 283) = 4.92, p = .05$.

It seems that expressed violence is associated with the perception of being squeezed between work and family demands and is accompanied by psychological discomfort. These results seem to suggest that violent individuals see themselves as having lost control of their lives. Classification with the discriminant function indicated that 98.9% of nonviolent and 85.7% of violent participants were correctly classified. It should be noted that the classification performance for expressed violence was superior to the classification of potentially violent parents. Consequently, it appears to be easier to discriminate between actually violent and nonviolent parents than between potentially violent and nonviolent parents.

Potential Violence Toward Partners

In Sample 2, fewer workers described themselves as potentially violent ($n = 181$) than described themselves as nonviolent ($n = 253$). It should be noted that proportionally fewer people reported being potentially violent toward partners (41%) than toward children (49%). Once again, the classification function was highly discriminant, $F(15, 418) = 7.40, p < .0001$. The univariate tests indicated that most of the variables were significant: emotional distress, $F(15, 418) = 97.93, p = .0001$; stressful financial events, $F(15, 418) = 20.37$, $p = .0001$; work conflict, $F(15, 418) = 7.59, p = .01$; aggressive colleagues, $F(15, 418) = 7.08, p = .01$; decisional latitude, $F(15, 418) = 6.69, p = .01$; gender, $F(15, 418) = 6.29, p = .01$; lack of communication with superior, $F(15, 418) = 5.71, p = .05$; and income, $F(15, 418) = 5.71, p = .05$.

Participants who were potentially violent toward their partners experienced psychological discomfort and financial difficulties. However, work constraints and interpersonal relations at work were also important. Family demands did not distinguish the two groups. The classification function correctly classified 79.1% of nonviolent but only 60.2% of violent participants.

Expressed Violence Toward Partners

Only 15 workers in Sample 2 described themselves as violent, in comparison with 419 who described themselves as nonviolent. Once again, proportionally fewer workers reported being potentially violent toward partners (3.4%) than toward children (7.0%). As observed for violence toward children, fewer variables were significant for expressed violence than for potential violence, although the classification function was discriminant, $F(15, 418) = 2.02, p < .01$. Only three variables were significant: consumption of medication in the previous 2 days, $F(15, 418) = 9.82, p = .01$; emotional distress, $F(15, 418) = 7.84, p = .01$; and domestic load, $F(15, 418) = 4.55, p = .05$.

Health status appeared to be very important: Both situational psychological distress and health problems over the previous 2 days emerged. Health difficulties accompany high family demands. In this case, work and finances were not involved at all in the expression of violence, even though they did discriminate potentially violent participants from nonviolent participants. The discriminant function correctly classified 100% of both violent and nonviolent participants.

In summary, individuals who were potentially violent toward children or partners differed from nonviolent individuals on several variables. But individuals who expressed violence differed on only a few variables—namely, health status and work or family demands. There are reasons to believe that the profile differs according to the type of violence. Finally, the classification of violent subjects was superior to that for potentially violent subjects.

Among the variables that contributed most to discriminating between all groups, emotional distress was the most important. Because of its importance in all models and its relationships with other variables in the model, we repeated all analyses after eliminating emotional distress to examine whether emotional distress had masked the effects of other variables. The analyses indicated that variables that contributed significantly to discriminating between groups remained significant once the emotional distress variable was removed. However, although the explained variance decreased for all discriminant functions, the level of significance of three out of the four discriminant functions remained highly significant. In fact, only participants who expressed violence toward partners could not be discriminated if their level of distress was not known. Finally, the classification error increased slightly for the potential and expressed violence groups.

The linear functions identified by the analyses were also examined to see whether they could reclassify the participants to the same groups. Violent participants, whether their violence was directed toward children or partners, were correctly reclassified in the violent group in 85%–100% of the cases. Admittedly, the chance of being correctly reclassified was increased because the classification function was drawn from the same groups. Consequently, the classification criteria were severe—taking into account the disproportionate group size—such that the chance of correct classification for violent subjects was reduced whereas the chance of correct classification for nonviolent subjects was increased. The classification error was lower in the nonviolent group than in the violent group for both potential and expressed violence and for violence toward both partners and children. However, the classification error was lower for expressed violent participants than for potentially violent participants and for both targets of violence. More specifically, there was no classification error for expressed violence toward partners and a low error rate for expressed violence toward children.

Discussion

In this study, we concentrated mainly on stress factors in the workplace that may play a role in family violence. Generally, the workplace was an important influence for violence toward children but not for violence toward partners.

In the case of expressed violence toward partners, the results indicated that perceived stressors in the workplace do not help distinguish between violent and nonviolent partners. Barling and Rosenbaum (1986) did succeed in discriminating between violent men who were consulting a counseling service and nonviolent men when they took into account the number of stressful events experienced at work and the global subjective perception of the negative nature of these events. Straus (1980a) also identified a link between the number of stressful events related to finances and to work (three items on work: trouble with a superior, problems with colleagues, and increased workload) and the occurrence of marital violence, mainly for men, because many women were not employed outside the home. In comparison with these two studies, our workplace stress measures provided better coverage of the multiple aspects of stress in the workplace and used parameters that are better known in the field of work-related stress. These characteristics ensure a more powerful test of the stressor–violence model. On the other hand, we did not collect data with a list of work-related stressful events. The question remains about whether the number of work-related stressful events or the overall negative perception of the events is a better predictor of violence than the perceived intensity of specific stressors among a nonclinical population of workers.

This study also provides information on stressors that are not related to work. In fact, our data indicate that the number of stressful events not related to work did not help distinguish between violent and nonviolent partners. These results are at odds with Straus's (1980a) data. He found a link between marital violence and the number of stressful events taken either globally or analyzed in different non-work-life areas (interpersonal relations, health, relation with the partner, relation with children, and finances). He was also the first to note that 3 of the 18 items on the list of stressors concerned misunderstandings with the partner (sexual problems, separation or divorce, and increased arguments) and so could have artificially inflated the link with the measure of violence. Our study thus contributes substantially to the study of the influence of stressors not related to work in the field of family violence.

In the studies cited above (Barling & Rosenbaum, 1986; Straus, 1980a), the reference period for the measure of violence (the Conflict Tactics Scale) covered the previous year, in contrast with its use in our study, where we limited the reference period to the previous week. This difference could partly explain the divergence between our results and theirs. In addition, our study was different in that it measured the intensity of exposure to stressors rather than their frequency.

According to our results, the predictors of expressed violence toward partners are, in order of importance, the consumption of medication in the previous 2 days, emotional distress, domestic load, and the consumption of medication over the previous year. Among workers, it is people with psychological problems and chronic health problems who express their violence. The direction of the causal relation cannot be specified. The possibility cannot be ignored that it is violent actions that lead to distress and the consumption of medication. In fact, the question measuring expressed violence did not take the context of the act of violence into account, and it may well be self-defense. It is clear, however, that the sources of stress experienced at work do not distinguish violent partners from nonviolent partners, although the former seem to experience more stress related to greater domestic load (caring for the house and the children) than do the latter. The perception of domestic load may be influenced by the emotional state of the person, but this seems unlikely because emotional state did not seem to influence the person's perception of the workplace. In addition, it is possible that domestic load could be the object of conflict with the partner.

On the other hand, workers in our sample were characterized by the presence of work-related stress variables for expressed violence toward children. We should first note that all the heads of single-parent families in our sample ($n = 29$) were employed and did not seem more likely to act violently toward their children than parents living as couples. Therefore, single-parent status is not considered further in the following discussion. It is, however, important to mention the protective role that work may play for heads of single-parent families. Workers that are violent toward their children have problems of role conflict, role ambiguity, and workload in the workplace. On the other hand, the variables that better distinguish violent from nonviolent parents are domestic load and emotional distress. The last predictor was gender, which indicated that women were more abusive than men. Depression among mothers has been specifically identified in research as being linked with negative behavior toward children and with hostility, rejection, and confrontation in particular (Weissman & Paykel, 1974). If it is true that distress may lead to violent behavior, then the experience of violence may also lead to distress. As Patterson (1980) pointed out, it is possible that the mothers of violent sons may be more victims than aggressors or that they respond to violence by their children and it is violence by children that causes distress. The direction of the distress–violence relation is not obvious. The literature would benefit from future research in which the child's behavior is also measured. Furthermore, most studies that link parents' work and their behavior toward children have not taken the status as worker or nonworker into consideration. The results are ambiguous: Some researchers believe that there is a beneficial effect to working, others that there is a harmful effect (e.g., Belsky & Vondra, 1989). According to them, the difficulties in interpreting the results are due not only to methodological problems but also to the lack of precision about the child's gender and age as well as the family's social class. When considering subjective aspects of work, some researchers have shown that satisfaction with work is linked to the use of a less severe approach to discipline and to less feelings of hostility among mothers of primary school children (Hoffman, 1961) and among fathers of teenagers (Kemper & Reichler, 1976). The more usual measures of stress at work are typically derived from work involvement, that is, the time and energy consecrated to work or study. These studies have revealed that fathers more involved in their work are more impatient with their children (Belsky & Vondra, 1989). Such measures of workplace stress are far removed from the measures used in the current study, thus making comparison difficult. To our knowledge, this study is the first to use well-developed measures of workplace stress in the study of domestic violence.

We note that, together with emotional distress, a heavy domestic load was one of the most discriminating factors in both cases of expressed violence (toward children and toward partners). In the case of potential violence toward children, a heavy domestic load among women would be linked to violence. Gelles and Hargreaves (1981) stated that, at equal occupational status, mothers who reported having more responsibility than they wanted for family tasks had higher rates of expressed violence and abuse. Their results highlighted the importance of specifying the area where the overload was felt (e.g., child supervision, discipline, or management of the household budget). In the case of expressed violence toward partners, a high domestic load would be found as much among violent men as among violent women. Our measure of domestic load would need to be improved, because it only included time spent on domestic tasks or caring for children. It would also be important to add a subjective measure.

When we consider what we have called *potential violence*, it is important to recall that the measure was essentially a measure of feeling: "Have you been on the edge of losing control of your words or acts?" As many clinicians recognize, a feeling of anger or exasperation may be an adaptive response to some situations, and it is the choice to resort to aggressive behavior that is condemned. Note that almost half of those in Samples 1 and 2 had experienced such a feeling. However, experiencing such a feeling repetitively may indicate that the person does not manage to solve the problem at its source. The possibility of resorting to a violent act may be greater among such people than among people who do not feel this way. It is thus important in this context to identify the variables that predict anticipated loss of control.

Our predictive models of potential violence were, however, less powerful and had higher classification error rates than did the models for expressed violence. We only comment on the model predicting potential violence toward children, because the model for partners performed little better than chance in classifying potentially violent individuals.

In addition to variables linked to health, work, and family life, being a woman seems to contribute to discriminating between violent and nonviolent parents, whether the violence is potential or expressed. On the other hand, the gender variable did not differentiate between people who acted violently toward their partners and those who did not. Using a longitudinal design with newlyweds, MacEwen and Barling (1988) were able to show that high perceived stress in the areas of the family and the workplace (a global score) could predict violence by women toward their husbands a year later but not violence by men who were violent regardless of stress levels. Two questions may be raised from our data: Are women more inclined to be violent toward their children than men? and Are women just as violent toward their partners as men? In the sample studied, we conducted chi-square tests of the hypothesis that a greater proportion of women would report expressing violence than men. For expressed violence toward partners, there was no significant difference between the sexes; almost as many women as men reported violence. We note that with the equivalent rates of violent behavior for men and women detected by our measures, we find the same difficulty as many other researchers in the domain of family violence. Although the rates of homicide and complaints are greater for violence inflicted by men, surveys relying on self-report—which take into account neither the gravity of the consequences of violence nor the context (self-defense or other)—have detected equivalent rates of violent behavior for both men and women. However, very slightly higher rates of violence toward children among women have been documented, as Zigler and Hall (1989) mentioned. This was confirmed by the chi-square test on expressed violence and is found indirectly in our multivariate analyses. The higher rates among women may be partly explained, according to workers in the field, by the much greater number of hours that women spend with their children. Given the greater number of hours spent with children even among women who work outside the home, the data possibly indicate that women are, in fact, less likely to be violent toward children than men (Zigler & Hall, 1989).

One possible explanation for the reports of greater or equivalent violence by women is the propensity of women, in comparison with men, to either greater self-disclosure or to greater recognition of a problem as a problem of violence. Our measure of potential violence supports this interpretation because more women than men reported such feelings about relations with their children and their partner.

The expression *loss of control* that we have used throughout in no way indicates that we share the idea of violent men who identify their problem as a loss of control (Stets, 1988). We refer more closely to Schechter's (1982) definition stating that domestic violence is violence constructed by the society and chosen individually. Furthermore, although we studied stressors in a more systematic manner in our study, this does not indicate in any way that we believe violence should be explained only by stress-related variables. A multicausal model should also integrate variables from individual, family, and social levels.

However, some ideas drawn from our data may be addressed to work organizations. First, although they were studied separately in our study, overload at work and overload at home highlight the possible existence of a problem at the interface of private and public as far as relations with children are concerned. These include problems with child care or with parental leave where the organization could act for the benefit of its workers and thus contribute to stress reduction. Second, organizations should consider the possibility that among the clients in employee aid programs there will be workers who are currently violent toward their children or partners; this must not be ignored, and counselors should be open to discussing such concerns.

Some limitations must be taken into consideration when interpreting our data. The overall sample was composed of full-time workers; thus, people working at home and people with an uncertain or part-time status were excluded. The sources of stress for these others would be different, and our conclusions cannot be extended beyond the full-time workers in our sample. In addition, we did not take into account the partners' respective occupations. Numerous studies in the field have indicated the interest of taking this factor into account in further research. This should be done not only objectively (e.g., presence or absence in the job market) but also subjectively (e.g., the partners' opinions on their own and their partner's involvement in the workforce). Other limits to our study are the rather moderate response rate (40%), the use of volunteer participants, and the use of subjective measures that could potentially elicit socially desirable responding. Because our questionnaire was on work stress and because there were only 4 questions about violence out of more than 200 questions, it is very unlikely that our low response rate implies a self-selection of the participants on the basis of violence. As far as the measures that call on the participants' perception are concerned, the volunteer status of participants did not seem to be a major problem here. This type of measure can be justified because violence is an emotional, irrational phenomenon that is based on the abuser's interpretation of the situation. The fact that so many participants reported potential violence suggests that the effect of social desirability was not major. Finally, our cross-sectional study does not provide an answer about whether workplace problems are brought home or vice versa. Among the strengths of this study is the fact that the questions about violence were embedded in a large study on the workplace, which decreased the potential for reactivity to the violence measures. Furthermore, in our questionnaire, the questions on stressors preceded the questions on violence, so the latter could not have been affected by the former.

The content of questions about violence in research should be reconsidered. The question on expressed violence is usually limited to the least frequent form of violent action, namely, physical violence. Thus, the influence of workplace variables on psychological and sexual violence remains to be established. Also, the measure of perceived potential violence needs to be better defined in the future. Is it a measure of violence? A measure of distress? A measure of feeling overwhelmed? Other stressors should be integrated to complete the study of family violence, according to recommendations by Greenhaus and Parasuraman (1986) and by Small and Riley (1990). These stressors involve the interface between work and nonwork—that is, the conflict between these two major life domains—while also taking into account the burden experienced by women. Studying the perceptions of both partners simultaneously in a longitudinal design also seems promising (Bolger, DeLongis, Kessler, & Wethington, 1989).

References

Barling, J., & Rosenbaum, A. (1986). Work stressors and wife abuse. *Journal of Applied Psychology, 71,* 346–348.

Belsky, J., & Vondra, J. (1989). Lessons from child abuse: The determinants of parenting. In D. Cicchetto & V. Carlson (Eds.), *Child maltreatment: Theory and research on the causes and consequences of child abuse and neglect* (pp. 153–202). Cambridge, England: Cambridge University Press.

Bolger, N., DeLongis, A., Kessler, R. C., & Wethington, E. (1989). The contagion of stress across multiple roles. *Journal of Marriage and the Family, 51,* 175–183.

Browne, D. H. (1986). The role of stress in the commission of subsequent acts of child abuse and neglect. *Journal of Family Violence, 1,* 289–297.

Desfossés, E., & Bouchard, C. (1987, April). *Using coercive behaviors with children: Stressors, conflictual relationships and lack of support in the life of the mothers.* Paper presented at the Biennial Convention of the Society for Research in Child Development, Baltimore, MD.

Dolan, S., & Arsenault, A. (1983). *Le stress au travail et ses effets sur l'individu et l'organisation* [Work stress and its effects on the individual and the organization]. Montreal, Quebec, Canada: Quebec Institute for Research on Health and Security.

Dutton, D. G. (1988). *The domestic assault of women: Psychological and criminal justice perspectives.* Boston: Allyn and Bacon.

Farrington, K. (1986). The application of stress theory to the study of family violence: Principles, problems, and prospects. *Journal of Family Violence, 1,* 131–147.

Finkelhor, D. (1983). Common features of family abuse. In D. Finkelhor, R. J. Gelles, G. T. Hotaling, & M. A. Straus (Eds.), *The dark side of families: Current family violence research.* Beverly Hills, CA: Sage.

Finn, J. (1985). The stresses and coping behavior of battered women. *Journal of Contemporary Social Work, 66,* 341–349.

Garbarino, J. (1976). A preliminary study of some ecological correlates of child abuse: The impact of economic stress on mothers. *Child Development, 47,* 178–185.

Garbarino, J. (1977). The human ecology of child maltreatment. *Journal of Marriage and the Family, 39,* 721–735.

Gelles, R. J. (1973). Child abuse as psychopathology: A sociological critique and reformulation. *American Journal of Orthopsychiatry, 43,* 179–187.

Gelles, R. J., & Hargreaves, E. (1981). Maternal employment and violence toward children. *Journal of Family Issues, 2,* 509–530.

Goldberg, D. P. (1972). *The detection of psychiatric illness by questionnaire.* London: Oxford University Press.

Greenhaus, J. H., & Parasuraman, S. (1986). A work–nonwork interactive perspective of stress and its consequences. *Journal of Organizational Behavior Management, 8,* 37–60.

Hoffman, L. W. (1961). Effects of maternal employment on the child. *Child Development, 32,* 187–197.

Howze, D. C., & Kotch, J. B. (1984). Disentangling life events, stress and social support: Implications for primary prevention of child abuse and neglect. *Child Abuse and Neglect, 8,* 401–409.

Ilfeld, F. W., Jr. (1976). Further validation of a Psychiatric Symptom Index in a normal population. *Psychological Reports, 39,* 1215–1228.

Insel, P. M., & Moos, R. H. (1974). *Health and social environment.* Lexington, MA: Heath.

Justice, B., Calvert, A., & Justice, R. (1985). Factors mediating child abuse as a response to stress. *Child Abuse and Neglect, 9*, 359–363.

Kemper, T. D., & Reichler, M. L. (1976). Father's work integration and types and frequencies of rewards and punishments administered by fathers and mothers to adolescent sons and daughters. *Journal of Genetic Psychology, 129*, 207–219.

Kovess, V. (1982). Les indicateurs de santé mentale [Mental health indicators]. Montreal, Quebec, Canada: Government of Quebec, Ministry of Social Affairs.

Lazarus, R. S., & Folkman, S. (1984). *Stress, appraisal, and coping.* New York: Springer.

MacEwen, K. E., & Barling, J. (1988). Multiple stressors, violence in the family of origin, and marital aggression: A longitudinal investigation. *Journal of Family Violence, 3*, 73–87.

Patterson, G. (1980). Mothers: The unacknowledged victims. *Monograph of the Society for Research in Child Development, 186.*

SAS Institute. (1985). *SAS user's guide: Statistics.* Cary, NC: Author.

Schechter, S. (1982). *Women and male violence.* Boston: South End Press.

Seltzer, J. A., & Kalmuss, D. (1988). Socialization and stress explanation for spouse abuse. *Social Forces, 67*, 473–491.

Small, S. A., & Riley, D. (1990). Toward a multidimensional assesment of work spillover into family life. *Journal of Marriage and the Family, 52*, 51–61.

Stets, J. E. (1988). *Domestic violence and control.* New York: Springer-Verlag.

Straus, M. A. (1973). A general systems theory approach to a theory of violence between family members. *Social Science Information, 12*, 105–123.

Straus, M. A. (1979). Measuring intrafamily conflict and violence: The Conflict Tactics (CT) Scales. *Journal of Marriage and the Family, 41*, 75–88.

Straus, M. A. (1980a). Social stress and marital violence in a national sample of American family. In F. Wright, C. Bahn, & R. W. Rieber (Eds.), *Annals of the New York Academy of Sciences, Vol. 347. Forensic psychology and psychiatry* (pp. 229–250). New York: New York Academy of Sciences.

Straus, M. A. (1980b). Stress and child abuse. In C. H. Kempe & R. E. Heler (Eds.), *The battered child* (3rd ed., pp. 86–103). Chicago: University of Chicago Press.

Straus, M. A., Gelles, R., & Steinmetz, S. (1980). *Behind closed doors: Violence in the American family.* New York: Doubleday.

Vézina, A. (1988). Le travail et le réseau de support comme facteurs d'adaptation chez les veuves d'âge moyen [Work and support systems as adaptive factors in middle-aged widows]. Unpublished doctoral dissertation, Laval University, Montreal, Quebec, Canada.

Weissman, M. M., & Paykel, E. S. (1974). *The depressed woman: A study of social relationships.* Chicago: University of Chicago Press.

Zigler, E., & Hall, N. W. (1989). Physical child abuse in America: Past, present, and future. In D. Cicchetto & V. Carlson (Eds.), *Child maltreatment: Theory and research on the causes and consequences of child abuse and neglect* (pp. 38–75). Cambridge, England: Cambridge University Press.

14

Child-Care Difficulties and the Impact on Concentration, Stress, and Productivity Among Single and Nonsingle Mothers and Fathers

Lois E. Tetrick, Rebecca L. Miles, Lyne Marcil, and Christine M. Van Dosen

The importance of quality child care for working parents is a well-researched topic (Presser, 1986; Terborg, 1985). Gutek, Repetti, and Silver (1988) have argued that a mother's employment experience cannot be understood without considering child-care arrangements. They cited the results of a survey in which women described the lack of quality child care as a major problem, one that places a constraint on the number of hours mothers are able to work. In addition, Harrell and Ridley (1975) asserted that mothers find their work more enjoyable and involving when they have confidence in the care their children are receiving while they are at work. Surprisingly, little research has looked at the effect of child care on mothers' work performance or productivity other than how it relates to absenteeism. Also noticeably missing from the research on the effects of child-care difficulties on employees is any mention of fathers. In the present study, we looked more closely at the impact of child-care difficulties among both fathers and mothers and the potential impact on their coworkers.

Child Care, Gender, and Marital Status

Most employees recognize that their family lives influence them at work (Crouter, 1984; Terborg, 1985). However, this influence will be determined in part by that person's role in the family. Therefore, women may be at prime risk. Even though one would expect that the division of labor for men and women (in terms of family responsibilities) has become more equitable, evidence shows that a working mother actually holds two jobs because she is often the sole person responsible for the care of children (Russo & Denmark, 1984). Although men are getting more involved in family matters, child-care responsibility has traditionally been, and still is, treated as a women's issue. Despite their increase in the paid labor market, women still assume most of the workload within the family, spending nearly twice as many hours as men on household duties (Coverman, 1983; Fernandez, 1986; Goff & Mount, 1989; Greenberger, Goldberg, Hamill, O'Neil, & Payne, 1989; Gutek et al., 1988). Men have not increased their participation in housework and child-care responsibilities proportionally to women's increased participation in the labor force (Nieva & Gutek, 1981). Also, Pleck (1977) suggested that men are expected to separate family and work, but women are not. Women are expected to allow family matters to interfere with their work lives (Pleck, 1977). This may explain why most of the literature in the area has examined the effect of child-care problems on working mothers, often overlooking its effect on fathers. However, it is important to examine whether there are differences between working mothers and fathers in their experiences of child-care difficulties.

Given the escalating divorce rate and increased number of children born out of wedlock, experts have estimated that approximately half of the children born in the 1980s will live with a single parent before they reach adulthood (Fernandez, 1990). Although the majority of single parents are women, Meyer and Garansky (as cited in Otten, 1992) estimated that there are 1.4 million father-only families and that this number is increasing at a far more rapid pace than mother-only families. It has been reported, not surprisingly, that single mothers have more problems related to child care (e.g., being able to pay for child care and traveling on overnight business trips) than two-parent families (Fernandez, 1990), but little is known about the child-care experiences of single fathers. Fernandez argued that single fathers and mothers have similar difficulties. Therefore, we examined the differences in child-care difficulties and the effect of these difficulties for single fathers, single mothers, married fathers, and married mothers.

Child-Care Difficulties

Child-care problems take a variety of forms. Such problems include the inability to find a conveniently located and affordable child-care center and the difficulties of making special arrangements when the child is ill, when the parent is required to work overtime, or when the parent must go out of town on business. Much of the research on child care has investigated the negative effect of child-care difficulties on work behaviors in an attempt to assess how much this problem costs organizations in terms of productivity (Bedeian, Burke, & Moffet, 1988; Fernandez, 1986, 1990; Mize & Freeman, 1989). Very often, the cost to the company is measured as a function of absenteeism. It has been shown that parents, especially mothers, are more likely to experience increased absenteeism because a child is not in school or is ill (Fernandez, 1986, 1990; Goff, Mount, & Jamison, 1990; Mize & Freeman, 1989). This link between child-care problems and work performance, as reflected by number of days absent from work, has been the most widely reviewed in the literature (Goff et al., 1990; Kossek & Nichol, 1992; Miller, 1984). However, other types of detrimental behaviors have been mentioned. For example, it has been reported that parents experiencing child-care difficulties are more likely to arrive late or leave early because of the need to adjust to day-care-center schedules (Fernandez, 1986, 1990; Mize & Freeman, 1989). Therefore, our investigation examined the effect of child-care difficulties, but differentiated between missing an entire day of work, arriving late, leaving early, and taking leave without pay. In addition, we looked at other factors that may reduce an employee's productivity on the job. These included interruptions at work because of child-care difficulties, difficulty concentrating, stress, and considering working part-time or quitting as a result of child-care difficulties (Crouter, 1984; MacEwen & Barling, 1991; Spruell, 1986; Terborg, 1985).

To the extent that child-care problems have negative consequences for working parents as suggested above, it also is possible that there may be indirect effects on others in the organization (Fernandez, 1990). For example, if a parent misses work when his or her child is ill, if he or she arrives late because the babysitter was late, or if his or her concentration is impaired because of concern about whether a child gets safely from school to a child-care provider, then others in the organization may have to compensate for this reduction in productivity.

Although most of the child-care literature has not addressed the issue of the effect of child-care problems on coworkers, a few studies have addressed the question of whether a person's work is affected by other people's child-care problems. Crouter (1984) mentioned that the spillover of family to work could, in turn, affect coworkers and team members. However, she did not provide any data that could support this claim. Fernandez (1990) found that 40% of the employees in one study believed they were negatively affected by other members of their work group who were experiencing dependent-care problems and, as a consequence, were absent or distracted at work. Only 38% of this sample reported not being affected. Surprisingly similar results were reported by Mize and Freeman (1989). Of the employees in their study, 38% reported that the child-care problems of others caused mild or moderate disruption of their own work, and approximately 10% reported this to be a major or fairly major inconvenience (Mize & Freeman, 1989). Therefore, we expected to find evidence that child-care difficulties of parents not only negatively affect their own productivity but also negatively affect their coworkers.

The present study was descriptive in nature, exploring potential differences and similarities among single and nonsingle fathers and mothers in the type of child-care difficulties encountered as well as the effect of these difficulties on their productivity. In addition, we explored the potential effect that the child-care difficulties of parents may have on their coworkers.

Method

Sample

Data from three organizations were obtained as a result of child-care needs-assessment projects conducted by the Work and Family Unit of the Merrill-

Palmer Institute at Wayne State University. The sample included 2,017 participants from a heavy equipment manufacturing company (from which we had a response rate of 87%). An additional 250 respondents were from eight plants of a large manufacturing company; surveys were sent to a random sample of 10% of the employees in this organization, and 69% of the surveys were returned. Last, 506 individuals of a large communications organization, representing a response rate of 64%, were included. The total number of respondents ($N = 2,773$) represented a range of hourly and salaried employees in a variety of occupations, including skilled trades, clerical, professional, and managerial personnel. Fifty-four percent were men, and 67% were between the ages of 26 and 45 years. Thirty-seven percent of the respondents were parents with children living at home; 23% of these had children below the age of 18 months, 7% had children between 18 months and 5 years of age, and 70% had children between the ages of 6 years and 18 years. Of these parents, 25% described themselves as "single parents"; 47% of these single parents were men.

Measures

Surveys were distributed by the individual organizations to their employees and returned through interoffice mail. Participation was voluntary and anonymous. To assess the type and extent of child-care difficulties encountered, we asked respondents to indicate whether they had experienced difficulties with any of the following in the past 12 months: (a) paying for child care; (b) finding affordable child care; (c) finding a convenient child-care location; (d) transporting a child to or from child care; (e) arranging child care to match their work schedule; (f) finding safe, quality child care; (g) finding reliable child care; and (h) obtaining child care when a child was sick. The response scale ranged from 1 (*no problem*) to 3 (*major problem*). In addition, respondents were asked how many times in the previous 12 months they had missed an entire day of work, been late to work, left work early, taken leave without pay, been interrupted at work, considered part-time work, and considered quitting their job because of child-care problems. The response scale ranged from 1 (*none*) to 4 (*more than 6 times*). Respondents were also asked if problems related to child care affected their concentration on the job or caused stress during the previous 12 months. The response scale used for these two questions ranged from 1 (*no problem*) to 3 (*major problem*). Finally, all respondents were asked if their work had been made more difficult because of other workers' child-care problems at any time during the previous 6 months. The response scale ranged from 1 (*no problem*) to 4 (*not aware of the problems*).

Results and Discussion

Child-Care Difficulties and Other Employees' Productivity

Before examining the child-care difficulties of the parents included in the study, we first looked at the extent to which parents' child-care problems affected their coworkers. Of the 2,773 respondents in our study, 28% indicated that other people's child-care problems had made their jobs more difficult, whereas 17% said they were not aware of any problems. There were basically no differences in the proportion of men and women indicating that their jobs had been made more difficult. When we restricted the sample to parents only, 31% indicated that their jobs had been made more difficult by the child-care problems of their coworkers. There was no difference in the proportion of fathers and mothers who indicated that their jobs had been made more difficult. However, only 22% of the single parents reported that their jobs had been made more difficult by the child-care problems of their coworkers, whereas 32% of the nonsingle parents indicated that their jobs had been made more difficult. These results support the notion that employees' child-care difficulties do affect their coworkers and are surprisingly consistent with results from previous studies (Fernandez, 1990; Mize & Freeman, 1989). These results also indicate that, to the extent that this increased difficulty in job performance results in reduced productivity, results of previous research on how child-care difficulties affect organizations have been underestimated because those accounts typically only considered effects on working parents.

Types of Child-Care Difficulties

The mean levels of experienced difficulties are shown in Table 1 for single fathers, single mothers, nonsingle fathers, and nonsingle mothers along with the general means for fathers and mothers and single and nonsingle parents. Overall, the parents in this sample reported the most difficulty in (a) getting a child to and from child care ($M = 2.46$), (b) finding affordable child care ($M = 2.19$), (c) finding reliable child care ($M = 2.15$), and (d) arranging for child care that matched their work schedules ($M = 2.03$). They reported less difficulty in (a) obtaining child care for an ill child ($M = 1.90$); (b) paying for child care ($M = 1.78$); (c) finding safe, quality child care ($M = 1.70$); and (d) finding child care that was conveniently located ($M = 1.43$). However, the extent of difficulty encountered differed depending on the marital status and gender of the parents.

There were no differences by gender or marital status in terms of experiencing difficulty paying for child care or for finding affordable child care, although the mean level of difficulty for finding affordable child care was higher overall ($M = 2.19$) than was difficulty paying for child care ($M = 1.78$). The picture changes when noneconomic child-care problems are examined. With respect to finding safe, quality child care, there was a significant interaction between marital status and gender, $F(1, 877) = 50.06, p < .01$, with single fathers reporting more difficulty in finding safe child care ($M = 2.27$). Nonsingle mothers reported the next highest difficulty ($M = 1.71$) and single mothers and nonsingle fathers reported the least difficulty ($Ms = 1.62$ and 1.61, respectively). A similar but weaker relation was evidenced for difficulty in finding reliable child care, with a significant interaction between marital status and gender, $F(1, 860) = 12.12, p < .01$. Again, single fathers reported experiencing the most difficulty ($M = 2.51$). Mothers, whether nonsingle or

Table 1. Mean Level of Child-Care Difficulty Experienced by Single and Nonsingle Mothers and Fathers

Difficulty	Marital status		Total
	Single	Nonsingle	
Paying for child care			
Men	1.83	1.77	1.78
Women	1.72	1.79	1.77
Total	1.77	1.78	1.78
Finding affordable child care			
Men	2.09	2.17	2.16
Women	2.31	2.21	2.24
Total	2.22	2.18	2.19
Finding a convenient child-care location			
Men	1.99	1.41	1.51
Women	1.41	1.30	1.34
Total	1.65	1.67	1.43
Getting a child to or from care			
Men	2.71	2.51	2.55
Women	2.38	2.33	2.35
Total	2.51	2.45	2.46
Arranging child care to match your schedule			
Men	2.40	1.97	2.04
Women	2.02	2.03	2.03
Total	2.17	1.99	2.03
Finding safe, quality child care			
Men	2.27	1.61	1.72
Women	1.62	1.71	1.68
Total	1.88	1.65	1.70
Finding reliable child care			
Men	2.51	2.05	2.12
Women	2.22	2.18	2.19
Total	2.34	2.10	2.15
Arrangements for sick child care			
Men	2.49	1.86	1.96
Women	1.77	1.83	1.81
Total	2.06	1.85	1.90

single, had the next highest difficulty (Ms = 2.22 and 2.18, respectively) and nonsingle fathers reported the lowest level of difficulty in finding reliable child care (M = 2.05). These same patterns held in response to difficulty arranging child care to match work schedules, finding a convenient child-care location, and finding care when a child was ill. Single fathers reported experiencing the most difficulty with these situations (Ms = 2.40, 1.99, and 2.49, respectively), with very similar levels of difficulty reported by single mothers and nonsingle parents. The last child-care problem that we examined was difficulty getting a child to or from child care. Here the relation changed from that in the prior analyses. Fathers reported having greater difficulty than mothers, regardless of marital status (Ms = 2.55 and 2.35, respectively; $p < .01$), and there was no significant difference between nonsingle parents and single parents (Ms = 2.45 and 2.51, respectively; $p > .05$).

Child-Care Difficulties and Work Performance

We asked the respondents in our study how frequently they had missed an entire day of work, been late to work, left work early, taken leave without pay, or been interrupted at work in the previous 12 months because of child-care problems. Overall, the respondents reported leaving work early the most frequently, an average of 4 to 6 times during the year (M = 2.84); this was followed by being late for work, an average of 4 to 6 times in 12 months (M = 2.74), and missing an entire day of work, on average slightly more than 1 to 3 times in 12 months (M = 2.27). Furthermore, the respondents indicated that they had been interrupted at work because of child-care problems an average of 1 to 2 times during the previous 12 months (M = 2.00), and 63% of the parents reported taking leave without pay at least once during the 12-month period (M = 1.73).

The mean responses by gender and marital status to the effects of child-care difficulties on productivity are shown in Table 2. There were significant differences in missing an entire day of work, arriving late, and leaving early because of child-care problems, depending on marital status and gender: for missing a day, $F(1, 569)$ = 5.14, $p < .05$; for arriving late, $F(1, 567)$ = 14.95, $p < .01$; for leaving early, $F(1, 75)$ = 6.88, $p < .01$. The pattern of relations was strikingly similar. Nonsingle fathers reported the most frequent absences (Ms = 2.14, 2.94, and 3.01, for missing an entire day, arriving late, and leaving early, respectively), followed by mothers (regardless of marital status; Ms = 2.19, 2.71, and 2.76, respectively). Single fathers reported the least absences because of child-care problems (Ms = 1.98, 2.09, and 2.46, respectively). There was no significant interaction between gender and marital status concerning taking leave without pay and no significant difference between single and nonsingle parents. However, men reported a slightly higher incidence of taking leave without pay than women (Ms = 1.80 and 1.63, respectively), $F(1, 457)$ = 17.766, $p < .01$. Relative to the extent of interruptions at work reported by the parents, there was a significant interaction between gender and marital status, $F(1, 414)$ = 23.019, $p < .01$; however, the pattern of the interaction was different from those for missing an entire day of work, arriving late, or leaving early. Single mothers reported the most frequent number of interruptions (M = 2.25), and single fathers reported the least number of interruptions (M = 1.75). There was virtually no difference in the number of interruptions because of child-care problems for nonsingle mothers and fathers (Ms = 1.97 and 2.06, respectively).

In addition to the lost time resulting from child-care problems, there appear to be costs associated with parents experiencing difficulty concentrating on the job, increased levels of stress, and attrition, either through formally reducing their hours (e.g., working part-time) or quitting their jobs. The respondents in our study were asked to indicate the effect of child-care problems on their ability to concentrate on their work and the level of stress they ex-

Table 2. Impact of Child-Care Difficulties on Job Performance and Productivity

	Marital status		
Effect	Single	Nonsingle	Total
Missed an entire day			
Men	1.98	2.41	2.32
Women	2.20	2.19	2.19
Total	2.10	2.33	2.27
Arrived late			
Men	2.09	2.94	2.76
Women	2.66	2.74	2.71
Total	2.39	2.86	2.74
Left work early			
Men	2.46	3.01	2.89
Women	2.79	2.75	2.76
Total	2.61	2.92	2.84
Took leave without pay			
Men	1.86	1.77	1.80
Women	1.65	1.62	1.63
Total	1.77	1.71	1.73
Interrupted at work			
Men	1.75	2.06	1.96
Women	2.25	1.97	2.08
Total	1.95	2.03	2.00
Had difficulty concentrating at work			
Men	1.64	2.14	2.04
Women	1.67	1.82	1.77
Total	1.65	2.02	1.92
Experienced stress			
Men	1.97	2.27	2.21
Women	1.86	1.99	1.94
Total	1.91	2.17	2.09
Considered part-time work			
Men	1.98	1.73	1.83
Women	1.69	1.62	1.65
Total	1.87	1.69	1.76
Considered quitting			
Men	1.93	1.78	1.83
Women	1.70	1.67	1.68
Total	1.83	1.74	1.77

perienced. They were also asked if they had considered working part-time or quitting because of child-care problems. These data also are presented in Table 2. There were no significant interactions for marital status and gender for either concentration or stress, $F(1, 545) = 3.25$ and 1.22, respectively, $p > .05$. However, there were significant differences between fathers and mothers, $F(1, 545) = 6.26$ and 8.91, respectively, $p < .01$, and between single parents and nonsingle parents, $F(1, 545) = 10.393$ and 5.864, respectively, $p < .05$. Fathers reported more difficulty in their ability to concentrate and the level of stress attributed to child-care problems ($Ms = 3.04$ and 3.21, respectively) than mothers (Ms = 2.77 and 2.94, respectively). Nonsingle parents reported more difficulty with concentration and stress (Ms = 3.02 and 3.17, respectively) than did single parents (Ms = 2.65 and 2.91, respectively).

With respect to respondents' considering working part-time or quitting their jobs altogether, a somewhat different pattern emerged. Again, there were no significant interactions between gender and marital status, whereas there were significant differences between mothers and fathers as well as between single parents and nonsingle parents. Fathers reported considering working part-time and quitting more frequently (Ms = 1.83 and 1.84, respectively) than did mothers (Ms = 1.65 and 1.68, respectively). However, somewhat surprisingly, single parents reported considering working part-time and quitting because of child-care problems more frequently (Ms = 1.87 and 1.83, respectively) than did nonsingle parents (Ms = 1.69 and 1.74, respectively). Unfortunately, we do not have the necessary data to examine whether the differences in considering these alternatives resulted in any employees actually working part-time or quitting their jobs.

Summary and Conclusions

That child care is an issue for working mothers is hardly surprising, as this has been demonstrated time and again. However, our data highlight that child care is not exclusively an issue for working mothers. Rather, working fathers also experience these same difficulties, and single fathers appear to have more difficulty in many areas. Fathers reported more problems with concentration at work because of child-care problems than did mothers. Similarly, fathers reported greater stress from child-care problems than did mothers. Furthermore, our results indicated that fathers experience child-care difficulties similarly to mothers. In fact, the fathers in this sample actually reported experiencing more difficulty obtaining transportation to and from child care for their children than did the mothers.

One of the unique aspects of the data we have presented is that it included responses from single parents (115 men and 128 women). Results of analyses comparing single fathers and mothers with nonsingle parents revealed that single parents—regardless of gender—reported less difficulty concentrating on work because of child-care problems. Also, single parents reported less stress resulting from child-care difficulties than did nonsingle parents. These results seem to run counter to the perception of many that single parents are most affected by child-care responsibilities. This may be a result of the type of occupations and work environments the respondents were in or it may reflect differences in adaptation to the roles of being a parent and an employee.

In addition to the above gender and marital status differences in the experience of child-care difficulties and their effect on the parents' productivity, there was a significant interaction between gender and marital status of the parent with respect to interruptions at work. Single fathers reported fewer interruptions, followed by nonsingle mothers and nonsingle fathers. Single mothers indicated the most interruptions at work because of child-care problems. Single fathers, on the other hand, reported more difficulty obtaining safe, reliable child care that matched their work schedules than did nonsingle fathers or mothers. Nonsingle fathers reported taking time off because of child-care problems more frequently than mothers, and single fathers reported taking time off the least frequently. In addition, male and female single parents as well as both single and nonsingle fathers reported considering working part-time or quitting their jobs more frequently than did nonsingle parents or single or nonsingle mothers. Clearly, the effect of child-care problems, contrary to much popular perception, does not appear to be a reality for mothers only.

The data from this study are generally consistent with prior investigations of the effect of child-care difficulties. However, the inclusion of sufficient numbers of single fathers as well as single mothers provides a better description of the effect of child-care responsibilities on work life. The data clearly suggest that it is not only the single mother who suffers from inadequate child care, given the vagaries of work schedules, children's health, and so on. In fact, the pattern of results were much more complex. Of the 2,773 respondents in this study—including those individuals who did not have children living with them—15% of the men and 13% of the women reported that their jobs were more difficult to perform because of other employees' child-care problems. This suggests that child-care responsibilities affect the productivity of others in the organization beyond those parents who have problems obtaining safe and reliable child care for their children. The view that child care is relevant only to a few is too narrow. Rather, the effect of child-care problems would appear to be greater in terms of productivity as well as quality of work life than what has been suggested so far.

References

Bedeian, A. G., Burke, B. G., & Moffet, R. G. (1988). Outcomes of work–family conflict among non-single male and female professionals. *Journal of Management, 14,* 475–491.

Coverman, S. (1983). Gender, domestic labor time, and wage inequality. *American Sociological Review, 48,* 623–637.

Crouter, A. C. (1984). Spillover from family to work: The neglected side of the work/family interface. *Human Relations, 37,* 425–442.

Fernandez, J. P. (1986). *Child care and corporate productivity.* Lexington, MA: Lexington Books.

Fernandez, J. P. (1990). *The politics and reality of family care in corporate America.* Lexington, MA: Lexington Books.

Goff, S. J., & Mount, M. K. (1989, August). *Work/family conflict and the need for child care while at work: Some findings of interest to managers.* Paper presented at the Academy of Management Meeting, Washington, D.C.

Goff, S. J., Mount, M. K., & Jamison, R. L. (1990). Employer supported child care, work/family conflict, and absenteeism: A field study. *Personnel Psychology, 43,* 793–809.

Greenberger, E., Goldberg, W. A., Hamill, S., O'Neil, R., & Payne, C. K. (1989). Contributions of a supportive work environment to parents' well-being and orientation to work. *American Journal of Community Psychology, 17,* 755–783.

Gutek, B. A., Repetti, R. L., & Silver, D. L. (1988). Nonwork roles and stress at work. In C. L. Cooper & R. Payne (Eds.), *Causes, coping and consequences of stress at work* (pp. 141–174). New York: Wiley.

Harrell, J. E., & Ridley, C. A. (1975). Substitute child care, maternal employment and the quality of mother–child interaction. *Journal of Marriage and the Family, 37,* 556–564.

Kossek, E. E., & Nichol, V. (1992). The effects of on-site child care on employees' attitudes and performance. *Personnel Psychology, 45*, 485–509.

MacEwen, K. E., & Barling, J. (1991). Maternal employment experiences, attention problems and behavioral performance: A mediational model. *Journal of Organizational Behavior, 12*, 495–505.

Miller, T. I. (1984). The effects of employer-sponsored child care on employees' absenteeism, turnover, productivity, recruitment or job satisfaction: What is claimed and what is known. *Personnel Psychology, 37*, 277–289.

Mize, J., & Freeman, L. C. (1989). Employer-supported child care: Assessing the need and potential support. *Child and Youth Care Quarterly, 18*, 289–301.

Nieva, V. G., & Gutek, B. A. (1981). *Women and work: A psychological perspective.* New York: Praeger.

Otten, A. L. (1992, November 4). People patterns. *The Wall Street Journal*, p. B1.

Pleck, J. H. (1977). Work–family role system. *Social Problems, 63*, 81–88.

Presser, H. R. (1986). Shift work among American women and child care. *Journal of Marriage and the Family, 48*, 551–563.

Russo, N. F., & Denmark, F. L. (1984). Women, psychology, and public policy. *American Psychologist, 39*, 1161–1165.

Spruell, G. (1986). Business planning for parenthood. *Training and Development Journal, 40*, 30–35.

Terborg, J. R. (1985). Working women and stress. In T. A. Beehr & R. S. Bhagat (Eds.), *Human stress and cognition in organizations* (pp. 245–286). New York: Wiley.

15

Stress, Control, Well-Being, and Marital Functioning: A Causal Correlational Analysis

E. Kevin Kelloway and Julian Barling

Since the early 1970s, there has been growing recognition that work and family roles are intertwined (Barling, 1990). Most commonly, this recognition is expressed as a "spillover" hypothesis whereby reactions to working conditions are transferred to another, nonwork domain. Although typically expressed in terms of positive work reactions, the spillover hypothesis may be extended to negative reactions as well (Barling, 1990; Zedeck & Mosier, 1990). Thus, impaired well-being resulting from work stress may be reflected in decrements in marital functioning.

Although the empirical literature has tended to support the spillover hypothesis (Staines, 1980), most of the supporting evidence has come from cross-sectional research. Indeed, in one recent review it was concluded that causal inferences regarding the links between employment and family functioning are premature (Barling, 1990). Thus, the first goal of our research was to specify the relationships and temporal ordering of work stressors and marital functioning. In doing so, we follow previous research in suggesting that (a) work stress predicts individual well-being (Kelloway & Barling, 1991) and (b) the resulting quality of individual well-being predicts both marital satisfaction (Higginbottom, Barling, & Kelloway, 1993) and marital functioning (Mac-Ewen, Barling, & Kelloway, 1992).

In addition, a great deal of research has been devoted to explicating the relationships between characteristics of the working environment and personal well-being. Researchers have commonly relied on measures of work-related stress or job design as predictors of psychological well-being (e.g., Kelloway & Barling, 1991). There has also been a growing recognition that perceptions of individual control contribute to well-being (e.g., Miller, 1979; Thompson, 1981). Most relevantly, organizational researchers have increasingly recognized the potential of control at work to ameliorate the negative outcomes associated with work stress (Ganster & Fusilier, 1989). Unfortunately, laboratory-based

This research was supported by Grant 410-88-0891 from the Social Sciences and Humanities Research Council of Canada and by a grant from Imperial Oil to Julian Barling.

findings supporting the link between control and well-being have not consistently generalized to the workplace. In one recent review, it was concluded that there is a need for prospective studies with a meaningful, longitudinal component to assess the contribution of work-related control to individual well-being (Ganster, 1989).

Accordingly, the second major goal of our research was to investigate the contributions of work stress and perceived control at work to individual well-being. In doing so, we used a longitudinal design with two time lags (6 months and 12 months) to provide a rigorous test of competing models of work stress, control, and individual well-being.

Employment and Marital Functioning

Barling (1990) has concluded that there is strong empirical support for the link between work experiences and marital functioning. Specifically, he suggested that positive work experiences are associated with positive marital functioning whereas work stress is associated with marital dysfunction.

More recently, researchers have considered the mechanisms through which marital functioning is affected by employment experiences and, more specifically, by work stress. The results of two longitudinal investigations (Higginbottom et al., 1993; MacEwen et al., 1992) suggested that stressors exert an effect on marital functioning through their effect on well-being. In essence, exposure to stress decreases individual well-being, which in turn results in more negative evaluations of marital functioning.

MacEwen et al. (1992) examined the impact of role overload on marital functioning in a weekly diary study. Participants provided weekly reports of role overload, anxiety, depression, and marital interactions. As hypothesized, role overload resulted in increased anxiety and depression, which in turn resulted in more negative marital functioning (e.g., increased withdrawal and angry interactions).

Similar findings were reported by Higginbottom et al. (1993) in their longitudinal examination of marital satisfaction in retirement. The quality of the retirement experience significantly predicted depressive symptomatology, which, in turn, predicted marital satisfaction over a 6-month time lag. Support for the temporal ordering emerged from cross-lagged regression analyses that suggested that depression is a predictor rather than an outcome of marital dissatisfaction.

Thus, we examined the linkages between work stress, control at work, individual well-being, and two measures of marital functioning: marital dissatisfaction and divorce propensity. Consistent with the evidence supporting a mediational link between work stress and marital functioning, we (MacEwen et al., 1992) expected depression to emerge as a predictor of both measures of marital functioning. Neither stress nor control at work was hypothesized to affect marital functioning directly.

Stress, Control, and Well-Being

In his review, Frese (1989) identified various theoretical models of stress, control, and well-being. Drawing on this framework, we proposed and evaluated four models of stress, control, and well-being that differ in terms of both the functional relationship they imply (e.g., moderation, mediation, and main effect) and the causal ordering of the variables in each. The four models are presented in Figure 1 and are more fully described below.

The most parsimonious model of how control might affect individual well-being is one that posits a direct main effect of control on well-being. Thus, although work-related stress is associated with impaired well-being, control at work would be seen as a countering force, positively associated with well-being. Frese (1989) suggested that this main-effect model is based on a need for control: If the need is not satisfied then negative outcomes will ensue. Certainly, there is a wealth of empirical data suggesting that autonomy, a construct related to control, is associated with measures of affective well-being such as job satisfaction (Kelloway & Barling, 1991; Loher, Noe, Moeller, & Fitzgerald, 1985). Similarly, Warr (1987) identified the opportunity for control as one of the nine features of the work environment that contribute to job-related mental health. In our study, support for the main-effect model would be evidenced by a significant cross-lagged prediction of individual well-being by perceptions of control at work. Because of the problems in inferring causal direction from cross-sectional data, a significant cross-sectional correlation cannot be interpreted as supporting the main effect of control on individual well-being.

Perhaps the most widely cited model of stress and control is the job demand–decision latitude model proposed by Karasek and his colleagues (Karasek, 1979; Karasek, Baker, Marxer, Ahlbom, & Theorell, 1981; Karasek & Theorell, 1990). Essentially, the demand–latitude model suggests that perceptions of decision latitude (i.e., skill discretion and task authority; Karasek & Theorell, 1990) moderate the impact of job demands on individual well-being. Thus, deleterious consequences of job demands are predicted when decision latitude is low, whereas no such negative effects are expected for individuals with considerable decision latitude (Karasek, 1979). Despite the popularity of this interactive model, supporting evidence for it has been relatively weak (Ganster & Fusilier, 1989). Problematic aspects of the research supporting the model include the confounding of worker control with other aspects of job design (e.g., skill variety), the conduct of analysis at the occupational rather than the individual level, and the failure to explicitly test for an interaction term when one is implied by the model (Ganster & Fusilier, 1989). In our study, support for the interactive model would be evidenced by a significant interaction (of the appropriate form) between stress and control, which would predict individual well-being.

Frese (1989) identified a model that suggests that control at work is used to decrease the occurrence or intensity of job stressors and, thereby, to enhance individual well-being. Empirically, support for this stressor reduction model would be evidenced by an effect of control on individual well-being that is

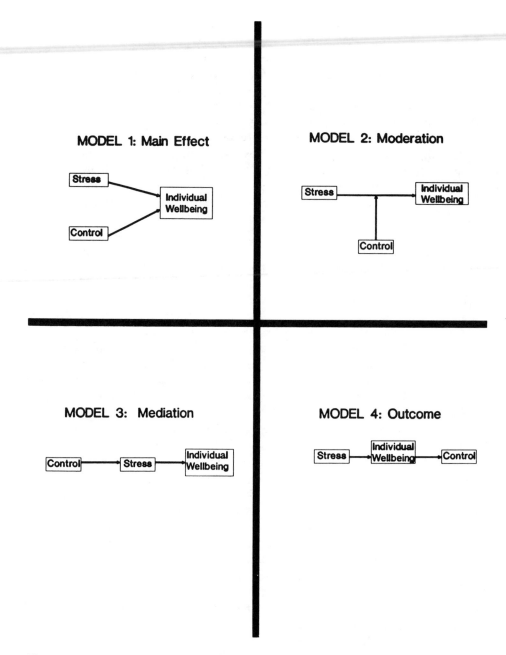

Figure 1.   Four models of stress, control, and well-being.

either fully or partially mediated by stress. In our research, support for such a mediational model would be gained if (a) there was a significant cross-lagged prediction of stress by perceptions of individual control and (b) there was a significant cross-lagged prediction of individual well-being by stress.

Finally, we considered a fourth model suggesting that perceptions of control at work are an outcome rather than a predictor of individual well-being.

Organizational researchers have increasingly recognized the role of affect and affectivity in predicting self-reports of job characteristics (e.g., Brief, Burke, George, Robinson, & Webster, 1988; Lewin & Stokes, 1989; Staw & Ross, 1985). Moreover, feelings of hopelessness and fatalism (i.e., decreased control) are associated with depressive symptomatology. Support for this outcome model in our study would emerge from a significant cross-lagged prediction of control perceptions by individual well-being.

Thus, we empirically contrasted four models of stress, control, and well-being. Each of the models (main effect, moderation, mediation, and outcome) is a plausible description of the relationships among these three constructs. Empirically, the models may be distinguished by both the functional relationships and temporal ordering that they imply among stress, control, and well-being. By using a three-wave panel study and cross-lagged regression analyses, we were able to contrast these four models over a significant longitudinal period.

The Current Study

The literature relating employment experiences to marital functioning is by no means unequivocal with regard to causal direction (Barling, 1990). Similarly, the main-effect, moderation, mediation, and outcome models of work, control, and well-being posit not only different functional relationships but also different temporal orderings among the variables.

Campbell, Daft, and Hulin (1982) have identified the establishment of proper time lags in longitudinal research as one of the most vexing problems in organizational research. In our study, we used data drawn from a three-wave panel study, incorporating both a 6-month and a 12-month time lag into our tests. The selection of appropriate time lags is based on previous research (e.g., Higginbottom et al., 1993) as well as on the need to identify significant longitudinal periods over which to evaluate the effects of work stress and control (Frese, 1989).

We chose to use data from a nationally representative sample to enhance the external validity of our findings. Collection of data from individuals employed in diverse occupations minimizes the danger of capitalizing on organizationally specific conditions.

Method

Subjects

Data for this study were taken from a three-wave panel study of married couples in Ontario, Canada. Respondents ($N = 224$) reported a mean age of 38 years and had been married for an average of 13 years. Mean organizational tenure was 8.6 years, and respondents reported completing 13 years of formal education on average. Fifty-three percent of the respondents were women.

Measures

At each time period, respondents completed two measures of work stress. First, respondents completed the organizational stress checklist (Sarason & Johnson, 1979). Next, they completed the 20-item short form of the Industrial Relations Events Questionnaire (Bluen & Barling, 1987). Bluen & Barling presented evidence for the convergent, discriminant, and known group validity of this scale. Although developed in South Africa, the scale has performed acceptably in Canadian studies of chronic stress (Kelloway & Barling, in press), acute stress (Barling & Milligan, 1987), and daily industrial relations stress (Kelloway, Barling, & Shah, 1994). Both stress measures provide indexes of the occurrence of stressors and of individuals' negative and positive evaluations of these stressors. In this study, we used only the negative stress scores.

Respondents also completed Tetrick and LaRocco's (1987) six-item scale of perceived control at work. The scale has demonstrated acceptable internal consistency ($\alpha = .83$) in previous research.

Respondents also completed a six-item measure of depressive symptomatology drawn from the Center for Epidemiological Study—Depression Scale (Radloff, 1977). This scale was developed to assess depressive symptomatology in the general population. The six items used in the current study were those loading on Radloff's depressive affect factor.

Finally, respondents completed two measures of marital functioning. These were the Short Marital Adjustment Test (Locke & Wallace, 1959), a widely used measure of marital satisfaction, and a five-item measure of divorce propensity (Booth, Johnson, & Edwards, 1983). The latter scale assesses the extent to which respondents are considering divorce.

Procedures

Qualified participants in the Canadian study (i.e., couples with at least one member employed) were asked in a public opinion survey if they would be willing to participate in a further study of married couples. Individuals who indicated a willingness to participate were sent an initial package containing the questionnaire and a cover letter from the researchers. Respondents were given a $15.00 honorarium for their participation. This procedure resulted in a response rate of 72% at Time 1 ($N = 467$).

Six months later, all respondents who had originally agreed to participate were sent another questionnaire package and cover letter. Again, participants were provided with an honorarium for their participation. At Time 2, 355 questionnaires (55%) were returned.

Finally, 6 months after the Time 2 distribution, questionnaire packages were sent to those respondents who had participated at either Time 1 or Time 2. Again, respondents received an honorarium for their participation. This procedure resulted in 264 questionnaires (57%) being returned at Time 3.

We used only data from those respondents who were employed and responded at all three time periods ($N = 224$) in the current study.

Results

Employment and Marital Satisfaction

The cross-lagged regression analyses for the marital functioning measures are presented in Table 1. As hypothesized, depressive symptoms at Time 1 emerged as a significant precursor of both marital satisfaction 6 months later (β = $-.14$) and divorce propensity 6 months later (β = .24) and 12 (β = .23) months later.

Neither measure of stress offered a direct, cross-lagged prediction of marital satisfaction or divorce propensity. Perceptions of control at work, however, significantly predicted divorce propensity at Time 2 (β = $-.12$).

Stress, Control, and Well-Being

To evaluate the four models of stress, control, and well-being described earlier, we conducted a series of cross-lagged regression analyses across the 6-month and 12-month time periods. Results of these analyses are presented in Table 2.

The model proposing a main effect of control on individual well-being received little support from the data. In neither the 6-month nor the 12-month analysis did control make a significant prediction of depressive symptoms after we controlled for depression at Time 1.

Similarly, the model proposing a moderation of work stress by control was not supported. As shown in the cross-lagged regression analyses, the interaction of control with either negative organizational stress or negative industrial relations stress did not significantly contribute to the prediction of depressive symptomatology.

The model predicting a mediated relationship between control and individual well-being was also not supported. Both negative organizational stress

Table 1. Cross-Lagged Regression Results for Marital Functioning

Measure	Time 1 (6 months)	Time 2 (12 months)
Divorce Propensity × Marital Satisfaction	-0.247***	-0.212***
Depression	0.228***	0.214***
Control at work	-0.119*	-0.047
Organizational stress	0.032	0.041
Industrial relations stress	0.037	0.023
Marital Satisfaction × Depression	-0.136**	-0.088
Control at work	-0.007	0.010
Organizational stress	0.052	0.063
Industrial relations stress	0.065	0.056

Note. In all regressions, the dependent variable was controlled for at Time 1. All values are standardized betas.
*$p < .05$.   **$p < .01$.   ***$p < .001$.

Table 2. Cross-Lagged Regression Analyses for Stress, Control, and Well-Being

Model	Time 1 (6 months)	Time 2 (12 months)
1. Main effect		
Depression (D) × Control (C)	0.031	0.016
D × Industrial Relations Stress (IRS)	0.067	0.089*
D × Organizational Stress (OS)	0.068	0.085*
2. Moderation		
D × OS × C[a]	0.233	−0.084
D × IRS × C[a]	0.178	−0.191
3. Mediation		
OS × C	−0.016	0.001
IRS × C	−0.017	0.002
4. Outcome		
C × D	0.014	−0.124**

Note. In all regressions, the dependent variable was controlled for at Time 1. All values are standardized betas.
[a]Controlling for stress and control at Time 1.
*$p < .05$. **$p < .01$.

($\beta = .09$) and negative industrial relations stress ($\beta = .09$) significantly predicted depression for the 12-month time lag. These effects were not significant for the 6-month time lag. Control predicted neither organizational stress nor industrial relations stress in the two cross-lagged regression analyses.

Finally, the fourth model, suggesting that control perceptions were an outcome of depressive symptoms, was supported for the 12-month but not for the 6-month time lag. Control perceptions were significantly predicted by depressive symptoms ($\beta = -.12$) for the 12-month analyses.

Discussion

Our goals in this study were to clarify the relationships among measures of stress, control, and well-being and to examine the relationship of these constructs to marital functioning. First, our analyses suggest that the effects of work stress on marital functioning are indirect, being mediated by the effects of stress on individual well-being. Second, of the four models we considered here, cross-lagged regression analyses offered support for only Model 4, which posited stress as a predictor and control as an outcome of individual well-being. As discussed below, these results have implications for both the study of work stress and the relationship between work stress and marital functioning.

With respect to our first goal, our findings supported the hypothesized links between work stress and marital functioning. These results are consistent with the spillover hypothesis suggesting that experienced work stress will spill over and have negative consequences on marital functioning (Barling, 1990; Zedeck & Mosier, 1990). Moreover, our results support and extend previous research (Higginbottom et al., 1993; MacEwen et al., 1992) suggesting that these effects are indirect, being mediated by individual well-being. Thus, our findings extend the basic notion of the spillover hypothesis by suggesting one such mechanism through which spillover may occur. Work stress had a direct effect on depressive symptomatology, which in turn predicted both marital dissatisfaction and divorce propensity.

These results echo and extend those reported by Higginbottom et al. (1993) showing that characteristics of the retirement experience predicted depressive symptoms, which, in turn, predicted marital satisfaction. In the current study, the same indirect effects were observed for the quality of the employment experience (i.e., work stress).

Our results offer little support for models positing control as either a moderator or a predictor of individual well-being. Rather, our results suggest that perceptions of decreased control are an outcome of impaired well-being that results from work stress. The failure to support a moderating role of control in our study was not entirely unexpected. Although the moderation hypothesis offers considerable appeal through its implications for job design, empirical support for a moderating role for control perceptions has been limited at best (Ganster & Fusilier, 1989). Our results also did not suggest that control perceptions offered either direct or indirect predictions of well-being.

Our findings imply that prescriptions for ameliorating the negative effects of stress on well-being by increasing employee control are, in themselves, unlikely to be effective. Rather, job design strategies focusing on the elimination or reduction of stressors are more likely to have a stronger effect on individual well-being. Although the need for further investigations of worker control continues, our results suggest considerable caution in assuming that increased control at work will ameliorate the effects of stress on individual well-being.

Consistent with the general strain model (House, 1981), our results support the hypothesized relationship between organizational and industrial relations stress and individual well-being. Moreover, they suggest that organizational and industrial relations stress may have long-term effects on well-being: The hypothesized effects did not emerge at Time 2 (a 6-month time lag) but were statistically significant at Time 3 (a 12-month time lag). These findings support the association between stress and general mental health and extend the research by demonstrating the temporal ordering of stress and depressive symptomatology.

Finally, our use of two time lags in the current study illustrates the utility of multiple time lags for similar research. The relationship between stress and well-being did not emerge with a 6-month time lag but was significant at 12 months. Similarly, the temporal ordering of marital satisfaction and divorce propensity was ambiguous with a 6-month time lag: Divorce propensity predicted, and was predicted by, marital satisfaction. At 12 months, however, no bidirectional causality was apparent: Marital satisfaction emerged as a predictor of divorce propensity.

There are several potential limitations to our study, each suggesting areas for further research. First, although we considered both 6-month and 12-month time lags, it is possible that the consideration of alternative time lags would result in different conclusions. Although our choice of time lags was based on previous research suggesting the utility of a 6-month time lag (e.g., Higgin-bottom et al., 1993), researchers and theoreticians should begin attempting to specify the appropriate time lags for posited effects.

Second, several reviews have included comments on the multidimensional nature of control perceptions. For example, *control* may refer to control over the timing of work, the nature of work, the ordering of specific tasks, or the selection of tools and materials (Ganster, 1989). We chose to focus on more generalized perceptions of control, that is, the extent to which respondents see themselves as being able to alter events at work. Our choice was based on the matching of control with the types of stress under consideration. Both the Industrial Relations Events Scale and the Organizational Events Scale assess respondents' perceptions of events in the workplace. Further research is required to assess the contribution of other forms of control to the stress—well-being relationship.

In summary, our results imply that organizational and industrial relations stress contribute to depressive symptomatology. Perceptions of control at work were an outcome rather than a predictor of depressive symptoms. Finally, both marital dissatisfaction and divorce propensity were related to depressive symptoms. These results support the mediational models of stress and marital function proposed earlier (e.g., Higginbottom et al., 1993; MacEwen et al., 1992) by suggesting that the relationship between work stress and marital functioning is mediated by psychological well-being.

References

Barling, J. (1990). *Employment, stress and family functioning.* New York: Wiley.

Barling, J., & Milligan, J. (1987). Some psychological consequences of striking: A six-month longitudinal study. *Journal of Occupational Behavior, 8,* 127–138.

Bluen, S. D., & Barling, J. (1987). Stress and the industrial relations process: Development of the Industrial Relations Event Scale. *South African Journal of Psychology, 17,* 150–159.

Booth, A., Johnson, D., & Edwards, J. N. (1983). Measuring marital instability. *Journal of Marriage and the Family, 45,* 387–393.

Brief, A. P., Burke, M. J., George, J. M., Robinson, B. S., & Webster, J. (1988). Should negative affectivity remain an unmeasured variable in the study of job stress? *Journal of Applied Psychology, 73,* 193–198.

Campbell, J. P., Daft, R. L., & Hulin, C. L. (1982). *What to study: Generating and developing research questions.* Beverly Hills, CA: Sage.

Frese, M. (1989). Theoretical models of control and health. In S. L. Sauter, J. J. Hurrell, & C. L. Cooper (Eds.), *Job control and worker health* (pp. 107–128). New York: Wiley.

Ganster, D. C. (1989). Worker control and well-being: A review of research in the workplace. In S. L. Sauter, J. J. Hurrell, & C. L. Cooper (Eds.), *Job control and worker health* (pp. 3–23). New York: Wiley.

Ganster, D. C., & Fusilier, M. R. (1989). Control in the workplace. In C. L. Cooper & I. Robertson (Eds.), *International review of industrial and organizational psychology, 1989* (pp. 236–280). New York: Wiley.

Higginbottom, S. F., Barling, J., & Kelloway, E. K. (1993). Linking retirement experiences and marital satisfaction: A mediational model. *Psychology and Aging, 8,* 508–516.

House, J. S. (1981). *Work stress and social support.* Reading, MA: Addison-Wesley.

Karasek, R. A. (1979). Job demands, job decision latitude, and mental strain: Implications for job design. *Administrative Science Quarterly, 24,* 285–306.

Karasek, R. A., Baker, D., Marxer, F., Ahlbom, A., & Theorell, T. (1981). Job decision latitudes, job demands and cardiovascular disease: A prospective study of Swedish men. *American Journal of Public Health, 71,* 694–705.

Karasek, R. A., & Theorell, T. (1990). *Healthy work: Stress, productivity, and the reconstruction of working life.* New York: Basic Books.

Kelloway, E. K., & Barling, J. (1991). Job characteristics, role stress, and mental health. *Journal of Occupational Psychology, 64,* 291–304.

Kelloway, E. K., & Barling, J. (in press). Industrial relations stress and union activism: Costs and benefits of participation. *Proceedings of the 46th annual meeting of the Industrial Relations Research Association.*

Kelloway, E. K., Barling, J., & Shah, A. (1994). Industrial relations stress, daily mood and job satisfaction: Concurrent effects and mediation. *Journal of Organizational Behavior, 14,* 447–458.

Lewin, I., & Stokes, J. P. (1989). Dispositional approach to job satisfaction: The role of negative affectivity. *Journal of Applied Psychology, 74,* 752–758.

Locke, H. J., & Wallace, K. M. (1959). Short marital adjustment and prediction tests: Their reliability and validity. *Marriage and Family Living, 21,* 251–255.

Loher, B. T., Noe, R. A., Moeller, N. L., & Fitzgerald, M. P. (1985). A meta-analysis of the relation of job characteristics to job satisfaction. *Journal of Applied Psychology, 70,* 280–289.

MacEwen, K. E., Barling, J., & Kelloway, E. K. (1992). Effects of acute role overload on marital functioning. *Work and Stress, 6,* 117–126.

Miller, S. M. (1979). Controllability and human stress: Method, evidence, and theory. *Behavior Research and Therapy, 17,* 287–304.

Radloff, L. S. (1977). The CES-D Scale: A self-report depression scale for research in the general population. *Applied Psychological Measurement, 1,* 385–401.

Sarason, I. G., & Johnson, J. H. (1979). Life stress, organizational stress, and job satisfaction. *Psychological Reports, 44,* 57–59.

Staines, G. L. (1980). Spillover versus compensation: A review of the literature on work and nonwork. *Human Relations, 33,* 111–129.

Staw, B. M., & Ross, J. (1985). Stability in the midst of change: A dispositional approach to job attitudes. *Journal of Applied Psychology, 70,* 469–480.

Tetrick, L. E., & LaRocco, J. M. (1987). Understanding, prediction, and control as moderators of the relationships between perceived stress, satisfaction, and psychological well-being. *Journal of Applied Psychology, 72,* 538–543.

Thompson, S. C. (1981). Will it hurt less if I can control it? A complex answer to a simple question. *Psychological Bulletin, 90,* 89–101.

Warr, P. B. (1987). *Work, unemployment, and mental health.* New York: Oxford University Press.

Zedeck, S., & Mosier, K. (1990). Work in the family and employing organization. *American Psychologist, 45,* 240–252.

16

Family-Friendly Workplaces, Work–Family Interface, and Worker Health

Nancy L. Marshall and Rosalind C. Barnett

The last 40 years have seen dramatic social changes in the United States. Spurred by the shift from a manufacturing economy toward a service economy, as well as by other demographic and economic changes (Oppenheimer, 1974, 1982), women's rate of participation in the labor force has steadily increased. Although significant proportions of single mothers have been in the labor force throughout this century—with almost two thirds of all single mothers employed in 1986 (Rix, 1988, p. 376)—the rise in women's employment rates now also reflects the participation of married women with young children. In 1960, less than 20% of married-couple families with children under 6 were two-earner families; by 1985 more than half of such families were two-earner families (U.S. Bureau of the Census, 1985).

These two-earner couples face certain challenges that the traditional single-earner, two-parent family did not face. Most obviously, they have less time in which to complete all the tasks of maintaining and nurturing a family. Although two-earner couples can respond to this situation by making some changes in their home life, such as sharing household chores more equitably, and enlisting or buying support services, these adaptations are not always enough.

As two-earner couples become the norm, there is greater interest in workplaces that facilitate the fit or interface between work and family. Workplaces are considered to be "family friendly" when they (a) help workers manage the time pressures of being working parents by having policies such as vacation time, sick leave, unpaid or personal leave, or flexible work schedules, or (b) help workers meet their continuing family responsibilities through such programs as maternity and paternity leave, leave that can be used to care for sick children or elders, affordable health insurance, and child-care or elder-care programs. However, being family friendly also includes the informal practices and culture of the workplace. For instance, can workers receive and make

Data for this study were collected with funding from the National Institute of Mental Health (MH 43222). We want to thank our dedicated research team: Carol Anello, Joyce Buni, Lillian Coltin, Connie Festo, Carla Fink, Lorraine McMullin, Pam Miller, Jennifer Rochow, Rosalind Sandler, Martha Sherman, Nathalie Thompson, Susan Wellington, and Kathryn Wheeler.

phone calls to take care of family matters? If the babysitter is sick, or a child is sick, can the worker take time off on short notice? Are workers' careers penalized if they take time off, or do they risk losing their jobs?

Although there has been attention paid to work–family programs and benefits, there is still little research on the effect of these benefits and programs on employees. What research exists primarily focuses on the effect such programs have on employers (Aldous, 1990; Galinsky & Stein, 1990; Raabe, 1990). The few studies that have been done that concern employees suggest that family-friendly workplaces do have an effect, although it is sometimes small and often confined to specific categories of workers. Research on the effects of flexible work schedules has generally found them to be positive (Pleck, 1992). Employees with flextime report less work–family conflict and more time for home chores and family (Bohen & Viveros-Long, 1981; Lee, 1983; Winett, Neale, & Williams, 1982). A recent study by Staines (1990) suggested that the level or type of flexibility is important. Staines found that employed mothers of newborns who could change their starting and ending times on a daily basis reported lower work–family conflict in comparison with those who could choose a work schedule but then had to keep that schedule for some minimum period of time (the more typical formal flextime arrangement).

In this chapter, we examine the importance of workplace flexibility in the broader sense, defined as having a job with sufficient flexibility to allow the worker to respond to nonwork situations. This might include specific work schedules that are compatible with family needs or the right to vary work schedules as needed, but would also include the general culture of the workplace. We also examine the role of more formal benefits, such as paid sick leave and paid parental leave, in creating family-friendly workplaces.

Method

The data for these analyses come from the first wave of a three-wave longitudinal study (over 2 years) of a random sample of 300 couples in which both the men and the women were employed full time. The couples were randomly selected from town lists of all adults living in two towns in the greater Boston area. The sample was stratified on parental status (60% of sample members were parents at the time of recruitment) and was limited to couples in which the man was between the ages of 25 and 40 years. The response rate was 68% of those couples contacted for the study (see Barnett, Marshall, & Pleck, 1992, for more information about the sampling procedures).

The respondents in this study were interviewed separately in their homes or offices by a trained interviewer. The interviews lasted approximately 2 hours and covered respondents' experiences in their major social roles (i.e., worker, parent, and spouse), their experiences combining employment and family roles, and indexes of mental and physical health. Each couple was paid a fee of $25 for participating.

Sample Description

Most of the respondents were in their 30s; the average age was 35 years for men (SD = 4.3) and 34 years for women (SD = 4.9). The sample reflected the racial composition of the two towns from which the respondents were recruited; 98% of the men and 97% of the women were White. About a quarter of the respondents (27% of the men, 25% of the women) had a high school diploma or less; one third of the respondents (33% of men, 38% of women) had 4-year college degrees, and more than one third had some graduate training or a graduate degree (40% of men and 36% of women).

All respondents were employed full time. Both men and women had been at their current jobs an average of 5 years, ranging from less than 1 year to 25 years. Men had been employed in the same occupation for an average of 9 years, and women for an average of 8 years. Almost one quarter of the respondents were employed as managers (21% of men, 23% of women), and more than one third were professionals (38% of men, 39% of women). Twenty-one percent of the women and 7% of the men were employed in administrative support occupations, an additional 1-in-20 were in technical support occupations (6% of men, 5% of women). Thirteen percent of the men and 1% of the women were employed in blue-collar occupations (e.g., in production, crafts, or repair, or as operators or fabricators). The remaining respondents were employed in sales (11% of men, 9% of women), or service occupations (4% of men, 3% of women).

The sample was stratified on parental status; 180 couples had children. Of these couples, 119 had one or more children under the age of 6, 69 had school-age children (6–11 years old), and 47 had teenagers (12–18 years old). Parents had an average of 1.74 children.

Measures

In the present study, we examined characteristics of the job that contribute to family-friendly workplaces. Specifically, we considered such benefits as paid sick leave, paid vacation, paid or partially paid health insurance, and paid maternity and paternity leave. We also considered the flexibility of the job. Additionally, we examined whether individuals in family-friendly workplaces report greater job satisfaction, reduced work interference with home life, and better mental health.

Job flexibility. Job flexibility was measured by a scale consisting of three items. Respondents were asked, on a scale ranging from 1 (*not at all*) to 4 (*extremely rewarding*), how much each of the following items was a rewarding part of their job: (a) being able to set their own work schedule, (b) having hours that fit their needs, and (c) having a job flexible enough that they can respond to nonwork situations. The Cronbach's alpha for this scale was .74.

Benefits. To measure benefits, we asked respondents if they were eligible for paid sick leave, paid vacation, paid or partially paid health insurance, or paid maternity and paternity leave through their jobs. Respondents who did not know whether these benefits were available to them were excluded from the relevant analyses.

Job satisfaction. We measured job satisfaction by asking respondents "All things considered, how satisfied are you with your current job?" They rated their jobs on a scale ranging from 1 (*completely dissatisfied*) to 7 (*completely satisfied*).

Work–family interface. The quality of the work–family interface was measured with the Work Interference Scale (Wortman, Biernat, & Lang, 1991). The scale consists of two items: (a) because of the requirements of your job, you have to miss out on home or family activities that you would prefer to participate in, and (b) because of the requirements of your job, your family time is less enjoyable and more pressured. Respondents were asked to answer these two items on a 4-point scale ranging from 1 (*not at all true*) to 4 (*extremely true*). The Cronbach alpha for the Work Interference Scale was .61.

Psychological distress. Psychological distress was assessed with the depression and anxiety subscales of the SCL-90-R (Derogatis, 1975). The depression and anxiety subscales were combined because they are strongly correlated with each other and showed similar patterns of relationship to other variables of interest. The alpha for the combined scale was .90. The SCL-90-R has high levels of both internal consistency and test–retest reliability.

Results

Workplaces vary in the benefits they provide and in the extent to which they are family friendly. The respondents in this sample worked in a variety of occupations and industries. Of the sample, 15% were self-employed, the greatest number of them (40%) working in the professions as doctors and other health professionals, lawyers, and therapists or in the trades as electricians, plumbers, carpenters, cabinetmakers, and general contractors.

Of the 506 respondents who were not self-employed, almost one third (31%) were also professionals in professional services, primarily elementary and secondary schoolteachers, college professors, doctors, nurses and other health professionals, scientists, lawyers, therapists, and engineers. Other common occupations and industries included managers and technical or administrative support occupations in health care, education, and other professional services and in manufacturing; managers in business services and finance; professionals in manufacturing; and production workers in construction. Because our emphasis in this study was on employer-provided benefits, we restricted our analyses to data from those respondents who were not self-employed.

Table 1 shows the proportion of respondents in each industry and occupation who were eligible for paid sick leave or paid vacation or who reported that (a) their jobs allowed them to set their own work schedules, (b) their jobs

Table 1. Percentage of Non-Self-Employed Respondents With Flexibility and Benefits by Industry and Occupation

Industry & occupation	n	Set own schedule[a]	Hours fit needs[a]	Can respond to nonwork situations[a]	Sick leave[b]	Vacation[b]
All workers	506	68	71	74	93	92
Construction						
Production	7	$57_{a,b,c}$	86	71	17_{a-r}	57_{a-r}
Manufacturing						
Manager	25	84_d	72	60	92_a	$96_{a,s}$
Professional	20	70_e	70	80	100_b	$100_{b,t}$
Support	18	$94_{a,f}$	100	94	100_c	$100_{c,u}$
Utilities & transportation						
Manager	6	83_g	50	50	100_d	100_d
Wholesale trade						
Support	6	67	67	83	83_e	100_e
Sales	6	100_h	67	100	100_f	100_f
Retail trade						
Sales	7	86_b	57	71	86_g	100_g
Finance & real estate						
Manager	15	80_i	73	73	100_h	100_h
Professional	6	83_j	83	100	100_i	100_i
Support	9	67_k	78	78	100_j	100_j
Sales	9	67	67	56	89_k	89_k
Business services						
Manager	16	63	63	63	94_l	94_l
Professional	8	75_l	88	88	100_m	100_m
Support	7	57	86	100	100_n	100_n
Professional services						
Manager	37	$76_{m,p}$	68	81	97_o	$97_{o,v}$
Professional	134	$56_{n,p,q}$	71	69	91_p	$84_{p,s-v}$
Support	28	$75_{c,o,q}$	82	89	96_q	93_q
Public administration						
Service	9	22_{d-o}	67	67	100_r	100_r
F		1.70*	1.03	1.05	4.31***	2.02**
N		373	373	373	364	371

Note. Percentages in the same column with similar subscripts were significantly different from each other at $p < .05$. For example, construction workers are significantly less likely to be able to set their own schedule than are support workers in manufacturing.

[a]Percentage of workers who reported this variable to be a considerably or extremely rewarding part of their job.

[b]Percentage of workers who reported having this benefit.

*$p < .05$.   **$p < .01$.   ***$p < .001$.

had hours that fit their needs, or (c) their jobs were flexible enough to allow them to respond to nonwork situations. Only industry-by-occupation categories for which we had information on job flexibility and benefits from six or more respondents of the same gender are shown in the table. Because there were no significant gender differences in job flexibility, paid sick leave, or paid vacation, responses from men and women were combined in Table 1.

The majority of the sample had paid sick leave and paid vacation benefits (93% and 92%, respectively). However, we found sick leave and vacation benefits to be very low among production workers in the construction industry, a difference that is statistically significant. In addition, 16% of professionals working in professional services did not have paid vacation benefits. A closer examination of the data indicated that, in this sample, more than three quarters of the professionals working in physicians' and other health practitioners' offices, more than half of the college teachers outside of the "core" departments (e.g., music, art, and industrial teachers), and one third of professionals in legal firms did not have paid sick leave or paid vacations. In addition, 29% of elementary and secondary schoolteachers did not have paid vacations.

Many of the respondents in this sample also had at least some job flexibility (i.e., they reported that the job flexibility items were a considerably or extremely rewarding part of their job). Two thirds of the respondents could set their own work schedules and reported that their hours fit their needs. Almost three fourths reported that their jobs were flexible enough to allow them to respond to nonwork situations. Job flexibility did vary by industry and occupation, although the differences in whether the hours fit the respondents' needs and in the ability to respond to nonwork situations were not statistically significant. However, certain workers were significantly less likely to be able to set their own work schedules. Service workers in public administration— primarily firefighters and police officers in this sample—were significantly less likely than almost all other workers to be able to set their own hours. Construction workers were less likely to be able to set their own hours than were technical and administrative support workers in manufacturing or professional services or sales workers in retail trade. Within the professional services industry (primarily health and education), managers and technical or administrative support workers were significantly more likely to be able to set their own work schedules than were professionals. A more detailed examination of the data revealed that, among professionals in professional services, those in elementary and secondary schools and those working in hospitals were less likely to be able to set their own schedules than were professionals in colleges, doctors' offices, law firms, libraries, museums, and other professional services industries.

Information about paid parental leave benefits is presented separately for men and women in Table 2. Because many parental leave policies differentiate between women and men, there were significant gender differences in the availability of parental leave for workers. As shown in Table 2, the majority of men in this sample did not have paid paternity leave benefits. However, men who were employed as professionals in manufacturing or business services or as salesmen in wholesale trade were significantly more likely than men

Table 2. Percentage of Non-Self-Employed Respondents With Paid Parental Leave by Gender

Industry & occupation	Men	Women
All workers	35	56
Construction		
Production	$0_{a,b,c,d}$	—
Manufacturing		
Manager	31_e	71_a
Professional	58_a	40_b
Support	50	75_c
Utilities & transportation		
Manager	—	83_d
Wholesale trade		
Support	—	$100_{b,e,l}$
Sales	60_b	—
Retail trade		
Sales	$0_{a,b,c,d}$	—
Finance & real estate		
Manager	33	$88_{f,m}$
Professional	—	83_g
Support	—	78_h
Sales	—	75_i
Business services		
Manager	$0_{a,b,c}$	$88_{j,m}$
Professional	$80_{c,e,f}$	—
Support	—	50
Professional services		
Manager	17_f	56_k
Professional	40_d	$33_{a,c-k}$
Support	—	$46_{l,m,n}$
Public administration		
Service	17_f	—
F	2.04*	2.90**
N	113	189

Note. Dashes indicate that there were not six or more respondents of this gender in this industry and occupation. Percentages in the same column with the same subscript were significantly different from each other at $p < .05$. Parental leave information was missing for 46 of the men and 25 of the women.
*$p < .05$. **$p < .001$.

employed in construction, a retail trade, or as managers in business services to have such benefits.[1]

Women were more likely to receive paid parental leave benefits than were men. However, considerable variation across industries and occupations existed in this sample. In general, women in professional services (primarily health and education), particularly professionals, were least likely to have paid maternity leave. A detailed examination of the data suggested that female

[1] The differences by occupation within industry are possible because these industry categories include a variety of subcategories of industries.

professionals in hospitals and other health care industries were least likely to receive paid parental leave (only 15% had paid leave). In addition, female professionals in manufacturing were significantly less likely than female support workers in wholesale trade to have paid maternity leave.

Family-Friendly Workplaces, Job Satisfaction, and Work Interference

We next examined the relationship between job flexibility and benefits and respondents' job satisfaction and reports of work interference with home life among those who were not self-employed. We first regressed job flexibility on each of these variables and then added each of the formal benefits to the regression equation. Because sick leave and vacation tend to occur together (they were correlated at .63), we combined them into one variable: paid time off. Respondents who had sick leave, vacation, or both were coded as having paid time off. We also controlled for several variables that might be associated with job satisfaction, work interference, or worker health: age, occupational prestige, and family income. Finally, we tested whether the relationships between flexibility or benefits and job satisfaction or work interference were different for four classes of workers: women without children, men without children, mothers, and fathers. The final models, with controls and the significant independent variables included, are shown in Table 3.

As can be seen in Table 3, workers with more flexible jobs reported greater job satisfaction as well as reduced work interference in their home lives. After we considered flexibility, paid time off and paid parental leave were not significant predictors of job satisfaction or work interference. However, there are two caveats to this: First, 93% of the respondents had paid time off, making it unlikely that an actual association with job satisfaction or work interference could be identified, and second, paid parental leave is a benefit that is only needed by certain workers at certain specific times in their lives. Therefore, paid parental leave might reasonably be expected to have little effect on the lives of other workers.

We examined these models to determine if there were differences by gender or parental status in the relationship between flexibility or benefits and job satisfaction or work interference. We found no significant differences among

Table 3. Significant Predictors of Work Interference and Job Satisfaction

Predictor	Work interference			Job satisfaction		
	b	SD	β	b	SD	β
Age	-0.00	0.01	$-.02$	-0.02	0.01	$-.07$
Occupational prestige	0.00	0.00	.05	0.00	0.00	.04
Family income	1.06	0.96	.05	3.52*	1.65	.10
Flexibility	$-0.22**$	0.04	$-.23$	0.45**	0.07	.27
R^2	$-.06**$			.08**		

Note. $N = 501$. Data were for all respondents who were not self-employed.
$*p < .05.$ $**p < .001.$

Table 4. Significant Predictors of Psychological Distress Measured With the SCL-90

Predictor	b	SD	β
Age	0.01	0.09	.00
Occupational prestige	0.02	0.03	.03
Family income	− 1.87	12.89	.01
Flexibility	− 0.44	0.58	.03
Work interference	4.18*	0.61	.29
Job satisfaction	− 1.76*	0.36	− .22
R^2	.18*		

Note. $N = 501$. Data were for all respondents who were not self-employed.
*$p < .001$.

the four groups: Flexibility was associated with greater job satisfaction and reduced work interference for all workers.

Worker Health

We next asked whether job flexibility was associated with the psychological distress of workers. We posited that such an association might take a direct path; that is, workers with more flexible jobs would report reduced psychological distress. However, flexibility might also take an indirect path, through its association with job satisfaction and work interference. To examine these questions, we regressed job satisfaction, work interference, and flexibility on psychological distress. The results of this regression, which included the same control variables used in the earlier models, are shown in Table 4.

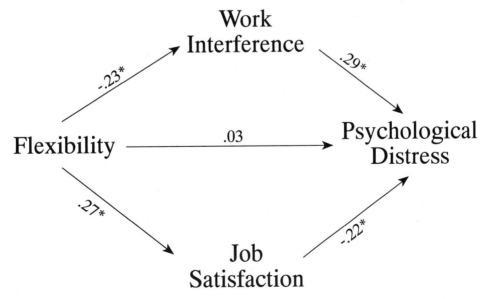

Figure 1. Path diagram of the relationship between flexibility and health. Standardized betas are given for each path. *$p < .001$.

To illustrate the direct and indirect effects more clearly, we have drawn a path model, using the standardized betas from the regression models but excluding the control variables. As shown in Figure 1, job flexibility did not have a significant direct effect on workers' psychological distress. However, flexibility did have an indirect effect on psychological distress, through its associations with work interference and job satisfaction.

Conclusion

As the U.S. workforce includes more and more members of two-earner couples, the issue of family-friendly workplaces will become increasingly important. Two-earner couples can sometimes manage the demands of work and family through adjustments at home, such as sharing household chores, relying on family and friends, or paying for paid support services. However, these couples are increasingly looking to their workplaces for the support they need.

In this chapter, we examined the links among job benefits, job flexibility, job satisfaction, work interference, and worker mental health. We found that, for two-earner couples, greater job flexibility is associated with greater job satisfaction and reduced work interference with family life. Furthermore, through indirect routes, job flexibility also affects workers' mental health.

Although working mothers are typically assumed to need job flexibility, in fact, in this study, we found that working fathers as well as women and men without children are just as likely as working mothers to benefit from job flexibility. Members of two-earner couples, with the extra demands of two jobs and home, benefit from job flexibility regardless of gender or whether they have children.

We also found that some industries and occupations are more family friendly than others. Although the majority of the workers in this sample had the flexibility to set their own schedules, construction workers, service workers in public administration (primarily firefighters and police officers), and professionals in elementary and secondary schools and in hospitals were less likely to be able to do so. The majority of these latter occupations involve direct service to vulnerable consumers of their services (schoolchildren, patients, or people in need of fire or police protection). This suggests that there are limits on flexible schedules for certain workers in a service economy; other forms of flexibility may be important to these workers.

We also found differences in the provision of paid time off. Although most of the workers in this sample had paid sick leave and vacation time, construction workers, professionals working in physicians' offices or law firms, and certain college teachers were less likely to have paid sick leave or paid vacations. In addition, many elementary and secondary schoolteachers did not have paid vacations. Similarly, women in these professions, as well as other female professionals in professional services, were less likely to have paid maternity leave than were other female workers. Interestingly, men were less likely than women to have paid parental leave, yet among professionals in professional services, men were as likely (or unlikely) as women to have paid leave.

We did not find that these variations in benefits were associated with job satisfaction, work interference, or mental health. However, as noted above, one must consider two caveats when interpreting this finding. First, 93% of the respondents had paid time off, making it unlikely that an actual association with job satisfaction or work interference could be identified. A proper evaluation of the importance of paid time off would require the use of a sample with a greater proportion of workers who do not have such paid benefits.

The same caveat does not apply to paid parental leave; only one third of men and a little more than half of women had paid parental leave benefits. However, paid parental leave is a benefit that is only needed by certain workers at certain specific times in their lives and might reasonably be expected to have little effect on the lives of other workers. This study does demonstrate that paid parental leave policies are not significant predictors of job satisfaction or work interference for workers in general. However, a proper evaluation of the significance of parental leave for those workers likely to use such a benefit would require the use of a sample of workers who vary in their access to paid parental leave and who have recently had a child or are anticipating having a child in the near future.

Finally, it must be noted that the majority of the respondents in this study were White and college educated. The connections between benefits and worker health may be very different for people of color and for workers with less education. Further research is needed in this area.

In summary, the findings reported in this chapter suggest that as the labor force includes greater numbers of workers who are in two-earner couples, it will become increasingly important to have workplaces that are family friendly and that allow workers the kind of flexibility discussed here. Such job flexibility directly contributes to greater job satisfaction and reduced work–family strain while indirectly contributing to worker health.

References

Aldous, J. (1990). Specification and speculation concerning the politics of workplace family policies. *Journal of Family Issues, 11*, 355–367.

Barnett, R. C., Marshall, N. L., & Pleck, J. H. (1992). Men's multiple roles and their relationship to men's psychological distress. *Journal of Marriage and the Family, 54*, 358–367.

Bohen, H. H., & Viveros-Long, A. (1981). *Balancing jobs and family life: Do flexible work schedules help?* Philadelphia: Temple University Press.

Derogatis, L. R. (1975). *The SCL-90-R.* Baltimore, MD: Clinical Psychometrics.

Galinsky, E., & Stein, P. J. (1990). The impact of human resource policies on employees. *Journal of Family Issues, 11*, 368–383.

Lee, R. A. (1983). Flextime and conjugal roles. *Journal of Occupational Behavior, 4*, 297–315.

Oppenheimer, V. K. (1974). Demographic influence on female employment and the status of women. In J. Huber (Ed.), *Changing women in a changing society* (pp. 184–199). Chicago: University of Chicago Press.

Oppenheimer, V. K. (1982). *Work and family: A study in social demography.* San Diego, CA: Academic Press.

Pleck, J. H. (1992). Work–family policies in the United States. In H. Kahne & J. Z. Giele (Eds.), *Women's work and women's lives: The continuing struggle worldwide* (pp. 248–275). Boulder, CO: Westview Press.

Raabe, P. H. (1990). The organizational effects of workplace policies. *Journal of Family Issues, 11,* 477–491.

Rix, S. E. (Ed.). (1988). *The American woman 1988–89: A status report.* New York: Norton.

Staines, G. L. (1990, August). *Flextime and the conflict between work and family life.* Paper presented at the 98th Annual Convention of the American Psychological Association, Boston.

U.S. Bureau of the Census. (1985). *Statistical abstract of the United States: 1986.* Washington, DC: U.S. Government Printing Office.

Winett, R. A., Neale, M. S., & Williams, K. R. (1982). The effects of flexible work schedules on urban families with young children: Quasi-experimental, ecological studies. *American Journal of Community Psychology, 10,* 49–64.

Wortman, C. B., Biernat, M. R., & Lang, E. L. (1991). Coping with role overload. In M. Frankenhaeuser, U. Lundberg, & M. Chesney (Eds.), *Women, work and health: Stress and opportunities* (pp. 85–110). New York: Plenum.

Part V

Work–Nonwork Conflict

Introduction

There is little doubt that people experience a daily struggle between their obligations at work and at home. The four chapters in this part focus primarily on the effects of conflicts that arise from simultaneously occupying work roles and such nonwork roles as spouse, parent, or caregiver. As these chapters show, the effects are numerous, and such conflicts greatly influence aspects of job, life, and marital satisfaction. The complexity of these relationships is not fully understood; therefore, this seems to represent a fertile area for future research.

First, Roskies and Carrier focus on women who have given their careers priority over marriage and childbearing and examine the consequences of that choice. They compare the career achievement patterns and personal well-being of three groups of professional women: never married and childless, married and childless, and married with children.

Next, Chapman, Ingersoll-Dayton, and Neal describe their study of how occupying both work and caregiving roles affects employees' absenteeism and reported stress. Their sample was broad, including 9,500 male and female employees from 33 business agencies.

The influences of marriage and family on the careers and life satisfaction of female graduates of a Canadian university are reported by Burke and McKeen. Their results are in some ways dissimilar to those reported by Roskies and Carrier, and together these two studies suggest the need for caution in drawing conclusions about the effects of marriage and family on well-being.

Finally, Grant and Barling examine the increasingly important problem of stress resulting from unemployment. Specifically, what happens to marital functioning when the work role is lost? Using data from unemployed and employed respondents, the authors reveal how unemployment affects depressive symptoms and, ultimately, marital dissatisfaction.

17

Marriage and Children for Professional Women: Asset or Liability?

Ethel Roskies and Sylvie Carrier

In recent years, much attention has been paid to the role strains experienced by women who add the new role of worker to the more traditional roles of wife and mother (Hochschild, 1989; Wortman, Biernat, & Lang, 1991). In sharp contrast, there has been almost no research on the stress affecting women who substitute new roles for old ones, for example, by embarking on professional careers while remaining childless or single (Allen, 1989; Fong, 1992). Nevertheless, this is a sizable and growing population. Not only are more women entering historically male professions each year (Marshall, 1989) but, in comparison with both their male colleagues and women in general, professional women are less likely to marry or bear children (Marshall, 1989; Statistics Canada, 1989). Moreover, this tendency to refrain from marriage, childbearing, or both is not restricted either to specific professions or to Canadian women but has been repeatedly reported in recent studies of managerial, professional, and academic women (Fong, 1992; Houseknecht, Vaughn, & Statham, 1987; Howard & Bray, 1988; Jagacinski, LeBold, & Linden, 1987; Nicholson & West, 1988).

In making the decision to marry or not, to bear children or remain childless, professional women are caught between the proverbial rock and a hard place. On the one hand, popular opinion and even some empirical research support the view that women are obliged to choose between top-level careers and the mommy track (Abella, 1984; Schwartz, 1989; Uhlenberg & Cooney, 1990). Indeed, one of the common explanations for the frequently reported discrepancy in income between male and female professionals has been women's distraction by family responsibilities. But just as marriage and children are seen as obstacles to career success, so are single status and childlessness commonly perceived as harmful to personal well-being; stereotypes of the unhappy old maid or the empty womb are widespread (see Faludi, 1991, for a review of recent media coverage of the issue). Here, too, there are supporting

Financial support for this research was provided by Grant 882-91-0013 from the Social Sciences and Humanities Research Council, Ottawa, Ontario, Canada, to Ethel Roskies. We acknowledge Adèle Karamanoukian's help in collecting and coding data and Maria Rosa's help with some of the data analyses.

data indicating poorer health, lower life satisfaction, and increased depression in unmarried women (Gove & Zeiss, 1987; Thoits, 1986; Verbrugge, 1982, 1983).

For a significant number of women who have recently gained entry into historically male professions, the choice has been to favor career aspirations at the cost of traditional family ties. But is this choice necessary, and if so, are these women making the right choice? The answers to these questions have important social ramifications not only because of the key economic and social positions occupied by the women themselves but also, and even more important, because these pioneer women will inevitably serve as role models for the steadily growing number of women following in their path.

In the present study, we examined the data relevant to this crucial decision by comparing the career patterns and personal well-being of three groups of professional women: never married and childless, married without children, and married with children. On the basis of the existing literature and popular assumptions, we formulated two hypotheses: First, we expected the three family groups to be rank ordered in terms of career achievement, with single, childless women placing highest; married women without children being intermediate; and married women with children being the lowest. Second, we expected that for personal well-being variables, in contrast, the order would be reversed: Married women with children would be at the top and single, childless women would be at the bottom.

Method

Sample Selection

Medicine, law, accounting, and engineering were chosen as the professional population base for the study because these professions share common key characteristics (lengthy preparation, high commitment, high status, and high income) while, at the same time, each has its own specific mode of operation. Hence, as a group, the four provide a good picture of the traditionally male upper-level occupations to which women are beginning to gain access in substantial numbers. Furthermore, the legal obligation for practicing members to belong to their professional corporation ensured that the corporate membership lists we consulted did, in fact, cover the entire population of women active in these professions.

Our aim was to recruit a representative sample of women in these four designated professions who were roughly between 35 and 40 years old. This age range was selected because by the late 30s (a) sufficient time has elapsed since graduation for differences in career patterns and achievement to manifest themselves, (b) the probability that never-married individuals will subsequently marry is small (Statistics Canada, 1985), and (c) the ticking of the biological clock is presumed to become salient to childless women. Practically, too, this is the oldest age group in these historically male professions where women are available in sufficient numbers to permit analysis by family status.

Potential participants were identified through the membership lists of the Quebec corporations governing the four professions in question: the Order of

Engineers, the Order of Chartered Accountants, the Professional Corporation of Physicians, and the Bar.[1] The first three corporations were able to identify members in our target age group, whereas the Bar, which does not categorize membership by age, allowed us to infer age by targeting members with initial registration between 1975 and 1980.

Solicitation was restricted to members with current Quebec addresses; the four lists contained 2,019 eligible names. Using survey procedures developed by Dillman (1983), we solicited participants in three steps between May and June 1991. Prospective participants were first sent a kit (with a questionnaire, cover letter, and postage-paid return envelope), a week later were sent a reminder postcard, and 3 weeks later were sent a second kit. Of the women contacted, 1,294 usable replies were received—a response rate of 64.1%. The response rate was similar across the four professions: medicine, 62.3%; law, 63.1%; accounting, 69.6%; and engineering, 68.3%.

Women not currently in the labor force (i.e., who were unemployed, on maternity leave, or homemakers; $n = 36$) or whose marital status could not be clearly deduced from their questionnaire replies ($n = 7$) were excluded from the sample. We then drew three groups of women from the remaining pool of 1,251 potential subjects: *Never-married women* were operationally defined as women who had never been married, were not currently living with a partner, and had never borne children ($n = 162$). *Married without children* identified women who were currently living with a partner (through legal marriage or consensual union)[2] but had no children ($n = 218$). *Married with children* identified women who were currently living with a partner (through legal marriage or consensual union) and who had one or more children ($n = 743$). Divorced, separated, and widowed women ($n = 108$), as well as never-married women with children ($n = 20$), were not included in these analyses because their situations were too diverse and their numbers were too small to permit valid comparisons.

Participants

The final sample contained 1,123 women: 66% married with children ($n = 743$), 19% married without children ($n = 218$), and 14% never married and childless ($n = 162$). This sample was homogeneous not only in educational level and age (83% were in the target age range of 35–40 years and the rest were within a few years either way) but also in cultural background (over 90% were Canadian born and spoke French as their first language) and in professional experience (over 90% had 10 or more years of professional experience).

---

[1] We should like to express our appreciation to these professional organizations for making this study possible by providing us with the relevant membership lists.

[2] In Quebec, consensual union has become an increasingly acceptable alternative to legal marriage, particularly in the younger age ranges. Statistics Canada, 1991 ("Changes in demographics," 1993), census data indicated that one out of every five couples in Quebec was living in a consensual union and that half of firstborn children were the offspring of a mother who was not legally married.

The majority of the sample (over 80%) was concentrated in the two largest urban areas of Quebec.

Physicians and lawyers were overrepresented in the sample (39.4% and 36.9%, respectively) in comparison with accountants and engineers (15.2% and 8.6%, respectively), but these differences accurately reflect the relative numerical strength of women in each of the four professions. There were no significant demographic differences among professions, except for a higher percentage of married women without children among lawyers, $\chi^2(1, N = 1,123) = 13.31, p < .001$.

Measures

Career patterns. The analysis was based on four measures: job satisfaction, job involvement, number of hours worked weekly, and annual professional income.

The Index of Job Satisfaction (Brayfield & Rothe, 1951; Cook, Hepworth, Wall, & Warr, 1981) consists of general evaluative statements concerning one's job situation. We used the abbreviated six-item version (Hirsch & Rapkin, 1986) here. Index items are rated on a 7-point Likert-type scale ranging from *strong disagreement* (1) to *strong agreement* (7). Possible scores ranged from 6 to 42, with higher scores indicating greater satisfaction. Cronbach's alpha for this sample was .80.

We used the 10-item Job Involvement Questionnaire (Kanungo, 1982) to evaluate the degree to which participants' jobs were central to their self-concept or sense of identity. Responses were made on 7-point Likert-type scales, as described above. Possible scores ranged from 10 to 70, with higher scores indicating higher job involvement. Cronbach's alpha for this sample was .86.

Number of hours worked weekly was based on the woman's own categorization of herself into one of the following groups: less than 19, 19–34, 35–50, 51–70, or 71 or more. For purposes of our analyses, we subsequently collapsed the scale into three categories: (a) fewer than 35 hours a week, (b) 35–50 hours, and (c) more than 50 hours.

Annual professional income was also based on the respondent's self-report, in this case, of the appropriate income category: less than $25,000, $25,000–$39,999, $40,000–49,999, $50,000–$74,999, $75,000–$99,999, $100,000–199,999, or more than $200,000. Because of small frequencies in the extreme categories, we subsequently collapsed the scale into four groups: less than $50,000, $50,000–74,999, $75,000–$99,999, and more than $100,000.

Personal well-being. This evaluation included self-report measures of basic personality disposition and physical health, as well as three indexes of current psychological state.

We used the Spielberger Trait Anxiety Scale (Spielberger, Gorusch, & Lushene, 1970; French–Canadian version validated by Bergeron, Landry, & Bélanger, 1976), which is considered to be an excellent measure of negative affectivity—a stable personality disposition to view and react to the world in a negative fashion (Watson & Clark, 1984). Individuals scoring high on this scale typically manifest a chronic high level of psychological distress, regardless of the particular stresses they are experiencing at any given time. Responses to the 20-item measure are scored on a 4-point Likert-type scale (1 = *practically never* to 4 = *practically always*), with possible scores ranging from 20 to 80. Higher scores indicate higher levels of negative personality disposition.

Current physical health was assessed by the four-item version of the General Health Rating Index (Davies & Ware, 1981; Read, Quinn, & Hoefer, 1987). Rather than detailing specific symptoms or dysfunctions, the statements reflect general evaluations of overall health. Respondents are asked to rate the applicability of each statement to themselves on a scale ranging from *completely false* (1) to *completely true* (4). Possible scores range from 4 to 20, with higher scores reflecting greater health. Cronbach's alpha for this sample was .77.

Because of recent suggestions that mental health is best viewed as a multidimensional concept (Bryant & Veroff, 1982; Diener, 1984; Diener, Emmons, Larsen, & Griffin, 1985), we used three different measures to evaluate the different facets of psychological well-being. The Rosenberg Self-Esteem Scale (Rosenberg, 1965; French–Canadian version validated by Vallières & Vallerand, 1990) consists of 10 items scored here on a 7-point Likert-type scale (1 = *strong disagreement* to 7 = *strong agreement*), with higher scores indicating greater self-esteem. Possible scores ranged from 10 to 70.

The Satisfaction With Life Scale (Diener et al., 1985; French–Canadian version validated by Blais, Vallerand, Pelletier, & Brière, 1989) is designed to have each individual evaluate his or her life as a whole, rather than sum individual satisfaction with specific domains. Moreover, this cognitive–judgmental evaluation is based on a comparison that each person sets for himself or herself rather than based on criteria judged to be important by the researcher. Both the English and French validations have indicated satisfactory reliability and validity as well as confirmed the unifactorial nature of the scale. The measure contains five items scored on a 7-point Likert-type scale, ranging from *strong disagreement* (1) to *strong agreement* (7) (range = 5–35), with higher scores indicating greater life satisfaction.

The General Health Questionnaire (Goldberg, 1978; Goldberg & Hillier, 1979; Payne, Warr, & Hartley, 1984) is a widely used measure of nonpsychotic psychological distress; the seven-item subscale we used here deals specifically with depression. This questionnaire focuses on the more severe signs of disturbed affect, including suicidal tendencies. There are four possible responses for each question, ranging from *practically never* (0) to *practically always* (3). Possible scores ranged from 0 to 21, with higher scores indicating higher levels of depression. Cronbach's alpha for this sample was .90.

Statistical Procedures

We used two main statistical procedures in these analyses. For measures yielding nominal data, we performed overall chi-square tests. In cases where it proved statistically significant, we then partitioned the contingency table to pinpoint discrepancies between expected and obtained values (Castellan, 1965;

Siegel & Castellan, 1988). These analyses were conducted separately for each of the two independent variables: family status and professional affiliation.

For each of the two groups of scaled measures (relating to career and personal well-being, respectively), we performed separate multivariate analyses of variance (MANOVAs), using family status and professional affiliation as the independent variables. Where MANOVA proved significant, we followed it with analyses of variance for each measure, using the conservative Scheffé procedure to localize differences between group means (Tabachnick & Fidell, 1983). As an additional safeguard against Type I error, we used an alpha level of .01 throughout the analyses.

Results

Career Patterns

The modal woman in our sample worked between 35 and 50 hours per week (67%) and earned between $50,000 and $74,999 per year (43%). Job satisfaction

Table 1. Hours Worked Weekly by Women According to Family Status and Professional Affiliation

Profession & hours worked	Family status			χ^2
	Never married	Married without children	Married with children	
Medicine				39.82**
n	52	77	311	
<35	7.7%$_a$	14.3%$_a$	35.4%$_b$	
35–50	65.4%	51.9%	52.7%	
>50	26.9%$_a$	33.8%$_a$	11.9%$_b$	
Law				14.37*
n	74	94	244	
<35	1.4%$_a$	6.4%$_a$	12.3%$_b$	
35–50	74.3%	74.5%	75.4%	
>50	24.3%$_a$	19.1%$_a$	12.3%$_b$	
Accounting				19.76**
n	24	32	113	
<35	8.3%$_a$	9.4%$_a$	34.5%$_b$	
35–50	75.0%	75.0%	62.8%	
>50	16.7%$_a$	15.6%$_a$	2.7%$_b$	
Engineering				NA[a]
n	11	15	71	
<35	0.0%	6.7%	7.1%	
35–50	81.8%	93.3%	88.7%	
>50	18.2%	0.0%	4.2%	

Note. Different subscripts indicate significant differences between groups.
[a]The frequencies in some cells were too small to permit statistical analysis.
*$p < .01$. **$p < .001$.

Table 2. Family Status Means for Measures of Career and Personal Well-Being

| | Family status | | | | | | MANOVA |
| | Never married | | Married without children | | Married with children | | |
Measure	M	SD	M	SD	M	SD	F
Career							13.94*
Job satisfaction	33.10	6.01	33.92	6.07	34.48	5.66	3.97
Job involvement	43.34$_a$	11.66	42.14$_a$	10.29	37.97$_b$	10.36	25.16*
Personal well-being							10.71*
Physical health	16.72	3.50	17.29	2.99	17.13	3.38	1.41
Personality							
disposition	39.39	8.46	38.00	8.38	37.31	7.73	1.05
Life satisfaction	23.86$_a$	6.29	26.80$_b$	5.76	28.22$_c$	5.32	41.97*
General Health							
Questionnaire—							
Depression	2.76$_a$	3.68	2.13	3.52	1.68$_b$	2.85	8.42*
Self-esteem	56.99$_a$	9.67	58.98	9.20	60.44$_b$	8.11	11.62*

Note. Different subscripts indicate significant differences between groups.
MANOVA = multivariate analysis of variance.
*$p < .001$.

was uniformly high in the sample ($M = 34.17$, $SD = 5.81$), but the level of work involvement varied considerably ($M = 39.55$, $SD = 10.77$).

Professional groups varied significantly in income and number of hours worked weekly. Physicians earned significantly more than lawyers, who in turn had higher incomes than accountants and engineers, $\chi^2(9, N = 1,116) = 239.84, p < .0001$. There were also more physicians and lawyers working more than 50 hours per week (18% and 16%, respectively) in comparison with accountants and engineers (7% and 5%, respectively). Job satisfaction and job involvement did not vary across professional groups.

There were no differences between single women and married childless women in number of hours worked, income, job satisfaction, or job involvement. Thus marriage, per se, does not seem to have an impact on work effort or involvement. The presence of children, however, definitely does. Women without children, married or not, worked significantly longer hours and reported significantly higher levels of job involvement than did their counterparts with children (Tables 1 and 2).

Surprisingly, however, this greater investment does not yield larger rewards. Childless women did not earn significantly more than those with children (Table 3) nor did they report increased job satisfaction (Table 2). The one exception to this finding that raising effort does not boost rewards was found among physicians earning more than $100,000 a year, where the percentage of childless women (married or not) was significantly higher than that of childbearing women. Results of a hierarchial log-linear analysis combining

Table 3. Annual Professional Income of Women According to Family Status and Professional Affiliation

Profession & income	Family status			χ^2
	Never married	Married without children	Married with children	
Medicine				16.41*
n	52	77	311	
<$50,000	3.8%	7.8%	14.1%	
$50,000–$74,999	23.1%	31.2%	30.9%	
$75,000–$99,999	30.8%	16.9%	27.3%	
$100,000 & up	42.3%$_a$	44.2%	27.7%$_b$	
Law				4.64
n	74	93	244	
<$50,000	18.9%	18.3%	22.5%	
$50,000–$74,999	60.8%	51.6%	54.1%	
$75,000–$99,999	9.5%	14.0%	13.5%	
$100,000 & up	10.8%	16.1%	9.9%	
Accounting[a]				5.32
n	24	32	112	
< $50,000	37.5%	28.1%	50.0%	
$50,000 & up	62.5%	71.9%	50.0%	
Engineering[a]				2.78
n	11	15	71	
<$50,000	45.5%	20.0%	42.3%	
$50,000 & up	54.5%	80.0%	57.7%	

Note. Different subscripts indicate significant differences between groups.
[a]There were insufficient frequencies in the cells above $75,000 to permit chi-square tests; accordingly, all salaries above $50,000 were combined into one group.
*$p < .01$.

number of hours worked, income, and presence or absence of children suggested that the greater income of childless physicians was largely attributable to the greater number of hours they worked.

Personal Well-Being

In comparison with the general population, the sample as a whole ranked high on physical and psychological health status; in view of their favored socioeconomic status, this is hardly surprising. Neither personality disposition nor physical health, with one exception,[3] showed any significant variation across groups, either by family status or by professional affiliation. In sharp contrast, all three indexes of current psychological state (self-esteem, life satisfaction, and depression) showed significant differences according to family status. There was a clear progression, with never-married women consistently faring worst, married childless women faring better, and married women with children

---

[3] Physicians scored significantly higher on the physical health measure than did lawyers.

faring best of all (Table 2). In the case of life satisfaction, differences between all three groups were statistically significant, whereas for depression and self-esteem it was only between the two extremes (never married and married with children) that the differences reached statistical significance.

Pursuing this analysis further, we separated higher scorers on the depression scale from the rest of the sample by using a cutoff score of four. A chi-square test for the number of cases according to family status indicated that there were almost twice as many single women in the high-depression group (28%) as there were married women with children (15%), $\chi^2(1, N = 1,106) = 14.54, p < .001$.

Discussion

By popular belief, backed by some empirical data, marriage and children are considered barriers to career advancement, and single status and childlessness are considered to impede personal well-being. The findings of this study contradict the first statement, but reinforce the second one. Marriage does not impede career in any of the ways measured (number of hours worked, income, job satisfaction, or job involvement). Even the presence of children has only selective effects: lower work involvement but no impairment of work satisfaction, and reduced hours of work (which, in only one profession was accompanied by lowered income). On the other hand, single women in the sample reported the lowest levels of self-esteem and life satisfaction and the highest levels of depression. Thus, the single professional woman appears to derive no career benefits from her lifestyle choice but pays a high personal price for it. Married childless women fare somewhat better, but even they have significantly lower life satisfaction than married women with children.

Before discussing the implications of these findings, we feel that the sensitive nature of this topic[4] makes it important to clearly acknowledge their limitations. First of all, we did not address the issue of the comparative mental health of working women and homemakers. The entire sample was composed of actively employed professional women, some of whom had family ties and others who did not. Thus, our results cannot legitimately be used to support a back-to-the-home movement.

Second, the findings were based on a sample designed to be homogeneous in gender, educational level, age, and employment status. In doing this, we eliminated many of the confounding variables that have clouded previous research on family roles, but in sharpening the acuity of our study we also limited its scope. For instance, it is possible that the higher satisfaction of the working mothers in this sample derived in part from their ability to purchase

---

[4] The initial presentation of this report at the November 1992 conference of the American Psychological Association and the National Institute for Occupational Safety and Health was prominently reported in the media. Interestingly enough, the vast majority of reports focused on the "good" news: the findings that married women with children reported greater life satisfaction and, on the whole, did not earn any less than their single or married and childless colleagues. Interest in the "bad" news—the finding that greater work effort by women did not necessarily yield greater rewards—was virtually nonexistent.

services (e.g., household help, dining out, and babysitting), a luxury not available to women in lower-paying jobs. Alternatively, even though the single women in this sample displayed poorer mental health than their married counterparts with children, they may still be above average in comparison with women in general. The restriction of the sample to a narrow age range imposed a further limitation by restricting the findings to a single cohort operating in a specific social climate. Further verification is required before we can generalize these results to the next generation of professional women, that is, those now beginning their careers.

Nevertheless, even with these limitations our results raise some disturbing questions. The first is why the greater number of hours worked by childless women and their greater involvement in work were not generally reflected in increased incomes. If women with children are commonly believed to lag behind because of family ties, should not women without these distractions forge ahead? One possible answer is that family responsibilities serve more as a convenient rationalization for the gap in income between male and female professionals, rather than constituting a real cause (Jagacinski et al., 1987; Ogle, Henry, & Zivick, 1986; Podomore & Spencer, 1982; Rochette, 1990). Following this line of reasoning, one would hypothesize that even though women are now freed from the overt discrimination that previously barred entry into historically male professions, they may still be restricted in career progression beyond a certain level by insidious forms of discrimination (see Morrison, White, & Van Velsor, 1987, for a discussion of the "glass ceiling"). If one accepts this interpretation, then the lack of income differential in favor of childless women becomes easier to understand. For, regardless of how whole-heartedly or single-mindedly a woman devotes herself to her profession, possibilities for increased income are limited by factors outside her control.

The one instance in which childless women in the sample did earn more than child-rearing women—physicians earning more than $100,000 annually—provides additional support for this hypothesis. Of the four professions sampled, it is medicine—and specifically, medical practice, in which the majority of physicians in the sample were concentrated—that has the fewest structural barriers to increased income. The nature of medical practice in Quebec (i.e., predominantly private practice, female physicians relatively common and widely accepted, and government payment provided per medical "act") largely removes sex bias as a limiting factor on income. Therefore, paradoxically, it is only because female physicians in this environment are free to "reach for the sky" that the decision of some to limit working hours for childbearing is reflected in lowered income. Ironically, before women in the other professions will be financially penalized by the presence of children, they first have to overcome a host of other barriers to income growth.

The second major question posed by these findings is why the single women—and, to a lesser degree, married women without children—are less satisfied with their lives than their married counterparts with children. This ordering of life satisfaction according to family status is consistent with a similar ranking reported by Baruch and Barnett (1987) for their subsample of employed women. It also accords with other reports of greater happiness in married individuals in comparison with unmarried ones, men as well as women (Glenn & Weaver, 1988; Gove & Zeiss, 1987). What makes it worthy of note, however, is the high socioeconomic status of the women involved. This would appear to contradict reports indicating that "the more economically independent women are, the less attractive marriage becomes" (Westoff, 1986, p. 1; see also Simenauer & Carroll, 1982).

One possible explanation, of course, is that it is precisely because of low self-esteem and high depression that these women failed to find partners in the first place; that is, their single status is the result, rather than the cause, of their dysphoria. However, the lack of significant differences between the three groups on negative personality disposition (see Table 2) would constitute a strong argument against invoking prior pathology as a causal factor in current distress.

Much more likely, therefore, is that the comparative dissatisfaction of the single women and the married childless women in this sample results from, rather than causes, their single or childless status. For instance, it is possible that single or childless professional women are less content with their lives because their lack of normative roles (wife or mother) places them in a position of deviance, creating dissonance with both their own and society's expectations for women (Adams, 1976; Cargan & Melko, 1982; Malley & Stewart, 1988). Thus, in spite of their professional success, they consider themselves and believe themselves to be viewed by others as failures.

Another possibility is that the reduced satisfaction of the single women or childless women is linked to disillusionment concerning their career prospects. The first generation of women to enter in large numbers into the historically male professions, they may have believed initially that total engagement in their careers would result in unlimited rewards. Now, however, as they confront the specific limitations placed on women's advancement—in addition to the general "plateauing trap" confronting baby boomers in an age of downsizing (Bardwick, 1986)—they may feel that their bargain has yielded inadequate rewards for the sacrifices entailed. From this would result lower self-esteem and life satisfaction, accompanied by higher levels of depression.

Still another explanation of lower satisfaction, for single women specifically, would focus on their restriction to a single role, rather than on the nature of the role itself. In the same way that marriage and childbearing fail to meet women's needs for social achievement and recognition, so may work—even challenging and satisfying work—fail to meet their needs for social support (Malley & Stewart, 1988; Wethington, McLeod, & Kessler, 1987). Thus, just as putting all of one's eggs in the basket of domestic felicity produces depression and self-devaluation in homemakers (Friedan, 1963), so might focusing all of one's energies on work—to the detriment of close personal ties—produce the same results in professional single women.

Further research is required, of course, to confirm and establish the mechanisms for the dissatisfaction reported by the single women and the married childless women in this sample. Whatever the causes, however, their psychological discomfort is worthy of more concern than it has received to date. What are the reasons that lead a sizable number of professional women to remain unattached, childless, or both? And what can be done to make this forced choice unnecessary? After all, if most professional men are able to combine career and family ties, why should this combination be unattainable for many of their female counterparts? A more equitable distribution of family obligations (see Hochschild, 1989) might indeed make it easier for professional women, like their male colleagues, to "have it all." Alternatively, if career ladders were made less rigid (e.g., there is no natural law decreeing that the access to partnership in legal and accounting firms must occur at ages 30–40 or not at all), then women might feel less pressure to choose between career and family. Simply increasing awareness that marriage and children do not constitute the only, or necessarily the most important, barriers to women's professional success might also reduce the perceived necessity for ambitious women to choose between family and career, concentrating their energies instead on removing these other barriers.

Even if these changes were effected, some career women might still elect single status or childlessness. Must women who abstain from traditional family ties necessarily suffer lowered self-esteem and higher depression? Or are there conditions under which single or childless women could also attain high life satisfaction? For instance, changing outdated beliefs could remove some of the social stigma and consequent self-devaluation of single or childless women. A second possibility is to foster alternative ways among women for obtaining the gratifications habitually subsumed under the marital or maternal roles so that absence of traditional family ties need not mean emotional deprivation. Finally, if the glass ceiling on career rewards for women were removed, then women who made the choice to devote themselves single-mindedly to their careers would have less cause to feel that their bargain was a bad one.

Some people may be uncomfortable applying the term *disadvantaged minorities* to women who present themselves in power suits and carry leather attaché cases. On the basis of our findings, however, the professional woman without traditional family ties—and, specifically, the single professional woman—may indeed constitute a neglected pocket of distress. It is time that these women receive their due share of attention from those concerned with social equity and mental health.

References

Abella, R. S. (1984). *Employment equity: Royal Commission Report.* Ottawa, Ontario, Canada: Commission on Employment Equity.

Adams, M. (1976). *Single blessedness: Observations on the single status in married society.* New York: Basic Books.

Allen, K. R. (1989). *Single women/family ties.* Newbury Park, CA: Sage.

Bardwick, J. M. (1986). *The plateauing trap.* New York: Bantam Books.

Baruch, G. K., & Barnett, R. C. (1987). Role quality and psychological well-being. In F. J. Crosby (Ed.), *Spouse, parent, worker: On gender and multiple roles* (pp. 63–73). New Haven, CT: Yale University Press.

Bergeron, J., Landry, M., & Bélanger, D. (1976). The development and validation of a French form of the State–Trait Anxiety Inventory. In C. D. Spielberger & R. Diaz-Gurro (Eds.), *Cross-cultural anxiety* (pp. 41–50). New York: Halstead Press.

Blais, M. R., Vallerand, R. J., Pelletier, L. G., & Brière, N. M. (1989). L'Échelle de Satisfaction de Vie: Validation Canadienne–Française du "Satisfaction With Life Scale" [Satisfaction With Life Scale: A French–Canadian validation]. *Canadian Journal of Behavioural Science, 21,* 210–223.

Brayfield, A. H., & Rothe, H. F. (1951). An index of job satisfaction. *Journal of Applied Psychology, 35,* 307–311.

Bryant, F. B., & Veroff, J. (1982). The structure of psychological well-being: A sociohistorical analysis. *Journal of Personality and Social Psychology, 43,* 653–673.

Cargan, L., & Melko, M. (1982). *Singles: Myths and realities.* Beverly Hills, CA: Sage.

Castellan, N. J. (1965). On the partitioning of contingency tables. *Psychological Bulletin, 64,* 330–338.

Changes in demographics. (1993, January 23). *Montreal Gazette,* p. 1.

Cook, J. D., Hepworth, S. J., Wall, T. D., & Warr, P. B. (1981). *The experience of work.* San Diego, CA: Academic Press.

Davies, A. R., & Ware, J. E. (1981). *Measuring health perceptions in the health insurance experiment* (R-2711-HHS). Santa Monica, CA: Rand Corporation.

Diener, E. (1984). Subjective well-being. *Psychological Bulletin, 95,* 542–575.

Diener, E., Emmons, R. A., Larsen, R. J., & Griffin, S. (1985). The Satisfaction With Life Scale. *Journal of Personality Assessment, 49,* 71–75.

Dillman, D. A. (1983). Mail and other self-administered questionnaires. In P. H. Rossi, J. D. Wright, & A. B. Anderson (Eds.), *Handbook of survey research* (pp. 359–378). San Diego, CA: Academic Press.

Faludi, S. (1991). *Backlash: The undeclared war against American women.* New York: Doubleday.

Fong, M. L. (1992, August). *Single professional women and stress: High risk yet overlooked.* Paper presented at the 100th Annual Convention of the American Psychological Association, Washington, DC.

Friedan, B. (1963). *The feminine mystique.* New York: Norton.

Glenn, N. D., & Weaver, C. N. (1988). The changing relationship of marital status to reported happiness. *Journal of Marriage and the Family, 50,* 317–324.

Goldberg, D. P. (1978). *Manual of the General Health Questionnaire.* Windsor, England: National Foundation for Educational Research.

Goldberg, D. P., & Hillier, V. F. (1979). A scaled version of the General Health Questionnaire. *Psychological Medicine, 9,* 139–145.

Gove, W. R., & Zeiss, C. (1987). Multiple roles and happiness. In F. J. Crosby (Ed.), *Spouse, parent, worker: On gender and multiple roles* (pp. 125–137). New Haven, CT: Yale University Press.

Hirsch, B. J., & Rapkin, B. D. (1986). Multiple roles, social networks, and women's well-being. *Journal of Personality and Social Psychology, 51,* 1237–1247.

Hochschild, A. (with Machung, A.). (1989). *The second shift: Working parents and the revolution at home.* New York: Penguin Books.

Houseknecht, S. K., Vaughn, S., & Statham, A. (1987). The impact of singlehood on the career patterns of professional women. *Journal of Marriage and the Family, 49,* 353–366.

Howard, A., & Bray, D. W. (1988). *Managerial lives in transition: Advancing age and changing times.* New York: Guilford Press.

Jagacinski, C. M., LeBold, W. K., & Linden, K. W. (1987). The relative career advancement of men and women engineers in the United States. *Work and Stress, 1,* 235–247.

Kanungo, R. N. (1982). Measurement of job and work involvement. *Journal of Applied Psychology, 3,* 341–349.

Malley, J. E., & Stewart, A. J. (1988). Women's work and family roles: Sources of stress and sources of strength. In S. Fisher & J. Reason (Eds.), *Handbook of life stress, cognition and health* (pp. 175–191). New York: Wiley.

Marshall, K. (1989). Présence accrue des femmes dans les professions depuis le début des années 80 [Increased presence of women in the profession since the beginning of the 1980s]. *Tendances sociales canadiennes, 12,* 13–16.

Morrison, A. M., White, R. P., & Van Velsor, E. (1987). *Breaking the glass ceiling: Can women reach the top of America's largest corporations?* Greensboro, NC: Center for Creative Leadership.

Nicholson, N., & West, M. (1988). *Managerial job change: Men and women in transition.* Cambridge, England: Cambridge University Press.

Ogle, K. S., Henry, R. C., & Zivick, J. D. (1986). Gender-specific differences in family practice graduates. *Journal of Family Practice, 23,* 357–360.

Payne, R., Warr, P., & Hartley, J. (1984). Social class and psychological ill-health during unemployment. *Sociology of Health and Illness, 6,* 152–174.

Podomore, D., & Spencer, A. (1982). Women lawyers in England: The experience of inequality. *Work and Occupations, 9,* 337–361.

Read, J. L., Quinn, R. J., & Hoefer, M. A. (1987). Measuring overall health: An evaluation of three important approaches. *Journal of Chronic Disease, 40,* 7S–21S.

Rochette, M. (1990). *Les femmes dans la profession juridique au Québec: De l'accès à l'intégration, un passage coûteux* [Women in the legal profession in Quebec: From entry to integration, a difficult passage]. Ste-Foy, Quebec: Laval University, Feminist Multidisciplinary Research Group.

Rosenberg, M. (1965). *Society and the adolescent self-image.* Princeton, NJ: Princeton University Press.

Schwartz, F. N. (1989). Executives and organizations: Management women and the new facts of life. *Harvard Business Review, 89,* 65–76.

Siegel, S., & Castellan, N. J. (1988). *Nonparametric statistics for the behavioral sciences.* New York: McGraw-Hill.

Simenauer, J., & Carroll, D. (1982). *Singles: The new Americans.* New York: Simon & Schuster.

Spielberger, C. D., Gorusch, R. L., & Lushene, R. (1970). *Manual for the State–Trait Anxiety Inventory.* Palo Alto, CA: Consulting Psychologists Press.

Statistics Canada. (1985). *Marriages and divorces: La statistique de l'état civil* (Publication No. 84–205). Ottawa, Ontario, Canada: Ministry of Supplies and Services.

Statistics Canada. (1989). *Les Canadiens et leurs professions: Un profil* [Canadians and their professions: A profile] (Publication No. 89–503F). Ottawa, Ontario, Canada: Ministry of Supplies and Services.

Tabachnick, B. G., & Fidell, L. S. (1983). *Using multivariate statistics.* New York: Harper & Row.

Thoits, P. A. (1986). Multiple identities: Examining gender and marital status differences in distress. *American Sociological Review, 51,* 259–272.

Uhlenberg, P., & Cooney, T. M. (1990). Male and female physicians: Family and career comparisons. *Social Science and Medicine, 3,* 373–378.

Vallières, E. F., & Vallerand, L. J. (1990). Traduction et validation Canadienne–Française de l'Échelle de l'Estime de Soi de Rosenberg [French–Canadian translation and validation of Rosenberg's Self-Esteem Scale]. *International Journal of Psychology, 25,* 305–316.

Verbrugge, L. M. (1982). Women's social roles and health. In P. E. Berman & E. Ramey (Eds.), *Women: A developmental perspective* (Publication No. 82-2298) (pp. 49–78). Washington, DC: U.S. Government Printing Office.

Verbrugge, L. M. (1983). Multiple roles and physical health of women and men. *Journal of Health and Social Behavior, 24,* 16–30.

Watson, D., & Clark, L. (1984). Negative affectivity: The disposition to experience aversive emotional states. *Psychological Bulletin, 96,* 465–490.

Westoff, C. (1986, September 25). Families staging a comeback: It's probably a mirage. *The Wall Street Journal,* p. 1.

Wethington, E., McLeod, J. D., & Kessler, R. C. (1987). The importance of life events in explaining sex differences in psychological distress. In R. C. Barnett, L. Biener, & G. K. Baruch (Eds.), *Gender and stress* (pp. 144–158). New York: Macmillan.

Wortman, C., Biernat, M., & Lang, E. (1991). Coping with role overload. In M. Frankenhaeuser, U. Lundberg, & M. Chesney (Eds.), *Women, work and health: Stress and opportunities* (pp. 85–110). New York: Plenum.

18

Balancing the Multiple Roles of Work and Caregiving for Children, Adults, and Elders

*Nancy J. Chapman, Berit Ingersoll-Dayton,
and Margaret B. Neal*

My husband is 68 and has Parkinson's disease. He is very dependent on me, as is his mother who is 88—she has had three operations in the last year and lived at my home for all three of them. I also have my mother who is 78. My daughter has a two year old which I babysit frequently—and is expecting another in September. It seems sometimes I am the only healthy one in the family—still I suffer from stomach problems and arthritis. I also have my son in college (22 years old) who I am supporting financially. Stress? Yes!

The combination of work and family roles is a major concern for many employees as well as for their employers. The quotation above from a female employee included in our survey illustrates the complexity of family role demands that many employees must balance with their work roles. Such concerns will be growing, according to demographic trends showing an increasing percentage of the population over 65 years of age (Subcommittee on Human Services, 1987), a decreasing number of children per family (National Center for Health Statistics, 1990), medical advances that have lengthened the life span of those with disabilities and chronic illnesses (Trieschmann, 1980), an increasing percentage of women in the workforce (Bureau of National Affairs, 1988), an increasing number of single-parent families (Subcommittee on Human Services, 1987), and a declining workforce size (Ontario Women's Directorate, 1990). These trends point to an increasing proportion of the population requiring assistance from family members at the same time that there are growing pressures for potential caregivers to enter and remain in the workforce.

Although the problems of balancing work and family are likely to affect increasing numbers of employees and employers, a dominant myth exists both

Preparation of this chapter was supported in part by Meyer Memorial Trust Grant 86064020 to Margaret B. Neal. We gratefully acknowledge our collaborator in this project, Arthur C. Emlen, for his contribution to the research and to our thinking as well as Nancy Perrin for her consultation regarding statistics and psychometrics.

in the literature and in the minds of most Americans that work and family are (or should be) separate spheres of life (Kanter, 1977). According to Kanter,

> The myth goes like this: In a modern industrial society work life and family life constitute two separate and nonoverlapping worlds, with their own functions, territories, and behavioral rules. Each operates by its own laws and can be studied independently. (p. 8)

The notion that the worlds of work and family are separate must be replaced by a recognition of work and family as open systems in constant interplay.

In this chapter, we take the view that work and family are overlapping spheres and explore how well employees are able to balance their overlapping responsibilities. We begin by reviewing theory and research relevant to employment and caregiving. We then report findings from our own research comparing the experiences of employees caring for one or more dependents (children, adults with disabilities, and the elderly) with employees who had no dependent-care responsibilities. In doing so, we are able to identify those groups of employees who are most in need of assistance in balancing their work and family responsibilities.

Caregiving and Employment

There is a growing body of research connecting employees' caregiving responsibilities with absenteeism and stress on the job. In the following paragraphs, we briefly summarize the research findings to date on the negative impacts that caring for children, adults with disabilities, or elders can have on employees' work and stress.

In studies of the aversive consequences of having children on employees' work and stress, it has been found that, in comparison with employees without children, employees with children miss more days of work (Emlen, 1987; Emlen & Koren, 1984; Scharlach & Boyd, 1989), have more conflict between work and family (Scharlach & Boyd, 1989; Voydanoff, 1988), and take more time off during the workday (Scharlach & Boyd, 1989). Married female employees with children experience more depression than do those without children (Cleary & Mechanic, 1983). There can be adverse effects on physical health as well. Employees with children have been found to experience more physical ailments and fatigue than childless employees (Haynes & Feinleib, 1980; Karasek, Gardell, & Lindell, 1987), as have employees providing elder care (Wagner & Halsey, 1987).

Scharlach and Boyd (1989) found that employees caring for elders had more conflict between work and family, missed more days of work, and took more time off during the workday than did their noncaregiving coworkers. Executives have reported that employees with elder-care responsibilities experience more stress, take more unscheduled days off, are more likely to be late for work or to leave early, and use the telephone for personal business more often during the workday (*Fortune Magazine* and John Hancock Financial Services, 1989; Warshaw, Barr, Rayman, Schachter, & Lucas, 1986).

Caregiving responsibilities also affect employees' decisions to remain in the workforce. In some cases, the financial burden of caregiving may force employees to remain in the workforce when they would prefer to retire (Creedon, 1987). Caregiving also forces many employees to leave work in order to provide care. Among women whose husbands had suffered heart attacks, one quarter stopped work temporarily (Skelton & Dominian, 1973); an equal proportion of family members of persons with chronic mental illness reduced or stopped work temporarily (Sainsbury & Grad, 1962). Stone, Cafferata, and Sangl (1987) reported that between 5% and 14% of male and female adult children and spouse caregivers of elders quit work to become full-time caregivers.

Multiple Caregiving Roles

Many caregivers take responsibility for more than one type of care recipient at the same time. The combination of caregiving roles that has received the most attention is that of caring for aging parents while still having children at home. These caregivers, who are mostly women, have been referred to as the "sandwich generation" (Miller, 1981; Shanas, 1980) and "women in the middle" (Brody, 1981) and are likely to experience significant role conflict. They are not only in the middle in a generational sense, but are also caught between the traditional value placed on family care and the new value placed on employment and careers for women (Brody, 1981). Additional role conflict may occur when caring for aging relatives occurs at the same time that caregivers are confronting personal developmental issues (e.g., their own aging and the "empty nest") and are looking forward to a time of "relaxation and self-indulgence" (Miller, 1981). These issues of timing and developmental stages are likely to be relevant to other combinations of caregiving roles as well, although less attention has been directed toward other role combinations.

In addition to role conflict, role ambiguity may also be associated with the role of caregiver. As Brody (1985) pointed out, although parent care is increasingly common, society has not developed clear expectations and behavioral norms for adult children who care for their parents. Indeed, Pratt, Schmall, and Wright (1987) found that a common form of ethical concern among caregivers of persons with dementia was the conflict with other obligations, such as family, career, and personal well-being. Such caregivers lack clear roles or moral principles to help them resolve their sense of ambiguity. These conflicts may be particularly salient for women, who tend to define themselves in the context of relationships and to judge themselves with respect to their ability to care for others (Gilligan, 1982).

Although empirical research on the effects of occupying multiple caregiving roles has been very limited, a few studies have explored this topic. For example, in a study of the amount of help that sons and daughters provided to their elderly parents (Stoller, 1983), employed daughters did not significantly reduce the amount of care they provided to the elder in comparison with daughters who were not employed. Among the sons, however, employment had more impact on reducing hours of assistance than any other variable except marital status. In addition, the number and ages of the children in the home had no impact on the amount of help that daughters provided to elders. In contrast, men with more children under the age of 6 provided more hours of elder care, perhaps because their wives were involved in child care. A few other studies have examined the relationship between multiple caregiving responsibilities and work. Gibeau and Anastas (1989) reported findings from a study of women who were working full-time and caring for an elderly family member. Although having children at home increased the level of conflict experienced between work and family, it did not increase absenteeism from work. Similarly, in a study of accommodations in work schedules (working fewer hours, rearranging work schedules, and taking time off without pay), Stone and Short (1990) found that having both child-care and elder-care responsibilities did not significantly increase work accommodations.

Some studies have explored the relationship between multiple roles and psychological well-being. On the one hand, multiple caregiving roles can have negative effects. Multiple responsibilities among caregivers to the elderly were associated with increased physical strain (Stull, Bowman, & Smerglia, 1991) and caregiver burden (Stoller & Pugliesi, 1989). Conversely, Stoller and Pugliesi (1989) found that multiple roles were associated with decreased psychological distress. Similarly, Stull et al. (1991) found evidence that work had a positive impact on women's ability to continue in their caregiving roles. Thus, existing research has suggested that occupying multiple roles may have both positive and negative effects.

Hypothesized Effects of Multiple Roles

Within role theory there are contrasting hypotheses about how employees combine the demands of caregiving with employment. The first of these is the scarcity hypothesis (Baruch, Biener, & Barnett, 1987; Goode, 1960), which assumes that the sum of human energy is fixed, so that more roles create a greater likelihood of overload, conflict, and strain and of associated negative consequences for well-being. A major source of role conflict is the competition between time spent at work versus time spent in caregiving. For example, Morycz (1980) found that role conflict (competing roles and conflicting demands) and role overload (too many roles) were associated with objective assessments of burden among caregivers. In contrast, the enhancement hypothesis (Marks, 1977; Sieber, 1974; Thoits, 1983) argues that multiple roles may augment one's energy by increasing sources of identity, self-esteem, and privileges. An important element of this hypothesis is the expectation that people holding multiple roles can negotiate reductions in one role because of the press of competing roles. However, Long and Porter (1984) argued that this ability to negotiate reductions in role demands may be more applicable to men than to women because of the lower status afforded to women's roles. Baruch et al. (1987) pointed out that neither of these hypotheses takes into account individual differences in the quality of work and family roles that may influence whether the caregiving role reduces or increases stress.

In addition to role theory, the scarcity hypothesis also is closely tied to a stress and coping paradigm (e.g., Lazarus & Folkman, 1984). Within that paradigm, it is expected that the combination of working and caregiving serves as a stressor, the severity of which is in part a function of how demanding the specific work and caregiving roles are for the employee. Resources deriving from the job (e.g., income and schedule flexibility) and from the family (e.g., a spouse or partner) may help the employee cope with these demands. The stress-buffering hypothesis (Gore, 1981; Thoits, 1982) argues that these resources will only act as such when the individual is under stress. That is, the resources will have no direct effect on stress outcomes in the absence of stress but will serve as buffers in the presence of stress.

Previous research has established some of the impacts of caregiving on work, family life, and personal well-being. Our study, however, is unique in assessing simultaneously the effects of different kinds of caregiving responsibility (child, adult, and elder) and different combinations of these caregiving roles. Several research questions have guided the analyses reported here. First, do employed caregivers report different amounts of absenteeism and stress than employed noncaregivers (the scarcity hypothesis vs. the enhancement hypothesis)? Second, are there specific combinations of caregiving roles that are more likely to be associated with absenteeism and stress? Third, are work and family resources more helpful in alleviating stress and absenteeism for employees with multiple caregiving roles than they are for other employees (the stress-buffering hypothesis)?

Research Methodology

Sample

The research presented here was based on a survey of employees concerning their informal caregiving responsibilities. Specifically, we surveyed employees of 33 businesses and agencies in the Portland, Oregon, metropolitan area. This convenience sample was selected to represent small, medium, and large employers and to represent employers within each of the seven major categories of the Standard Industrial Classifications. The 1987 Standard Industrial Classifications (U.S. Office of Management and Budget, 1987) were modified for the industrial mix of the Portland metropolitan area and included the following: nonmanufacturing (agriculture, mining, and construction); manufacturing; transportation, communications, electric, gas, and sanitary services; wholesale trade; retail trade; finance, insurance, and real estate; and services. Surveys were distributed through interoffice mail to 27,832 employees and were returned by 9,573 employees of these 33 businesses and agencies, for an overall return rate of 34%. This rate is comparable to the response rates of other studies that have used similar kinds of distribution methods in surveys of multiple employers (see Wagner, Creedon, Sasala, & Neal, 1989). The response rate varied dramatically by company, from a low of 10% to a high of 78%, and even varied by department within companies. In summary, our sample represented employees from a wide variety of work settings. To achieve this breadth, however, it was necessary to sacrifice some control over distribution and return of questionnaires, which resulted in a lower return rate than is achievable when focusing on a single work setting.

Because of the low overall return rate, it is important that we note some general characteristics of the sample. This was a relatively affluent sample, with an average household income between $30,000 and $40,000 and a majority (64%) working as professionals, technical workers, managers, or administrators. Ninety percent of the respondents were employed full-time; that is, they worked at least 35 hours per week. Eighty-seven percent worked a day shift. Only 7% of the sample represented a minority group, which was less than the 10% present in the metropolitan area as a whole. The sample also included more women (59%) than would be expected.

We determined different types of caregiving responsibilities in different ways. Employees were identified as providing child care if they reported having children under the age of 18 years living in their households. To assess adult-care or elder-care responsibilities, we asked respondents the following question:

> Do you have responsibilities for helping out adult relatives or friends who are elderly or disabled? This includes persons who live with you or who live somewhere else. By "helping out" we mean help with shopping, home maintenance or transportation, checking on them by phone, making arrangements for care, etc.

Respondents were identified as providing adult care if they were helping someone 18 through 59 years of age; they were identified as providing elder care if they were helping someone aged 60 years and over. This definition of care for elders and adults with disabilities, which is relatively broad in comparison with that used in some of the caregiving literature, was chosen based on our notion that becoming a caregiver is often a gradual process and that employees may not define themselves as caregivers even though they may provide a great deal of assistance. It should also be noted that employees with children in the household did not report how much care they personally provided to the children in the household, whereas employees designated as *adult-care* or *elder-care providers* identified themselves specifically as providing assistance to an adult or an elderly person.

Figure 1 shows the numbers and percentages of individuals in our sample providing each of these types of care and the overlap for those providing more than one type of care. Child care was the most common caregiving responsibility, shared by 46% of the sample. Almost one quarter (23%) provided elder care, and 4% provided care to adults with disabilities. Overlapping care was also common, with 21% of those with children also providing care to an elder and 42% of those providing elder care having children in the household. In addition, 25% cared for multiple children and 16% cared for multiple adults with disabilities or elders. Thirty-nine percent of the sample reported no caregiving responsibility.

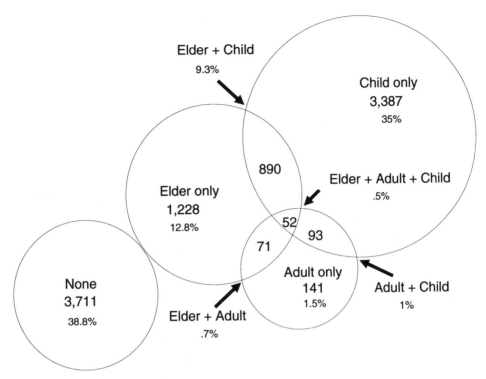

Figure 1. Number and percentage of employees with responsibility for each type of caregiving group and overlapping caregiving responsibilities. $N = 9,573$. From *Balancing work and caregiving for children, adults, and elders* (p. 41) by M. B. Neal, N. J. Chapman, B. Ingersoll-Dayton, and A. C. Emlen, 1993, Newbury Park, CA: Sage. Copyright 1993 by Sage. Reprinted with permission.

Male and female caregivers differed on several dimensions. In our sample, female employees with multiple caregiving roles were in their 20s or 30s (56%), whereas 60% of the men were in their 40s or 50s. Most often, these employees had one or more children over the age of 9 years (67% of men and 61% of women); a sizable minority, however, had at least one child under the age of 9 (47% of men and 45% of women). Men and women with multiple roles were also differentially likely to have no spouse or partner: 28% of the women did not have a mate in comparison with only 7% of the men.

Conceptual Framework and Measures

The conceptual framework we used in our research is illustrated in Figure 2. The research questions posed above were examined in the context of this framework, which ties employees' rates of absenteeism and levels of stress to the caregiving roles they perform, their personal characteristics, the demands placed on them at work and in the family, and the resources available at work and in the family to cope with these demands.

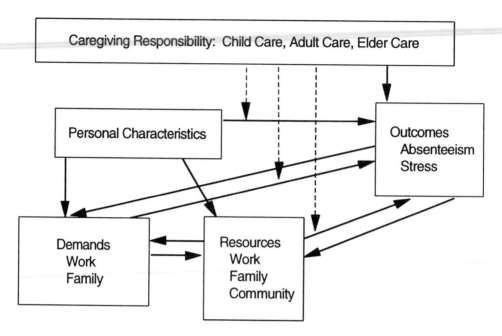

Figure 2. Conceptual framework used to study multiple roles of work and caregiving. From *Balancing work and caregiving for children, adults, and elders* (p. 33) by M. B. Neal, N. J. Chapman, B. Ingersoll-Dayton, and A. C. Emlen, 1993, Newbury Park, CA: Sage. Copyright 1993 by Sage. Reprinted with permission.

Predictive measures. The three kinds of caregiving roles considered were child care, adult care, and elder care. The personal characteristics were gender, age, ethnicity (White vs. all others), and occupation (professional-managerial vs. all others). The demand variables included number of hours worked per week and work shift (day vs. other). Finally, the resource variables were household income, work schedule flexibility, and a set of dummy variables representing whether or not the employee had a spouse or partner and whether or not that partner was employed outside the home.

Outcome measures. Two scales were developed to assess the effects of combining work and family. The first was a measure of time lost from work, or absenteeism, and the second was a measure of stress. Four aspects of absenteeism were assessed: how many times in the preceding 4 weeks the respondent had missed a day from work, had been interrupted at work (including telephone calls) to deal with family-related matters, had arrived at work late, or had left work early. Because the items were severely skewed, with most respondents reporting no absenteeism, we tried using both logarithmic and inverse transformations to normalize the distributions. The inverse transformation yielded a distribution closest to normality, and the resulting scores were then standardized. A principal-axis factor analysis of these scores yielded one factor, but the "days missed" item was dropped because of a relatively low loading on the factor. The absenteeism scale was developed by summing the standardized scores for the remaining three measures. Cronbach's alpha for the scale was .51. Although the reliability of the scale was low, we would argue that employees whose absenteeism is due to caregiving may exhibit one specific kind of absenteeism that allows them to cope with their specific circumstances and, thus, that correlations among the types of absenteeism may be low.

The stress measure was a composite of six items assessing stress emanating from the personal, family, and work contexts. Five of the items, measured on 4-point scales ranging from *no stress at all* to *a lot of stress*, assessed stress associated with "your health"; "health of other family members"; "personal or family finances"; "your job"; and "family relationships, including extended family." These items were presented after the following introductory question: "We would like to know which areas of life are creating difficulty, worry, and stress for people. In the past 4 weeks, to what extent have any of the following areas of life been a source of stress to you?" The final stress measure concerned the difficulty of combining work and family: "Circumstances differ and some people find it easier than others to combine working with family responsibilities. In general, how easy or difficult is it for you?" This item was recoded from a 6-point to a 4-point scale, and the six items were summed to create the stress scale. Principal-components analysis, followed by principal-axis factor analysis, revealed the presence of only one factor. The reliability of the resulting scale based on Cronbach's alpha was .66.

What Are the Effects of Occupying Multiple Caregiving Roles?

With the initial set of analyses, we addressed two of our research questions: Do employed caregivers report different amounts of absenteeism and stress than employed noncaregivers? and Are there specific combinations of caregiving roles that are more likely to be associated with absenteeism and stress? The scarcity hypothesis would predict that employees with multiple caregiving roles would experience more absenteeism and stress than those with no caregiving roles, whereas the enhancement hypothesis would predict the opposite.

The analytic approach taken to answer these questions was to categorize the sample into eight groups on the basis of their caregiving responsibilities: those having (a) no dependent-care responsibilities, (b) child care only, (c) adult care only, (d) elder care only, (e) both child and adult care, (f) both child and elder care, (g) both adult and elder care, and (h) all three types of caregiving roles. The relative levels of absenteeism and stress experienced by these eight groups were examined by graphing each group's mean absenteeism and stress scores. Figure 3 shows how the average scores of the employees in each of the eight groups compared with the average scores for the entire sample of employees. Thus, the mean score of each caregiving (and noncaregiving) group is represented in terms of how much higher or lower it was than the overall mean score of the sample. Because the caregiver groups were likely to differ on a number of other characteristics that also influence levels of absenteeism and stress (e.g., younger people are more likely to be absent), we adjusted the mean scores for each group by controlling for personal characteristics, resources, and demands. We accomplished this by conducting multiple classifi-

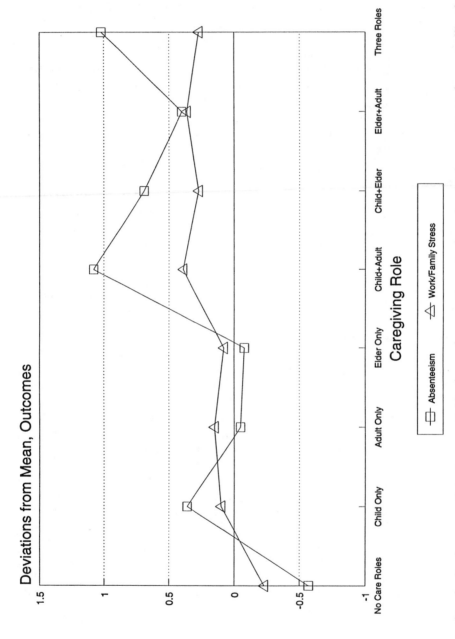

Figure 3. Standardized scores on the outcome variables for employees with no, single, and multiple caregiving roles, controlling for personal characteristics, demands, and resources. From *Balancing work and caregiving for children, adults, and elders* (p. 157) by M. B. Neal, N. J. Chapman, B. Ingersoll-Dayton, and A. C. Emlen, 1993, Newbury Park, CA: Sage. Copyright 1993 by Sage. Reprinted with permission.

cation analyses to predict stress and absenteeism, using variables representing each of the eight caregiving groups as the independent variables and the personal characteristics, demands, and resources as covariates. A separate analysis was carried out for each outcome measure. These analyses predicted the mean absenteeism and stress scores for each group after we controlled for the effects of personal characteristics, demands, and resources. The results of the multiple classification analyses are shown in Figure 3.

Figure 3 can be inspected to address a number of issues about multiple roles. First, did those with no dependent-care responsibility have lower rates of absenteeism and stress? The answer was clearly yes. Second, were multiple roles associated with more absenteeism and stress than one role? The answer was "almost always"; the only exception was for employees caring only for children, who were absent almost as often as employees caring for both adults and elders. All of the employees with multiple roles averaged higher levels of stress than those with only one role. Third, was occupying three caregiving roles associated with more absenteeism and stress than occupying two roles? Employees occupying all three roles showed higher absenteeism than all other groups except those caring for both adults and children; their stress levels, however, were comparable to those for employees with two caregiving roles. Fourth, which of the dual roles were associated with the most absenteeism and stress? Employees with child- and adult-care responsibilities had the highest absenteeism rates, but there were no clear differences in stress scores among employees with dual roles. Fifth, which single role was the highest in absenteeism and stress? Caring for children was associated with the most absenteeism, but there was little difference between the three single roles in their stress scores. Taken together, these findings offer support for the scarcity hypothesis.

Do Work and Family Resources Serve as Stress Buffers for Those With Multiple Caregiving Roles?

The second set of analyses allowed us to examine our third research question, concerning whether resources and demands function differently for employees with different numbers of caregiving roles. On the one hand, it may be that having resources such as a high income and a nonworking partner decreases absenteeism and stress for all employees, regardless of their caregiving responsibilities. On the other hand, stress theorists have argued that resources (such as social support) function as buffers against stress rather than directly affecting it (Gore, 1981; Thoits, 1982). Thus, such resources as work flexibility might have little impact on those with minimal or no caregiving responsibilities but great impact for those experiencing multiple caregiving roles.

This hypothesis is best tested by returning to our conceptual framework. Specifically, in these analyses, both of the dependent variables were regressed on personal characteristics, demands, resources, and the number of caregiving roles occupied by the employee. In addition, interaction terms were added to test whether the relationships of these personal characteristics, demands, and resources to the dependent variables differed depending on level of caregiving responsibility. The variables were entered in sets into hierarchical multiple regression analyses. In our model, the variables representing the personal characteristics of the employee were entered first, followed by the variables representing work demands placed on the employee and then the variables representing the resources available to the employee.

In the context of this study, stress as a predictor was represented by the number of caregiving roles, ranging from zero to three roles. This variable was entered into the regression equation after the personal characteristics, demands, and resources. Interaction terms were calculated by multiplying the number of caregiving roles occupied by each of the 10 measures of personal characteristics, demands, and resources. These 10 interaction terms were entered in the final step of the hierarchical regression analyses. The results of these analyses are shown in Table 1 and address a number of issues. Before considering the issue of main interest—resources as buffers to stress—we need to briefly review the relationship between personal characteristics, demands, and resources for all employees, not just for those with caregiving responsibility. In the first three issues raised below, then, we address these main effects for all employees, whereas in discussing the final issue we directly address the relationship of these variable sets to absenteeism and stress for only those employees with caregiving responsibility. Within this final discussion, we address the stress-buffering hypothesis.

First, do employees with particular personal characteristics experience more stress and absenteeism? The most consistent findings were that women and younger workers had significantly more absenteeism and stress. Professional and managerial workers were also more likely to report stress.

Second, are particular workplace demands predictive of higher levels of stress and absenteeism among employees in general? The only demands included in these equations were related to work because of the lack of comparable caregiving demand measures across the caregiving subgroups. Employees working a day shift reported more absenteeism and more stress than those working evening or night shifts. Those who worked more hours per week also reported experiencing more stress.

Third, are particular resources predictive of reduced levels of absenteeism and stress for employees in general? For the variables we used to be considered to be acting as resources, we would expect their regression coefficients to be negative. In other words, as resources increase, absenteeism and stress should decrease. Only two of the four significant coefficients were in the expected direction, so these variables were not acting consistently as resources. The only variable that served solely as a resource was household income, which was associated with lower stress. Work-schedule flexibility was associated with decreased stress but with increased rather than decreased absenteeism. In addition, having a working partner increased rather than decreased stress in comparison with having no partner.

Finally, which resources are most helpful in alleviating stress and absenteeism for those with multiple caregiving responsibilities? The number of caregiving roles was a significant predictor of only one of the outcome measures:

It was associated with higher levels of work and family stress. The interaction terms, however, are the most germane to the final research question. They represent the effects of personal characteristics, demands, and resources specifically on employed caregivers rather than on employees as a whole. As shown in Table 1, the interaction terms added significantly to the prediction of both absenteeism and stress, although they accounted for less than 1% of the variance in both cases. Only two of the interaction terms were significant predictors of both outcome variables. Women with caregiving responsibilities were

Table 1. Effects of Personal Characteristics, Caregiving Demands, Caregiving Resources, Multiple Roles, and Interaction Terms on Outcome Variables

	Absenteeism		Stress	
Predictor	β	B	β	B
Step 1. Personal characteristics				
Gender (female)	.29	.06**	.14	.10**
Age of employee	−.05	−.18**	−.01	−.07**
Ethnicity (White)	−.01	−.00	.00	.00
Occupation (professional)	−.04	−.01	.06	.04*
ΔR^2		.05**		.03**
Step 2. Demands				
Hours worked	−.00	−.02	.01	.09**
Shift (day)	.99	.13**	.10	.05**
ΔR^2		.02**		.00**
Step 3. Resources				
Household income	−.00	−.01	−.00	−.12**
Work-schedule flexibility	.20	.06**	−.16	−.18**
Working partner	.09	.02	.11	.08**
Nonworking partner	.05	.01	−.07	−.03
ΔR^2		.01**		.05**
Step 4. Caregiving roles				
No. of caregiving roles	.28	.07	.33	.31**
ΔR^2		.03**		.06**
Step 5. Interaction terms				
Roles × Gender	.26	.06**	.08	.07**
Roles × Age	−.00	−.06	−.00	−.01
Roles × Ethnicity	−.10	−.03	−.00	−.00
Roles × Occupation	.14	.04	.01	.01
Roles × Hours Worked	.00	.06	−.00	−.07
Roles × Shift	.18	.05	.00	.00
Roles × Income	−.00	−.00	−.00	−.00
Roles × Work Flexibility	.09	.07	.00	.01
Roles × Working Partner	−.23	−.06*	−.07	−.06*
Roles × Nonworking Partner	−.36	−.06*	.04	.02
ΔR^2		.00**		.00**
Total R^2		.114		.152
R^2 adjusted		.112		.150
Overall F		49.93**		69.37**

Note. For overall F, *df*s = 21 and 8114.
*$p \leq .05$.   **$p \leq .01$.

more likely than men to be absent (i.e., to arrive at work late or leave early or to be interrupted at work to care for family matters) and showed higher levels of stress. Caregivers with working partners showed lower levels of both stress and absenteeism than those without partners. Finally, caregivers with nonworking partners were less likely than those without partners to be absent from work.

We can thus conclude that resources, as well as the demands included in these analyses, do not consistently function as such for caregivers. The finding most consistently in line with the stress-buffering hypothesis was that having a partner, whether that partner is employed or not, serves as a resource for caregivers with multiple roles. In addition, employed women who are caregivers were more likely than men to bear the consequences of multiple roles in the form of absenteeism and stress.

Discussion

This study of employees from a wide range of work sectors resulted in a number of suggestive findings. It should be noted, however, that our return rate was quite low, so any results should be interpreted with caution and further tested in other large-scale studies in which more attention is devoted to increasing the response rate. It appears that the results of our comparison of caregivers with noncaregivers and of our exploration of the effects of multiple roles provide evidence more in line with the scarcity hypothesis than with the enhancement hypothesis. That is, we generally found that having caregiving responsibility— especially having responsibility for more than one age group—is associated with increased absenteeism and stress rather than with the increased well-being that would be consistent with the enhancement hypothesis. This finding contrasts with a literature that, although inconsistent, has tended to find more evidence that multiple roles are associated with positive outcomes. We think that the difference between our findings and those in the larger literature is due, in part, to differences in the dependent variables included in the various studies. Many of the positive findings in the literature have focused on the effects of multiple roles on general well-being and happiness rather than on measures of time lost from work, family- or job-related stress, or reports of difficulty in combining the roles. We argue that the latter measures are more directly tied to the conflicts between work and family than are overall morale and life satisfaction.

Occupying multiple roles may, in fact, involve satisfactions as well as costs, as was pointed out by Baruch and Barnett (1986), and these conflicting feelings may be differentially reflected in the outcome measures selected. The stresses involved in providing care to children, elders, and adults with disabilities may contribute to personal growth and self-esteem at the same time that they pose difficult problems on a day-to-day basis. Horowitz (1978) and Brody (1990), for example, are among the researchers who have provided qualitative evidence of the benefits as well as the burdens experienced by some providers of elder care. Providing care to family and friends is in itself evidence that these employees are embedded in social networks and in the web of re-lationships and exchanges that those networks entail. At the same time, em-ployed caregivers are caught in a conflict between these informal ties and the workplace for their limited time and commitment. Such conflicts may neces-sitate some adjustment in the work schedule (arriving late, leaving early, or interruptions from family members) that allows the employee to honor com-mitments to both work and family.

It appears that in addition to the number of caregiving roles occupied, the specific combination of roles has an impact on absenteeism and stress. We found that those employees with no dependent-care responsibility had the lowest levels of absenteeism and stress. Employees with responsibility for all three care-recipient groups and those with responsibility for children and adults with disabilities had the most consistently elevated levels of absenteeism and stress. Among employees with only one caregiving role, caring for children was the most consistent predictor of absenteeism and stress.

Finally, we examined whether resources can buffer the effects of multiple roles for employed caregivers and whether workplace demands have more impact on absenteeism and stress for caregivers than for noncaregivers. The combination of being a caregiver and being a woman was associated with increased absenteeism and stress. Among the resources, having a nonworking partner was associated with reduced absenteeism, and having a working part-ner was associated with decreased absenteeism and stress for caregivers. This finding is consistent with the stress-buffering hypothesis—that resources such as having a partner are more beneficial for employees under stress. In contrast, flexible work schedules seem to serve as a resource for all employees. They are associated with lower levels of stress, but it appears that stress is lowered by increasing absenteeism.

The results of this study may shed some light on critical practice and policy questions. First, is a response to employed caregivers really necessary? Our findings indicate that employees with caregiving responsibilities of any kind (child, adult, or elder) experience more absenteeism and stress than do employees with no caregiving responsibilities. Their higher levels of absen-teeism and stress suggest a need for assistance in balancing their work and family roles.

Second, assuming that employed caregivers need additional assistance, which group or groups of employed caregivers are in greatest need? We found that the group of employees who care for multiple dependents (either providing three kinds of caregiving simultaneously or caring for children and adults) experienced the most problems. Among those who cared for only one kind of dependent, those caring for children experienced the most difficulty. Such findings suggest that special efforts to target employees in these caregiving situations might be beneficial.

Third, what types of programs and policies are needed and who should implement them? Although we did not directly address this question, we would suggest that change is needed in many sectors—the workplace, the family, and the community. In the last few years, employers have assumed increasing responsibility for helping employees attend to their caregiving responsibilities, especially in regard to child care. Growing numbers of companies are offering educational and supportive services, benefits, and work-scheduling policies that ease work and family conflict (Neal, Chapman, Ingersoll-Dayton, & Emlen, 1993; Scharlach, Lowe, & Schneider, 1991).

One cannot, however, expect employers to shoulder all of the responsibility for helping employees balance their work and family obligations. Some of this responsibility must also be carried by employees' families and the communities in which they live. Our study shows that women are most negatively affected by balancing work and family, indicating that for many women there is a need for greater flexibility within the family. This flexibility may involve the assumption of more caregiving or domestic responsibilities by other family members. Within the community, a greater variety of services (e.g., home care and respite services) offered more flexibly (e.g., extended hours of service and summer programs for school-age children) might reduce absenteeism.

The changing demographic, social, and economic trends reviewed at the outset of this chapter point to the need to broaden the focus of the field of work and family. In particular, integrated conceptual models that include all types of dependent care—care for children, adults with disabilities, and elders—must be developed. Solutions must be sought in the family, the workplace, and the formal institutions in the community. All sectors of society having a stake in how care is provided should be included in the dialogue about solutions to balancing work and family responsibilities. The division of responsibility within and among the family, the workplace, the community, and the nation in providing care must be reassessed. In the words of one of our respondents,

> I think it is very important that, as a society, we make it easier for people to care for their responsibilities regarding their elders and children. If more people were able to do this on their own, it would reduce government costs and give the individual the satisfaction of discharging his responsibilities to parents and children, which is what I think most adults really want to do anyway. People will do better work if they are contented with their lives, and job satisfaction is only a small part of how we measure our self-worth. Besides, if it weren't for our parents, we wouldn't be here, and if it weren't for our children, all our striving would have no purpose.

References

Baruch, G. K., & Barnett, R. (1986). Role quality, multiple role involvement, and psychological well-being of mid-life women. *Journal of Personality and Social Psychology, 51*, 578–585.

Baruch, G. K., Biener, L., & Barnett, R. C. (1987). Women and gender in research on work and family stress. *American Psychologist, 42*, 130–136.

Brody, E. M. (1981). "Women in the middle" and family help to older people. *The Gerontologist, 21*, 471–480.

Brody, E. M. (1985). Parent care as a normative family stress. *The Gerontologist, 25*, 19–29.

Brody, E. M. (1990). *Women in the middle: Their parent-care years.* New York: Springer.

Bureau of National Affairs. (1988). *33 ways to ease work/family tensions—an employer's checklist* (Special Rep. No. 2; Product Code BSP-84). Rockville, MD: Buraff Publications.

Cleary, P. D., & Mechanic, D. (1983). Sex differences in psychological distress among married people. *Journal of Health and Social Behavior, 24*, 111–121.

Creedon, M. (1987). Introduction: Employment and eldercare. In M. Creedon (Ed.), *Issues for an aging America: Employees and eldercare: A briefing book* (pp. 2–4). Bridgeport, CT: University of Bridgeport, Center for the Study of Aging.

Emlen, A. C. (1987, August–September). *Child care, work, and family*. Panel presentation made at the 95th Annual Convention of the American Psychological Association, New York.

Emlen, A. C., & Koren, P. E. (1984). *Hard to find and difficult to manage: The effects of child care on the workplace*. Portland, OR: Portland State University, Regional Research Institute for Human Services.

Fortune Magazine and John Hancock Financial Services. (1989). *Corporate and employee response to caring for the elderly: A national survey of U.S. companies and the workforce*. New York: Time Magazine and John Hancock Financial Services.

Gibeau, J. L., & Anastas, J. W. (1989). Breadwinners and caregivers: Interviews with working women. *Journal of Gerontological Social Work, 14,* 19–40.

Gilligan, C. (1982). *In a different voice: Psychological theory and women's development*. Cambridge, MA: Harvard University Press.

Goode, W. J. (1960). A theory of role strain. *American Sociological Review, 25,* 483–496.

Gore, S. (1981). Stress-buffering functions of social supports: An appraisal and clarification of research models. In B. S. Dohrenwend & B. P. Dohrenwend (Eds.), *Stressful life events and their contexts* (pp. 202–222). New York: Prodist.

Haynes, S. G., & Feinleib, M. (1980). Women, work and coronary heart disease: Prospective findings from the Framingham Heart Study. *American Journal of Public Health, 70,* 133–141.

Horowitz, A. (1978, November). *Families who care: A study of natural support systems of the elderly*. Paper presented at the meeting of the Gerontological Society of America, Dallas, TX.

Kanter, R. M. (1977). *Work and family in the United States: A critical review and agenda for research and policy*. New York: Russell Sage Foundation.

Karasek, R., Gardell, B., & Lindell, J. (1987). Work and non-work correlates of illness and behaviour in male and female Swedish white collar workers. *Journal of Occupational Behaviour, 8,* 187–207.

Lazarus, R. S., & Folkman, S. (1984). *Stress, appraisal, and coping*. New York: Springer.

Long, J., & Porter, K. L. (1984). Multiple roles of midlife women: A case for new directions in theory, research, and policy. In G. Baruch & J. Brooks-Gunn (Eds.), *Women in midlife* (pp. 109–160). New York: Plenum.

Marks, S. R. (1977). Multiple roles and role strain: Some notes on human energy, time and commitment. *American Sociological Review, 42,* 921–936.

Miller, D. A. (1981). The "sandwich" generation: Adult children of the aging. *Social Work, 26,* 419–423.

Morycz, R. K. (1980). An exploration of senile dementia and family burden. *Clinical Social Work Journal, 8,* 16–27.

National Center for Health Statistics. (1990). *Advance report of final natality statistics, 1988. Monthly vital statistics report* (Vol. 9, No. 4, Suppl.). Hyattsville, MD: U.S. Public Health Service.

Neal, M. B., Chapman, N. J., Ingersoll-Dayton, B., & Emlen, A. C. (1993). *Balancing work and caregiving for children, adults, and elders*. Newbury Park, CA: Sage.

Ontario Women's Directorate. (1990). *Work and family: The crucial balance*. (Available from Consultative Services Branch, Suite 200, 480 University Avenue, Toronto, Ontario, Canada M5G1V2).

Pratt, C., Schmall, V., & Wright, S. (1987). Ethical concerns of family caregivers to dementia patients. *The Gerontologist, 27,* 632–638.

Sainsbury, P., & Grad, J. (1962). Evaluation of treatment and services. In *The burden on the community: The epidemiology of mental illness: A symposium* (pp. 69–116). London: Oxford University Press.

Scharlach, A. E., & Boyd, S. L. (1989). Caregiving and employment: Results of an employee survey. *The Gerontologist, 29,* 382–387.

Scharlach, A. E., Lowe, B. F., & Schneider, E. L. (1991). *Elder care and the work force: Blueprint for action*. Lexington, MA: Lexington Books.

Shanas, E. (1980). Older people and their families: The new pioneers. *Journal of Marriage and the Family, 42,* 9–15.

Sieber, S. D. (1974). Toward a theory of role accumulation. *American Sociological Review, 39,* 467–478.

Skelton, M., & Dominian, J. (1973). Psychological stress in wives of patients with myocardial infarction. *British Medical Journal, 2,* 101–103.

Stoller, E. P. (1983). Parental caregiving by adult children. *Journal of Marriage and the Family, 45,* 851–858.

Stoller, E. P., & Pugliesi, K. L. (1989). Other roles of caregivers: Competing responsibilities or supportive resources. *Journal of Gerontology: Social Sciences, 44,* S231–S238.

Stone, R., Cafferata, G. L., & Sangl, J. (1987). Caregivers of the frail elderly: A national profile. *The Gerontologist, 27,* 616–626.

Stone, R. I., & Short, P. F. (1990). The competing demands of employment and informal caregiving to disabled elders. *Medical Care, 28,* 513–526.

Stull, D. E., Bowman, K., & Smerglia, V. (1991, October). *Women in the middle: A myth in the making?* Revised version of paper presented at the 1990 annual scientific meeting of the Gerontological Society of America, Boston.

Subcommittee on Human Services of the Select Committee on Aging, U.S. House of Representatives. (1987). *Exploding the myths: Caregiving in America* (Committee Publication No. 99–611). Washington, DC: U.S. Government Printing Office.

Thoits, P. A. (1982). Conceptual, methodological, and theoretical problems in studying social support as a buffer against life stress. *Journal of Health and Social Behavior, 23,* 145–159.

Thoits, P. A. (1983). Multiple identities and psychological well-being: A reformulation and test of the social isolation hypothesis. *American Sociological Review, 48,* 174–187.

Trieschmann, R. B. (1980). *Spinal cord injuries: Psychological, social and vocational adjustment.* New York: Pergamon.

U.S. Office of Management and Budget. (1987). *Standard Industrial Classification manual.* Washington, DC: Office of Management and Budget.

Voydanoff, P. (1988). Work role characteristics, family structure demands, and work/family conflict. *Journal of Marriage and the Family, 50,* 749–761.

Wagner, D. L., Creedon, M., Sasala, J., & Neal, M. (1989). *Employees and eldercare: Designing effective responses for the workplace.* Washington, DC: National Council on Aging.

Wagner, D. L., & Halsey, J. H. (1987). Corporate eldercare project: Findings. In M. A. Creedon (Ed.), *Issues for an aging America: Employees and eldercare—a briefing book* (pp. 25–29). Bridgeport, CT: University of Bridgeport, Center for the Study of Aging.

Warshaw, L. J., Barr, J. K., Rayman, I., Schachter, M., & Lucas, T. G. (1986). *Employer support of employee caregivers.* New York: New York Business Group on Health.

19

Work, Career, and Life Experiences Associated With Different Career Patterns Among Managerial and Professional Women

Ronald J. Burke and Carol A. McKeen

Lee (1993) has argued for new approaches to understanding women's career patterns because of the diversity of women's experiences in professional careers and family life. She identified six models of involvement in professional careers and family over the life span and discussed potential benefits and costs of each model from the perspective of women themselves, the family, organizations, and society. These six patterns were a function of the degree of women's involvement in their careers, degree of involvement in their families, the presence of children, and their timing.

Lee (1993) considered the following six models: career preeminent sustained, career preeminent modified, simultaneous career and family, sequencing career–family–career, sequencing family–career, and family preeminent sustained. The career preeminent sustained pattern involves high involvement in career and low involvement in family throughout women's adult lives. These women may or may not have partners or children. The career preeminent modified pattern resembles the career preeminent sustained pattern until the arrival of children. At this point there is a shift in career involvement; these women do not take a break from their careers, however. The simultaneous career and family pattern also includes high involvement in career and family with mutual accommodation of career and family. These women try not to let career interfere with family or let family interfere with career. Their careers are demanding yet allow some flexibility to permit the desired balance. The sequencing career–family–career pattern involves alternating priorities, as opposed to clear trade-offs, or trying to juggle high career and high family simultaneously. This pattern begins

This research was supported in part by the National Center for Management Research and Development, University of Western Ontario, London, Ontario, Canada; the School of Business, Queen's University, Kingston, Ontario, Canada; and the Faculty of Administrative Studies, York University, Toronto, Ontario, Canada. We thank Jeff Greenhaus, Lianne Joanette, Nora Kalb, and Jacob Wolpin for their help in preparing the study and in collecting and analyzing the data.

with an early focus on career, which is followed by a shift in focus to family and then by a return focus on career. The family focus results in a career interruption, a period of part-time work, changing careers, or a combination of these. The sequencing family–career pattern begins with a focus on family and, then later, launching of a high involvement career. Women in this pattern may not work at all when children are young. Finally, in the family preeminent sustained pattern, the family takes priority; the career is pursued only if it can be fit in with the family needs.

Lee (1993) suggested that each pattern has its own costs and benefits. She discussed each in terms of outcomes for women (e.g., adult development, career development, psychological well-being, and maternal role satisfaction), outcomes for the family (e.g., husband's well-being, marital solidarity, children's development and well-being, and quality of the parent–child relationship), and implications for organizations and society (e.g., use of women's skills, gains to society from women being involved in their communities, and organizations' needs to be flexible to accommodate women's needs).

Schwartz (1989) distinguished between career-primary women and career–family women. She noted that some managerial and professional women—those who both have children and want to spend time with them—have periods of their work lives when they are unable to be fully committed to their organizations. She proposed that organizations consider assigning these women less demanding jobs or allow them to take a break from work (or even work part-time) until they were ready to reenter the workforce fully committed. These assignments would result in work and career experiences more compatible with some women's needs in the short run, while in the long run availing organizations with a large pool of talented women, some of whom have spent some time in less demanding jobs.

Do women choose various career-priority patterns or do organizations place women in them? What are some of the personal and organizational antecedents of being in various career-priority patterns? What are some of the consequences, if any, of being in various career-priority patterns? Little research has been carried out that directly addresses such issues. Hochschild (1989) discussed the disproportionate amount of work outside of paid employment undertaken by dual-career women as opposed to dual-career men. The question of whether managerial women choose various career-priority patterns or are forced into them by societal realities of who does household, or "second-shift" work needs to be addressed (Konrad & Cannings, 1990).

The present investigation was somewhat exploratory in nature. One objective was to determine where managerial and professional women placed themselves on a career-primary and career–family continuum. A second objective was to examine potential antecedents (personal, career, and organizational) of this placement. Third was the consideration of both individual and organizational outcomes of this placement. Our final objective was to identify potential issues raised by our findings for managerial and professional women and their employing organizations.

Method

Respondents

Respondents were 792 female graduates (Bachelor of Commerce, MBA) of a single Canadian university. Demographic characteristics of this sample are shown in Table 1. There was considerable diversity in most of the demographic and situational characteristics. However, women in the sample tended to be early in their careers (1–10 years of work experience); fairly young ($M = 30$ years); married (about two thirds), but without children (about two thirds); and employed in diverse functions in a variety of industries.

Procedure

We obtained the names of every female business graduate ($N = 1,444$) from the university's central alumni records office. We sent questionnaires to these women at the preferred address (business or home), along with cover letters indicating the purpose of the study. All questionnaires were completed anonymously and were returned to a university address in the stamped, self-addressed envelope that had been included. Seven hundred ninety-two completed questionnaires were returned—a response rate of 55%, which was quite high given the length of the questionnaire (17 pages). To collect a variety of data, we used three versions of the questionnaire, each of which had a common and a unique component. There were no differences on the common measures between the three versions, so the three subsamples were combined for these measures.

Measures

Career-primary versus career–family patterns. We assessed patterns of women's involvement with career and family by posing the following scenarios.

> The following paragraphs describe two professional women. Please answer this question using your current or most recent employment.
>
> *Jane:*
> Jane's career is the most important thing in her life. She is ready to make the same trade-offs made by men who seek top management positions. She has made a career decision to put in extra hours, to make sacrifices in her personal life, and to make the most of every opportunity for professional development.
>
> *Betty:*
> Betty wants to pursue a career while actively participating in a personal life and the rearing of children. She is willing to trade some career growth and compensation for freedom from the constant pressure to work long hours and weekends.

I am . . . (circle one number)

Exactly Like Jane	A Lot Like Jane	Somewhat Like Jane	Halfway Between Jane & Betty	Somewhat Like Betty	A Lot Like Betty	Exactly Like Betty
1	2	3	4	5	6	7

Jane and Betty represented the career-primary and career–family ends of the continuum, respectively.

Antecedents. Three types of demographic and situational antecedents of career-priority patterns were considered: personal, career, and organizational. Most were measured with standard one-item measures.

Personal demographics. We collected data on age, current employment status, current marital status, length of marriage (if married), presence of children, number of children (if present), time children spent at home, time woman spent on household duties, number of university degrees, number of professional designations, years since bachelor's degree, hours worked per week, and extra hours or overtime hours worked per week.

Career demographics. To measure career demographics, we asked subjects whether they had ever worked part-time, and if they had been continuously employed since graduation, as well as about their number of breaks from work, the length of breaks from work, and the number of jobs they had held with different employers.

Organizational demographics. We collected data on years with present employer, years in present position, level of present position, numbers of employees supervised, size of organization, and size of department.

Consequences. Two kinds of consequences were considered: work outcomes and individual psychological well-being.

Work outcomes. We considered five work outcomes. Job satisfaction was measured with a five-item scale developed by Quinn and Shepard (1974). A sample item is "In general, how well would you say that your job measures up to the sort of job you wanted when you took it?"

We also used Burke's (1991) Intention to Quit Scale, consisting of two items: "At this time in your career, would you want to quit this job if it were possible?" and "If you are presently employed, please indicate whether you have ever had thoughts of leaving."

Our job involvement scale had three items taken from earlier work by Lodahl and Kejner (1965). A sample item is "The most important things that happen to me involve my work."

We also included the Career Satisfaction Scale—developed by Greenhaus,

Table 1. Demographic Characteristics of the Sample ($N = 792$)

Measure	n	$\%$	Measure	n	$\%$
Age (years)			Current marital status		
20–25	120	15.2	Single (never married)	70	34.1
26–30	320	40.4	Single (divorced, separated, or widowed)	20	2.5
31–35	223	28.1	Married or living together	501	63.3
36–40	93	12.7	Length of marriage (years)		
41–45	11	1.4	0–5	254	49.9
46–50	8	1.1	6–10	162	31.8
51 and over	17	2.1	11–15	61	12.0
No. of degrees			16–20	12	2.4
1	517	65.3	21 or more	20	3.9
2	241	30.4	Children		
3	31	3.9	Yes, my own	255	32.9
4	3	0.4	Yes, partner's	14	1.8
No. of professional designations			My own & partner's	2	0.3
0	559	70.6	No	504	65.0
1	227	28.7	Breaks from work		
2	6	0.8	0	384	48.7
No. of jobs			1	240	30.3
1	239	30.1	2	109	13.8
2	246	31.1	3	43	5.4
3	193	24.4	4 or more	14	1.8
4 or more	114	14.4	Size of organization		
Years in present position			1–50	144	19.6
1–5	725	95.6	50–250	136	18.5
6–10	25	3.3	250–500	86	11.7
11–15	5	0.7	500–1,000	45	6.1
16–20	2	0.3	1,000–2,500	115	15.6
Over 20	1	0.1	2,500–5,000	47	6.4
Own income			5,000–10,000	38	5.2
<$20,000	95	12.5	Over 10,000	124	16.9
$20,000–$29,999	71	9.3	Years with employer		
$30,000–$39,999	147	19.3	1–5	622	79.4
$40,000–$49,999	167	21.9	6–10	125	16.0
$50,000–$59,999	137	18.0	11–15	33	4.2
$60,000–$69,999	64	8.4	16–20	1	0.1
$70,000–$79,999	23	3.0	Over 20	2	0.3
$80,000 and over	58	7.6	Worked part-time?		
Level of position			Yes	206	26.7
Senior management	114	14.8	No	565	73.3
Middle management	259	33.5			
Junior management	189	24.5			
Nonmanagement	210	27.2			

Note. Sample sizes varied because of missing data. Total percentages varied because of rounding.

Parasuraman, and Wormley (1990)—which has five items. A sample item is "I am satisfied with the success I have achieved in my career."

Our final work-outcome measure was the Future Career Progress Scale, also developed by Greenhaus et al. (1990), which has four items. A sample item is "I have very good prospects for promotion in this company."

Psychological well-being. We measured life satisfaction with the three-item scale by Caplan, Cobb, French, Harrison, and Pinneau (1975). One item is "I am very satisfied with life."

Psychosomatic symptoms were measured with the 20-item scale developed by Derogatis, Lipman, Rickels, Uhlenhuth, and Covi (1979). Sample items include "poor appetite," "headaches," and "pains in my stomach."

Finally, we assessed emotional exhaustion with the nine-item scale developed by Maslach and Jackson (1981), one of three subscales constituting the Maslach Burnout Inventory. A sample item is "I feel burned out by my work."

Results

Reliabilities of Measures

All multi-item measures had internal consistency reliabilities (Cronbach's alphas) exceeding .70, a level of reliability considered acceptable. The reliabilities for each were as follows: life satisfaction, .90; psychosomatic symptoms, .84; emotional exhaustion, .87; intent to quit, .75; job satisfaction, .84; satisfaction with career success, .84; job involvement, .70; and satisfaction with career progess, .71.

Career-Priority Patterns

A mean of 4.5 was observed on the one-item measure of career-priority patterns. This placed the sample, as a whole, closer to the career–family end than to the career-primary end of the continuum. Women did, however, place themselves at each of the 7 scale points.

Personal Antecedents of Career–Family Priority

Table 2 shows the correlations between the various demographic characteristics and the career-priority measure. Almost 70% of these correlations reached statistical significance ($p < .05$), even given the large sample size. Career–family women were less likely to be currently employed and were more likely to be married; to have a greater number of university degrees; to have children; and, if children were present, to have more children. The children of these women spent more time at home, and the women spent more time on household

Table 2. Correlations Between Personal Antecedents and Career–Family Priority

Personal characteristic	r
Age	.05
Current employment status	$-.24^{**}$
Current marital status	.27**
Length of marriage	.05
No. of degrees	.10*
No. of professional designations	.04
Year of bachelor's degree	$-.05$
Children	.38**
No. of children	.34**
Time children at home	.16*
Time spent at household duties	.30**
Own income	$-.26^{**}$
Hours worked	.49**
Extra hours worked	.47**

$^*p = .01.$ $^{**}p = .001.$

duties, earned less income, worked fewer hours per week, and worked fewer extra hours per week.

No correlation was found between career-priority pattern and age, length of marriage (if married), number of professional designations, length of time since bachelor's degree, or spouse's income (if married).

Career Antecedents of Career–Family Priority

Table 3 shows correlations between career antecedents and career–family priority. Career–family women were more likely to have worked part-time, were less likely to have worked continuously, had taken a greater number of breaks from work, and had taken longer breaks from work. There was no relationship between the career-priority pattern measure and number of different jobs held.

Table 3. Correlations Between Career Antecedents and Career–Family Priority

Career characteristic	r
Worked part-time	.19*
Employed continuously	$-.25^*$
No. of work breaks	.28*
Length of work breaks	.26*
No. of jobs	$-.00$

$^*p = .001.$

Table 4.   Correlations Between Organizational Antecedents and
Career–Family Priority

Organizational characteristic	r
Years with present employer	.02
Years at present position	.14***
Level of position	−.13***
Employees supervised	−.08*
Size of organization	−.10**
Size of department	.06

*p = .05.   **p = .01.   ***p = .001.

Organizational Antecedents of Career–Family Priority

Table 4 shows correlations between some organizational antecedents and career–family priority. Managerial and professional women with career–family priorities had spent a longer time in their present positions, were in lower-level positions, had supervised fewer employees, and had worked in smaller organizations. There was no relationship between length of tenure with present employer or size of current department and the career–family priority measure.

Consequences of Career–Family Priority

Table 5 shows correlations between various individual measures of psychological well-being and career priority and between work outcomes and career priority. Career–family women were more satisfied with their lives and reported fewer psychosomatic symptoms. In addition, managerial and professional women with greater career–family priorities reported greater intention

Table 5.   Correlations Between Consequences and
Career–Family Priority

Consequences	r
Psychological well-being	
Life satisfaction	.10*
Psychosomatic symptoms	−.06*
Emotional exhaustion	−.06
Work outcome	
Intention to quit	.14**
Job satisfaction	−.16**
Satisfaction with career success	−.18**
Job involvement	−.53**
Satisfaction with career progress	−.22**

*p = .01.   **p = .001.

to quit, less job satisfaction, less career satisfaction, less job involvement, and less satisfaction with their future career progress.

Discussion

Do Different Career-Priority Patterns Exist?

The managerial and professional women in our study were able to place themselves on a career–family and career-primary continuum. Interestingly, a slight majority of the sample—all business graduates of a leading Canadian school of business—placed themselves on the career–family priority end of the continuum.

There were several personal, career, and organizational antecedents that related to the career-priority measure in ways that provided construct validity (see Tables 2–4). Career–family women were more likely to be married and to have children (and more children, who also were more dependent), and they spent more time on household duties—what Hochschild (1989) has called the *second shift*. These characteristics were matched by a correspondingly lower investment in work: Career–family women worked fewer hours per week, worked fewer extra hours per week, and were more likely to be currently unemployed. Employed career–family women also earned less income.

Career–family women also had more career interruptions, and these interruptions were of longer duration. These women also were more likely to have worked part-time at some point in their careers.

Despite having identical university credentials and working for employers for just as long as career-primary colleagues, career–family managerial and professional women held lower-level positions and held these positions for longer periods of time.

These patterns are consistent with other conclusions (Schwartz, 1989) that managerial and professional women successful at advancing their careers are likely to be single or, if married, to be childless. In addition, such women must seemingly pursue their careers with single-minded focus (i.e., without breaks or part-time work).

Costs of the Career–Family Pattern

There are several costs one might consider of the Career–Family pattern. At the individual level, one cost would be the diminished satisfaction and work commitment of career–family women. These women envisioned fewer career advancement opportunities in their futures (Morrison & Von Glinow, 1990; Morrison, White, & Van Velsor, 1987). On the other hand, work-and-family women reported greater life satisfaction and fewer psychosomatic symptoms. A second cost, at the organizational level, would be potentially greater turn-over; more dissatisfied, "stuck" managerial and professional women; and managerial and professional women who are less interested in career development initiatives and challenging, demanding jobs.

The Challenge

Women and organizations are left with the following dilemma. Talented women prepare themselves for managerial and professional careers by pursuing their education in leading university business programs. Some of these women—perhaps half—who choose to have partners and children find themselves in positions where they are unable or unwilling to commit to their employing organizations at a level equal to their male counterparts and equal to some female counterparts. Both they and their employing organizations endure costs.

These findings highlight some interesting dilemmas. Managerial and professional women equip themselves for a career yet find themselves unable to commit to this career for a period of time (in some cases, forever). Organizations hire these women—in some cases, going to great lengths to do so—and then find that they are unable to get an intense commitment from them for a period of time. It should be noted that some men also find it difficult to make such an investment—all men are not alike, as all women are not alike.

One possibility is for organizations to allow greater flexibility to managers and professionals during that period of time when work and family concerns peak. This might reduce job dissatisfactions of career–family women in particular. There is evidence (Morrison, 1992) that such initiatives may make it easier for women (and men) to pursue their careers in a more satisfying way.

References

Burke, R. J. (1991). Early work and career experiences of female and male managers and professionals: Reasons for optimism? *Canadian Journal of Administrative Sciences, 8*, 224–230.

Caplan, R. D., Cobb, S., French, J. R. P., Harrison, R. V., & Pinneau, S. R. (1975). *Job demands and worker health* (Research Rep.). Cincinnati, OH: National Institute for Occupational Safety and Health.

Derogatis, L. R., Lipman, R. S., Rickels, K., Uhlenhuth, E. H., & Covi, L. (1979). The Hopkins Symptom Checklist (HSCL): A self-report symptom inventory. *Behavioral Science, 19*, 1–15.

Greenhaus, J. H., Parasuraman, S., & Wormley, W. (1990). Organizational experiences and career success of black and white managers. *Academy of Management Journal, 33*, 64–86.

Hochschild, A. (1989). *The second shift*. New York: Avon Books.

Konrad, A. M., & Cannings, K. (1990). Sex segregation in the workplace and the mommy track: Sex differences in work commitment or statistical discrimination? In L. R. Jauch & J. L. Wall (Eds.), *Academy of Management best paper proceedings*, 369–373.

Lee, M. D. (1993) Women's involvement in professional careers and family life: Themes and variations. *Business and the Contemporary World, 5*, 106–127.

Lodahl, T., & Kejner, M. (1965). The definition and measurement of job involvement. *Journal of Applied Psychology, 49*, 24–33.

Maslach, C., & Jackson, S. E. (1981). Measurement of experienced burnout. *Journal of Occupational Behavior, 2*, 99–113.

Morrison, A. M. (1992). *The new leaders*. San Francisco, CA: Jossey-Bass.

Morrison, A. M., & Von Glinow, M. A. (1990). Women and minorities in management. *American Psychologist, 45*, 200–208.

Morrison, A. M., White, R. P., & Van Velsor, E. (1987). *Breaking the glass ceiling*. Reading, MA: Addison-Wesley.

Quinn, R. P., & Shepard, L. J. (1974). *The 1972–73 Quality of Employment Survey*. Ann Arbor: University of Michigan, Institute for Social Research.

Schwartz, F. N. (1989). Executives and organizations: Management women and the new facts of life. *Harvard Business Review, 89*, 65–76.

20

Linking Unemployment Experiences, Depressive Symptoms, and Marital Functioning: A Mediational Model

Sally Grant and Julian Barling

Despite the belief that unemployment is associated with marital dissatisfaction and spousal aggression, results from studies on the marital functioning of the unemployed have been inconsistent (Barling, 1990). Some studies have reported no differences in marital satisfaction as a function of husbands' employment status (Brinkerhoff & White, 1978; Kessler, Turner, & House, 1988; Perrucci & Targ, 1988). Others have documented lower marital satisfaction (Aubry, Tefft, & Kingsbury, 1990) and family cohesion (Liem & Liem, 1988; Perrucci & Targ, 1988) and more marital distress (e.g., Aubry et al., 1990; Komarovsky, 1940; Voydanoff & Donnelly, 1988) and spousal abuse (Straus & Gelles, 1986; Straus, Gelles, & Steinmetz, 1980) among the unemployed.

We suggest that two factors account for the inconsistent relationship between unemployment and marital functioning found in previous research. First, by focusing primarily on between-groups studies of unemployed and employed individuals, researchers have treated unemployment as a homogenous psychological experience. Instead, unemployment is best conceived as a set of heterogenous experiences, each of which is characterized by considerable variation. Second, we suggest that the effects of unemployment on marital functioning are indirect: Unemployment experiences directly influence depressive symptoms, which affect marital functioning. The idea of an indirect effect of unemployment on marital functioning is not recent. Komarovsky (1940) noted that wives' decreased sexual contact with unemployed husbands was a function of the extent to which their respect for their husbands had decreased following unemployment. In this study, we tested these two factors in a model positing that the psychological experience of unemployment affects mental functioning through its effects on depressive symptoms.

The present study was supported, in part, by Grant 410-88-0891 from the Social Sciences and Humanities Research Council of Canada to Julian Barling. We express particular appreciation to E. Kevin Kelloway for assistance throughout this research and to E. Kevin Kelloway, Frank Fincham, and K. Dan O'Leary for constructive comments.

The Experience of Unemployment

The psychological experience of unemployment is a complex process that varies across individuals (Jahoda, 1982). To understand the experience, we rely on recent research (see Feather, 1990; O'Brien, 1986; O'Brien & Feather, 1990; Warr, 1987) and theory of the psychological consequences of unemployment (cf. Jahoda, 1982, 1988; Jahoda, Lazarsfeld, & Zeisel, 1933) that highlight critical aspects of the subjective experience of unemployment: financial strain, meaningful time use and structuring, and attributions concerning unemployment. We also believe that an understanding of unemployment must include negative life events experienced during unemployment.

Financial Strain

Within Jahoda's (1982) framework, unemployment threatens the manifest function of employment—namely, pay. The prediction that income loss during unemployment results in psychological distress has been supported by studies from the 1930s through the 1980s (e.g., Bakke, 1940; Jahoda, 1982). Lower income has also been associated with poorer marital functioning (Elder & Caspi, 1988; Voydanoff & Donnelly, 1988) and increased family violence (Straus & Gelles, 1986; Straus et al., 1980). The effects of objective financial hardships also extend beyond the unemployed themselves, influencing spouses' marital dysfunction and conflict (Aubry et al., 1990; Brinkerhoff & White, 1978; Broman, Hamilton, & Hoffman, 1990; Liem & Liem, 1988).

The effects of perceived financial change may be more significant than levels of objective financial change during unemployment (Barling, 1990). Studies have repeatedly demonstrated the salience of perceived financial changes or financial worries to psychological distress in the unemployed (Broman et al., 1990; Kessler et al., 1988) and the general population (McConagle & Kessler, 1990). Perceived financial strain also predicts marital dissatisfaction (Aubry et al., 1990) and parental functioning (Simons, Lorenz, Conger, & Wu, 1992) among the unemployed. Conger et al.'s (1990) study established links between financial strain and objective ratings of marital interactions. Thus, we predict that perceived financial strain—rather than objective income— affects depressive symptoms, which then mediate the effects of financial strain on marital aggression and marital dissatisfaction (see Figure 1).

Meaningful Time Use

Paid work contributes to mental health by forcing a structure to one's waking day; any negative impact of job loss is due partially to the loss of a sense of structure and purpose in daily life (Jahoda, 1982). Unemployed men describe their time as being without purpose and structure more frequently than do employed men (e.g., Bond & Feather, 1988; Feather, 1990). Moreover, the way in which time is used by the unemployed (Bond & Feather, 1988; Feather,

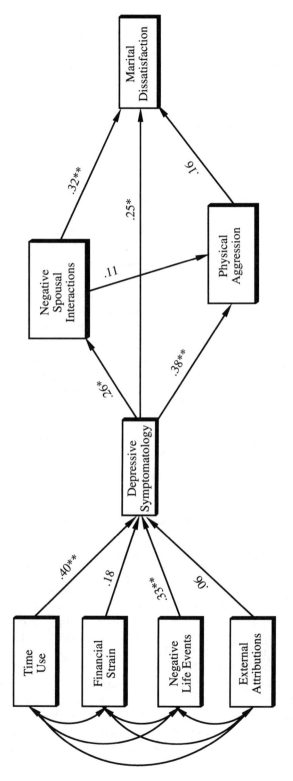

Figure 1.   Results of the confirmatory path analysis for the proposed mediational model. *$p < .05$. **$p < .01$.

1990; Fryer & McKenna, 1987) and nonemployed (i.e., those who do not wish to work; Barling, MacEwen, & Nolte, 1993; Higginbottom, Barling, & Kelloway, 1993) is associated with psychological distress and depressive symptoms.

These consistent findings validate the inclusion of time use as an integral aspect of the subjective experience of unemployment. Although there have been no studies linking time use and marital functioning, we predict that ineffective use of time directly influences depressive symptoms and, through the mediating action of depressive symptomatology, exerts indirect effects on marital aggression and marital dissatisfaction.

Negative Life Events

Unemployment ranks in the upper quartile of unpleasant events that generate life stress and leads to other events that exacerbate the negative effects of job loss (e.g., foreclosure of a mortgage or loan or experiencing changes in one's social activities or living conditions; McConagle & Kessler, 1990). Moreover, the unemployed are more vulnerable to negative life events than the employed, even when those events are not directly related to job loss (e.g., illness of a child; Hamilton, Broman, Hoffman, & Renner, 1990; Vinokur, Caplan, & Williams, 1987).

Negative life events (MacEwen & Barling, 1988a; Straus et al., 1980) and negative work events (Barling & Rosenbaum, 1986) have been correlated with spouse abuse. Researchers have repeatedly confirmed the association between negative life events and depressive symptoms in community samples (e.g., McConagle & Kessler, 1990), and we suggest that any effect of negative life events on marital dysfunction is mediated by depressive symptoms. Thus, we include negative life events as an integral aspect of the psychological experience of unemployment.

Attributions for the Causes of Unemployment

In addition to investigating the effects of time use during unemployment, Feather and his associates (e.g., Feather & Barber, 1983; Feather & Davenport, 1981) have also studied causal attributions for unemployment. They predicted that individuals making stable and global external attributions would experience depressive outcomes caused by a generalized belief in their inability to control negative events. In comparison with the employed, the unemployed make more external, stable, and global attributions for unemployment (Feather & O'Brien, 1986), but their attributional style appears to be self-serving: The employed attribute their status to personal qualities, such as competency and motivation, whereas the unemployed attribute their status to factors beyond their control (e.g., government, unions, or chance; Feather & O'Brien, 1986).

These findings suggest that external attributions for unemployment should be included in a mediational model linking unemployment and marital functioning. The model hypothesizes that external causal attributions will predict depressive symptoms among the unemployed. No direct link is hypothesized between causal attributions for unemployment and either marital aggression or marital dissatisfaction.

Depressive Symptoms

There is a consistent association between unemployment and depressive outcomes (see Dew, Penkower, & Bromet, 1991), and depressive symptoms among the unemployed have been related to misuse of time, to causal attributions for unemployment, to financial pressures, and to negative life events. Thus, we posited that depressive symptoms act as gatekeepers or mediators for any effects of the subjective experience of unemployment on marital functioning.

Depressive Symptoms and Marital Functioning

As there is no separate literature on unemployed individuals, we used the literature on community and clinical samples as the basis for our predictions concerning the relationships between depressive symptoms and marital functioning. As shown in Figure 1, a direct link is predicted between depressive symptoms experienced during unemployment and negative spousal interactions. Depressive symptoms have been linked to negative spousal interactions in cross-sectional self-report studies (Barling & MacEwen, 1992; MacEwen & Barling, 1991), daily self-report studies (MacEwen, Barling, & Kelloway, 1992), and observational studies (Ruscher & Gotlib, 1988). Examples of negative spousal interactions range from passive behaviors, such as refusal to comply with a partner's request; to verbal criticism and nonverbal demonstrations of contempt for one's spouse; to more actively aggressive behaviors, such as making hostile gestures and verbal threats toward one's spouse (O'Leary & Curley, 1986).

We predicted that depressive symptoms experienced during unemployment directly influence the level of negative spousal interactions and, through those interactions, indirectly affect marital dissatisfaction. Our mediational model also predicts that depressive symptoms experienced by the unemployed partner directly influence physical spousal aggression during unemployment. This is consistent with findings from studies of community couples (i.e., volunteers from the community not seeking or receiving marital treatment) during early marriage (Murphy & O'Leary, 1989), of couples seeking marital therapy (Beach, Sandeen, & O'Leary, 1990), and of men who are physically aggressive toward their spouses (Maiuro, Cahn, Vitaliano, Wagner, & Zegree, 1988).

We also predicted that depressive symptoms would exert an indirect effect on physical spousal aggression through negative spousal interactions. Murphy and O'Leary (1989) showed that negative spousal interactions preceded new instances of physical aggression. In addition, in both community and clinical samples, physical spousal aggression has been related negatively to marital satisfaction (Murphy & O'Leary, 1989; Straus & Gelles, 1986; Straus et al., 1980). Thus, we predicted that indirect effects of depressive symptoms on marital dissatisfaction would arise from physical spousal aggression.

Because many previous studies have been cross-sectional in nature, conclusions about the causal relationships between depressive symptoms and marital functioning remain somewhat ambiguous. In this study, we make causal hypotheses for several reasons. First, separate studies of retired and nonemployed individuals have shown that depressive symptoms predict marital dissatisfaction (Higginbottom et al., 1993). Also, in comparison with the employed, unemployed individuals often report normal levels of marital satisfaction (Brinkerhoff & White, 1978; Kessler et al., 1988; Perrucci & Targ, 1988) but heightened levels of depressive symptoms (Dew et al., 1991). Therefore, we predicted that depressive symptoms experienced during unemployment would lead to marital dysfunction, and we explicitly tested this hypothesis.

Last, several general issues should be raised. First, some researchers have argued that the effects of socioeconomic status should be retained in studies to reflect the real rather than artifactual variance in vulnerability to social stressors in general (Pearlin, 1989) and to unemployment in particular (Hamilton et al., 1990). Socioeconomic factors are conceived as contributing to the context within which people make subjective interpretations about their unemployment (Pearlin, 1989): Lower levels of education, occupational status, and personal income limit an individual's financial resources before unemployment, curtail opportunities for reemployment (Hamilton et al., 1990), elevate the risk of experiencing objective and perceived financial strain after job loss (Broman et al., 1990; Leana & Feldman, 1990), and increase exposure to negative life events (Hamilton et al., 1990; Vinokur & Caplan, 1986).

Second, we suggest that unemployed individuals are more likely to suffer from poor time use, greater financial strain, higher external attributions, and more negative life events. To test this, we contrasted employed and unemployed individuals on these four variables. Third, when path analysis is used, support for the model does not preclude the possibility that other models might fit the data equally well. Thus, alternative models should also be tested (Pedhazur, 1982). Because the literature is not conclusive as to the causal direction between depressive symptoms and marital dysfunction, we tested an alternative model in which the experience of unemployment was hypothesized to affect marital functioning, which then influences depressive symptoms. Additional support will be gained for the hypothesized model if alternative models can be excluded.

Method

Subjects and Procedure

The unemployed and employed groups we studied were accessed with two different methods. At the end of a telephone survey of a random sample of Canadians, a marketing organization asked respondents to provide names of individuals who met the research criteria (unemployed from 3 to 24 months or continuously employed for the previous 12 months and in a spousal or partner relationship for at least 12 months). Those who met the criteria were asked if their names could be forwarded to us to participate in this study, and we mailed each of them questionnaires. Questionnaires were returned by 34 of the 115 unemployed volunteers and by 48 of the 123 employed volunteers (in a spousal relationship and employed for 12 months) contacted in this manner.

Because the provision of names was slow, we also contacted participants meeting the research criteria in one eastern Ontario community (population 45,000) that was experiencing high unemployment. In the total sample, 52 of the 86 unemployed respondents and 37 of the 85 employed respondents were volunteers from this community. The overwhelming majority of respondents were White. Five unemployed individuals and 3 employed individuals contacted in the community chose not to participate.

Respondents in the unemployed group (24 women and 62 men) had a mean duration of unemployment of 29.85 weeks (mode = 21.5 weeks). On average, they were 43.17 years old (SD = 11.46 years). Their mean level of education was 11.66 years (SD = 2.03 years), and their mean annual income in the year preceding unemployment had been $23,501 ($SD$ = $11,450).

The mean age of the employed group (22 women and 63 men) was 37.31 years (SD = 8.84 years), and members of this group had completed an average of 13.26 years of education (SD = 2.43 years). Mean annual income in the past 12 months had been $31,763 ($SD$ = $12,254). As a group, the employed respondents were significantly younger, had higher annual incomes, and were more educated than their unemployed counterparts. There were no differences between the two groups in terms of the proportion of male and female respondents.

Assessment

Table 1 shows descriptive data for each of the study variables. Perceived financial strain was assessed by combining two measures. The first was a nine-item composite developed by Pearlin, Lieberman, Menaghan, and Mullan (1981) that measures the perceived difficulty in paying bills and in providing the home, furniture, car, food, medical care, clothing, and leisure activities for one's family. Although Pearlin et al. did not report the reliability of the scale, Kessler et al. (1988) showed a six-item version to be reliable. The second measure of perceived financial strain was a single item: "Thinking back over the past month, how often have you had serious financial worries?" (Jackson & Warr, 1984). Responses on this item could range from 0 (*never*) to 4 (*all the time*). This item has been used effectively in previous studies (Warr, 1984).

We measured time use with Feather and Bond's (1983) 17-item Time Use Scale. Each item (e.g., "Do you have a daily routine which you follow?") is rated on a 7-point scale (1 = *yes, always* and 7 = *no, never*). Internal consistency of this scale is satisfactory (Feather, 1990). Higher scores indicated better time use.

Table 1. Descriptive Data and Intercorrelations for the Study Variables

Variable	1	2	3	4	5	6	7
1. Age	—	NA	.11	−.23*	−.12	−.04	−.04
2. Duration of employment or unemployment	−.12	—					
3. Time use	.03	−.07	—	−.19	−.20	−.24*	−.39**
4. Perceived financial strain	−.22*	.34**	−.22	—	.44**	.23*	.21
5. Negative life events	−.03	−.05	−.27*	−.09	—	.20	.51**
6. External attributions for unemployment	.25*	−.06	.07	.01	.10	—	.23*
7. Depressive symptoms	−.12	.18	−.54**	.43**	.08	.23	—
8. Negative spousal interactions	.07	.28**	−.22	.09	.06	−.06	.31**
9. Physical spousal aggression	−.26*	.11	−.21	−.08	.21	−.14	.38**
10. Marital dissatisfaction	.01	−.13	.20	−.02	−.20	.09	−.34**

Note. Correlations are above the diagonal for the employed group and below the diagonal for
p < .05.   **p* < .01.

External attributions for unemployment were measured with Feather's (1990) subscale. Similar scales of causal attributions for unemployment have been used effectively with adults (Payne & Furnham, 1990). Respondents rated items on a 5-point scale (ranging from 1 = *not at all important* to 5 = *very important*) to indicate the perceived salience of each item for explaining current causes of unemployment.

We assessed negative life events with the 47-item Life Experiences Survey (Sarason, Johnson, & Siegel, 1978), which provides subjective ratings of the impact of commonly experienced life changes. Respondents reported the presence of each event in the past 3 months (the shortest time period to satisfy the criterion for the experience of unemployment) and rated the impact of the event at the time it occurred. We used the negative life change score (the summed impact of all negatively rated items). Because the items on the Life Experiences Survey measure independent events, assessing internal consistency would not be appropriate.

Depressive symptoms were measured with the Beck Depression Inventory (Beck, Steer, & Garbin, 1988). This widely used and highly reliable self-report measure comprises 21 items assessing cognitive, motivational, behavioral, affective, and somatic symptoms of depression. Scores less than nine are considered "normal" (Kendall, Hollon, Beck, Hammen, & Ingram, 1987).

We measured negative spousal interactions with the Spouse Specific

8	9	10	Unemployed		Employed		Univariate F	dfs
			M	SD	M	SD		
−.18	−.26*	.11	43.11	11.64	38.34	9.58	8.53**	1, 169
			29.85	20.10	NA	NA	NA	NA
−.30**	.07	.27*	4.47	0.88	4.89	0.85	9.14**	1, 158
.14	.06	−.12	6.72	2.24	4.87	2.10	22.81**	1, 164
.30**	.41**	−.24**	5.07	6.17	2.71	3.68	7.61**	1, 162
.23*	.02	.01	13.33	2.48	11.93	2.55	8.81**	1, 167
.27*	.17	.26*	8.16	7.16	4.72	5.18	15.09**	1, 168
—	.38**	.24*	2.51	.93	2.25	0.84	3.89	1, 164
.21	—	−.18	0.04	.14	0.04	0.14	0.11	1, 169
−.37**	−.33**	—	110.62	28.19	113.10	24.10	0.83	1, 168

the unemployed group. NA = not applicable.

Aggression Scale (O'Leary & Curley, 1986). Respondents use a 6-point scale to rate psychologically coercive acts, such as "I often yell back when my mate yells at me." The 12-item scale is highly reliable and is used to discriminate physically abusive couples from happily married couples (Murphy & O'Leary, 1989; O'Leary & Curley, 1986).

Physical spousal aggression was measured with a modified, eight-item version of Straus's (1979) Conflict Tactics Scale. According to a factor analysis of community and clinical samples (Barling, O'Leary, Jouriles, Vivian, & MacEwen, 1987), Items 11–17 (which are internally consistent; Straus, 1979) measure physical aggression between spouses. Item 18, "used a knife or gun," was excluded here because reports of that act are too infrequent in a community sample (Barling et al., 1987). However, an eighth item—"choked partner"—was added to the Conflict Tactics Scale by Straus and Gelles (1986). For our study, respondents provide self-reports for the last 3 months (rather than for the more typical 12 months) to reflect the shortest period of unemployment experienced by any of our subjects and to provide consistency across questionnaires. Instead of the traditional 7-point rating scale, we used a 4-point rating scale, ranging from 0 = *never* to 3 = *more than twice.*

Finally, we assessed marital dissatisfaction by using the 15-item Short Marital Adjustment Test (Locke & Wallace, 1959), a self-report measure of global relationship satisfaction that yields high internal reliability (O'Leary

& Turkewitz, 1978) and temporal stability over a 3-month period (MacEwen & Barling, 1988b). With a cutoff score of 90, the Short Marital Adjustment Test discriminates between distressed and nondistressed couples (Barling & Rosenbaum, 1986). Mean scores of the unemployed and employed samples were in the satisfied range (>100).

Results

We computed a multivariate analysis of variance (MANOVA) between the employed and unemployed groups on the four variables reflecting the psychological experience of unemployment (time use, financial strain, external attributions, and negative life events). The overall MANOVA effect was significant, Pillai's Exact $F(4, 144) = 8.82$, $p < .001$, and analyses of variance revealed consistent between-groups differences. In a second MANOVA, we contrasted the marital functioning (negative interactions, physical spousal aggression, and marital dissatisfaction) of the two groups. The overall MANOVA effect was nonsignificant, Pillai's Exact $F(3, 162) = 1.35$, $p > .05$, and no differences emerged on the three outcome variables (see Table 1).

We used confirmatory path analysis to test our proposed model. Before doing so, we satisfied several assumptions underlying this technique (no measurement error; all measures of an ordinal nature; and none of the relationships between the study variables violated the assumptions of linearity, multicollinearity, or additivity of effects). Although scores on the physical spousal aggression scale were positively skewed, we still included these data because the low frequency and restricted variance of the scores are functions of the behavior being measured (Barling et al., 1987; O'Leary et al., 1989). Moreover, regression analysis is generally robust in the absence of measurement or specification errors (Pedhazur, 1982).

We assessed the significance of the path model in three ways. First, we evaluated the goodness of fit of the model with Specht's (1975) Q, which approaches unity when the difference between the hypothesized and alternative models is minimal, that is, when the nonpredicted paths account for little of the generalized variance. Second, we assessed the significance of each predicted path. Conventional levels of statistical significance were not used in isolation, because of recommendations that "meaningful" paths be retained: Schumm, Southerly, and Figley (1980) have recommended retaining path coefficients if $p < .20$; Billings and Wroten (1978) and Pedhazur (1982) have recommended retention of paths when the path coefficient is greater than .05. Thus, all predicted paths were retained and presented for illustrative purposes. Third, we tested the goodness of fit of an alternative model in which marital dissatisfaction served as the mediating variable. In all analyses, unemployment duration was controlled statistically because of its significant association with many of the variables in the model (see Table 1).

Specht's Q statistic ($Q = .86$) suggested that the proposed model provided a reasonable fit to the data. This inference was supported by an examination of the magnitude of the individual paths (see Figure 1). Time use ($\beta = -.40$), negative life events ($\beta = .33$), and perceived financial strain

(β = .18) all predicted depressive symptoms. Of the variables reflecting the experience of unemployment, the effect of external attributions for unemployment was smallest (β = .06). Negative spousal interactions were predicted by depressive symptoms (β = .26), and physical spousal aggression was predicted both by depressive symptoms (β = .25) and by negative spousal interactions (β = .11). Last, depressive symptoms (β = .25), negative spousal interactions (β = .32), and physical spousal aggression (β = .16) all predicted marital dissatisfaction.

The third test entailed an examination of the alternative model, in which marital dissatisfaction functioned as the mediator and depressive symptoms was the outcome variable. Although a direct contrast of the two models was not possible, Specht's Q (.62) was substantially lower for the alternative model, suggesting that this model did not provide an acceptable fit to the data.

Discussion

The goal of our research was to develop and test a mediational model of the process linking the subjective experience of unemployment to marital functioning through depressive symptoms. Before discussing the fit of the model, it is worth noting that the variables proposed to reflect the experience of unemployment evidenced construct validity: The unemployed and employed groups differed significantly in terms of financial strain, time use, external attributions, and negative life events. The groups also differed in mean levels of depressive symptoms. The mean level of depressive symptoms within the unemployed group (7.95; SD = 7.02) was within the upper normal range on the Beck Depression Inventory and was similar to levels found for unemployed groups in previous research (Bond & Feather, 1988; Feather & Davenport, 1981). These heightened yet normal levels of depressive symptoms support Jahoda's (1988) argument that within community samples life stress does not result in clinical depression but, rather, in lowered positive mental health. In contrast, the two groups did not differ in marital functioning. These outcomes support the central thesis of our study—namely, that unemployment status alone is not a sufficient explanation of marital functioning. The challenge of this study, then, was to demonstrate that within an unemployed group, depressive symptoms mediate the relationship between the psychological experience of unemployment and marital functioning.

The proposed model provided a good fit to the data. First, the overall goodness-of-fit statistic was high. Second, the magnitude of the individual paths supported most of the specific links in the model. (Because these path coefficients were standardized, it is possible to contrast the relative importance of the various paths within the model.) Third, an alternative model, in which depressive symptoms was the outcome variable and marital dissatisfaction was the mediator, provided a poor fit to the data.

The Experience of Unemployment and Depressive Symptoms

Financial strain influenced depressive symptoms in the unemployed sample. This relationship is consistent with research from the 1930s and the 1980s in which financial strain or reduced income was shown to contribute to psychological distress during unemployment. Although not statistically significant, the meaning of the path linking financial strain and depressive symptoms is enhanced by several factors. First, the path coefficient reflects the influence of financial strain on depressive symptoms after time use, negative life events, and external attributions are controlled for. Second, financial strain worsens with increasing durations of unemployment (Warr, 1984), and the influence of the duration of unemployment was excluded statistically. Third, the duration of unemployment in our sample was relatively low (minimum = 3 months, M = 7 months), suggesting that the negative effects of depressive symptoms might be conservative. Like previous research documenting the importance of subjective perceptions of events rather than their objective occurrence (Barling, 1990), the present results suggest the primacy of the detrimental effects of perceived financial strain on mental health rather than of objective financial change during unemployment.

Time use demonstrated the strongest relationship with depressive symptoms among the unemployed. This extends previous research by showing that unproductive time use exerts a greater impact on depressive symptoms than that exerted by perceived financial strain. Conceptually, this should not be underestimated, because it represents the unique contributions of time use to depressive symptoms, after effects of the duration of unemployment, financial strain, negative life events, and external attributions are controlled for.

Negatively perceived life events also predicted depressive symptoms. This is consistent with studies documenting the effects of negative life events on psychological distress among unemployed and community samples. In most studies, life events have been rated over a 12-month period. In our research, the negative effects of negative life events were evident over a 3-month period, suggesting that the magnitude of the path coefficients may again underestimate the effects of negative life events.

Unlike previous researchers (e.g., Feather, 1985, 1990; Feather & Barber, 1983; Feather & Davenport, 1981; Feather & O'Brien, 1986), we did not find that external causal attributions for unemployment influenced depressive symptoms: The beta associated with this relationship was statistically insignificant and trivial. Even the zero-order correlation between external causal attributions for unemployment and depressive symptoms was not significant. Nonetheless, the unemployed subjects did manifest significantly higher external attribution scores than their employed counterparts. Perhaps this is because their unemployment is initiated and maintained by factors beyond their control and because being unemployed accurately describes their economic and social reality (Feather, 1990; Payne & Furnham, 1990; Pearlin, 1989).

In future research on unemployment, depressive symptoms, and marital functioning, it will still be useful to include causal attributions for unemployment. However, for depressive symptoms to be affected, it is possible that unemployed individuals should feel personally responsible for their unemployment as well as that they are somehow failing personally by being unemployed (Feather, 1990).

Depressive Symptoms and Marital Functioning Among the Unemployed

Consistent with prior findings, we found that depressive symptoms substantially predicted negative spousal interactions. Unemployed individuals reporting higher levels of depressive symptoms also reported being more critical and more verbally coercive toward their spouses.

Beach et al. (1990) suggested that depression is the product of physical spousal aggression. In contrast, our model posits that depressive symptoms predict physical spousal aggression, and the data from the unemployed respondents support our prediction. Despite restricted variance of physical spousal aggression, the path linking depressive symptoms to physical spousal aggression was statistically significant. Although the modal aggressive behavior is at the "low level" of pushing, shoving, and slapping one's partner, depressive symptoms remain a substantial predictor of physical spousal aggression among the unemployed.

In contrast, the path linking physical spousal aggression and marital dissatisfaction was not statistically significant. Nonetheless, this path was retained because of its conceptual meaning. Also, the measure of physical spousal aggression was substantively constrained by floor effects caused by its low base rate and by the shortened period over which aggression was rated. The link between physical spousal aggression and marital dissatisfaction might have been supported if the usual rating period of 12 months had been used for the Conflict Tactics Scale. These possibilities should be investigated in future research.

These data supported a direct link between depressive symptoms and marital dissatisfaction. Depressive symptoms also exert indirect effects on marital dissatisfaction through the mediation of negative spousal interactions, which negatively influence marital dissatisfaction. Thus, among the unemployed, the effect coefficient representing the relationship between depressive symptoms and marital dissatisfaction is quite strong.

With the exception of the link between external attributions and depressive symptoms, our data were consistent with predictions in our mediational model. However, cross-sectional, correlational data cannot support causal inferences between the variables within the mediational model because alternative models using those same variables would prove equally effective in explaining the variance in the data observed in the unemployed group. One method of supporting this mediational model is to disconfirm other alternative models. To test this, the proposed roles of depressive symptoms and marital dissatisfaction were reversed, allowing marital satisfaction to assume the mediator role in the relationship between the subjective experience of unemployment and depressive symptoms (Beach et al., 1990). The failure of this alternative (and theoretically viable) model strengthens the inference in our research that depressive symptoms mediate the relationship between subjective experience and marital functioning among the unemployed.

The results of the present study emphasize several conceptual issues. First, the utility of a within-group approach to studying the subjective experiences of the unemployed is evident. In adopting such an approach, we were able to show how the experience of unemployment predicts depressive symptoms. In future research, consideration could be given to expanding the conceptualization of the experience of unemployment. For example, losing the opportunity to use one's skills is an important component of the experience of unemployment (O'Brien & Feather, 1990), and this explanation is consistent with the three theoretical approaches identified earlier (Feather, 1990; Jahoda, 1982; Warr, 1987). Second, both path analyses clearly show the mediating influence of depressive symptoms in the relationship between unemployment experiences and marital functioning. As a result, an understanding of how different unemployment experiences influence depressive symptoms will advance understanding of the process by which joblessness affects marital functioning. This intragroup focus is perhaps especially important given that there were no statistically significant differences between the marital functioning of the unemployed and employed groups in our study.

Several suggestions for interventions can also be offered. Because depressive symptoms in our model served a mediating function and because levels of depressive symptoms and marital functioning were typically within the normal range, factors threatening depressive symptoms during unemployment should be addressed through preventive efforts. In most retirement and unemployment counseling packages, priority is given to financial issues. However, perceived financial strain had less impact on depressive symptoms than either time use or negative life events in this study, and so aspects such as time use warrant more attention in preventive efforts if well-being is to be enhanced.

In conclusion, the utility of adopting a within-group approach to understanding the nature and effects of unemployment experiences was supported. The data highlighted the mediating role of depressive symptoms and showed how the detrimental effects of the psychological experience of unemployment are transmitted to marital functioning.

References

Aubry, T., Tefft, B., & Kingsbury, N. (1990). Behavioral and psychological consequences of unemployment in blue-collar couples. *Journal of Community Psychology, 18,* 99–109.

Bakke, E. (1940). *The unemployed worker: A study of the task of making a living without a job.* New Haven, CT: Yale University Press.

Barling, J. (1990). *Employment, stress, and family functioning.* New York: Wiley.

Barling, J., & MacEwen, K. E. (1992). Linking work experiences to facets of marital functioning. *Journal of Organizational Behaviour, 13,* 573–583.

Barling, J., MacEwen, K. E., & Nolte, M. L. (1993). Homemaker role experiences affect toddler behaviors via maternal well-being and parenting behavior. *Journal of Abnormal Child Psychology, 21,* 213–229.

Barling, J., O'Leary, K. D., Jouriles, E., Vivian, D., & MacEwen, K. (1987). Factor similarity of the Conflict Tactics Scales across samples, spouses, and sites: Issues and implications. *Journal of Family Violence, 2,* 37–54.

Barling, J., & Rosenbaum, A. (1986). Work stressors and wife abuse. *Journal of Applied Psychology, 71,* 346–348.

Beach, S., Sandeen, E., & O'Leary, K. D. (1990). *Depression in marriage.* New York: Guilford Press.

Beck, A., Steer, R., & Garbin, M. (1988). Psychometric properties of the Beck Depression Inventory: Twenty-five years of evaluation. *Clinical Psychology Review, 8,* 77–100.

Billings, R., & Wroten, S. (1978). Use of path analysis in industrial/organizational psychology: Criticisms and suggestions. *Journal of Applied Psychology, 63,* 677–688.

Bond, M., & Feather, N. (1988). Some correlates of structure and purpose in the use of time. *Journal of Personality and Social Psychology, 55,* 321–329.

Brinkerhoff, D., & White, L. (1978). Marital satisfaction in an economically marginal population. *Journal of Marriage and the Family, 40,* 259–267.

Broman, C., Hamilton, V., & Hoffman, W. (1990). Unemployment and its effects on families: Evidence from a plant closing study. *American Journal of Community Psychology, 18,* 643–659.

Conger, R., Elder, G., Lorenz, F., Conger, C., Simons, R., Whitbeck, L., Huck, S., & Melby, J. (1990). Linking economic hardship to marital quality and stability. *Journal of Marriage and the Family, 52,* 643–656.

Dew, M., Penkower, L., & Bromet, E. J. (1991). Effects of unemployment on mental health in the contemporary family. *Behavior Modification, 15,* 501–544.

Elder, G., & Caspi, A. (1988). Economic stress in lives: Developmental perspectives. *Journal of Social Issues, 44,* 25–45.

Feather, N. T. (1985). Attitudes, values, and attributions: Explanations of unemployment. *Journal of Personality and Social Psychology, 48,* 876–889.

Feather, N. T. (1990). *The psychological impact of unemployment.* New York: Springer-Verlag.

Feather, N. T., & Barber, J. (1983). Depressive reactions and unemployment. *Journal of Abnormal Psychology, 92,* 185–195.

Feather, N. T., & Bond, M. (1983). Time structure and purposeful activity among employed and unemployed university graduates. *Journal of Occupational Psychology, 56,* 241–254.

Feather, N. T., & Davenport, P. (1981). Unemployment and depressive affect: A motivational and attributional analysis. *Journal of Personality and Social Psychology, 41,* 422–436.

Feather, N. T., & O'Brien, G. (1986). A longitudinal analysis of the effects of different patterns of employment and unemployment on school leavers. *British Journal of Psychology, 77,* 459–479.

Fryer, O., & McKenna, S. (1987). The laying off of hands: Unemployment and the experience of time. In S. Fineman (Ed.), *Unemployment: Personal and social consequences* (pp. 37–73). London: Tavistock.

Hamilton, V., Broman, C., Hoffman, W., & Renner, D. (1990). Hard times and vulnerable people: Initial effects of plant closing on autoworkers' mental health. *Journal of Health and Social Behavior, 31,* 123–140.

Higginbottom, S. F., Barling, J., & Kelloway, E. K. (1993). Linking retirement experiences and marital satisfaction: A mediational model. *Psychology and Aging, 8,* 508–516.

Jackson, P., & Warr, P. (1984). Unemployment and psychological ill health: The moderating role of duration and age. *Psychological Medicine, 14,* 605–614.

Jahoda, M. (1982). *Employment and unemployment: A social psychological analysis.* Cambridge, England: Cambridge University Press.

Jahoda, M. (1988). Economic recession and mental health. *Journal of Social Issues, 44,* 13–23.

Jahoda, M., Lazarsfeld, P., & Zeisel, H. (1933). *Marienthal: The sociography of an unemployed community.* London: Tavistock.

Kendall, P., Hollon, S., Beck, A., Hammen, C., & Ingram, R. (1987). Issues and recommendations regarding use of the Beck Depression Inventory. *Cognitive Therapy and Research, 11,* 289–299.

Kessler, R., Turner, J. B., & House, J. (1988). Effects of unemployment on health in a community survey: Main, modifying, and mediating effects. *Journal of Social Issues, 44,* 69–85.

Komarovsky, M. (1940). *The unemployed man and his family.* New York: Arno Press.

Leana, C., & Feldman, D. (1990). Individual responses to job loss: Empirical findings from two field studies. *Human Relations, 43,* 1155–1181.

Liem, R., & Liem, J. (1988). Psychological effects of unemployment on workers and their families. *Journal of Social Issues, 44,* 87–105.

Locke, H., & Wallace, K. (1959). Short marital adjustment and prediction tests: Their reliability and validity. *Marriage and Family Living, 21,* 251–255.

MacEwen, K., & Barling, J. (1988a). Interrole conflict, family support and marital adjustment of employed mothers: A short-term longitudinal study. *Journal of Organizational Behavior, 9,* 241–250.

MacEwen, K., & Barling, J. (1988b). Multiple stressors, violence in the family of origin and marital aggression: A longitudinal investigation. *Journal of Family Violence, 3,* 73–88.

MacEwen, K. E., & Barling, J. (1991). Effects of maternal employment experiences on children's behavior via mood, cognitive difficulties and parenting behavior. *Journal of Marriage and the Family, 53,* 635–644.

MacEwen, K. E., Barling, J., & Kelloway, E. K. (1992). Effects of short-term role overload on marital interactions. *Work and Stress, 6,* 117–126.

Maiuro, R., Cahn, T., Vitaliano, P., Wagner, B., & Zegree, J. (1988). Anger, hostility, and depression in domestically violent versus generally assaultive men and nonviolent control subjects. *Journal of Consulting and Clinical Psychology, 56,* 17–23.

McConagle, K., & Kessler, R. (1990). Chronic stress, acute stress, and depressive symptoms. *American Journal of Community Psychology, 18,* 681–706.

Murphy, C., & O'Leary, K. D. (1989). Verbal aggression as a predictor of physical aggression in early marriage. *Journal of Consulting and Clinical Psychology, 57,* 579–582.

O'Brien, G. (1986). *Psychology of work and unemployment.* New York: Wiley.

O'Brien, G., & Feather, N. (1990). The relative effects of unemployment and quality of employment on the affect, work values, and personal control of adolescents. *Journal of Occupational Psychology, 63,* 151–165.

O'Leary, K. D., Barling, J., Arias, I., Rosenbaum, A., Malone, J., & Tyree, A. (1989). Prevalence and stability of physical aggression between spouses: A longitudinal analysis. *Journal of Consulting and Clinical Psychology, 57,* 263–268.

O'Leary, K. D., & Curley, A. (1986). Assertion and family violence: Correlates of spouse abuse. *Journal of Marital and Family Therapy, 12,* 281–289.

O'Leary, K. D., & Turkewitz, H. (1978). Methodological errors in marital and child treatment. *Journal of Consulting and Clinical Psychology, 46,* 747–758.

Payne, M., & Furnham, A. (1990). Causal attributions for unemployment in Barbados. *Journal of Social Psychology, 130,* 169–181.

Pearlin, L. (1989). The sociological study of stress. *Journal of Health and Social Behavior, 30,* 241–256.

Pearlin, L., Lieberman, M., Menaghan, E., & Mullan, J. (1981). The stress process. *Journal of Health and Social Behavior, 22,* 337–356.

Pedhazur, E. (1982). *Multiple regression in behavioral research* (2nd ed.). New York: Holt, Rinehart & Winston.

Perrucci, C., & Targ, D. (1988). Effects of a plant closing on marriage and family life. In P. Voydanoff & L. Majka (Eds.), *Families and economic distress: Coping strategies and social policy* (pp. 55–71). Newbury Park, CA: Sage.

Ruscher, S., & Gotlib, I. (1988). Marital interaction patterns of couples with and without a depressed partner. *Behavior Therapy, 19,* 455–470.

Sarason, I., Johnson, J., & Siegel, H. (1978). Assessing the impact of life change: Development of the Life Experiences Survey. *Journal of Consulting and Clinical Psychology, 46,* 932–946.

Schumm, W., Southerly, W., & Figley, C. (1980). Stumbling blocks or stepping stone? Path analysis in family studies. *Journal of Marriage and the Family, 42,* 251–262.

Simons, R. L., Lorenz, F. O., Conger, R. D., & Wu, C.-I. (1992). Support from spouse as mediator and moderator of the disruptive influence of economic strain on parenting. *Child Development, 63,* 1282–1301.

Specht, D. (1975). On the evaluation of causal models. *Social Science Research, 4,* 113–133.

Straus, M. (1979). Measuring intrafamily conflict and violence: The Conflict Tactics (CT) Scales. *Journal of Marriage and the Family, 41,* 75–78.

Straus, M., & Gelles, R. (1986). Societal change and change in family violence from 1975 to 1985 as revealed by two national surveys. *Journal of Marriage and the Family, 48,* 465–479.

Straus, M., Gelles, R., & Steinmetz, S. (1980). *Behind closed doors.* New York: Anchor Press.

Vinokur, A., & Caplan, R. (1986). Cognitive and affective components of life events: Their relations and effects on well-being. *American Journal of Community Psychology, 14,* 351–370.

Vinokur, A., Caplan, R., & Williams, C. (1987). Effects of recent and past stress on mental health: Coping with unemployment among Vietnam veterans and nonveterans. *Journal of Applied Social Psychology, 17,* 710–730.

Voydanoff, P., & Donnelly, B. (1988). Economic distress, family coping, and quality of family life. In P. Voydanoff & L. Majka (Eds.), *Families and economic distress: Coping strategies and social policy* (pp. 97–116). Newbury Park, CA: Sage.

Warr, P. (1984). Reported behaviour changes after job loss. *British Journal of Social Psychology, 23,* 271–275.

Warr, P. (1987). *Work, unemployment, and mental health.* New York: Oxford University Press.

Author Index

Numbers in italics refer to listings in reference sections.

Subject Index